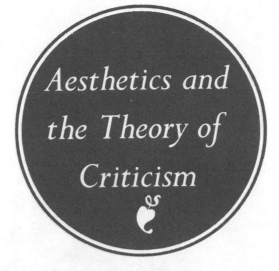

Aesthetics and the Theory of Criticism

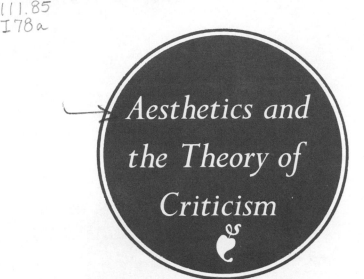

Aesthetics and the Theory of Criticism

SELECTED ESSAYS OF
ARNOLD ISENBERG

Edited by William Callaghan, Leigh Cauman
Carl Hempel, Sidney Morgenbesser, Mary Mothersill
Ernest Nagel, and Theodore Norman

With an Introduction by Mary Mothersill
and a Biographical Sketch by William Callaghan

THE UNIVERSITY OF CHICAGO PRESS
CHICAGO AND LONDON

The late ARNOLD ISENBERG was professor of philosophy at Michigan State University. His articles, reviews, papers, and addresses appeared in a variety of publications.

[1973]

THE UNIVERSITY OF CHICAGO PRESS, CHICAGO 60637
THE UNIVERSITY OF CHICAGO PRESS, LTD., LONDON
© 1973 by the University of Chicago
© 1973 by Frederic D. Camper and Shirley C. Soman,
Custodian of Frances A. Camper
All rights reserved. Published 1973
Printed in the United States of America
INTERNATIONAL STANDARD BOOK NUMBER: 0-226-38511-6
LIBRARY OF CONGRESS CATALOG CARD NUMBER: 73-77133

Contents

Arnold Isenberg: Some Recollections, by William Callaghan
vii

Introduction by Mary Mothersill
xix

PART I. AESTHETICS
1. Music and Ideas
3

2. Formalism
22

3. Perception, Meaning, and the Subject Matter of Art
36

4. The Technical Factor in Art
53

5. The Aesthetic Function of Language
70

6. The Problem of Belief
87

7. On Defining Metaphor
105

PART II. CRITICISM
8. Cordelia Absent
125

9. A Poem by Frost and Some Principles of Criticism
138

10. Critical Communication
156

11. 'Pretentious' as an Aesthetic Predicate
172

12. Superlatives
184

13. Some Problems of Interpretation
199

PART III. ETHICS AND MORAL PSYCHOLOGY
14. Natural Pride and Natural Shame
216

15. Deontology and the Ethics of Lying
245

16. Ethical and Aesthetic Criticism
265

Appendix A: Analytical Philosophy and the Study of Art
285

Appendix B: Notebooks and Letters
302

Index
317

Arnold Isenberg:
Some Recollections

Arnold Isenberg's accidental death occurred on 26 February 1965.[1] I learned of it by cablegram the next day (I was in Italy, on leave from the university we both served). The news came as a shock, a painful one; Isenberg and I had been friends for nearly forty years. Later a newspaper obituary arrived. It made sad reading, of course, but it also left me feeling displeased and disputatious. The general tone or tenor was what disturbed me, a tenor established by the quoted remark of an unidentified colleague. He described Isenberg as a slight, lonely man, adding that "the life in him seemed to come to the surface only in philosophical discussions."

The frail, pale, and monkish scholar, excited only by questions moot within his field—that is a genuine type, and a good enough one too. But Isenberg, I found myself protesting, wasn't that type. Time and troubles had indeed changed his manner and appearance. Even in his last years, however, he retained to an uncommon degree the traits and style which were his as a young man. The cabled news had set me to recalling such matters, to remembering Isenberg as I had first known him. That Isenberg was clearly and vividly much more a fledgling Samuel Johnson than a Leslie Stephen or an Isaac D'Israeli in pinfeathers. And he was already very much what he always remained.

Isenberg was in Class II at the Boston Public Latin School when I entered its Class IV, that is, became a freshman there, in 1926. The

1. A smouldering fire had started in his apartment during the previous night. He died, probably in the early morning, from smoke-inhalation.

school was old, older than Harvard, and used harsh old-fashioned ways to produce scholars of an old-fashioned sort. Students were exercised in languages, literature, history, mathematics, and—with a little disdain—science. The teachers, accurately (as well as by tradition) called "masters," trusted more in sticks than carrots as motivating stimuli. Almost penal standards of diligence and discipline were maintained. Class performances were assessed with scant mercy, and many masters thought it salutory that the identity of a boy on the brink of failure should be known to his fellows. Lapses in discipline or decorum earned their perpetrators "misdemeanor marks." The acquisition of seven of these led to suspension, and suspension could be followed by expulsion. Everyone knew of several walking dead, almost visibly dwindling away under the burden of six marks and failures in two subjects. It was a sad and frightening thing to pass such a one in a corridor, possibly for the last time.[2]

One would have supposed the official program to be demanding enough and more than sufficiently competitive. In addition, however, there was a mélange of extracurricular activities, all bookish, in which it was a shame not to achieve at least some small success: the Latin, French, German, and history clubs (as—God save the mark—they were called); the school's very literary magazine, the *Latin School Register* (Santayana had been one of its earlier editors); a long list of prizes, awards, and medals, with or without palms. Sports were tolerated, but it was possible (to use an old friend as an example) to be All New England Interscholastic Tennis Champion in Singles and a person of no consequence in the school.

Isenberg was a person of major consequence in it. He and some few others of similar talents and achievements both dazzled and depressed new arrivals. They easily mastered their subjects; were unintimidated by the system;[3] won prizes in debating, declamation,

2. Not all, or even most, of the masters were as frightful by nature as I have suggested. And some few had human and scholarly qualities so fine as quite to defeat the pressure of the school's institutions. A prime example (and a man most influential in the careers of Isenberg and others) was Philip Marson. His book, *A Teacher Speaks* (New York: David McKay, 1960), a fairer account of the Latin School than mine could be, is most interesting in itself, and makes many references to Isenberg and his contemporaries.

3. At least they appeared unintimidated. When I met Isenberg some-

and essay-writing; acted roles in the productions of the dramatic society; edited the *Register*; and Lord knows what besides. They read whole libraries; spoke with easy knowledgeableness of Freud, Marx, Spengler, Darwin, Shaw, Wells, Joyce, Mann, Dreiser, O'Neill, Yeats, Conrad, James, Galsworthy, Dostoevski, Turgeniev, Nietzsche; and they disputed about theories and social proposals whose names were meaningless to me. Later on it was a relief to find that not all of them were equally informed on all these matters. And, of course, constant inquisitions by our masters had taught all survivors how to make the maximum display of any knowledge they possessed. Even after these allowances, they still seemed to me a remarkable group: bright, intensely and widely curious, and voracious consumers of books.

That they retained so much spontaneity and independence was remarkable. The Latin School's heavy-handed style of instruction scarcely encouraged such traits. All the emphasis was upon the accumulation of hard facts, upon accuracy, thoroughness, and order. Nearly half the working day was spent in translating foreign languages, ancient and modern. The translations were constantly subject to challenge, on grounds semantical, syntactical, rhetorical, and historical. Work in English went much the same way. The author might be Shakespeare instead of Virgil; still, we parsed and paraphrased line by line with careful attention to glossary and footnotes. Too frequently the method of teaching deprived the material taught of all possibility of pleasing. When this did not happen, the method produced scholars with precociously high standards. It certainly developed respect for texts, and inhibited idle chatter about or around literature.

This was impressed on me, rather strongly, during the course of some talk in the *Register*'s office (known as the Sanctum, and off-limits to masters). Isenberg was then, and remained all his life, an assiduous reader of poetry. Someone in the office that day deprecated this devotion; poetry, he suggested, nourished vague and vapid sentimentality, gave exercise to no faculties that were seriously and properly intellectual. Isenberg was outraged. A standard

---

time during the war, he happened to mention a nightmare that had steadily recurred to him. In it he was walking the dim and totally empty main corridor of the Latin School, aware that something deadly impended. It had always the same climax. The voice of the Headmaster, booming off the tiled walls, would deliver the horrendous sentence: "I-SEN-BERG! SEV-EN MARKS!!"

anthology was handy, and Isenberg challenged his dour critic to pick from it, at random, the titles of any five poems, wagering that he could quote substantially from at least four. He also guaranteed to point out five poetic passages which his prosy friend could not satisfactorily analyze and interpret. Isenberg carried out the first part of the bargain; the second part, predictably, broke up in a wrangle.

Isenberg's performance was an exceptional one, displaying a phenomenally quick and retentive memory.[4] But there were others who performed at equally surprising levels. A gaunt young Irishman, John Wright, debated ethical and theological propositions with a sardonic wit and a dialectical ingenuity that were diabolically effective. (He is now a cardinal of the Roman Catholic church.) William E Harrison was another remarkable person. Black, frail, humorous, a delightful companion (for all his incorrigible uprightness), he wrote and talked with grace, drollery, and erudition. (Harrison took politics as seriously as letters. When McCarthyism arrived in Massachusetts, he came—much to his credit—under constant attack by super-Americans.)

These remarks may seem peripheral and overextended. I am anxious, though, to sketch a situation that, early and to an unusual extent, formed or deformed the characters of those immersed in it. That situation mainly accounts for the fact that my earlier and later memories of Isenberg are so much of a piece. *Haec studia adolescentiam aleunt* was the Latin School's official motto. It very often proved true (sometimes in a grimmer sense than Cicero had intended). But those studies and that setting did cause Isenberg to form the style and attitudes which marked him for the rest of his life.

The style featured more than scholarly talents, interests, and habits. The Latin School severely tested both vigor and confidence. Isenberg had ample supplies of both. Rather below medium height, he was stocky, sturdy, even something of an athlete. He swam

---

4. His memory remained prodigious. In his first month at Michigan State, he joined some colleagues who happened to be discussing *The Locomotive-God* and William Ellery Leonard, its somewhat strange author. Stranger still was his poetry, Isenberg remarked, and went on to quote verbatim a running series of sonnets from the "Man and Wife" part of Leonard's autobiographical sonnet-sequence, *Two Lives*. Not an unusual sort of thing for Isenberg to do, but first performances left his auditors goggling.

strongly and, from my hydrophobic point of view, daringly. He played tennis well—his service and forehand were fast, though erratic, and hit in good style—although he did not move very well on court (even then he had a noticeably ponderous gait, rather like a wrestler or a policeman). He was good at baseball and always remained fond of it. Much later (around 1940, I think) this proved a comfort to another baseball fan, Arthur Oncken Lovejoy. Lovejoy was at Harvard that year and was enchanted to find in Isenberg another philosopher willingly and informedly ready to undertake extended on-the-spot observations of the Boston Red Sox' seasonal agony.

The physical appearance, in short, did not suggest prize scholar, bookworm, aesthete, or intellectual. Neither did the voice, conversational style, or social manner The voice had a rasp, rather consciously (I think) varied in pitch and abrasiveness. An argument or anecdote would begin in the middle range and with pauses; as a denouement approached, the pitch would rise, the tempo would accelerate; interrogative, incredulous, or amused grunts would interpolate themselves; the finale—the point of the joke or of the rebuttal—had a buzz-saw quality. The accent had no regional or class qualities. When amused, he laughed rather like a department store Santa Claus, but the "ho! ho's!" came out "huh! huh!", much as though this Santa were strangulating.

Neither then nor later did Isenberg's dress and manner particularly suggest a university person. A few years ago he told me, with pleased and innocent chuckles, that he had been said to have the appearance of a decadent Polish aristocrat. He did not give many strangers that impression. More commonly he was classified as a business or professional type, well established in management, civil branches of the law, a school superintendancy, or something of that sort. Very short conversations were enough to get him reclassified.

Isenberg's conversation had a kind of Johnsonian solidity. Like the great Samuel, he detested cant, and maudlin or mock-philosophical clichés. Quite early he scandalized some relatives at a funeral where there had been a good deal of the teleological talk which, according to Spinoza, leads to gloomy suspicions that "nature, the gods and men are all mad together." Turn by turn, people remarked antiphonally (and truly enough) on the kindness, honesty, fortitude, and so forth, of the deceased. Each encomium was capped by much the same expression of puzzlement: "This good man, why did he have to die?" Isenberg remarked, "I understand it was heart failure." The explanation was considered heartless.

He had no use for the cant of false modesty either, and his rejection of it earned him in some quarters an undeserved reputation of conceit. As a young man, he exploited this by writing for the *Register* an essay upon the trait, and the ease with which he had become one of its outstanding exemplars:

"Were you first in your class last year?," asked a young lady of me a year or so ago. "No," I replied, "I was second." "Well, that's good too," she ventured. "Of course, it's good," I said. "Oh!" she murmured, "aren't you conceited." Was I then expected to conceal my thoughts, to reply to her with a modest disclaimer? What profound hypocrisy!

Isenberg all his life derived pleasure from this ploy, as some folks do from distributing explosive cigars. Two years before his death, he was introduced (and identified as, among other things, an aesthetician) to a colleague in the English department. "Ah," said the latter, "no doubt you keep up with the work of Kenneth Burke?" The reply came with an evil chuckle: "Keep up with it? I'm far, far ahead of it!"

Quasi-automatic compliments are closely related to cant, and Isenberg had a definite, perhaps excessive, distaste for them. Speaking about a person, he was quick to express admiration and liking, warmly and perceptively. He would never, or scarcely ever, speak in that fashion to the person concerned. As a consequence of these scruples, he may have struck some people as more reserved, less open to friendship, than was truly the case.

Isenberg had little use for small talk, was uncomfortable when much of it was required, and adroit at turning it off. The range of his interests and knowledge was so wide that banalities about, say, the weather, could be smoothly and spontaneously attached to some less humdrum proposition (as when, in one case, he attached it to Milton's argument that bad weather and bad teeth accounted for the way Englishmen pronounced Latin). Usually, once the talk had been jostled out of conditioned-reflexive grooves, it stayed out. When this failed to be the case, Isenberg grew progressively more and more silent, more and more the picture of stoic melancholy.

Another news clipping (from the Michigan State University

daily) reached me in Italy that spring. It was a letter concerning Isenberg written by a graduate student of his, a very fine one, J. Peter Meloney. I quote a bit that set me thinking about a number of things. "Some weeks ago, while reviving from a lecture at the departmental coffee-urn, [Isenberg] took pleasure and gave pleasure by sharing the following epigram which he had been polishing: 'Academic' in the worst sense of the word means 'detached' in the worst sense of the word. 'Academic' in the best sense of the word means 'detached' in the best sense of the word.' Dr. Isenberg was academic in the best sense of the word."

Meloney's comment was perfectly true: Isenberg steadily preserved an admirable, even-handed objectivity about himself, about his talents, failings, troubles, and successes. And the event reported was most typical: the artful insertion into the flow of talk of some epigram or gnomic saying, carefully elaborated in advance. One clearly visualized its delivery—Isenberg solemn-faced and oratund at the start (heavy-lidded eyes lowered to prevent a premature leak of the conclusion); the tone sharpening through the last clause; the quick, round-eyed stare at the end, intent on seeing whether he had surprised and pleased the listener.

I suspect, in fact, that it would be difficult to remember Isenberg without remembering his remarkable expressiveness, the variegated, quick but controlled gestures of the hands, the highly mobile eyes and mouth, the adjustment of the tone and pace of the voice to the topics and the intentions he had in mind. The effects produced, given an insufficiency of art, could have been displeasing or ludicrous. But Isenberg's steady fascination with the theater reflected a natural grasp of, and delight in the actor's skills. His own use of them was expert and legitimate. They made him a most effective lecturer and a formidable participant in philosophical symposia, colloquia, and other such exercises. What might be called the text, the matter transferable without loss to a written transcript, was accompanied by a subtle running gloss and commentary on it, communicated through means which elude stenographic notation.

I shall make only a few remarks on Isenberg's life and professional career. It was nearly inevitable that he should go on to Harvard from Latin School, and unsurprising that he should shift from literary to philosophical studies. He had a natural gift for and delight in the construction and criticism of close-knit arguments. And he found literary scholars (fairly or not, he took Irving Babbitt as a prime example) overly impressionistic and idiosyncratic in their views. His new interests by no means usurped the old ones. He went on reading novels, plays, and poems in English, French, and German, developed a new and strong concern for painting, continued an old one for music. Philosophic work in aesthetics and in general value theory connected smoothly with such preoccupations. But, then as later, philosophy had a nearly across-the-board fascination for Isenberg; logic perhaps not so much, though he did his duty by the subject.[5]

I saw Isenberg from time to time when he was an instructor at Harvard. (His office was in the old Divinity Hall and contained the corpse of a baby shark, glumly afloat in a sealed jar of formaldehyde.) Talk and argument might revolve about topics ethical and aesthetical. Certainly it often turned to the continuing, friendly, and mutually enlightening controversy which he carried on with David Prall on the matter of method in aesthetics. But it was just as likely to involve Whitehead's organicism (which, unfathomably and almost comically, enraged him), Popper's *Logik der Forschung* (a work he also disliked, though less heatedly), the proper understanding of Spinoza's theory of attributes, and so forth.

Isenberg did much of his work in ethics and aesthetics (and, later, in philosophy of mind). This was not because other branches of philosophy proved uninteresting or awkward in his hands. Rather it was because his empiricism was of a somewhat special sort. He took seriously empirical data and their links with the validating and interpreting of factual statements, their role in the formation of concepts, and so on. He took a livelier interest in *empeira*, experience that, in Dewey's phrase, came as "*an* experience." Things (all sorts of them: persons, actions, traits of personality, objects natural and artificial) seldom present themselves with solidity and vividness. Good artists and good moralists (a scarcer species) are uncommonly prone to emphatic experiences, to encounters with things realized as individuals. To be good they need to be alert to nuances, to fine discriminations.

Such nuances excited Isenberg's curiosity, and he was good at

5. According to Henry Leonard, Isenberg took logic under the brilliant but sadly short-lived Ralph Eaton. Isenberg scarcely ever attended classes but submitted all the written assignments for 100s, and calmly accepted an "A" for the course. I do not know what later work he did, or how expert he was in symbolic operations. He was certainly well up on what one might identify as the philosophy of logic, and knowledgeable about contributions made to it by such experts as Carnap, Tarski, Hempel, and Quine.

spotting them. He had, of course, full professional competency in managing ethical concepts and ethical theories. He had an additional, much less usual competence: a sharp eye for the differences between the individual cases that must somehow be all crammed together in the same conceptual file-compartment.

He sometimes claimed that morals and ethics would be much advanced if their work were carried on in Yiddish. According to him, Yiddish was as enviably rich in a vocabulary directed at conduct and character as Eskimo was in terms applying to snow, sleet, slush, and ice. As for the terms he cited in support of this thesis, I never knew which were genuine and which mere spoofs. The argument had this general drift: English (and French, German, and so on) were inferior media for ethical inquiry because they were inefficiently circumlocutory. In English, for example, one would need to speak roundaboutly of the sort of man who, if he should steal all that you have and leave you destitute, and if you were then to beg a loan of him, would indeed make you a loan—but the interest-rate would be terrible. Yiddish, Isenberg would assert, had a single substantive denoting this very special general type. (Unfortunately, I've forgotten the word.) I always, perhaps ignorantly, doubted that Yiddish was all that rich. However, listening to Isenberg read his paper "Deontology and the Ethics of Lying," it occurred to me that he was precisely the man to enrich the moralizing vocabulary of Yiddish, supposing it needed enrichment. He identified more varieties of lies and liars, all (if I may be permitted to say so) entirely believable, than I had ever clearly distinguished in the flow of my own experience. His papers in aesthetics and art criticism show the same taxonomic talents, the same intent and sensitive curiosity.

One connects Isenberg's papers in part (sometimes in large part) with his talk, because talking—which he did so well—was an integral part of his continuous work of inquiry. His conversation ranged sociably over a broad front, but the opinions expressed in it were almost always considered, not impromptu. The interchanges in which they were presented, elaborated, revised, or retracted were tied directly to his peculiar mode of composition. They led to rather fully worked-up notes, which got grouped (and often later regrouped) by topics and assembled in folders. As one such assemblage grew and began to exhibit an embryonic skeleton, it was taken up and became the basis for a paper or essay. A method rather like Bentham's.

That kind of absorption in a subject matter is sometimes said to be incompatible with good teaching. For the people who believe this, "good teaching" probably has a salvational-therapeutic significance. Isenberg was, at least, an outstandingly good teacher of philosophy. He not only knew philosophy but could do it, so to speak, and exhibit what that consisted in. His lecturing was not only lucid but provocative of response. He insisted on that. Once, at Queens College, I passed a room in which one of his classes was meeting, and heard a familiar, hectoring voice: "Speak to me, somebody, for God's sake!" He was thoroughly professional about techniques—syllabi, reading lists, assignments, examinations were developed and used with care and ingenuity. He was unexpectedly patient, and—though not prepared to do plastic surgery on psyches or bugle in society's new day—he wanted philosophy to have for his students more than just scholastic importance. Once, in an earlier era when students professed fewer vital commitments, he came out of a class in a state of angry disgust. "Not one of those people think there's anything wrong with him which a million dollars couldn't cure." He was not content that teaching leave them in such a state.

The teaching went on for a long time, at Cornell, Harvard, Queens College, and finally Michigan State, with visiting appointments at several other schools. The period at Queens was, for the most part, a happy one. Isenberg was there with people he liked and respected enormously—John Goheen, Carl Hempel, Donald Davidson, Herbert Bohnert. New York then, war and all, was the perfect urban environment for him. He knew there many, though by no means every one, of the bright and handsome girls and women who figured in his life.

The period was not all gas and gaiters. There was illness; a hemorrhaging stomach ulcer proved nearly fatal. The radical surgery then popular saved his life but left him in pain for many years after, and altered his life-routine unhappily.[6] Moreover, community tensions turned Queens College into something quite different from what its beginnings promised. First Goheen and David-

6. The attack was sudden and without advance warning. It occurred (in relating this, Isenberg used to mime superstitious awe) at the Toronto meeting of the American Philosophical Association, during Quine's reading of his essay "Two Dogmas of Empiricism." The after effects of the illness persisted for a very long while. They contributed to the severe bouts of melancholy depression which Isenberg had to struggle with at intervals over the rest of his life.

son left; after a miserable year as department chairman, Isenberg
joined them at Stanford. He came to Michigan State in 1962.

My final reunion was with a battered but still indomitable Isenberg. He arrived (and I found this absurdly but deeply touching)
carrying the briefcase he had used since his high-school days. Like
an ancient camel, it had become pouched and wrinkled, and its
hide had turned furry with age. He viewed the new scene, this
newly huge midwestern university ("deep in the Great Plains," as
he put it) with round-eyed astonishment. His ironic-humorous
style was still in evidence, but with its function somewhat changed.
Pretty clearly, it now often served as a defense against self-pity
only too justifiable on grounds of ill health, loneliness, and frustration. He was initially an enigma to new colleagues and to students
of a sort new to him. He became very soon (to the surprise of none
who knew him well) an object of their deep and at the same time
delighted respect. Soon too he appeared to be flourishing better
than for many years before.

The latest and plainest visual recollection I have of Isenberg is
from the time I delivered him to the local airport for a flight to
California. A picture of Napoleonic gloom (the picture he commonly presented in the face of purely practical complications), he
stalks at the head of a little procession. Next comes a graduate student, next the junior, then the senior secretary of the department;
at the end of the line, the department chairman. Each bears a sep-
ate item of luggage or a separate assignment connected with the
mission—is charged with arranging insurance, verifying arrival
times and reservations, and so forth. Unlike the much too common
run of Napoleons, however, Isenberg heads a troupe of more than
willing volunteers. And they see him off affectionately, anticipa-
ting his return.

WILLIAM J. CALLAGHAN

Introduction

The individual merits of Arnold Isenberg's papers in aesthetics and theory of criticism are distinctive and widely recognized. What has been overlooked is the bearing they have, collectively, on the relation of philosophical analysis to the arts. My object in the following pages is to argue that the papers collected for the first time in the present volume provide counterevidence for a kind of skepticism that has come to be taken for granted. What is assumed to be, at the very least, doubtful is that an aesthetic theory that speaks to the actual interests of artists and critics can be of anything more than nominal interest to philosophers. What philosophers respect, so it is said, is repellent to lovers of the arts, who find more substance in—feel greater affinity with—fragments of prophetic thought than abstract exercises of logic. Discounting its frivolous aspects—it is one of the things people *say*, knowing little and caring less about either art *or* philosophy—the thesis is a serious one and can be defended both on inductive grounds and by appeal to arguments a priori.

I

Arguing inductively, one might begin by pointing to the de facto divisions of empire in the world of letters. Individual philosophers in the analytical tradition have written well on paticular topics, but their contributions have the air of occasional pieces and are few in number (as appears from the fact that the same essays appear in each new anthology). Also, none of them aims at the degree of generality required by "theory of criticism" as the term is understood by literary scholars. Standard textbooks on aesthetics do discuss such theories—art as imitation, expression, and the like—but the author of a textbook fulfills his responsibilities by presenting each competing theory fairly and calling attention to comparative strengths and weaknesses. Having surveyed the field, he is under no obligation to reconstruct it. Apart from a dozen or so papers addressed to particular issues, anthologies of analytical aesthetics lean heavily in the direction of metatheoretical questions discussed at the level of abstraction remote from critical practice. The programmatic suggestions that result are, by and large, either very vague (say, that the critic should study "the logic of the concept of art) or negative (that the critic ought not to classify or define works of art).

What nonphilosophers call "aesthetics" (or at any rate what nonphilosophers find worth reading) belongs (so the argument continues) under one of two headings: it is either genuine theory of criticism or philosophy of art. Genuine theory of criticism is normative, is anchored in an authoritative text, and is being tested in actual current practice. (A genuine theory thus stands in contrast to the theory-types canvassed in textbooks by philosophers.) Erwin Panofsky, Northrop Frye, and John Cage are representative of theorists of the visual arts, literature, and music, respectively. The difference between theories of criticism and philosophies of art is one of scope: the former are specific to one medium or artform, while the latter are addressed to the question that, according to. analytical philosophy, ought not to be raised, namely, "What is the nature of Art?" Examples of philosophies of art currently believed in are those of Sartre, Merleau-Ponty, Langer, Ingarden, Lévi-Strauss, and Collingwood. From the point of view of analytic philosophy, philosophies of art are deviant with respect to aims and methods, a fact that their authors acknowledge and indeed claim as a virtue.

A final point: wherever genuine critical theory has profited from contemporary philosophy, it has been due to the efforts of critics, not of philosophers. Richards and Empson learned and applied some of the insights of Cambridge analysis in literary theory; Gombrich recognized in the Wittgensteinian contrast between depicting and describing the nucleus for a new theory of comparative stylistic analysis. But where is the philosopher who has made a comparable contribution to the theory of criticism?

The case against aesthetics, as outlined above, is put as a matter of observation without any theoretical apparatus. The question of why philosophers and critics should have little to say to one another is left open; it may be a difference of temperament, training, or background, or perhaps inexplicable except as a symptom of the spirit of the age. The second and more formal argument can be put in the form of a dilemma:

1. If aesthetics has a distinctive subject matter for its province, it centers on questions relating to the beautiful in art and nature, to principles of critical reasoning, and to the grounds of aesthetic judgment.

2. If aesthetics is a branch of philosophy, then aesthetics consists of the choice of appropriate definitions for the concepts that determine its distinctive subject matter.

3. The beautiful depends on contingencies of perception, feeling, and taste; it is not governed by concepts. The grounds of aesthetic judgment are always particular, and hence there can be no principles of critical reasoning.

Therefore: Either aesthetics has no distinctive subject matter or aesthetics is not a branch of philosophy.

The conclusion of the argument allows for two possibilities that have historical instances. If the beautiful is taken to be one among other topics for metaphysics or psychology, as it was, for example, by Plato, or if the beautiful is assimilated, as by Dewey, to "value realized in experience," then aesthetics "has no distinctive subject matter." On the second alternative, aesthetics is identified with what was described above as "philosophies of art," speculative systems in a tradition alien to that of analytical philosophy.

There are three observations to be made about the argument as I have sketched it: (1) To tell what force it has, whether it presents a genuine and not a merely verbal challenge, would require a lengthy and detailed analysis. Such questions as how concepts are related to perceptions and feelings, or principles of reasoning to grounds of judgment, cannot be discussed to any purpose except in the light of explicit assumptions ranging over epistemology, theory of perception, and philosophy of language. The scale of such an enterprise is suggested by the fact that it would have to include a refutation of Kant's claim that there is an "Antinomy of Taste." The opposition in his summary is as follows:

Thesis: The judgment of taste is not based on concepts,

for, if it were, it would be open to dispute (decision by means of proofs).

Antithesis: The judgment of taste is based on concepts; for otherwise, despite diversity of judgment, there could be no room even for contention in the matter (a claim to the necessary agreement of others with this judgment).[1]

(2) The argument against aesthetics depends on affirming the thesis to be true and on assuming that the legitimacy of aesthetics requires the truth of the antithesis and further that the antithesis is false. None of the philosophers who have questioned the claims of aesthetics on a priori grounds has provided, even in outline, a justification for these two assumptions. Stuart Hampshire,[2] for example, has argued that aesthetics is otiose because (a) it purports to be a critique of critical methods and principles and (b) every work of art is "unique" in a sense that precludes any nontrivial application of principles. But Hampshire does not mention the judgment of taste, nor does he explain how he knows that every work of art is unique in the sense in question. (3) If it had been proved (as it has not) that the idea of a "theory" of art or a "theory" of the beautiful is logically incoherent, then the tendency on the part of contemporary philosophers to avoid dealing directly with the traditional problems of aesthetics would be understandable and a sign of prudence. Reading the other way, the de facto gap between philosophy and the art studies makes the a priori argument *seem* intuitively plausible and perhaps discourages attempts to analyze the basis of its claim.

Skepticism about aesthetics can be expressed either (a) as a doubt, in the light of past performance, that analytical philosophers are likely to contribute anything of substantive interest to aesthetics, or (b) as doubt that an analytical aesthetics is *possible*, that is, internally consistent. Skepticism of the later sort cannot be dispelled until it is clearly stated. Isenberg's example proves that it is possible to satisfy *some* of the interests of artists and critics without slighting the demands of philosophy. Whether in so doing he proves that analytic aesthetics is "possible" in the Kantian sense must be left an open question.

1. Immanuel Kant, *The Critique of Judgment,* trans. James C. Meredith (Oxford: Oxford University Press, 1964), p. 206.
2. Stuart Hampshire, "Logic and Appreciation," in William Elton, ed., *Aesthetics and Language* (Oxford: Blackwell, 1954), pp. 161–69.

II

Every philosopher who thinks he has something to say in aesthetics is confronted with the question, "For whom am I writing?" Isenberg's success can be described as his having found a way to answer that question that avoids the hazards and pitfalls surrounding it. Why should such a question, which arises (obviously) for anyone who writes anything, be particularly troublesome in aesthetics?

Imagine a philosophy student in a state of innocence, that is, a student not yet imbued with the skepticism discussed above. What would make aesthetics seem an attractive field to him? Primarily, no doubt, the subject matter; the arts are interesting in themselves, and he might feel that even if he made no great contribution to aesthetics, his time would not have been wasted. Also, the material is *available* and open to inspection in a sense that distinguishes aesthetic from ethical criticism. Whether it was wrong for Brutus to kill Caesar, whether tyrannicide is ever justified, are prima facie less auspicious than the question whether, for example, Shakespeare's presentation of the death of Caesar is dramatically convincing. Again, criticism and critical theory seem to need the kind of skills that philosophers have and yet not to demand proficiency in unfamiliar, highly technical subjects. (Philosophy of mathematics or philosophy of law are not attractive to amateurs.) In short, aesthetics looks like a reasonable choice for anyone with a sympathetic interest in the arts and a modest philosophical competence.

It may be true of philosophy in general that it is more exciting in prospect than in practice or at least that the satisfactions it provides are different from those it seems to promise. But a student might survive that discovery and still be disillusioned by aesthetics. The problem of choosing one's intended audience brings up in a new form the question of the relation of philosophy to the arts. Suppose that I, eager to dispel conceptual confusion, decide to address thoughts to an audience of critics. Since they cannot be assumed to know philosophy, I have to avoid technical vocabulary and professionalistic mannerisms (such as are developed by philosophers bent on avoiding technical vocabulary). What I write is going to sound like an introductory philosophy course and is unlikely to seem attractive to critics, particularly if the point of my efforts is to call their attention to their logical *gaffes*. Exactly what T. S. Eliot meant by the expression 'objective correlative'[3] has been a topic for discussion among literary scholars. A good case (I think) can be made for saying that it is impossible to make anything but the vaguest sense of the term, as he uses it. But why should I be listened to by scholars who think they *do* understand Eliot and believe the concept of the objective correlative to be a cornerstone of his theory? (Philosophers, of course, are even less likely to be interested in my exposition of elementary rules of definition.)

Suppose then, I undertake to write for philosophers: I find a topic that is anchored in critical literature and that seems to offer scope for philosophical inquiry. Yvor Winters[4] organizes a series of critical interpretations of "experimental" writers around an opposition between two views of "the morality of the artist." The doctrine he rejects, the "cult of romantic irony," he attributes to Kenneth Burke; his own view has to be reconstructed from the series of objections he makes to particular poems and authors. In the course of reconstruction, one comes to see in a *general way* what Winters is for and what he is against. But to get an arguable thesis requires introducing definitions and missing premises, deleting inconsistencies—in short, not editing, but rewriting, the original. One of the results of tidying up Winters' argument is that most of his examples, analyses of particular poems, are dropped. But these are what made his paper interesting in the first place, and without them it seems very thin. The sense of futility is similar to that induced by philosophers' attempts to make psychoanalytic theory into a coherent system. As in the case of criticism, the outcome may be an improvement in point of clarity, but to the extent that being clear involves isolating the theory from its de facto practical uses, the point of the philosophic enterprise becomes obscure.

One way—I suppose the most usual way—of solving the problem of finding an audience is to write for philosophers who themselves write about aesthetics, that is, for aestheticians. There are the various journals to be consulted and professional meetings to

3. T. S. Eliot, "Hamlet and His Problems," in T. S. Eliot, *Selected Essays: 1917–32* (New York: Harcourt Brace, 1932).
4. Yvor Winters, "The Experimental School in American Poetry," in Yvor Winters, *In Defence of Reason* (New York: New Directions, 1943).

attend; aesthetics is a going concern. But this solution has difficulties too. To the extent that one can recognize a common vocabulary for aestheticians, it seems to be a sort of Esperanto, with terms borrowed from technical philosophy, criticism, *and* philosophy of art. It is unsatisfactory as a vehicle for argument and leads to feelings of disorientation. Furthermore, the problem about standards is compounded. It is not, as critics of aesthetics claim, that the general intellectual level is uniformly low, but rather that there is no common standard. A symposium paper that would be good as a dissertation chapter appears side by side with a paper that would be good as an editorial in, say, the *Atlantic Monthly*.

A further difficulty is that while there are a number of relatively well-defined issues that are extensively discussed, the debate is isolated in a curious way from what is going on in philosophy outside aesthetics. Two examples illustrate this point:

1. Is there an "aesthetic attitude"? Although the term aesthetic attitude is a twentieth-century invention, the general idea that definitions of beauty must be intentionalistic is very old. It appears in Plato and Aquinas and is a commonplace of post-Kantian aesthetics. In the early years of the present century, the problem of characterizing and explaining the difference of response to what is believed to be real life and to what is taken as artistic fiction was given a psychological bias and discussed in the terms set by such authors as Edward Bullough and Vernon Lee. Since it was agreed that there was *some* difference that called for explanation, the point at issue, as appears from the writings of, say, Ducasse, Prall, Dewey, Pepper, and Richards, was how the distinction should be drawn. 'Aesthetic attitude' was a kind of blank check, to be filled in according to one or another theory.

In recent years, several philosophers have argued that the aesthetic attitude is an "illusion" or a "myth," and their claims have been opposed by aestheticians who follow the older tradition. But it is difficult to derive from the arguments and counterarguments any clear idea of the nature of the issue, what it is that is challenged by the claim that there is no such thing as an "aesthetic attitude."

2. What is the critical relevance of the artist's intention? The question of how much weight ought to be given, in interpreting and assessing a work, to an author's statement of what he intended in the work, was debated by literary critics before it was taken up

by aestheticians. In "The Intentional Fallacy,"[5] which appeared in 1946, Wimsatt and Beardsley stated the issue in clearer terms than had their predecessors and presented a series of objections to the assumptions of Crocean aesthetics ("Beauty is expression") and also to the practices of critics who claimed credence for their interpretations on the basis of biographical data and what was termed "author psychology." The controversy that ensued engaged the attention of literary scholars as well as aestheticians and has produced—since it continues to the present day—a substantial literature. On the whole, the discussion has been profitable and interesting. It is true that the extent to which opposing parties actually disagree is often hard to determine, since the concept of relevance itself was left unanalyzed. But in contrast to the debate about "aesthetic attitude," vagueness about what it would take to settle the issue did not make it seem verbal. There was enough agreement on an intuitive level about the difference between "relevant" and "irrelevant" criticism to support the use of examples and counterexamples and keep the problem of question-begging in the background.

What made the discussion gradually come to seem archaic from the point of view of observers was the treatment of "intention." In the question as originally set, the artist's intention was taken as one among other psychological factors—for example, his desires, emotions, temperament, and so forth—to be invoked in explaining and interpreting his work. And "author psychology" as a whole was classified along with historical information and sociological data as material for "external" criticism, as distinguished from "internal" criticism which was confined to what could be derived from considering characteristics of the authors diction, style, imagery, poetic form, and the like.

The publication of Wittgenstein's *Philosophical Investigations* in 1953 set philosophy in general off in a new direction, and, with the revival of interest in theory of action and philosophical psychology, the analysis of intention and intentional action became an object of intensive study. On Wittgenstein's view, as developed by Anscombe and others, the pattern of intentional explanation is idiosyncratic and totally unlike that of explanation by way of "mental causes." It was an issue that was (and is) very much in the

5. W. K. Wimsatt and Monroe C. Beardsley, "The Intentional Fallacy," *Sewanee Review* 14 (1946):468–88.

air, and yet it appears never quite to have been acknowledged by aestheticians.

III

Isenberg's strategy in aesthetics is consistent and in a sense simple. He exploits, one might say, the ambiguity of the question, "For whom am I writing?" He writes for philosophers in the sense that he uses the available resources without apologizing for (or trying to circumvent) technically difficult material. To say that he does not write exclusively for aestheticians is perhaps mildly tendentious: what I mean is, first, that nothing in his writing presupposes a knowledge of current topical disputes in aesthetics and, second, that he is sensitive to the logical bearing of aesthetic questions on issues in epistemology, theory of perception, and philosophy of language.

At the same time, Isenberg's concern is to give explicit statement to the goals that criticism sets for itself, and in that sense he writes for (that is, on behalf of) critics. For purposes of discussion, I shall distinguish professional "critic" in a narrow sense from "critic" taken in a broader sense, which would include artist, amateur, connoisseur, anyone preoccupied with the fine arts. A philosopher who treats the problems of critics in the narrow sense is, as we have seen, easily tempted to undertake "improvements" that lead in the end to triviality and failure. The cure, as Isenberg shows, is to forswear censorious judgment—confused thinking is common in criticism as elsewhere—and to concentrate on questions raised by criticism insofar as it is successful.

But to recognize successful criticism demands what few philosophers trouble to acquire: a thorough knowledge of critical literature plus a developed skill in critical practice. In 1950 Isenberg prepared a report on the status and future prospects of aesthetics in which he commended to philosophers with an interest in the arts a close study of contemporary critical writings. As is evident from the excerpts from the report which appear as appendix A of this volume, his aim was to turn philosophers away from the abstract and the programmatic toward concrete questions raised by particular passages of critical writing.

Isenberg's own talent for criticism is well displayed in the present volume in two of the papers in part 2: "Cordelia Absent" and " A

Poem by Frost." The latter is of particular interest as illustrating the kind of interaction he envisaged as between the practice and the theory of criticism. A genuine tour de force, it is divided into two sections: the first, a line-by-line exegesis of "A Star in a Stone Boat," and the second, a critique and commentary on his own interpretation. As a corrective for "philosophical remoteness," Isenberg had prescribed a thorough acquaintance with "the rich though incoherent reflections of men working in the mines."[6] A sure way —Isenberg's way—of gaining that knowledge is by working in the mines.

"Perception, Meaning, and the Subject Matter of Art" (hereafter "PMSA") is one of a group of papers, including "Music and Ideas," "The Aesthetic Function of Language," and "The Problem of Belief," each of which is addressed to questions about the relation of "form" to "content" or "subject matter" in the various arts. How to interpret the common focus of these papers, whether we are entitled to speak of "The Form-Content Problem" as one that emerges in different critical contexts, is a question that Isenberg leaves open. His view, I think, would be that to the extent that each issue can be settled in its specific context, the motivation for moving to a higher level of abstraction will be diminished. To put it another way: we do not *know* that there is some single metaphysical question relating to form and content, but we are confronted with a variety of particular and, from the critic's point of view, practical questions, and these take precedence.

The argument of "PMSA" is condensed and, in some places, difficult to follow. His essay "Formalism,"[7] an unpublished lecture outline, provides a good introduction to the topics discussed in "PMSA." It is discursive and colloquial in tone and illustrates some of the distinctive features of Isenberg's approach. He begins by explaining his choice of Roger Fry and Clive Bell as representatives of formalist theory. Their views, he observes, are not well developed and are far from novel.

Yet the modern formalist movement in the aesthetics of painting was unique in its *auspices*. We know what these auspices were: a great and seemingly progressive "retreat from likeness," as one writer has called it, in the practice of the foremost painters of the age. Hence the old thesis acquired new meanings. One could perhaps show that there was no idea in Fry that could not be found

6. See appendix A, p. 290.
7. See chapter 2 in this volume.

in Ruskin. But even Whistler, who passed for a formalist in his day, did not imagine any such work as Cézanne's; while Fry lived to see the work of the cubists, and vorticists, and suprematists. The range of application of the old terms changed; new and distinctive concepts of form and subject were developed and these have blanketed the age down to the present day.

I think there is more to Isenberg's point about the "auspices" of modern formalism than perhaps appears. No matter how humdrum or how wild it may be in itself, a doctrine acquires a certain interest just by virtue of being believed by a man of genius. T. S. Eliot makes us curious about Anglo-Catholicism, Rimsky-Korsakoff about theosophy. And, as Isenberg remarks in the sequel to the passage quoted, the "real sources" of the views put forward by Fry and Bell are the occasional writings of painters themselves—Chirico, Kandinsky, Leger, Matisse, Malevitch, Mondrian, Tanguy, and Moholy-Nagy.

But Fry and Bell are interesting not just because they offer a coherent resumé of the dark sayings of artists, but because they were able to put their doctrine to good pedagogical use and to bring about a genuine revolution of taste in the visual arts. (Nothing comparable has happened in music; what was regarded as avant garde in 1920 still sounds exotic to audiences today. Schoenberg is supposed to have predicted that, in thirty years, he would be regarded as no more "difficult" than Verdi, but his prediction has yet to be fulfilled.) The hunches of the formalist critics, as it happened, proved to be correct, and their intuitions communicable. They taught a whole generation to see and respond to the distinctive aesthetic merits of abstract art. And since we know and appreciate that art, we are in a position to explore the nature of their achievement, to study their theory not in the abstract, but as a functioning element of successful practice. The point could be put as follows: Roger Fry was no philosopher, but Plato, who also espoused the doctrine that Beauty resides in Form, was, to judge by what we have to go on, no critic, and, apart from unobservable circles and triangles, provides no examples of Beauty as Form. To understand what Plato *meant* by 'Form', we study metaphysics and logic; to understand what Fry meant by 'form', we study Cézanne. This is part of the thought expressed when Isenberg says, "the range of application of the old terms changed."

In recent aesthetic theory, the standard thing to say about formalism is that it illustrates the error of "essentialism." The motto of the movement—"Art is significant form"—is cited as a misguided attempt to impose a strict logical definition on an "open-textured" concept. Such attempts, in the words of one critic, "foreclose on the very conditions of creativity in the arts."[8] Moreover, inasmuch as the proposed definition is clearly circular, the formalists are exposed to the double ignominy of failing even by their own faulty standards. The high-handedness of such an objection, the strange picture of Bell and Fry driven by the desire to emulate Carnap, illustrates the hazards of aesthetics "done from above."

Isenberg, although he does not concede any merit to the theory as such, offers a persuasive interpretation of the formalists' aims. Their argument, as pieced together from various scattered passages, is simple:

Since there are great paintings with humble subjects and mediocre paintings with exalted subjects, it cannot be the subject of a painting that determines its value; but if not the subject, what could it be unless it were the "form," that is, the mode of organizing color areas on canvas?[9]

The formalists are not looking for a definition that will "close" the concept of art: they are trying to find some explanation that will cover the whole range of their own positive aesthetic response. Their reasoning is inductive and, in particular, causal. There is nothing, Isenberg observes, inherently absurd in such a project. If feelings and emotions in general have causes, then so do aesthetic likes and dislikes. And as to the features of a particular work that explain our feelings about it, part of what we expect of a critic is that he point these out. What is wrong with the argument is that it assumes, first, that "abstracting the subject matter describes some actual operation that can be performed, a sort of laboratory experiment," and, second, that all aesthetic responses must have the same explanation.

Philosophers who object to formalism on the grounds cited above find *all* traditional theories of criticism defective in the same way, that is, in virtue of their obsessive concern with the defining conditions of art. Since the most familiar "definitions," taken from their contexts, are no less vapid than "Art is significant form," there is a puzzle about why anyone should have taken them seriously.

8. Morris Weitz, "The Role of Theory in Aesthetics," *Journal of Aesthetics and Art Criticism* 15, no. 1 (September 1956): 27–35.

9. See chapter 2 in this volume.

The solution, according to Weitz, whose strictures were quoted above, is suggested in the following passage:

In each of the great theories of art, whether correctly understood as honorific definitions or incorrectly accepted as real definitions, what is of the utmost importance are the reasons proffered in the argument for the respective theory, that is, the reasons given for the chosen or preferred criterion of excellence and evaluation. . . . Look at the Bell-Fry theory again. Of course, "Art is significant form" cannot be accepted as a true, real definition of art; and most certainly it functions in their aesthetics as a redefinition of art in terms of the chosen condition of significant form. But what gives it its aesthetic importance is what lies behind the formula: *In an age in which literary and representational elements have become paramount in painting, return to the plastic ones since these are indigenous to painting.*

Thus, the role of theory is not to define anything but to use the definitional form, almost epigrammatically, to pin-point a crucial recommendation to turn our attention once again to the plastic values.[10]

Although what Weitz says is true, his way of expressing himself conceals questions of genuine philosophical interest, in particular the question of how "significant form" is related to "representational and literary elements." This was a problem with which Fry, at least, struggled continuously, and it is one that impinges on a variety of philosophical interests. Weitz's efforts to rehabilitate formalism end by trivializing it. What he says comes down to this: Despite the fact that the formalists fail to provide any coherent and nontrivial interpretation of 'plastic value' and 'significant form,' we must nonetheless be grateful to them for calling our attention to plastic values and significant form.

IV

The central insight of the formalists may be put briefly: whatever it is that makes a painting good must be something discernible in the painting, and not something *inferred* from what is discernible—that is to say, must be a visual feature. The issue under dispute between formalist critics and their opponents concerns the consequences of this principle for critical practice. To Clive Bell it appeared that the following two propositions were entailed: (1)

10. Weitz, "The Role of Theory in Aesthetics," p. 35; my emphasis.

The subject matter of a painting can be "of no importance," and hence abstract painting, being purged of irrelevance, has, so to speak, a better chance of being good than representational painting. (2) Anyone who offers as his reason for liking a painting a description couched in a nonformalist vocabulary (for example, a portrait admired for its expression, a genre scene for the mood it evokes) shows himself to have missed the values distinctive to painting and to have mistaken some private association that happens to please him for a genuine aesthetic response.

It is Isenberg's position in "PMSA" that both propositions are false and, hence, that if they are entailed by the formalist principle, it too is false. And yet the principle seems intuitively true and also fundamental. The aim of his paper is to resolve the apparent conflict.

I shall argue that an all but complete analysis of 'subject matter' can be given by a *presentational* aesthetic; and that we may, therefore, continue to identify the aesthetic with the immediate without submitting to the reductions of formalism.

The structure of Isenberg's argument is rather complex, and, rather than try to reproduce its various turns in a paraphrase, I shall simply summarize the main points.

1. Whatever is visible (for example, sitters as well as their portraits, natural as well as picture landscapes) can be described in the formalist vocabulary which refers only to shapes, colors, and organization of space.

2. When we identify or refer to a natural object that is familiar, we ordinarily do so by a "nonformalist" name or description, such as 'the moon', 'the barn I see from my window'. The formalist vocabulary serves a practical function in situations where we want to refer to something seen which either is unfamiliar (for example, what a novice sees through a microscope) or awaits classification ("those dark specks on the horizon").

3. Nonetheless, the features that the formalist vocabulary picks out, that is, shapes and colors, are those which enable us to identify familiar objects by name, as with the moon, a barn, and so on. By the same token, confronted by a representational painting, we can identify the picture-moon or picture-barn. (Isenberg adopts the convention of referring to the latter as "the moon," "a barn.")

4. Visual recognition requires the capacity to classify colored shapes on the basis of perceived and remembered similarity. Simi-

larity is a symmetrical relation. A picture may be said to "represent" a natural object in contexts where the former serves some practical, surrogate function, for example, passport photographs, aerial surveys. Such representation, fixed by convention, is an asymmetrical relation—is not a pictorial quality but a use to which pictures may be put.

5. The aesthetic interest of a picture is fully determined by its pictorial qualities, which include recognizable shapes such as "the moon," "a barn."

6. It follows that "subject matter" in pictures is a subclass of "form" distinguished only by its familiarity, that is, by its resemblance in greater or less degree to what we recognize by name (the moon). The notion of a contrast between "subject matter" and "form" is logically incoherent. The formalist vocabulary may nonetheless serve a critical or aesthetic purpose in relation both to pictures and to natural objects There is, however, no reason of principle for preferring this vocabulary to less ascetic idioms (for preferring "Arrangement in Grey" to "Whistler's Mother," for instance). Nor is there any reason to suppose that the many items, both pictorial and natural, which by virtue of their unfamiliarity invite description in formalist language, are of special, or indeed of any, aesthetic interest ipso facto.

Details and illustrations that are omitted from my summary are important, but some general lessons can be drawn from the argument in outline. Isenberg resolves the paradox set forth in the opening sections of the paper by showing not just that there *need* not be an opposition of opinion on the level of theory between formalists and their opponents, but also that there *cannot* (logically) be such an opposition. If the proof he offers withstands closer examination (as it seems to me it does), then one major problem in one area of aesthetics has been solved. Isenberg is certainly not the first to notice that the supposed dichotomy of form and content in the visual arts involves some kind of confusion, but his predecessors were unable to make the sources of confusion explicit. Many said simply that form is identical with content: but philosophical problems cannot be solved by fiat, and Isenberg is right to distinguish his position from that of philosophers who speak of a "fusion" of form and content. (A. C. Bradley somewhere recommends that we speak not of "meaning plus paint" but rather of "meaning in paint.")

Theoretical resolution of a controversial issue does not guarantee an end of controversy, but then nothing does. At best, it shifts the burden of proof; philosophers or critics who feel after reading Isenberg that important aspects of the Form-Content problem have not been touched, are now under at least some slight pressure to say what those aspects are.

In "Music and Ideas" Isenberg provides an exposition and analysis of the dispute between the advocates of "pure music" and critics who subscribe to one or another form of "expression" theory. The obvious—at any rate nominal—analogy with the topic of "PMSA," invites a comparison of the two papers. To trace the details of each argument, noting where they run parallel and at what points they diverge, is an exercise well worth undertaking, particularly for anyone who is interested in the semantics of critical description. Apart from questions of structure and organization, "Music and Ideas" differs from the earlier paper in style and in spirit. It is concerned less with the problems of professional critics —perhaps because the musical purists, Hanslick or Gurney, for example, show none of the critical gifts of the "formalists"—and more with the kind of question that is likely to be raised by what I called "critics in the broader sense," which includes artists and amateurs. The difficulty of finding a point of contact between *their* interests and what philosophy can offer is, in one sense, greater than that discussed above. With respect to the professionals, what I wanted to suggest, as the lesson to be drawn from Isenberg, was that to appreciate the problems of the critic, a philosopher must know the critic's trade as well as his own. (Where irrelevance is the product of ignorance, no "deep" explanations have to be sought.) Now to the extent that criticism is a trade, that is, a craft or *techné*, it can be taught and learned. Like any rule-governed skill, such as auto racing or dental hygiene, it offers a foothold for conceptual analysis. Where decisions have to be made, there is room for discussing criteria, a trivially general truth. But what we are apt to find puzzling in our transactions with the arts (outside of the classroom, that is) cannot always be clearly formulated. What might be called the "primitive questions" of aesthetics are characteristically vague, "subjective," inchoate—often little more than exclamations. I emerge from a performance of *Parsifal* thinking (or saying), "How can anyone sit through the *uncut* version?" This might be witless conversation-making, or it might express genuine puzzlement. And I myself may not quite know which; nor, since it is characteristic of the primitive questions of aesthetics to be nonpressing, may I be inclined to pursue the matter. Even questions that are in sharper focus, such as "Why does Michelangelo's sculpture make me uneasy?" are problematic in that it is not clear to whom they are or ought to be addressed. To be perplexed by the nature or degree of one's feeling response is, in the nature of the case, to be in doubt about what kind of explanation is in order. Should I scrutinize the stimulus-object or review my own emotional history? One of the primary values of criticism is that it can sometimes serve to dispel such doubts before they become articulate. But how can *philosophy*, except through the analysis of critical concepts, be responsive to the genuine, though unanalyzed concerns expressed in "primitive questions"?

One way is simply by taking account of them, giving them their due weight. The central issue of musical aesthetics, on Isenberg's view, can be expressed only in questions that are archetypally "primitive," for example, "What is it about music? Why does music have the effect that it has on emotions and feelings?" Given the difficulties of explaining, or even of describing in the first person, the impressions connected with listening to a particular composition, the question why music in *general* should have affective power appears to verge on vacuity. Nonetheless, Isenberg claims, all the varieties of critical theory may be seen as attempts to dispel or to rationalize the feeling that there is something essentially mysterious in the power of music. What gives "Music and Ideas" a dimension that is lacking in "PMSA" is that, in working out the technical problems raised by the opposition of critical theories, Isenberg is concerned throughout with the central and "primitive" question. The latter, it is true, cannot, strictly speaking, be *answered* except in the sense suggested by Wittgenstein, "when no questions remain . . . just that is the answer."[11]

The argument, in summary, is as follows:

1. The emotional effects of music seem to require explanation largely because they are unfamiliar; listening to music is, for most of us, an occasional diversion and, hence, not a model for ordinary thinking about emotion. To be overjoyed by the birth of a child seems natural; to be overjoyed by nothing more than a melody seems strange. This is an accident; were it not for the effect of habit, the one might seem no less astonishing than the other.

11. Ludwig Wittgenstein, *Tractatus Logico–Philosophicus* (London: Routledge & Kegan Paul, 1922), § 6.52.

2. "Metaphysical" accounts fail by attempting to explain the obscure by the more obscure: "The majesty of God, the salvation of the soul, the transcendence of suffering—whatever be the feeling quality of these ideas, it is not clearer but less clear than that of a military march." To show that music "contained a presentiment of luck at the races" would make more sense as an explanation of its effects than saying that it contained a presentiment of eternity.

3. The effects of music in general require no explanation. We are properly awe-struck by an individual work or genius even though we may, by having that work explained to us, come to understand it better.

4. A single note or a five-finger exercise has its own "expressive" character, and we are not tempted to ascribe *that* character to its philosophic content. There is a continuum between the simple exercise and the musical masterpiece; the latter has a more complex and interesting character, not a character linked to a thought. Similarly for literature: "as we pass from the first sentence we ever learned to the reading of *Paradise Lost*, we speak more words and better words, but there is no point at which speech transcends itself and takes on a new dimension."

Points 1 through 4 summarize what Isenberg takes to be true and consistent with doctrines of the advocates of "pure" music. What he rejects are the supposed consequences of 1 through 4. Accordingly:

5. The complaint against program music, if it relies on the claim that music cannot or ought not to be conjoined with ideas, is mistaken in principle, as is proved by the existence of song and opera, both legitimate art forms. And there is nothing in the difference between perception and imagery to warrant a prejudice in favor of what is seen (for example, the set of *Aida*) from what is imagined (a sorcerer's apprentice and his misadventures). The only aesthetically significant difference is purely contingent; the stage set was constructed by a designer and is the product of training, thought, and creative art. "Can an audience, prompted by a mere title, or a scrap of a program (and not one program has ever been written that was worth reading for itself) improvise . . . a landscape that can vie with this? Nothing can confer value that does not possess it." The thoughts and images that pass through my mind while half my attention is taken up by listening are unlikely to be such as will augment whatever value the music has.

6. Some music, such as the *Pastoral Symphony*, is plainly imitative, that is, contains sounds that are in some respects similar to nonmusical sounds (thunder, wind, breaking waves, and so forth). Music can imitate anything it can resemble: "if in music there are fine gradations of tone, then music can imitate anything else that, like the sunrise, proceeds by minute changes or barely perceptible shades."

7. Associated images are no more required for the appreciation of the musical imitation of a sunset than for the appreciation of a sunset. Rimsky-Korsakov's musical bee sounds enough like ordinary bees to account for our coming to accept, perhaps with the help of a title, that the two sounds fall under the same concept. The one need not "remind" us of the other; they are similar, although the ordinary bee is less interesting to listen to than the musical bee. Hence, "program music is a species of absolute music which is distinguished by its form and nothing but its form from other kinds of absolute music."

8. Although music is simply music, music may be sweet, bitter, morbid, gay, portentous, or melancholy. The effect of the vocabulary restrictions imposed by the formalists is to make it impossible for the critic to mention such qualities in describing music —a prohibition which is arbitrary and pointless. That music, tonal experience, can be described in language native to areas of experience other than tonal is a matter of fact and has no tendency to show that music is something other than music.

The human imagination is always at work. Metaphors are ubiquitous in language. Every area of experience borrows from nearly every other. *Light* and *gloom* come from visual experience; *light* and *heavy* from the sense of weight. It seems rather silly to ask how music can be *light-hearted*, as if you already knew how a *heart* can be *light*.[12]

Natural objects, no less than works of art, are topics of figurative description. We read of the inscrutable sea, the self-contemplative sea. Why, then, are there no philosophers who say, "This proves that water is not just water but a vehicle for profound spiritual concepts"?

The principles Isenberg establishes in the two papers I have discussed are applied, with modifications, to those which deal with

12. See "Music and Ideas," chapter 1 of this volume.

the question of aesthetic meaning and belief in the literary arts.[13]
The issues raised by the latter are less easily summarized than those
I have discussed, and I leave their interpretation to the reader.

Isenberg's career spanned the transition from the "old" aesthetics—the work of Prall, Ducasse, and Dewey, for example— to the
"new," first clearly recognizable in *Aesthetics and Language*, the
collection of essays edited by William Elton which appeared in
1954. Among the other incongruities of contemporary aesthetics
is that the two traditions continue to exist concurrently. The older
tradition is, broadly speaking, phenomenological and concerned
less with particular problems of critical theory than with discriminating the aesthetic from the moral and the cognitive "dimensions"
of experience. There were genuine theoretical differences (between Dewey and Ducasse, for instance), but in retrospect the
areas of agreement are striking. Few philosophers of the earlier tradition would have found reason to object to the conception of
aesthetics offered by Santayana:

A definition that should really define must be nothing less than
the exposition of the origin, place, and elements of beauty as an
object of human experience. We must learn from it, as far as possible, why, when, and how beauty appears, what conditions an
object must fulfill to be beautiful, what elements of our nature
make us sensible of beauty, and what the relation is between the
constitution of the object and excitement of our susceptibility.
Nothing less will really define beauty or make us understand what
aesthetic appreciation is.[14]

The distance that separates the "old" aesthetics from the "new"
is apparent if one puts Santayana's expansive conception side by
side with recent discussion of the role of definition in aesthetics.
As is suggested by the introduction to the Elton volume—"the
present collection attempts to diagnose and clarify some aesthetic
confusions, which it holds to be mainly linguistic in origin"[15]—the
"new" aesthetics had a strong polemical bias. Now it is certainly
true that the tradition of Dewey and Croce provides many examples of "confusions . . . mainly linguistic in origin," but inasmuch
as the real object of attack is the conception of philosophy in

13. See "The Aesthetic Function of Language" and "The Problem
of Belief," chapters 5 and 6 in this volume.
14. George Santayana, *The Sense of Beauty* (New York: Dover,
1955), p. 11.
15. Elton, *Aesthetics and Language*, p. 1.

general as espoused by the older generation, it is not clear what is to be gained by pointing to particular "confusions." To put it another way: the differences between the linguistic philosophers and their predecessors do not seem to be *specifically* relevant to aesthetics. It was as if the genuine and interesting problems got lost in the cross-fire. Isenberg took no part in the light-level, methodological debate and was therefore free to follow his own intuitions without being constrained by party loyalty. He was not the only philosopher to do so—and the picture I have presented is, of course, oversimplified. Nonetheless, Isenberg's contribution has a systematic breadth and richness of detail that makes it distinctive and assures him a unique place in the history of aesthetics.

MARY MOTHERSILL

PART I

Aesthetics

1

Music and Ideas

The great question in the aesthetics of music is the so-called problem of expression. It has always been a matter for wonder and exclamation that tones should be "expressive," that is, that they should have the power to arouse emotion. "Is it not strange," as someone says in Shakespeare, "that sheep's guts should hale souls out of men's bodies?" Strange indeed. A sense of the miraculous enters into the experience itself: it sometimes seems as if half the beauty of the music were in the astonishment.

Think of it a minute. A great novelist of this century tells us about a man who, having yielded up nearly every positive purpose in life, finds himself restored to youth and ambition through the influence of a short phrase in a sonata. A poet, apostrophizing the art of music, says that it transports him *into a better world*. Another poet declares:

> With you alone is excellence and peace,
> Mankind made plausible, his purpose plain.

But examples are hardly needful, for all who know music know it as an influence which radiates into every department of life.

But what *is* it that is so charged with implication for thought and feeling? Sounds without sense, saying nothing and meaning nothing, less significant than a call or a cry which draws the attention

---

Read at a meeting of the Bay Area Aesthetics Society in 1951; also delivered at Stanford University, autumn 1952. From a typed copy given by the author to Professor Sue Larson, Barnard College.

to some object or situation not itself. Is it any wonder that there should be so many writers who seem to say, "I can't believe it! I won't believe it! It cannot be just the music. Sounds never did any such thing to anybody. It must be something behind the music. It must be religion or poetry or painting or philosophy. Now *there's* something you really can get excited about."

The effects of music are doubtless in need of explanation. But everything is in need of explanation: the bawling of a child, the growth of a bean. Not everything, not even everything that taxes our curiosity, is accompanied by a sense of anomaly, as if *it should not be*. Music, merely as a topic of speculation, is saturated with just that sense. The first step, therefore, in musical aesthetics is not to answer the question, Why does music please?—a question that will still be on the hands of the psychologists ten thousand years from now—but to find out what kind of question it is: discover the source of the element of amazement, of incredulity, and if possible remove that element.[1]

I

Perhaps it is strange that there should be any joy or sadness at all. But common experience, associating these feelings with certain types of occurrence, makes us accept them as natural and prevents wonder. "Why is he so downcast?" "He has lost nearly all his fortune." "What is the celebration about?" "Our daughter has just been married." These are, in ordinary life, sufficient explanations. Why we are not so made as to bewail good fortune and rejoice over death and illness is a question that may bother the philosophical psychologist but will not interest another man, who is satisfied when he sees that an emotion has a reason such as he is

---

1. We need to make a distinction here between aesthetic surprise and another kind that might be called scientific or philosophical. As already noted in the text, a sense of the miraculous sometimes enters into the very hearing of a piece of music which, as we say, is *incredibly* beautiful. Great originality in any art must be, whatever else it be, astonishing. But the wonder of which I have been speaking occurs at a second moment, when the result is in, and the person finds himself marveling at what has happened to him. Music and its effects, including the astonishment, are then considered as a datum, a fact to be explained; and a new wonder is felt, which is that of the observer of nature. We marvel not at the music any longer but at the fact that the music should be found so marvelous.

used to finding for that kind of emotion. Of course, there are cases that will baffle him. If he comes upon a group of people somewhat tearful because, having acquired a lot of money, they are about to leave their home in the slums, he is given no pause; for his experience, supplying some maxim about "the effects of habit," helps him to understand such a mixture of feelings. But these mixtures can grow complicated; and when our attention is called to strange depressions and euphorias, "baseless" elations and melancholies, we admit that we do not understand them. For we feel that they *ought* to be about something tangible and external; but they are not visibly about anything at all. Yet the clinical psychologist, who analyzes just these peculiar constellations of feelings, will consider himself successful—when? When he has made them *as* or *nearly as* comprehensible as, say, the glee of a pitcher who has won a ball game or the indignation of a man whose watch has been stolen. These simple and direct discharges of feeling may, at some profound level of psychological thought, themselves require explanation; but they are *models of intelligibility* for all of the more customary researches into the structure of emotion. Freud's psychology, which deals with the weirdest things in life, takes for its basic concepts some of the simplest ideas of human nature: hunger, pain, and pleasure; fear of injury, dislike of frustration. These serve as a conceptual base in terms of which more complicated concepts are to be defined; but they also serve as poles of comparison, standards of psychological intelligibility.[2]

Now music, which has never been anything more than a diversion of mankind, secondary even to its concern with ghosts and a future life, is for that reason not the model in our ordinary thinking about emotion. We feel it natural to be overjoyed by the birth of a child, the end of a war, the discovery of a new country—not by a parade of sounds. This feeling is itself natural, reflecting as it does the difference in degree of familiarity between music and certain other

2. It is to be noted that the explanations cited in this paragraph are not necessarily of a "scientific" kind at all. They are perhaps better to be compared with the case of a man victimized by some mood for which he cannot give or find the reason, and who may say with Antonio in the *Merchant of Venice*, "In truth, I know not why I am so sad." If, later on, he realizes that he had probably offended a friend that morning and that the effect of this unpleasantness was still hanging over him, he will say to himself, "Now I know why I have been so depressed." He has acquired some understanding. It may not be "scientific." But the problem of expression in music may not be a "scientific" one.

things. But is it justified? When we comment curiously on the power of a sheep's gut, we take it to be quite in order for a woman or a political ideal to hale the soul out of a man's body; but is this to be taken for granted? I have just noted that it is open to question by the psychologist and the metaphysician, who by exploring our basic feelings restore the sense of their contingency, which had not been dispelled by demonstration but only allayed by habit. And everything contingent is wonderful. The power of sound is wonderful; but it is not, in this respect, anomalous. The poet who found music strange found almost everything else in human life very strange.

A philosopher who finds music strange and nothing else strange will hit on a device to explain the expressiveness of music. He will say that it tells us, albeit in a code that can never be deciphered, of other things, things that have a powerful appeal to our emotions. It exposes the secrets of the universe. It deals with Platonic Ideas. It states propositions concerning the ultimate nature of things. It is, as Beethoven said, "the one incorporeal entrance into the higher world of knowledge." It conveys to us ideas of man and nature and morality. The influence of music, a thing which we do not understand, is made intelligible as a special case of the influence of metaphysics, a thing which we understand very well!

It is well to remember that such explanations are meant to hold, if not for all music, at least for all great music, and perhaps primarily for the absolute music of Bach and Mozart and Beethoven.

As explanations, they are not impressive. Nearly everything that could be wrong with them *is* wrong with them. It is enough to observe that they explain the obscure by the more obscure. The starry heavens above, the moral law within, the majesty of God, the salvation of the soul, the transcendence of suffering—whatever be the feeling quality of these ideas, it is not clearer but rather less clear than that of a military march. The true model of an intelligible feeling is a child crying because it has lost its doll, not a philosopher pondering the paradoxes of the infinite. If a new Schopenhauer or a new J. N. W. Sullivan should arise to say that music contained a presentiment of good luck at the races, he might help to explain why so many people should be fond of it—better at least than by saying that it contains a presentiment of eternity. It makes much better sense to conceive the blessedness of the saints as a sort of prolonged musical ecstasy than to conceive the pleasure of music as a fore-glimpse of the blessedness of the saints.

Some works of music may have a greater *affinity* with meta-physics than they have with eating and drinking. Music is what is called a "spiritual" good; it is therefore akin to other spiritual goods —though we must also recognize various connections between music and the natural appetites, music and the emotions of every-day life, and so on. But all spiritual experiences are ethereal, refined, tenuous, and complicated. It cannot serve any purpose of explana-tion to interpret one of them by another.

Those who say that music is no mere pleasure, no mere pattern of sounds, but a form of knowledge and a revelation of reality, think they are paying homage to the art. There once was a man, not less an expert on stages of the soul than Susanne Langer or J. N. W. Sullivan, who thought it was *knowledge* that had to be dignified by comparison, and who wrote:

> How charming is divine philosophy!
> Not harsh and crabbed as dull fools suppose,
> *But musical as is Apollo's lute*—

not thinking it disgraceful to interpret knowledge as a food of the mind—

> And a perpetual feast of nectar'd sweets,
> Where no crude surfeit reigns.

II

Music, to become intelligible, need contain no *presentiment* what-ever; for it has its own model—a musical one. We should here draw a distinction between music in the mass, with our general expe-rience of its effects, and the individual work of genius. The latter has no model, no paradigm. It is proper to remain awestruck and incredulous at what Schubert has accomplished in his Ninth Sym-phony; and it is wrong to ask for a prototype or analogy. In a sense we can "explain" the work: we can analyze it into its parts and put it together again; thus the work becomes better "understood," that is, it comes to give the feeling that it is capable of giving. But the *fact* that it should in the end affect us as it does cannot (in this millennium) be explained. But this limitation is by no means peculiar to the aesthetics of music: it holds equally for any expe-rience of high creativity. At the time I write this, I have been reading H. J. C. Grierson on *Le Cid* of Corneille: "When in that play Rodrigue, the Cid, who has killed the father of Chimène to whom he is betrothed, killed him in defence of his own father's honour, meets her on the stage, 'a shudder,' it was said, 'ran through the audience assembled in Mondory's theatre indicating a marvellous curiosity, a redoubling of attention as to what they could have to say to one another in so pitiable a situation.' " It would be hard enough to explain the feelings of Rodrigue and Chimène. What else do they resemble? Grief? Hatred of an enemy? A mixture of grief, love, and hate? Surely these analogies do not carry us very far. But the shudder in the audience! What is there to say but that it is the shudder of *Le Cid*? "But can't it be analyzed into its psychological components, like curiosity, sympathy, and suspense?" Just so—no more, no less, and in no other way—can the Schubert be analyzed into effects of harmony, of melody, of rhythm, and so on. The force of the music is as intelligible or as unintelligible as the force of the play.

It is the general phenomenon of expressiveness, however, that has given the problem to aesthetics; and here we have models aplenty on which to base an interpretation. A single chord played on the piano does not exactly hale the soul out of your body; but it has a definite tone of feeling. A small finger exercise contains some of the simpler elements of musical appeal. Few persons have ever been tempted to ascribe to *these* experiences a literary or philosophic content. But the great masterpieces do not have a different *kind* of value: they have only different and greater values. As we pass from the first sentence we ever learned to the reading of *Paradise Lost*, we speak more words and better words; but there is no point at which speech transcends itself and takes on a new dimension. And there is no point in the development of absolute music at which the score suddenly opens up and admits a brand new order of ideation. Milton is greater than Hans Christian Andersen, but he is still only speaking and flying at once. The enormous disparity in thought and feeling between these two authors corresponds exactly to the range of utterance. And the formal differences between plainsong and sonata account completely for the differences in expressiveness.

III

But if music is simply music, why should it seem to require a description in nonmusical terms? Why should the critical lexicon be so largely drawn from the general field of thought and emotion? Again Shakespeare puts the question for us: "Then music with its silver sound." Why "silver sound"? Why "silver sound" unless the music has some content or connotation of color? But color is only one neighboring field of sensation. Music can also be sweet or bitter. Why "sweet," and why are there "sour" notes? Why "funereal" or "morbid," "gay," "solemn," "melancholy," or "portentous"? These terms do not come from tonal experience; but they seem to fit and belong there once they have been applied. How should that be so unless there were in the music some intimation of the things these terms originally named or described? If we can scarcely speak of music without ranging beyond the language of tone, must there not be an expression of something other than tone?

A good part of our critical usage seems to be the result of figurative thinking by the critics in the audience. You can know a piece of music and know it well even if you do not have to write a review; and it is absurd to suppose that you cannot have the experience unless at the same time words are coming to describe it with —for then what would there be for the words to describe? But the needs of discussion will force us to grope for metaphors and analogies. This is a semipoetical act of imagination that *follows* the enjoyment of music: it is a separate and independent aesthetic moment. For even if some comparisons should flock into your mind during the performance itself, you could not expect another person to have made them. You can, perhaps, ask someone to *agree* to the appellation 'silver': you cannot ask him to see or think of silver while he is listening—when, as a matter of fact, it took a great poet to think of the comparison in the first place.

One wonders why the question should come up with a peculiar force in the aesthetics of music. The human imagination is always at work. Metaphors are ubiquitous in language. Every area of experience borrows from nearly every other. *Light* and *gloom* come from visual experience, *light* and *heavy* from the sense of weight. It seems rather silly to ask how music can be *light-hearted*, as if you already knew how a *heart* can be *light*. Chirico's painting is filled with a sense of foreboding, as if omens were hanging in the very structure of the space. Why should one picture be entitled *Melancholy and Mystery of a Street* and another be called *Nostalgia of the Infinite,* and both seem to be aptly so called? Here, at least, we may receive the answer that there is a problem of expression in painting, like the one we have in music. But what about nature? When I pass a certain body of water not far from my house, I receive always the impression that it is *keeping its own counsel*. And this seems to be a standard impression, for we read of the inscrutable sea, the self-contemplative sea, and so on. Why are there no philosophers who say, "This proves that water is not just wet but is a vehicle for profound spiritual concepts"? and others who ask, "How can *water* have counsels or keep them to itself?"

Such questions *can* be asked; but they belong to the aesthetics of metaphor, not to the aesthetics of water. When Emily Dickinson speaks of "a certain slant of light/ On winter afternoons," that "Oppresses like the weight/ Of cathedral tunes," she gives us a third entity, the simile that she has invented, over and above the slant of light and the cathedral tunes—each an aesthetic object on its own part. We are at liberty, if we wish to speculate on the genesis of figures like this, to say that the rays of light and the organ music have an obscure affinity: *that they are similar in their expressiveness*. But this kinship would, but for Emily Dickinson, never have been noticed; and it is nonsense to say that the expressiveness of the organ music depends on its recalling the light, or vice versa. That way you soon rid the world of all its expressiveness: nothing retains a feeling quality of its own.

Let us say that a figure of speech can have an explicative value and contribute something more than beauty or eloquence to the exposition of a subject. Now when figures of speech occur in expository prose, the subject of the passage (and of the figures) is treated as the unfamiliar term, the idea that needs to be clarified; and the other term of comparison is treated as familiar and intelligible. We should not expect music and its emotions to be considered a primary and obvious sort of experience *while we are talking about music* and trying to explain it. Language has many examples of the reverse relationship between music and the other things of this world. I hardly need to mention the harmonious family and concord or discord in the commonwealth. Friends, as Thoreau said, live "not in harmony alone, but in melody." People speak of the "rhythm" of revolution and reaction. You strike a false note in conversation. A trial lawyer plays on the entire gamut of the jury's emotions. Rousseau and the writers who succeeded him exploit the full diapason of the self. A man's life can have a final cadence and many partial ones. Novels and treatises have been written in the form of theme and variations. Scholars have begun to speak of Shakespeare's "musical method." And in a depressed frame of mind—

Haply I think on thee, and then my state,
Like to the lark at break of day arising
From sullen earth, sings hymns at heaven's gate—

where one of the most familiar emotions is elucidated through a
musical simile. It would be fair to turn the tables on the advocates
of "substance" in music and say that here is proof that one cannot
love a mere girl or desire peace among the nations, but that they
must symbolize, the first a serenade, the second a blue Danube
waltz. And again we may ask: why is there no problem of expression in the psychology of love and hate or of logical reasoning,
where one encounters "neat" demonstrations—"deep" or "shallow" reasonings, and so on.

Besides all those locutions wherein musical experience appears
to be fundamental, there are terms whose root meanings are obscure and which apply just about as literally to music as to anything else. 'High tones' and 'low tones' may be figurative; but to
speak of fast music and slow music is to speak quite literally. And if
Bruckner's music is diffuse, if the structure of a Mahler symphony
is slack, one is surely not borrowing these terms from one's knowledge of clouds or ropes. A child wails, the wind wails, and Tchaikovsky wails—all of them quite literally.

IV

All this time we have been verging upon a question which cannot
be answered but must be mentioned here. What kind of truth or
untruth can a metaphor have? What sort of witness is borne to
the nature of a musical experience by the freely creative act that
likens it to something else? Why are some metaphors apposite and
"true" while others are not? Now metaphor is not the only means
by which music is compared with other things; and before leaving
this question, we should widen its scope.

If we had not so many bad plays and novels in our literature,
perhaps no one would have invented a name for the "sense of anti-
climax." Imagine someone then explaining to another how he felt
about the fourth act of a new drama. "It's like the time when you
see a friend off at the train and the whistle blows and you embrace
and promise to write and each bids the other to take care of himself. And then the train doesn't start for another twenty minutes."

When we cannot name an emotion and cannot or will not furnish
the very situation that gave rise to it, we can still explain what our
feelings were by describing another situation that evokes com-

parable feelings. This manner of elucidation by comparison is not very different at bottom from naming and describing; for there, too, you apply to an object words that have drawn their meaning from other objects.

Now consider Tchaikovsky's explanation of the *Andantino* in his *Fourth Symphony*:

The second movement shows suffering in another stage. It is a feeling of melancholy such as fills one when one sits alone at home, exhausted by work; the book has slipped out of one's hand; a swarm of memories arise in one's mind. How sad that so much has been and is gone, and yet it is pleasant to think of the days of one's youth. We regret the past and have neither the courage nor the desire to begin a new life. We are weary of life. We wish refreshment, retrospection. We think of happy hours when our young blood still sparkled and effervesced and life brought satisfaction. We think of moments of sadness and irrepressible losses. But these things are far away, so far away! It is sad, yet sweet, to pore over the past.[3]

We all know the story about the musician who, being asked the meaning of a piece he had just performed, sat down and played it again. Tchaikovsky could have replied in a like manner to the correspondent who asked him for the "program" of his work, but he seems to have felt that a verbal response would be serviceable. What is he saying? That these were the circumstances that had inspired the movement? But there is not the smallest sign of an autobiographical purpose in the entire passage.

And Tchaikovsky is not telling us what he thought when he made the music; what he thinks when he listens to it; what he hopes an audience will think when it hears the movement; or what an audience *ought* to think if it would understand the work. There is not the least suggestion that the idea of "a book slipping out of one's hand" or of "happy hours when our young blood sparkled" is to form any part of the musical experience.

And if he *had* instructed us to think of such things in the concert hall, we should have no special reason for heeding him. For his authority is only that of the reflective critic reaching for terms of comparison by which to shadow forth the emotional effect of the music—much like one who says, "Homer is to me like the ocean." The ideas come when he *writes* about the music, not when he lis-

3. From Lawrence Gilman, *Stories of Symphonic Music* (New York: Harper & Brothers, 1907), p. 322.

tens to it. If the music produces them, it is by stimulating the analogical imagination, not by "conveying," "communicating," or "signifying" these ideas. The ideas are somehow *like* the music. They are not what the music is *about*. Anyway they are not *in* the music.

The rambling letter by Tchaikovsky is really not different in purpose or effect from the inscription over a movement in one of Brahms's symphonies: *Andante giocoso*. When I first read this, I realized that I had not felt the jocosity of this music; but when I looked for it, it was there. Now the idea of the jocose, and of the heroic and of the pastoral, and of the melancholy, all have vague and diffuse tones of feeling in them; whereas some music has precise and definite tones of feeling. But the adjective 'jocose' denotes a *range* of feelings which circumscribes the feeling tone of the music and *excludes* certain expressive possibilities—possibilities which may not have been already excluded by the careless listener. Language never hits the bull's eye; but it can draw a circle which takes it in and, by leaving out the miscellaneous environment, can focus attention at least on the proper region. That is why we feel dissatisfied even with the idea that the heroic symphony is heroic or the pathetic symphony pathetic and yet admit that these are better than some other terms that might be used. It seems unwise to protest against literary analogy as such, in the criticism of music, seeing that some of these analogies are helpful because they "pinpoint" feeling response, while others are indeed dreadful, increasing the diffuseness of the listener's reaction.

V

So far we have said nothing about a special kind of music that is *certified* as a music of ideas and hence called imitative, descriptive, narrative, or programmatic. What we are going to say about this kind of music is that it is a species of absolute music which is distinguished by its form and nothing but its form from other kinds of absolute music. We shall see that this view has been now and then anticipated in the common criticism of program music. But it is another theory of the subject that has always prevailed among composers, critics, and students; to see what this theory is, we may quote the *Oxford Companion*: "It is music which, instead of being based, purely or primarily, upon a formal scheme of contrasting themes, development of them, repetition of them, etc., is based upon a scheme of literary ideas or of mental pictures which it seeks to evoke or recall by means of sound."[4] The idea of works' being "based" upon ideas or pictures does not tell us very much; but the next phrase makes it perfectly clear: program music "seeks to evoke or recall" certain ideas by means of sound. Ernest Newman says exactly the same thing: "All program music must be . . . suggestive of a certain external phenomenon, such as the wind, or the fire, or the water."[5] What these authorities agree on may be restated as follows: There is one kind of music, called absolute, which affords a single homogeneous experience, purely acoustical from start to finish. There is another kind of music, called programmatic, that affords a complex experience, acoustical on one plane, optical or intellectual on another.

Ernest Newman has been a life-long champion of program music. Certain older writers, like Schopenhauer and Hanslick, were harsh adversaries of program music. Sometimes these writers sound as if they were trying to prove that music cannot convey ideas; but if that were true, they would have had nothing to rave against. What Hanslick was really trying to prove was that music cannot convey ideas *to any good effect*. He was taking issue with the defenders of program music on aesthetic grounds. It would be easy to show that he held the same notion of program music that they did: it is a music that evokes ideas.

We have two questions: first, what is program music? second, is it any good? On the second question we have two schools of opinion: the representationalists, who say that program music is good, and the formalists, who say that it is no good. Both schools answer the first question by saying that program music is a music of ideas. And both schools confound the two questions by quarreling about whether ideas are to be admitted into music, without taking the trouble to *show* that absolute music is pure form and program music form plus ideas.

The questions, the answers, and the confusion are the same that come up in the criticism of painting. The only difference is this. Abstract easel painting is a late development, while abstract music came first upon the scene and established itself by great achievements. So that, in the criticism of painting, the formalists were an advance guard and the old fogies were the representationalists;

4. Peter A. Scholes, *Oxford Companion to Music* (New York: Oxford University Press, 1943), p. 757.
5. *Musical Studies* (London: John Lane, 1905), p. 112.

while in music criticism (at least in the nineteenth century) it was the representationalists who were the progressives and the formalists a conservative old guard.

If someone were to challenge the propriety of combining music with ideas, the answer is that in the combined arts, like opera, ballet, and song, we have a mixture of musical with extramusical ideas. And everybody admits that these arts are legitimate. It must then be legitimate for music to be combined with ideas. The ideas of opera and song are, however, like their music, given to us *through* the senses *by* an artist. The ideas that may be *provoked* by instrumental music are not sensory impressions but images; and they have to be supplied by ourselves. Even when the composer writes out a detailed program, it is meant to set us imagining or thinking while we listen; it is not meant to be read along with the music. And the program is *fitted* only roughly, if at all, to the score: there is no counterpart in instrumental music to the correspondence in a song between the very syllables of a word and the inflections of the music. It is the audience that must do the fitting—and that must furnish from its own imagination the face and body of the hero, the colors of his costume, in a word, everything that is specific and characteristic. Suggestion is only suggestion: we do the rest.

Yet there is no such difference between perception and imagery as to compel us to say that, while the former may well accompany music, the latter cannot and should not. There is no difference in aesthetic principle between the two. If, while I listen, I may see or think what another man has thought out for me, I may certainly see or think what I have imagined myself.

It just happens to be unlikely that I should imagine anything very good. The words of a song have been written by a person gifted in the art of verse. The dance movements and décor in the ballet are the work of skilled artists. I cannot think of any operatic libretto that is poetically distinguished; yet someone has at least taken pains to work out a story; other people have been at work on the scenery and costumes. Can an audience, prompted by a mere title, or a scrap of a program (and not one program has ever been written that was worth reading for itself), improvise a plot or a landscape that can vie with any of these? Can you write even bad verses like Richard Wagner's? Can you compose a plot as silly as one of his, while you are sitting in an auditorium with an orchestra playing at you? Or have you memorized *Thus Spake*

Zarathustra so as to have a worthy text for the music of Strauss?

Nothing can confer value that does not possess it. What is there about a peasant dance or a sunken castle or a lot of nasty little elves or pictures at an exhibition you have never seen that Beethoven's music or Debussy's or Liszt's or Moussorgsky's should stand in need of their support? Not that any of these subjects is contemptible in itself: there are great paintings and fine ballet movements that have little else in them than a bunch of peasants dancing. But how should *you* in ten minutes dream up anything comparable while with three-quarters of your mind you are doing something else? Notice that my point has nothing to do with program music as such. Goethe, hearing a fugue by Bach, saw in his mind's eye "a procession of stately persons descending a staircase." Abstract music can and does evoke ideas, while program music just as often is heard without any visual or mental accompaniment.

To accommodate this fact, some writers are led to seek a *differentia* for program music in the *fixity* of the ideas that accompany the music. The distinction is made to turn on the presence or absence of an explicit program prepared by the composer and published with the work. The music then becomes a conventional medium for meanings—like language, which certainly does convey ideas. If this or that person does not have them, it proves either that his understanding is weak or that the composer has been speaking obscurely. But the argument fails on several counts. Language really conveys its ideas and does not need any program to explain it: if musical tones (or musical phrases) had fixed meanings, they would not need any program either. Besides, program music does not always come with a program. Strauss did not provide a program for *Till Eulenspiegel:* it was cooked up later by the critics. Shall we say that the *Hebrides Overture* and *La Mer* are the less programmatic because only a title is provided with them? On the contrary, these are quintessential program music.

VI

Let us now make a serious effort to say what program music is. Many critics who approve of program music are scornful of "mere imitation." There are two reasons for this. The first is that by 'imitative music' they mean the reproduction of natural sounds, like a cockcrow or the noises of battle. The second reason is that they conceive this reproduction to be quite literal. Musical literature contains a number or such passages, and they are of course limited in their effect. For the sounds to be imitated are scarcely very interesting, and the reproduction does not improve them. Since program music *can* be interesting, the critics feel there must be some other principle than imitation by which to interpret it. It is customary to quote what Beethoven said of his *Pastoral Symphony*—"more expression of feeling than painting." This remark has led not only to the utterly confused idea that music depicts feelings but to many more wisely inspired attempts to show how the feelings produced by music (Schumann's *Rhine Symphony*, Hindemith's *Mathis der Maler*) can match or resemble or agree with the feelings produced by another object (Cologne Cathedral or Grünewald's alterpiece), so that in an indirect manner or in a figurative sense the music can be said to be "about" the object. But one should not appeal to such an elaborate method of interpretation unless the simpler principle of imitation has really proved inadequate. The fact is that a good part of the *Pastoral Symphony is* plainly imitative. The truth is that all program music is imitative. But this, as we shall see, need not be a limitation: there are, for example, greater and better things to be imitated than cockcrows and sounds of battle. A number of writers have tried to explain just what music can imitate and what it cannot; and we shall not repeat them except to say that music can imitate anything that it can resemble; so that if in music there are, for instance, fine gradations of tone, music can imitate anything else that, like the sunrise, proceeds by minute changes or barely perceptible shades. Our question for the moment then becomes: what is imitation in music?

Imagine yourself lying out on the lawn with a bee humming not far from your head. A good many people, including poets, seem to have found this a pleasant sound; and it is a musical sound, for the bee is emitting tones. Now you would not think of saying, when you are actually hearing the bee, that you are being *reminded* of a bee; though perhaps the hum reminds you of the bee's *body*, provided that you are not looking at it at the time. You could not identify the hum, or give it a name, if you had not heard some such sounds before: you are therefore (in the language of philosophy) bringing a concept to bear upon the material of the senses. This act of recognition by means of a concept is part of the act of hearing. But you are not thinking of any sound: You are hearing one.

It is quite true that one *could* be reminded of *another* bee that one had heard the day before. This would be "association by resemblance," and it would be a useful way of thinking if you went on to conclude, "There must be a hive in the vicinity," or asked yourself the question, "Why do they give notice of their where-abouts? How do the evolutionists explain it?" But if your object is merely to enjoy a sound, there is no point in remembering one when you have one right before you.

What would be the case if the same sound were produced by artificial means? This would be an imitation, first, because it is just like a bee and, second, because it is not a bee. But I cannot see that our experience of the imitation need be in any way different from our experience of the original. If the murmuring of bees were something good enough to be worth bringing to us on records, we should be in the position of *enjoying the same thing* that we enjoyed on the lawn, not of recalling what we enjoyed on the lawn. The sounds might be weakly evocative of the lawn or the hive or the pleasures of spring, that is, of anything they were not imitating; but they would not be *evocative* of a hum, because they *are* a hum.

The situation is in principle the same if it is a violin or an orches-tra that does the humming. Insofar as he is an imitator, the com-poser *brings* the sounds and motions of nature into his piece and *gives* them to his audience. He does not ask his audience to remember these sounds and motions. Why then should the critics, or the composer himself, think that the audience is being asked to muse as well as listen and fetch up ideas from its visual imagina-tion? It is because no composer is just an imitator, with nothing better to do than to vie with recording machines. A composer may be stimulated by what he hears: he will not stop with that, but try to make something more beautiful. It is beneath him to duplicate the mediocre rhythm of falling waves or the humming of a bee or the frantic sweeping of a sorcerer's apprentice. These rhythms, however, may save him from duplicating his classical predecessors (who in their day imitated their predecessors and were able to do so creatively); for they suggest patterns of which music had not been thought capable. This is the kind of suggestion that counts in music: the suggestion *by* ordinary natural figures *of* extraor-dinary musical ones; not the suggestion by finished music of objects inferior to itself. The humming of a bee is monotonous; it scarcely varies except in terms of distance from the ear; it has no beat or

accent; it does not state and relinquish and restate a melodic subject nor alternate, at calculated intervals, staccato with legato
passages. Rimsky-Korsakov has done all these things. He gives us,
as it were, a superior bee. His little piece retains a resemblance to
the object that inspired it; but it also retains a resemblance to classical music, with its modes of statement and development. The
first of these resemblances is, *in music,* apt to be slight: so slight
that a person to whom no clue is given would not be able to name
the class of natural objects to which it belongs. This explains the
almost boundlessly variable results obtained by those psychologists who ask their students to say what a given piece of program
music represents. But we know that a person who will never think
of the aunt whom his child resembles and will never be able to
say which relative it is, when asked, will often admit the resemblance when it is pointed out to him. And the students see the
pecking of a chicken in Couperin's piece once the comparison is
made. After that they will, in all probability, say that the piece
reminds them of a chicken. We do not say such things of a garden
by Rubens or Fragonard; but we say them of a garden by Miro or
Klee. It would sound strange to say that Klee paints a garden when
his garden is so unlike an ordinary garden and we have not yet been
taught to say that he paints a very odd and distorted garden; so we
say that he paints something which recalls a garden. It is a permissible though peculiar use of the word 'recall'; but it does not mean
that Klee, while providing one garden, wants us to think of another one; or that Rimsky-Korsakov is dealing with two hums, the
one of the instruments and the other on the lawn.

The principle of imitation can thus be reduced to another
principle: design. The word 'imitative' is not opposed to 'purely
formal'. An imitation has something of the *same form* as the thing
imitated. It need not evoke an idea of the thing imitated. Indeed,
the more imitative it is, the less need it has to evoke such an idea.
The imitation of nature or of literature in music is exactly like the
imitation of previous music: each is a source of formal patterns,
tamely borrowed or creatively reworked according to the genius
and temper of the composer. But the imitation of music tends to
keep music within fairly fixed limits. The inspiration provided by
nature and literature is by comparison heterogeneous: hence the
tendency of program music is libertarian and individualistic; it is
like the other arts of the nineteenth century, which are marked by
the dissolution of traditional forms. The waltz, for example, is a

pretty definite and repetitious form. It is music that everyone considers suitable for dancing to and that nobody would say tells us
about a dance. But a *Waltz of the Flowers*, it has been supposed,
must be accompanied by a play of ideas. There is no such difference between the two. The difference is that the *Waltz of the
Flowers* is exotic, idiosyncratic, and has a relatively unique inspiration and that it is *formally* specialized by comparison with the conventional waltz.

Hence there is a function for programs and titles. In principle
they are always dispensable, just as the formal vocabulary of music
theory is dispensable for purposes of appreciation. If the music
has a rhythm similar to the jogging of a horse, this is sooner or
later *bound* to be heard, whether one ever thinks of a horse or not;
just as the fugal structure is bound to be noticed if the composition
is a fugue. But, critically and pedagogically, both the formal and
naturalistic vocabularies may be valuable; for just as one could not
point out the structure of one piece without formal analysis, so
might it be hard to make someone understand the structure, say, of
Till Eulenspiegel without telling a story, or of the *Forest Murmurs*
without a reference to nature.

Let us consider a final question. Have I not been saying that
music is nothing but a pretty play of sounds? That question is often
put by those who, disregarding the enormous scope of the formal
dimension, imagine that if ideas and significances are once excluded, all music must sound like a finger exercise for children.
One such writer has said, "Great art is a significant phenomenon
and not a direct sensuous pleasure; for if it were the latter, then it
would appeal like cake or cocktails to the untutored as well as to
the cultured taste." This is like saying that if a cathedral were de-
stroyed except for the facade, that facade must be indistinguishable
from a two-inch line drawn on the blackboard. You ignore the
complexity of the one, the simplicity of the other, and then assume
that since there must be a difference, the difference is made by the
introduction of a foreign factor in one of the two cases. Thereby
you illustrate the most prevalent of all fallacies in aesthetics, which
consists in converting a difference of quality into a difference of
level.

It must be admitted that formalists in music criticism often
commit this fallacy themselves or give encouragement to it. When
Stravinsky says that "music is the domain where man orders the
elements of sound and of time," that it neither teaches nor ex-

presses anything at all, he sounds as if he were presenting the same thesis that has been presented in this paper. But really he is making a very different point. He is writing in a vein of reaction *against program music* and wants us to understand that only one kind of music is proper: the others are bad or illicit. Naturally, those whose tastes do not conform to his will insist that there are other brands of music besides Stravinsky's and will put this by *denying* that music is confined to sound and time. I hope we can now see some reason for refusing to believe that this issue is real.

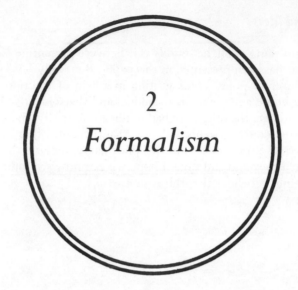

2

Formalism

Now I venture to say that no one who has a real understanding of the art of painting attaches any importance to what we call the subject of a picture—what is represented. To one who feels the language of pictorial form all depends on *how* it is presented, *nothing* on what. Rembrandt expressed his profoundest feelings just as well when he painted a carcass hanging up in a butcher's shop as when he painted the Crucifixion or his mistress. Cézanne whom most of us believe to be the greatest artist of modern times expressed some of his grandest conceptions in pictures of fruit and crockery on a common kitchen table.

Roger Fry

I say to Lidian that in composition the *What* is of no importance compared with the *How*. The most tedious of all discourses are on the subject of the Supreme Being.

Ralph Waldo Emerson

And doubtless I can be moved, as much as by the most expressive figure, by a certain "still life" of Chardin, a dish of plums on a copper fountain . . . ; doubtless I may even prefer some little canvas of Delacroix, representing the *Interior of the Duke de Morny's House*, I think, or a certain red-hot *iron stove*, to some pathetic composition where he falls into the declamatory. . . . This is *true painting* owing to its very absence of a subject; that is seeing painting divested of all spiritual

---

Read at the Annual Regional Meeting of the American Society of Aesthetics, University of California, May 1955. Two typed copies were found among the author's papers when he died; the present paper is a slightly cut and emended version.

virtue, so as to attach a value only to the qualities of the craft; it is seeing our greatest painters of today take care no longer to address themselves to our senses, to be nothing more than eye to brush. This stripping, voluntary omission, will remain, I believe, characteristic of our epoch without a hierarchy and risks causing it to be judged severely later; yes, all the more severely because these painters will have been all the more admirable because of their craft. It is by their lack of *significance* that the paintings of our time will be recognized.

André Gide

I

Early in this century critics of painting and sculpture were reviving an old debate of the aestheticians: Which is more important, the form of the work of art or its subject matter? Those who said the form were called formalists; those who said the subject were termed, hideously but inevitably, representationalists.

The issue was, in sound and appearance, an old one; also to some degree in substance. If one compares the passage I have quoted from Emerson—which could be matched by many others from Goethe, Kant, Reynolds, Burke, perhaps even Michelangelo— with the passage I have quoted from Roger Fry, one sees that the reasoning and the conclusions are not dissimilar. Yet the modern formalist movement in the aesthetics of painting was unique in its *auspices*. We know what these auspices were: a great and seem- ingly progressive "retreat from likeness," as one writer called it, in the practice of the foremost painters of the age. Hence the old theses acquired new meanings. One could perhaps show that there was no idea in Fry that could not be found in Ruskin. But even Whistler, who passed for a formalist in his day, did not imagine any such work as Cézanne's; while Fry lived to see the work of the cubists and vorticists and suprematists. The range of application of the old terms changed; new and distinctive concepts of form and subject were developed; and these have blanketed the age, down to the present day.

The leading documents of the formalist movement, in the English language, consist of three or four weakly reasoned essays, which have been reprinted in anthologies and quoted again and again. If we were asked who the leading formalists were, some would say Bell and Fry while others would say Fry and Bell. The display was not a very impressive one. But this does not measure the power of the movement. If one went to the real sources and culled passages from the occasional writings of Chirico, Kandinsky, Léger, Matisse, Malevitch, Mondrian, Tanguy, Moholy-Nagy, and hundreds of major and minor artists, one could assemble a formidable volume—one which would unquestionably represent the aesthetic climate of the age.

The formalists were the aggressors in the original controversy, simply because representationalism had for many years held the field both in art and in criticism. The formalists were also better critics and more interesting writers than their opponents were. Their judgments have, on the whole, been sustained. Though the issue was and remains a theoretical one, the two sides were associated each with a certain set of tastes and preferences. The formalists despised the academic paintings of the nineteenth century and were receptive to succeeding waves of abstractionism; while the representationalists, hostile to those whom one of them (Rhys Carpenter) termed the Outrageists, retained a fondness for painters like Bouguereau and Sir Lawrence Leighton. Both sides professed reverence for painters like Giotto and Rembrandt; but there, of course, the reasons were different, the formalists admiring mainly the form, the representationalists the subject matter.

The question of form and content gets started in the manner of almost any philosophical question. When I read, in one of the letters of Henry James, that "the facility and abundance" of William Dean Howells, which are (he says) "my constant wonder and envy," have been purchased by "throwing the whole question of form, style and composition overboard into the deep sea," it seems to me that I understand him perfectly and that I agree. But if someone should claim that he does not understand or should offer a different opinion, I would not know how to locate the characteristics that were being discussed. A certain type of curiosity, therefore, impels us to ask what is meant by form; and when we do this, it is natural to go beyond Howells' novels, consider many applications, and seek to frame general definitions; for James would probably not have thought of invoking the words 'form' and 'style' to apply to Howells unless they already possessed a general significance. But once embarked on the quest for general conceptions, we lose the easy and common understanding that we had and are caught in ambiguities and inconsistencies. In view of these deplorable confusions, which I shall presently review, the existence of some degree of mutual understanding among persons who confine themselves to limited contexts deserves some emphasis. It is surprising as well as gratifying that one can say with great hope of being understood that the painter Salvador Dali does not concern himself with the values of design—when one considers what preposterously vague and conflicting notions of design are current in aesthetics.

My object is as follows: first, to understand, if I can, what our authors meant by the word 'important'; for that word, or another that has the same meaning, has a key position in every discourse on form and subject matter. Secondly, to examine the reasoning by which they reach their conclusion—that the form is more important than the subject—in other words, to describe and criticize their *method*. It may well seem to you, however, that there is another point which takes precedence of either of these, and that I could not take a step without first addressing myself to this— namely, what is to be understood by the word 'form' and what by 'subject' or 'subject matter'? I agree that this is the chief question of all. But though I shall be alluding to certain definitions of form and subject, I shall not analyze these concepts. It is agreed on all sides that the subject of any work and its form, whatever else they may be, are aesthetic *characters*—more or less complex features of the work of art. Now, these two characters are doubtless of exceptional interest in aesthetics. But the question of their relative importance is exactly like a hundred other questions of relative importance—with many of which, indeed, it overlaps. Aristotle, for example, said that the action of a play is more important than the characterization—a remark which has baffled my intelligence since infancy. There have been those who said that line was more important than color or that color was more important than line. There have been, in the history of criticism, harmonists and polyphonists, romanticists and classicists, and many other groups divided on the importance of this or that. I should be well content if I were to explain what it means to say that one character is more important than another character and how one could proceed to show that this is so. But if we want to conceive our particular subject a little more vividly, we can use examples; and I am willing to follow our authors in choosing these examples. Thus we can say that smiles and frowns and tears and fainting spells and fervent gesticulations, in painters all the way from the Lorenzetti, through Correggio and the *Transfiguration* of Raphael, to the Baroque, are values of subject matter; and that the organization of the picture space in a Cézanne still life is an example of form.

II

Our desire to interpret the authors whom we have quoted makes it unnecessary to explore the full usage of the word 'important'. Often it has the connotation 'prominent', 'central', 'that which is emphasized'. Diatonic harmony is not important in Eastern music, since it doesn't exist at all. In the work of some Western composers, though present, it is only a minor thing. And some composers of the nineteenth century, who employ the full resources of diatonic harmony, do not employ them creatively: the harmony is not the distinctive and interesting feature of the style. So, one might say that subject matter is not important in certain contemporary painters and that form does not count for much in a painter like Dali. But I see no sign that the word 'important' is being used in this way in any of our passages.

As a first supposition, let us imagine that 'important' is being used (by Emerson and Fry) as a synonym for 'valuable'. The formalist thesis then would read: that it is the formal characters in art which are especially to be admired and that life, drama, facial expression, religious feeling are relatively indifferent.

There is reason to believe that this is at least part of what the formalists intend. Just as William Blake seems never to have been moved by the color of the Venetians so much as by the Florentine art of delineation, so Roger Fry could think of no gesture, no story, no beatific gaze or scowling caricature in all the world's painting that gave him as much pleasure as did the organization of the picture space in certain Renaissance and Baroque masters. The plastic values, he said, were the highest values; even the finest achievements of psychological portraiture were secondary.

But, for a number of reasons, I am forced to believe that 'good' could not have been, for Fry and his school, the *only* meaning of 'important'. Fry was a good judge of what he called "psychology" in art and has left many pages of appreciation of Dürer's and Rembrandt's and Daumier's skill in characterization. The judgment that subject matter was *less* important, aesthetically, than form would never lead you to say, as Fry says here, that subject matter was of *no* importance at all. Neither could it lead you to speak with the air of enunciating a *principle*. A person who attempted, from his knowledge of art, to estimate the importance of the use of light-and-dark in painting would have been in one position before Leonardo's time and in another afterwards; in still other positions after

Caravaggio and after Rembrandt. Artists are always doing what no one had dreamed of; and I do not know that anyone has ever been able to offer even a plausible guess as to the inherent potentialities or limitations of a medium, a general aspect of nature, or a dimension of art. If there were no *human* values in painting equal to the *architectural* values, that would not mean that there will not be any tomorrow. What Fry, as a critic, was able to offer was the opinion that there exist some treatments of space and light and color which are greater than any known treatment of individual passion or social action. But it is obvious that, in the passage we are now reading, he wants to say something stronger.

A study of the formalist writings would, I think, bring to light another meaning of 'important'. To say that the form is more important than the content is to say, not that formal qualities are good and the representative qualities less good, but something like the following: If the form is good, then the *work* will be on the whole good; and if the form is not good, the work will not be good. In other words, form makes a greater *contribution* to the merit of the work than the so-called "content" does. This idea could be illustrated by pages in Fry where he pays tribute to the dramatic qualities, for instance, of a picture by Breughel and then pronounces the picture nevertheless inferior; or where he shows what a clumsy student of the expression of human emotions Poussin was in pictures which are, notwithstanding this liability, great masterpieces. It is somehow more *necessary* that the form should be adequate than that the subjects should be interesting and well conceived.

Still a third and very important sense of the word 'important' is illustrated in our passages. This is borrowed from the casual usage of persons who are trying to dope out an explanation of some phenomenon, usually a recurrent phenomenon—in the sciences or police work. Its nearest synonym, perhaps, is the word 'effective', though it may also connote something like 'useful' or something like 'pertinent'—as when we speak of an important clue or an important lead. It can be applied either to the concept which is supposed to have explanatory value or to the natural events and forces which are adduced in explanation. All our authors are curious individuals, with speculative minds, who, though they are in the position of critics making value judgments, are also impressed with the general phenomenon of aesthetic value and wish to get some understanding of it. It appears to them that works of art have strange powers. They feel (for reasons we have yet to review) that the subjects of these works are totally incapable of explaining their effects; and they appeal to the form as possibly yielding an answer. The form, then, is the important element in the mixture, the thing that accounts for what we want to have explained to us, namely, the efficacy of the mixture.

But before we leave the concept of importance, there is still one thing to be noticed. I can bring this out best, perhaps, by saying that every one of our authors means to declare that it is not important that a work of art should have an *important* subject. We see this when we consider how we are meant to take the examples that they use. Emerson's example is the Supreme Being. One who said that the *What* is of no importance compared with the *How* might be taken to mean that it is of no importance, for instance, that *Moll Flanders* should be the story of a drab; all depends on the style, the organization, the elaboration, the artistic working. But Emerson's point is made by invoking the idea of a *majestic* subject and pointing out that this by no means assures us of a majestic discourse on that subject. Fry's examples are the carcass of an ox and crockery on a table; Gide's is an iron stove. We are to understand that these are mediocre if not base subjects; yet great works have been made in which they appear.

What is an important subject? Well, it is obvious that Fry does not think we need to *look* at Rembrandt's ox; Gide does not think we must *see* the iron stove in Delacroix in order to tell whether this naturalistic, imitative, or material element in the painting is a valuable quality or not. We are supposed to respond automatically to the *mention* of the thing. This suggests that the importance or unimportance of the article or object has been settled beforehand and perhaps long ago. So it has. The importance of the subject has been decided by its or his position in the universe or the state, its influence, its connections, its role in history, or its supposed rank in a hierarchy of eminence. Opinions on these matters vary; and they also change. While a peasant would have been thought a mean subject for painting in some French circles during the eighteenth century, a revolutionary sentiment can lift him above a king; his very shoes can begin to bespeak the dignity of labor. But while these estimates change, the idea of estimating the aesthetic importance of a subject, as a quality in the picture, survives. Thus Van Gogh could say that he loved such painters as Millet and Breton and all who painted the people.

It is a commonplace of the history of criticism that men have thought that artists should take only important subjects, independently qualified as such before the artist commences. For a long time nobody but an important subject could afford to have himself painted. Now our authors are opposed to all this, and instance the worthlessness of a work with an important subject, or the converse, just so as to prove how wrong it is. But they remain curiously beguiled by the idea which they are rejecting. They create a double impression. Gide, for example, speaks of the *absence of a subject* in a picture in which he has just mentioned the subject—an iron stove. It is as if someone had proved to him beforehand that the picture of an iron stove *ought* to be worthless and he finds himself contradicting a thing that he believes. The formalists believe that qualities of abstract construction and design are the valuable element in the picture. Now the painting of a small, homely, insignificant object can be as realistic, as little abstract, as a painting of the Battle of Marengo. But if the painting is felt to be a good one, then since a subject devoid of all worldly importance cannot have made it good, then there *must* be qualities of abstract design in the picture which account for its goodness whether you can see them there or not.

III

To proceed now to the question of formalist reasoning: If one takes the word 'important' in the sense of 'good' or 'valuable', there is little doubt as to the method by which the formalist tries to show that form is more important than subject matter. It is the method known as critical evaluation, or, as it might also be called, reflective preference. It was used again and again by Fry, in pages where he endeavors to convince us that one character in a work of art is superior to another.

Comparative evaluation is not without its snags; and I should think there were difficult questions, in particular, about the status of critical *generalizations*. Let us say there is a man who prefers the classical composers either to their predecessors or to the romantic composers who followed them. This preference is couched in the form of judgment about the superiority of classical music. I am inclined to think that such a judgment is at most only a summation of individual value judgments and the individual experience that lies behind them. In other words, if he is asked to vindicate his judgment, he will point (say) to a certain sonata of Mozart. If he is asked why it should be considered a great achievement, he will analyze the work, exhibiting its several qualities. If there are many such works which he can in this way show to be great, he is making his point. But in the way in which the qualities of the individual work substantiate the individual value judgment, there is no "classical" quality, common to all the classical works, which relates itself to these works collectively and supports a judgment of their value. I do not mean that the classical works do not have distinctive common qualities. But to appreciate such a general quality when it is pointed out in the pages of a book, and to see that it supports a judgment about the value of an art form, the reader must implicitly resolve this quality into the qualities experienced on individual occasions, and respond or recall his responses to those, then collect the results and announce his verdict. No *principle* of value is yielded by such a summation.

I am therefore in some doubt as to our ability to reach a general conclusion, inductively, on the comparative importance of form and subject. Notwithstanding these doubts, there is an obvious directness and simplicity in the method of comparative criticism. One is tempted to say now to the *representationalist* that the way in which he can prove his case (if at all) is simply to find some values, indisputably dramatic or psychological, which are indisputably very great. The dangers in this proceeding are those to which all criticism is liable. One may commit errors of taste. Thus when Berenson says, "At Assisi, in a fresco by Pietro [Lorenzetti] . . . the Madonna holds back heart-broken tears as she looks fixedly at her Child, who, Babe that he is, addresses her earnestly; but she remains unconsoled," I suspect a sentimental distortion that magnifies the trivial; and could not accept as a *great* human situation in painting one that perhaps does not even exist in the place where you are supposed to find it. But these are the confusions and distortions that eyes and brains are heir to; and no such mistake in a given instance prejudices any other case whatsoever.

This method, critical evaluation, together with the judgments of value or importance that the formalists make when they use it, is undoubtedly present in our passages, as in all the formalist writings. But the one real point I have to make is that there is also present a completely different method, bound up with the second and especially the third conceptions of importance, which passes itself off as critical evaluation and passes its conclusions off as value judgments.

Representation is said to be irrelevant not or not only because you have found the representative qualities inferior where they exist, but because you admire other works from which those qualities are absent, and because you do *not* admire still other works in which, as you conceive the matter, the "same" qualities are present. Thus you deduct from an admittedly great altarpiece or historical painting those factors which you think have been proved by experience either to be not necessary or not sufficient conditions of value in art; and since you believe that the principles which govern aesthetic effect must be the same everywhere, you identify these principles with the mystic remainder in the imitative work and call it the *how*. Your reader is persuaded by this proof to imagine that he does not see what he sees and does not like what he likes but is being affected in an uncanny manner by hidden relationships, the same in Giotto, Titian, Picasso, and Mondrian.

The method, in short, is *subtraction*. Since it has proved so useful in so many branches of science and has been consecrated by Mill in some of his canons of inductive inference, it may be worth the while of some person versed in arithmetic to see whether the formalists are using it properly. I shall, however, not endeavor to be precise and shall only enlarge upon my point with a few illustrations.

There have been worthless pictures with illustrious and resounding subjects—*Washington Crossing the Delaware* will do for example. There have been great works of art, for example, St. Paul's Cathedral and the *Chromatic Fantasy and Fugue* of Bach, that have had no subjects. And there have been good or great paintings that have had either no subjects at all; little subject matter—men and objects treated so abstractly as to be hardly recognizable; mean and humble subjects; or a psychological and dramatic subject matter that was either unattractive or positively ugly—Roger Fry thought, and I agree, that the stilted features and operatic poses of certain figures in Poussin were of this sort.

Value has been present when subject matter was absent and absent when subject matter was present. It has also been present in large amounts when subject matter was present in small amounts and present in small amounts when there was a lot of subject matter around.

It follows that when a picture by Giotto, Titian, Rubens, or Rembrandt greatly affects us, it cannot be the subject that does the affecting—no matter what the apparent zeal of the painter in depicting piety, mourning, horror, or fright; any more than it can be the soda in a Scotch-and-soda that does the affecting. For if either the subject matter or the soda had been effective, then it should have been effective in other concoctions previously administered; it should perhaps have been effective when taken by itself; and no recipe that omitted this ingredient should have proved successful.

What would happen if we applied this method quite generally in criticism? "They speak of the blues and greens in this picture by Tintoretto. But here is a splendid picture by Rembrandt which has no blues or greens at all. So it can't be the blues and greens that make the Tintoretto good." "They say that Titian is a great colorist. But there are fine engravings by Dürer which manage to do without color. So it can't be the color that makes Titian a good painter." The formalist movement has produced many an argument in defense of abstract painting that rested on the evidence of music, which has no subject matter. But we may, logically, go further and say that it is not essential to a painting that it should be *painted*, since there is value, though no paint, in music.

Many people, as it happens, think that Michelangelo was *not* a great colorist. Now if you believe this and also believe he was a great painter, you may not detect the absurdity of arguing that color does not count for much in painting since it counts not at all in sculpture. (Michelangelo did not detect this absurdity.) It is *because* the formalist aesthetic is accompanied by the declaration of honest preferences, which deserve attention, that people are taken in by it.

But now I am sure you all feel that there is, in the passages I have been criticizing, something sound and salubrious to which I have done scant justice, a corrective emphasis that is badly needed by some people, even some professional critics, if not all. Even if I am right (as I may not be) in believing that the formalists reason badly, we should still have to ask, What accounts for the endless repetition of the idea of which my three quotations are a very small sample? There must be something, some maddening provocation in the environment, to which intelligent men are forced to respond in this particular way. This brings us back to the conflicts in taste from which all problems in aesthetics are generated. Goethe in his day pointed out that "you can't expect the public to accept a work of art as such. Its attention is fixed entirely upon content, substance." (Goethe, incidentally, who had the privilege of many-sidedness, could also take the opposite side of the question, as in the famous passage where he says that though he values both rhythm and rhyme, yet that which is really, deeply, and fundamentally effective is what remains of that poet when he is translated into prose.) The average layman does not like Cézanne and if questioned will point out how undistinguished, unsoldierly, unstatesmanlike are his heads and bodies, how cheap and inglorious the crockery on the table, of which he believes himself to possess better specimens at home. The same persons are repelled by Rembrandt's ox and are apt to think well of a sermon that Emerson would consider dull just because it is on the subject of the Supreme Being. And they respond very favorably to tawdry advertising art because it displays an expensive punch bowl of sterling silver from which a fine old white-haired Negro butler is ladling punch. The intelligent critic, confronted with such tastes, is in despair and can think of no retort but, "It's not *what* is depicted but *how* it is depicted that matters." He sounds as if he were saying that the effect of some fine object in the picture is outweighed by another set of qualities, which is the drawing or the form; though in fact he finds the whole thing loathsome. What he is really doing is recommending attention *to the work of art*, as it fully and exactly is. And he might just as well have said, "It's not the punchbowl but *what* punchbowl it is." We may speak this way even when we have an object that, in formalists' jargon, is "all form"—for instance, a bank building with Ionic columns. Here too the layman is impressed; but the critic may say either, "It's not what the columns are but how they are done," or "It's not the Ionic columns but *what* Ionic columns."

In modern formalism we recognize a certain project, one which students of aesthetics have found irresistible since the beginning of time. I will call it the great inductive enterprise. It begins with the observation that all beautiful things have one thing in common: they are beautiful. If one holds a subjectivist theory of beauty, one would say that those works we call beautiful all elicit positive feeling response. But one notices also that they are all very different. Yet we believe in the principle "same effect, same cause." We suspect, therefore, that those works which *seem* so completely different one from another must nevertheless have common properties that account for their ability to work similar effects on us. These must be secret properties, since (as I say) they are not apparent; but for that matter gravitation, which accounts for so many diverse happenings in the world, was a secret property until it was discovered. The essential property must be something vastly general, something that is present *in* all the good cases of chiaroscuro, reference, harmony, and so forth. It would be, one would say at a guess, whatever it was that was expressed by some fearful set of differential equations to be discovered by some aesthetician of incalculable genius in the future.

There are two points to be noted briefly before we go any further. One is that it could not be necessary to know this undiscovered law in order to know what is valuable, since we can know what is valuable though we do not know any such law. Even a schoolgirl, poor in algebra, sometimes knows what is valuable in art. The inductive enterprise wants to discover the *law* of the valuable; and this virtually presupposes that the results of experience and of criticism should be in.

The second point is this. One could in a sense endorse the idea that where there is one common property, beauty, there must be another to be found by study, without endorsing the inductive enterprise. The theory of aesthetic value, in its own way, assumes some such notion. For example, in the *Hippias Major* Plato entertains the idea that wherever beauty is ascribed, there is a pleasure of sight or of hearing. The latter is a property which represents the articulated meaning of the word 'beauty' and is discovered by an analysis of that concept. But the inductive enterprise is only just starting where Plato, and the theory of aesthetic value, end; for Plato does not begin to ask what *makes* beautiful things beautiful, that is, what is it in the various objects that causes the pleasures of sight and hearing?

The inductive enterprise, which may now also be called the idea of a science of art, is very much to the fore in the pages of all the leading formalists. What is to be said of this enterprise and of its basic assumptions, namely, that there is one juice in all beautiful things which could be extracted if we sent them all to a mental refinery?

Perhaps we all agree that the potent stuff has not been squeezed or filtered out as *yet*—though in reluctant contradiction of all academicians and such distinguished men as Pope, who spoke of "those rules of old discovered, not devised."

But is it—is any aesthetic law—discoverable?

Two points of view have been expressed on this. One is associated with the name of Croce, who held that an inductive science
of art is in principle impossible. But though he appears to be
arguing from theoretical considerations, the only consideration he
ever *gives* is the fact that works of art —the *subjects* of the proposed study—are unique individuals. The opposite view, which
has been advanced by philosophers of science who turned their
thoughts momentarily to aesthetics, human history, the psychology of personality, and other places where an exceptional stress
has been laid on the uniqueness of the individual, consists simply
in pointing out that every *science* deals with unique individuals
and that this has not prevented the discovery of general laws. But
though this does counter Croce's reasoning and is what Bacon
called an argument of hope, it doesn't really give any hope, if only
because *until* a subject has been put on a scientific basis, its individuals must seem "more unique" than even the most unique things
that have already been subsumed under laws.

My own brain power and training are entirely inadequate to a
question of this kind. My one suggestion must be addressed to a
very limited branch of the question. Though it were true that
similar effects must have similar causes (and though a science of art
were indeed feasible), it would not follow that, since penicillin
cures the flu and electric shock is good for mental depressions and
a soft answer turneth away wrath and a sling will help to heal a
broken arm—since these four remedies all work an improvement
in the human organism, there must be another property which they
all have in common. You may think the comparison inept; but it is
not nearly so bad as to assume that the aesthetic situation is to be
compared, for instance, to visual sensation, where scientists look
for and find functional relationships between properties of the light
stimulus, chemical reactions in the retina, and recurrent qualities
of brightness and chroma. Works of art fire themselves at us
through selected sense organs; and they produce final effects which
do have a certain similarity; but they reach these effects by circulating each through its separate channels; and it may well be
precisely in virtue of the *differences* in the stimuli that the sameness
of effect, if any, is to be explained.

But if the stimuli did have common effective properties, these
would not be discovered by a critic holding up a Cézanne and
saying, "See. If we take from the *Bacchus and Ariadne*, Bacchus,
Ariadne, and everything else extraneous, what we shall have left is
is the same thing you see in this bowl of apples. Form."

3
Perception, Meaning, and the Subject Matter of Art

I propose, in these pages, to examine the distinction that is drawn between the contents and the form of a work of art—a distinction with which all are dissatisfied but no one, apparently, is ready to dispense. Commonly, it is given a psychological significance—for example, by Franz Boas: "It is essential to bear in mind the twofold source of artistic effect, the one based on form alone, the other on ideas associated with form."[1] This alludes to the ordinary classification of art objects as formal and representative; but the *principle* of classification is extraordinary. A composition is based on the repetition of a spiral motive, or on a scheme of interlocking lozenges, or on elements placed with exact symmetry on a rectangular field; in another there appears a mountain, a face, a tree. The first is called an abstract or pure design; in the second, called a representation, we find—I will not say a *familiar* form because the abstract figure is perhaps familiar in its way—the form which is characteristic of a familiar sort of object or situation lying about us in the world. Now comparing the rug on the floor with the picture on the wall, we are instantly aware of a difference which would seem to be *anterior* in the order of obviousness to the categories of

Originally published in *Journal of Philosophy* 41, no. 21 (October 1944): 561–75. Reprinted in Eliseo Vivas and Murray Krieger, eds., *The Problem of Aesthetics* (New York: Rinehart, 1953). Here reprinted by permission of the *Journal of Philosophy*.

1. *Primitive Art* (Cambridge, Mass.: Harvard University Press, 1927), p. 13.

psychology; and a child, we might suppose, who should be asked to explain the difference between these objects would wonder why they should be expected to be *alike*—so great is the disparity of visible form. Yet Boas has taken no account of this disparity. He finds that the examples are in one respect similar, since each presents a certain form to the eye, but that there is added something to the second in the nature of a contribution which it extorts from the mind; and it is implied that if this increment were somehow obviated, there would remain no fundamental difference to be marked. This implication is made explicit, in an essay designed to establish the aesthetic significance of subject matter, by Professor Walter Abell:

> Were we to limit painting and sculpture to elements provided in complete form by vision, then color, line, shape, and size would be the only elements available to them. . . . [Subject matter] cannot be legitimately excluded unless we wish to limit ourselves to visual stimuli uninterpreted by *any* of their meanings, in which case we should have to restrict art to the sphere of geometrical pattern.[2]

If painting and sculpture, in short, were perfectly formal, they would be perfectly abstract.

Appreciation is an activity that runs its course within the psychological framework. The question must therefore arise, What functions or faculties does it call into play; and what, in particular, is the role of direct perception on the one hand and of meaning, association, or thought on the other? There has also existed a controversy, from an early time, between the *Formaesthetiker*, as Fechner called them, and the *Inhaltsaesthetiker*, over the element of subject matter in the arts. The singular feature of the analysis from which I have quoted is that it combines the two issues by assuming that subject matter is imported through associative processes into the experience of art. It affirms the importance of the representative factor in art and, simultaneously, of the higher mental action in aesthetic experience. (Modern formalism joins issue very squarely on this ground, rejecting the double thesis in a single breath.[3]) Originating within the limits of a psychology of consciousness, it

2. *Representation and Form* (New York: Scribners, 1936), pp. 97–98.
3. "To appreciate a work of art we need bring with us nothing from life, no knowledge of its ideas and affairs . . . nothing but a sense of form and color and a knowledge of three-dimensional space" (Clive Bell, *Art* [London: Chatto & Windus; New York: Frederick A. Stokes, 1913], pp. 25–27).

tends to adopt an account of meaning in terms of sensory datum and associated image; but the same assumption has been couched in the terminology of behaviorism and in quasi-epistemological terms like 'designation', 'construction', and 'reference'.[4] It will not be material to my argument what theory of interpretation we may choose to endorse.

I shall argue that an all but complete analysis of "subject matter" can be given by a *presentational* aesthetic; and that we may, therefore, continue to identify the aesthetic with the immediate without submitting to the reduction of formalism. It will be convenient to press this thesis in a one-sided fashion, leaving the necessary qualifications to the end.

I must give notice that I shall be unable to propose definitions that will satisfy *every* element in the complicated usage of our leading terms. 'Form' we may here define with Santayana as "sensuous elements in combination."

I

We have a picture in which the moon is seen shining through leaves upon figures in a garden. If associations can be said to contribute to the effect of this scene, they must be called upon to bring the absent into the present—to render certain ingredients available that are not directly given to sense. But the moon could not be one of these, because it is already included within the direct impression. Nor any of these leaves—for the same reason; and I believe that we can pronounce them *sere* or *fragile* with a certainty equal to that with which we can say that they are *yellow* or *symmetrical*. In fact, if I may say so, the whole picture is already in the picture: since there is no question of a response on our part to outlying extensions of the picture landscape, there can be no need that these extensions (which do not even exist) should be made known to us.

It will be said that there are no leaves in the picture and no moon, but a collection of shapes—a geometrical pattern. Now nothing that exists in two dimensions or in three is not a shape and a geometrical pattern; but it may be just as arbitrary as it is accurate

4. I number among English and American partisans of this view Santayana, Bosanquet, Dewey, Alexander, Ducasse, Parker, Morris, Barnes, Bowers, and others.

to describe it so. A leaf is a geometrical, a botanical, a foliar, and finally a uniquely individualized, pattern. But the point is otherwise well taken: there is of course no leaf in the picture but something that looks like a leaf—a leaf-like shape. (Not some *other* shape, be it noted, such as a triangle; nor does the moon reduce itself to a "yellow disk"; nor does the painting as a whole assume the slightest tendency to resemble a composition by Kandinsky.) Not to confuse the "shape" (that is, the sense-datum) with the object, I shall refer to the first, whenever necessary, in quotation marks—as, the "leaf," the "moon."

The inside and the other side, the physical dimensions—in a word, the substance—of the moon finds no place in the representation. Let us therefore turn to the moon itself, which we will imagine ourselves to be admiring. The same associations, be it admitted, which are demanded of us by *this* situation will be demanded by the other. (We must suppose, in the interest of our problem, that the sense-data are exactly alike in the two cases—a condition that is perhaps never fulfilled.) Now it is not essential to the present argument that associations be ruled out of *either* situation: we are concerned with the question of associations only insofar as that question is raised in a *special* form by the topic of artistic representation. Yet it does appear to be just the peculiarity of the aesthetic outlook on nature that the normal processes of interpretation are in abeyance for its duration. To *admire* a natural object is to contract one's interest to its appearance; or, conversely, we may say that the appearance, relinquishing its several sign functions, achieves an intrinsic importance; so that precisely that substance which is lacking in the imitation is ignored in the original, where it really exists. All this, to be sure, is more easily said than understood, for the *analysis* of the aesthetic attitude is somewhat complicated. But a conception can be sound without being precise, and this is a conception upon which modern writers, with few exceptions, converge, saving their differences for the refinements. When they deal with the aesthetic experience *in general*, they find nothing to distinguish it save the aspect of absorption in the immediate. But the subject matter of *art*, as they insist, is drawn from nature. Do the forms, then, with which in nature we are said to traffic directly become symbolic and referential when they are translated into the experience of art?

The moon is said to be *represented* by a sense-datum, an impression. In the same sense, though less directly, it may be represented by a photograph or a drawing, for on such a figure we may base certain calculations concerning the moon. The function of representation in this sense, I suppose it granted, is utterly antagonistic to aesthetic appreciation. There remains only the sense in which the picture of the moon may be said to represent, not the moon itself, but the original impression. But why should the picture need to *represent* the "moon" when *ex hypothesi* it *is* the "moon"? What would in that case account for the ability of the original to act on us as it does? The "moon" as it appears to us this evening is certainly not unique—we have seen the "same thing" before. Yet no one will say that the present impression represents, or recalls, a past impression, much less a painting. The scene being here and now laid out before us with all its elements, there is nothing which recollection is needed to supply. But the same condition is met by the representation. We can not, perhaps, explain why certain cloud formations, hovering before the moon, should affect us with a sense of mystery; but no special problem, surely, is created by the same form (still supposing that it were the same) when it appears in painting.

To treat with a representative is to aim at a principal; but the aesthetic datum, artificial or natural, acts for itself alone, and our response is appropriate not to what the form may stand for but to what the form may *be*. Art, then, in its aesthetic capacity, is not representation; and we shall continue to refer to "representations" by that name only in the way that a senator retains his title when he leaves his office. Works of art may indeed retain their *power* of representation insofar as, being connected by a chain of events with various incidents or persons, they can form the basis of an inference respecting the latter. The so-called *iconic* emblem, such as a portrait, which bears a certified resemblance to an original, can tell us something about the appearance and character of that original. And this use to which the object lends itself has its familiar satisfactions, more renowned, perhaps, than those of beauty. A portrait of Erasmus possesses an interest which stems from the "subject," as we say, meaning the sitter; but if that interest could be said to contribute to the beauty of the picture, then its beauty would be subject to impairment—for example, by documentary evidence, which might show that the portrait was spurious. Which is absurd.

Does it follow that we must ignore what indubitably is *in* the picture, an aspect of its form—the human countenance with its moral expression, its smile, the light in the eye? Must we speak only of color areas, volumes, the relationship of planes?

We have by no means exhausted the question of the dependence of appreciation upon past experience, for past experience may function in recognition as well as in interpretation and recall. The concept of recognition, however, is ambiguous. One is said to have recognized somebody in a crowd. This implies a conviction of that person's physical presence. The act of recognition, in this sense, is predictive: it is equivalent to an act of inference. But it embodies a necessary first stage in which one "recognizes" a typical form, as one might in the case of a portrait; without this the inference would not be possible. I will reserve the term 'recognition' for the preliminary act by which we identify a mere impression as belonging by its character to a certain class. This act can occur without its customary sequel, and *does* occur, for example, when we recognize a figure on the blackboard as a circle or a musical interval as a fifth. Here the *name* that we use—'circle', for instance—has a meaning; but it will not be urged, on that account, that the circle has a meaning. What the shape or the tone may be *like* is one thing—its resemblance to certain other forms suffices to give it a name; what it *stands for* is something else. What we bring to the datum is one thing; it is another thing where we go from there. Interpretation digresses beyond the datum; while in the act of recognition the form which is being classified can remain the final *object* of attention.

Recognizability is hardly the differentia of subject matter since it is a prerequisite for the apprehension of any form whatsoever.[5] Percepts without concepts are blind; and while there can hardly exist such a thing in mature experience as absolute failure of recognition, since there is nothing that we can not classify under one head or another, yet a form which is at once original, complicated, and abstract will be greeted with bewilderment. But this difficulty is met simply by repeated exposure: we familiarize ourselves, say, with the style of a Mondrian as we digested long ago the abstract motives of an older art. To speak accurately, then, we cannot say that the abstract motive is unfamiliar but only that it has not been rendered familiar through our experience of nature—and there lies the basis for a definition of subject matter. A form may be entitled a "subject" if it bears a resem-

5. "For eyes unpracticed in the discriminating perceiving of shapes and lines, one Gothic arch will look much like another; it will not be felt in its own specific individual character; its felt character for discriminating eyes will not be expressed to the organism whose eyes do not discriminate" (D. W. Prall, from an unpublished manuscript).

blance, in specific respects, to certain *natural* forms. 'Form' refers to what is in the picture, and 'subject matter' to a resemblance borne by this form to some aspect of the real environment. "Representations" are works containing forms which are in certain respects like the forms of nature.

There is also a negative requirement. If we could make a genuine tree, as pins are made in the factory, on the model of those which exist already, it would not be called a representation. Artistic imitation exists by defect as well as by likeness. The representation will bear a double relationship to its model—a resemblance in appearance and a deficiency of the substance.

This criterion suggests the following remarks:

1. The criterion is not precise, for it is well known that the naturalistic grades off into the abstract. Resemblance is a matter of respects and degrees. A simple circle with a line extending beneath—is it a "flower"? The rigidly rectilinear "snake" pattern of an Indian basket—does it resemble a snake? The animal motive is "formalized," the flanks are brought into exact balance, the tail describes a regular scroll. Between the perfect oval and the human head a series of forms can be inserted; and whole styles —whole arts, one might say—flourish in this particular limbo.

2. The criterion is based on a circumstance extraneous to the form. It requires that a form shall (a) be similar to a form which (b) is natural. But natural forms are distinguished as a class by nothing save their connection with natural objects. The subjects of representation are as remote from one another as from various classes of abstraction; and if we had to define subject matter on the basis of intrinsic quality, we could proceed only by enumeration. It is an accident, so to speak, that there are no real musicians who resemble Picasso's. There may today exist seemingly abstract forms in painting which in fact have been adapted from little-known fishes or plants.

3. It follows that subject matter is not an aesthetic category. This point must not be misinterpreted. It is not a matter of indifference that heads and bodies should appear in painting rather than cubes and cones; and I can see no reason why the human shape, regarded purely as a shape, should be expected to affect us like a checkerboard. *What* the form may be that nature may contribute is significant; but it is immaterial that *nature* should be the source. Nature works as a purely decorative designer in the tortoise-shell, the skin of reptiles, the plumage of birds; in

the honeycomb and the snowflake it develops the geometrical style. To imitate such an aspect of nature is to deal with "reality"— but the effect is formalistic, minute, and precise. A tendency to abstraction, on the other hand, in some of the Italian painters is responsible for broadly structural and expressive values. Indeed, abstract compositions are themselves objects of nature and are, accordingly, imitable. Architecture, pottery, and dress are examples of formal design, which lean upon the naturalistic not at all. Let any such object be photographed and *pouf!* it is subject matter. What has happened? Nothing has been added, nothing has been altered. Something has been *omitted*—the physical body of the building or gown. But whatever was the aesthetic quality of the original, it will be held intact in the representation. It is therefore impossible to agree with those who, confusing an accident with the essence, hold that the decorative is to the expressive as the immediate to the "real."[6] Aesthetic distinctions (with a class of exceptions presently to be noted) are distinctions of quality *within* the field of the immediate.

To generalize this thesis somewhat beyond the present topic: If it had been Plato's intention to stifle the analysis as well as the production of art, he could not have adopted a better expedient than that conception of the archetype which he fixed on aesthetic theory. Let me briefly examine a single application of that idea. It is believed that there exists a realistic motive in art which is the antithesis of the motive of expression through design. I will take the example of Shakespearean acting. The last speeches of the dying Hamlet can be organized, in performance, into a rhythmic unity in which, with due emphasis and subordination, a range of feeling culminates and is brought to rest. *Or* they can be punctuated with stertorous gasps, heavy breathing, a death rattle, and so forth, gaining "conviction" of a sort but with a sacrifice in point of dramatic design. There is an example of the constructive versus the merely imitative aim. But the inferiority of the realistic version stems from the pattern of the original—the natural death,

6. "The expressive inclines to the side of meaning, the decorative to that of sense" (Dewey, *Art as Experience* [New York: Milton, Balch, 1934], p. 124).

"Expressive form, in other words, always involves the perception of something real. . . . The 'decorative arts' proper depend wholly on such qualities as are immediately apprehended" (Albert Coombs Barnes, *The Art in Painting* [New York: Harcourt, 1937], pp. 14–16).

as it happens, is not designed for aesthetic effect and seldom comes off very well. At bottom we have a contrast not between imitation and design but between one design and another. There is design in nature (if I am permitted the pun)—only that design is not always to our liking. Imitation reproduces, as imagination invents; and the significance of each lies in the nature of the content which it brings into art. A literally literal realism, if that could exist, would be raw and shapeless, vital or dull, according to the phase of nature which it duplicated; and if we search for the real effort of criticism beneath the label of 'realism' which it attaches to this trend or that, we find that it seeks to discriminate a particular *kind* of topic or of treatment—low subjects, minute detail, intimate emotions, casual arrangement. Certainly a work is not less momentous because its issues, its forms, are also to be found in the world that surrounds it. Art perpetually discloses value and significance that had existed independently in nature but had lain unnoticed; and I make no doubt that this connection is part of the special relevance borne by certain works to our lives. But such a *correspondence* between one experience and another is not a relationship of *dependence*, and it can not begin to account for the beauty of either.

II

Our language contains a number of *sensory terms*—those which refer to elements or forms that can be given in direct experience— as well as the wider *physical* vocabulary. Examples of the first are the names of the plane figures, musical tones, colors, tastes, and smells. (This could be called the language of recognition.) Now we are said to see "ourselves" in the mirror or to have seen a "friend" in a dream or, in a picture, a "group of fighting men." Here we wish to describe a specific appearance for which no sensory name exists, and it is convenient to borrow the name of the physical object with which that appearance is associated. Clearly, the name has dropped its physicalist function and is being used as a sensory term. Physical terms so imported into the sensory language make up what we shall call the language of subject matter.

Now appreciative criticism is subject inevitably to this limitation, that while form is individual and determinate, language is general and (in W. E. Johnson's sense) merely determinable. "In composition," wrote Emerson, "the *What* is of no importance compared with the *How*."[7] But the *How* is nothing but the determinate *What*. The language of subject matter can not express the *How* because it touches upon only those characteristics of the form which it shares with certain whole classes of forms. A swerve in the outline, the slightest variation in the shading of a head represents the gulf between the master and the dub, but no ready distinction of language corresponds to it. *Formalism* strives to repair this deficiency with the help of an explicitly sensory vocabulary—'line', 'plane', 'color', 'light', and their derivatives. The formalistic analysis of painting has often demonstrated its utility. The eye is arrested in its perfunctory grasp of the familiar form and persuaded, as if by a pointer, to follow the determinate course of the design. But the language of formalism, we must observe, is itself general and determinable. The following comment—a model of elucidation—on Seurat's *Poudreuse* employs a formalistic terminology combined with references to subject matter: "Table, plant, mirror, stylized bow are all conceived according to a succession of curves that are continued both in the color pattern of the wall behind and the form of the woman herself. The skirt is modeled by a series of curves that not only repeat the shapes of arms and shoulder-straps but complete the circular pattern of the shadows on the wall."[8] It is still necessary to look at the picture—we could not construct it from the description. Language does not communicate the determinate—'color pattern' and 'curves' get us hardly closer to the actual form than 'female figure', 'table', and 'skirt'.[9] *In the presence of the picture* certain geometrical designations (as for that matter certain figurative comparisons—'flame-like', 'gem-like', 'serpentine', and so on) may assist our vision to grasp the unique design where an inventory of subject matter would leave it fixed on the general type of object or situation.

When we speak of emaciated or swollen bodies, gnarled or pudgy fingers, grass, foliage, the bark of trees, we are talking

7. Quoted from Emerson's *Journals* by F. O. Matthiessen, in *American Renaissance* (Oxford: Oxford University Press, 1941).

8. Robert J. Goldwater, "Some Aspects of the Development of Seurat's Style," *Art Bulletin* 23 (1941): 120.

9. I do not raise the question whether it is *in principle* possible to communicate an aesthetic content by means of language. With the help of a set of co-ordinates like the color solid one can no doubt determine an exact shade of any color. But such precision is still impossible *in practice*, that is, where we are dealing with a form of the slightest complexity.

about areas, colors, and lines. The countenance is pale or florid, grim or gaunt, according to the relationship of colors, the arrangement of planes. To say that Brouwer's figures are "stunted," El Greco's "elongated," Tura's "contorted," Signorelli's "flayed" —these are limited but genuine expressions of aesthetic value *because they designate formal character*. The terminology of formalism represents simply another selection from the sensory language, convenient perhaps for further specification. It does not represent a distinct set of aesthetic attributes, to be set off as the "design" from the "material" values of subject matter. The very same form—often, indeed, the same characteristic of the form—can be designated in either way. The movement which engages the Three Graces in the *Primavera* is a linear rhythm. It is also a "lovely gesture of concord." We are not talking about different things— we are grouping the same thing either with one class of forms or with another. Undoubtedly there might be another "gesture of concord" which had little in common with this; but so are there linear rhythms which do not resemble this one. If the line were altered here, the gesture would not be the same; and if the gesture were altered, it would not be the same line.

Let us suppose there was a group of figures which served as the model for this detail. That group had its lines, its colors, its volumes, its shadows and lights. Composition, relation, pattern, proportion are *everywhere!* The significance of the act of imagination is that it brings *new* colors, new lines, new arrangements in place of the original qualities, that is, that it creates new "objects." The notion is preposterous that line, light, color, space are a set of properties peculiar to art, to be superimposed upon a formless matter supplied by nature. Yet Roger Fry could write: "The moment representation is introduced forms have an entirely new set of values. Thus a line which indicated the bend of a head in a certain direction would have far more than its mere value as line in the composition because of the attraction which a marked gesture has for the eye."[10] As if the attraction which a gesture has for the eye were conceivable apart from the *line* which it describes! As if a line could have a value "merely as line" and not as that determinate line which automatically takes membership in the class of "gestures"! Mr. Fry was no doubt thinking about the value of the gesture in isolation as against its value in the total composition;

10. *Vision and Design* (London: Chatto, 1929), p. 35.

but that is a distinction of part and whole, of figure drawing and space-composition. Representation introduces an entirely new set of forms. It contributes new designs. It does not intrude itself, with an effect of disturbance, into the midst of a set of abstract forms, which somehow hang on as pure line and color and shape.

I will submit two further examples of the same confusion: "As Mr. R. G. Collingwood has wittily said, a painter may be interested either in the volumes of a woman or in her femininity."[11] No painter, we may safely affirm, has ever been interested in a femininity without volumes. But there are painters who study volumes that are rather familiar to us from everyday life and there are painters who render relatively abstract, or fantastic, or stylized volumes. The volumes, in any two painters, are not alike.

"Whistler's *Mother* was called by the artist *Arrangement in Grey and Black*, but it has seldom been looked at simply as a pattern of colors."[12] But to look at the pattern of colors that Whistler painted is to see a "woman seated in a chair."

It will be observed, finally, that we do not align ourselves with those who insist that form and content are inseparable or, according to the appeal of the phrase, "inextricably intermingled," "indissolubly blended," or "indistinguishably fused." At bottom this formula represents an obscurantist protest against the comparison and analysis of different forms. 'Content', according to our definition, refers to certain general or class characteristics of the form. Now it is not senseless—though it is for various reasons pretty futile—to ask whether a class of forms may not be marked as a class by a particular value, whether "nudes" are not nobler than "apples," in other words, whether the "subject" does not contribute something to the effect. This question, to be sure, is apt to be complicated by another. For many people aesthetic forms are merely the pretext for the release of feelings which belong to the corresponding *objects*. *Any* mother or baby or sheep dog or venerable old man, any *Nativity* or *Crucifixion*, regardless of the individual treatment, elicits the stereotyped sentiment; and popular criticism, when it considers whether a *subject* is edifying or offensive, is thinking about the *thing portrayed*. Now the aesthetic value of a form does not necessarily correspond to the value which

11. Samuel Alexander, *Beauty and Other Forms of Value* (London: Macmillan, 1933), p. 79.
12. George Boas, *A Primer for Critics* (Baltimore: Johns Hopkins University Press, 1937), p. 62.

its bearer enjoys in real life. There may be representations of humanity which are grander than any rendering of still life, but not because of the superior station of the former in some non-aesthetic hierarchy of excellence. The painter who takes the heavenly choir or the Supreme Court for his subject does not start with the slightest advantage on that account, and we observe that religious pictures, figure studies, landscapes, interiors range all the way from supreme achievement to utter failure. Formalism is justified in seeking to eliminate this source of sentimental and didactic irrelevancy. But popular taste suffers from another limitation which is more nearly excusable. Children, horses, flowers, mountains, and waves do after all possess inherent aesthetic quality, and that quality will be carried into any reproduction. But that quality is apt to be trivial, elementary, crude. An area of shadow thrown over one side of a head, a relationship between the head and the positions of the hands, may create a mightier organization than anything known to us from nature: it may absorb, it may cancel whatever value the model may have possessed in isolation. The emphasis upon subject matter, the demand for the reproduction of "beautiful things," is therefore seen to represent a fixation upon the isolated detail and a blindness to the values of the total synthesis; an arrest at the *elementary* aesthetic quality and an insensibility to great achievement; a predilection for the standardized and an incapacity to comprehend the original. Genuine issues figure here, but they are issues of formal analysis. A thousand problems of formal analysis are agitated under the heading of subject matter versus form.

III

The depth effect, whether in nature or in painting, is measurably dependent upon habits of perception. The cube, drawn correctly on a piece of paper, can hardly be seen as another pattern on a plane with the square—it seems to have assumed a new dimension; and the conditions of this effect are not all innate. A large number in the list of elements which contribute to our sense of the bulk and location of objects in space—overlapping, perspective, distribution of light—could not function with that result apart from acquired adjustments of the optical mechanism. Meaning interpenetrates with sense to give the visual effect: it may be said that in the visual perception of space the datum is itself a function of learning. The depth phenomenon, incidentally, is not unique in this respect—the apparent color of a heavily shaded sheet of white paper, which is white when it "should" be gray, testifies equally to the influence of learning upon immediate effect.

The question we have to settle is a simple one. Suppose that we are standing on the seashore, looking out to a group of islands. Now the field is organized for us very differently from that field which might exist for a man who had just gained his vision, for the first time, by surgical means—for whom the islands might stand merely *above* the water in the vertical plane. Ours is a fuller experience of space, and it is at least in some degree our past experience that is our advantage. But we may further be led to judge that the islands are just two miles out, and in this we may turn out to have been mistaken. Our perception will then have been proved "illusory"; but, returning to our position on the beach, we find that the visual field has not changed. When we have once come to the end of one of those stair-cases or avenues of columns which are contrived to look longer than they are, our muscular preparation will not be the same another time round: the same phenomenal distance now "means" a shorter physical stretch. The habits which condition the phenomenon are not affected by the revision of those later judgments, relating to traversible distance and physical size, which are *based* on the visual phenomenon. All of the last are canceled, in the case of painting, by good and sufficient knowledge; yet the effect of depth and of solidity persists. Without intending to obscure the difference in kind between the flat and the "deep" order of composition, I hold, then, that the space which matters aesthetically is given and that the space which is not given does not count; or, in other words, that 'volume' and 'mass' are what we have called sensory terms in their application to painting.

Yet those who argue, on the strength of the depth effect, for a factor of interpretation in the appreciation of painting are thinking not of the "space" which indubitably appears in the picture but of the space which does not exist within it.[13] The meanings for which

13. "[Subject-matter] is *never immediately experienced as a whole,* but consists in part of qualities and relations whose presence can only be *inferred* or *assumed.* This is true if only because the subject-matter of all representational painting includes three-dimensional objects whereas the pictorial surface itself is necessarily two-dimensional" (D. F. Bowers, "The Role of Subject-Matter in Art," *Journal of Philosophy* 36 [November 1939]: 617–30, p. 618; my italics).

they plead are not those which, for example, help to create perspective but those which operate normally to correct perspective in the interest of physical action upon the environment. That a surface which exists in two dimensions should manage to express a third is a paradox in their eyes, to be resolved only by an appeal to the supplementary action of the mind. But to say that we are dealing with volumes and masses when we know that there is only a plane is not a paradox but a contradiction; on the other hand, it is but an axiom that a scene which only *seems* to recede does seem to recede. To utilize untouched resources of their direct experience, to duplicate upon wood or canvas the complete *appearance* of physical nature, was the task projected by those fifteenth-century masters who first achieved the conquest of naturalistic space.

We can now understand the strategy which is followed by representationalist and formalist alike, for the example of the third dimension is typical of the entire issue. Painting, they feel, so far as it is a matter of direct perception, *ought* to appear flat. So *in general* the first step is to conceive an impoverished caricature of the immediate: at the level of "sensation," we are told, there are only colors and lines and shapes. This causes us to imagine, in place of the obvious landscape or interior, a patchwork of abstractions. The formalist rests at this point, convinced of the supremacy of formal relationships—by which he secretly understands some other than the *given* scheme of relationships. Thus Birkhoff, seeking to apply his mathematical analysis to the art of painting, proposes to ignore the "connotative" factor, that is, the factor of meaning. As it turns out, what he ignores are those irregularities of the forms— by which we recognize them as "kneeling figures," "warriors," "slaves"—which refuse to fit into a purely *abstract* or geometrical analysis. The moment is ripe for someone to interpose with emphasis that we perceive not "isolated" colors and lines but the *real* objects of which they are qualities.[14] Meaning is invoked to supply what has been expelled from sense—a task which is beyond its power; for, if we saw nothing to begin with but a twisted system of planes, the mind would be impotent to assemble them into the form of a man.

Representation borrows the forms of nature without the substance, and that is everywhere the main source of confusion. For criticism seems unable to conceive a medium between real objects

14. Cf., for instance, Dewey, *Art as Experience*, pp. 86–89.

and abstract forms. Finding that space, body, reality are not included within the work, it does not concede the obvious—that these are not required for what the work is meant to do—because that seems to ignore the significant difference between representations and abstractions. In the face of material nature it is ready to admit the possibility of an aesthetic approach: where the reality is granted, we can readily see how it might be forgotten. Art is conceded no such independence, precisely because in art the form stands alone! Hence the appeal to an *extra* faculty to account for the *negative* factor, the factor of absence—that is, the aesthetically immaterial.

It may be well at this point to underscore our admission that to the extent to which a natural effect depends upon association, the representation of that effect does too. It is far from my purpose to deny, for example, that tactile quality is apprehended through the medium of vision. In general, the claim of this paper is positive: it seeks to show how much of what we understand by the subject matter of art can be rescued for the province of sense-perception, what an enormous range of aesthetic feeling can be explained through the power of form—not the "pure" pleasure of formalistic arrangement merely but the awe, the mystery, the excitement inherent in El Greco's landscape or the shadows and perspectives of Chirico or the quiver and vibration of Van Gogh's form. It would be quite a different matter to urge that associations are illicit, to banish the factor of meaning from the conception of aesthetic experience. I believe that almost any representation will excite at least a penumbral activity of meaning. The figures of men and women are not cut off at the edges; an arm which passes behind another body is not, for our feeling, thereby amputated. Moreover, the element of drama, which involves a sequence of incidents in time, can be condensed into the experience of painting only through a significance which attaches to the presented form. But painting *does* occasionally exploit the values of narrative and of drama; and it is only by a sacrifice of its own competence that a criterion of the aesthetic can dismiss this factor as irrelevant.

Aesthetic theory will now have to show how meanings, admitted as legitimate, can be reconciled with the conditions that define the aesthetic experience as such. Otherwise, it must continue to fluctuate between intolerable extremes, whereby the field is either reduced to the field of *sense*, with undue restriction of its scope, or assimilated to a mode of *cognition*, with consequent impairment of the very marks which delimit the aesthetic. In other words, it must

establish the existence of interpretations which are not fundamentally inferential and predictive. This task has been recognized
—the recognition is embodied in such expressions as 'immanent
reference'—but it has not been executed; and it can not be executed
here. But we may say that meaning functions, in aesthetic experience, so as to expand the field on which attention rests. The essential condition of the aesthetic experience is that attention should
rest on a certain content. It is by no means essential that that content
be supplied by sense. The fundamental thing is the nature of the
attitude that is aroused. What renders an attitude practical rather
than aesthetic is not the fact that it is based on past experience: it is
the fact that it turns away from a given content to obtain or avoid
what it does not yet possess. But in the contemplation of things
which we do not see but only imagine, we definitely possess those
things. Hence the *immediate* cannot be identified with the *sensuous*.
Through the play of meaning, a veritable universe can figure as an
object of contemplation. And we reach the conception of the total
imaginative experience, or the total *content* of the work, in which
questions of source are transcended.

4

The
Technical Factor
in Art

I

Croce says that art is spiritual activity, complete in the aesthetic imagination; and the physical exertions of the artist, which are obvious to the naked eye, he thinks secondary and dispensable: they *follow* the essential work of expression but remain outside of it and without influence upon it:

The aesthetic fact is altogether completed in the aesthetic elaboration of impressions. When we have achieved the word within us, conceived definitely and vividly a figure or a statue, or found a musical motive, expression is born and is complete; there is no need for anything else. If after this we should open our mouths— *will* to open them to speak, or our throats to sing, that is to say, utter by word of mouth and audible melody what we have completely said or sung to ourselves; or if we would stretch out—*will* to stretch out our hands to touch the notes of the piano, or to take up the brush and chisel, thus making on a large scale movements that we have already made in little and rapidly, in a material in which we leave more or less durable traces; this is all an addition, a fact which obeys quite different laws from the former . . . a *practical* fact, or fact of *will*. . . . The work of art is always *internal;* and what is called *external* is no longer a work of art.[1]

Originally published in *Journal of Philosophy* 43, no. 1 (January 1946): 5–19. Reprinted with permission.

1. Benedetto Croce, *Aesthetic as Science of Expression and General Linguistic*, trans. Douglas Ainslie, 2d ed. (London. Macmillan, 1922), p. 50.

The reader promptly contributes observations from his own mind which seem to verify and extend this analysis. Have we not always doubted that penmanship belongs to the essence of poetry—or even speech, understood as talking aloud? Does not either presuppose something to be spoken or set down (or to be rendered in clay or stone), and what is this but the work of art? Do we not see beneath the convention which assigns to the objects locked up in the museum at night the name of art? Does not *every* art, and not music or drama alone, require in the truest sense a continual re-creation, so that it exists as art only intermittently, in performances as it were, that is, in discrete moments of human experience?

But the question is, What becomes of the artist's *training*, on such a theory of aesthetic, of that proficiency which in years of study he has taken for his goal and which serves later as his professional hallmark? What is the aesthetic significance of technique? Croce replies as follows. The artist's intuitions would soon be forgotten if there were no physical medium for recording them. Now the labor of composition springs not alone from the disinterested motive of expression. Artists are human, and having shaped something in the spirit, they want to communicate and to preserve—not to mention any such incentive as money, applause, or fame. So they perform exercises which teach them to handle pigments or instruments or notations or stones, and know how to produce "stimuli to aesthetic reproduction" corresponding in some manner to their visions—means, that is, by which other spirits, if they so desire, can obtain an experience of art, identical with the author's or similar to it. All this belongs to the "activity of externalization"; and technique is nothing but "knowledge at the service of the practical activity directed to producing stimuli to aesthetic reproduction."

Let me offer an example which Croce himself does not give. Phonograph records are a sort of archive by which we preserve the works of the past; and we know that the work is finished before the reproduction can begin. Now we can easily imagine circumstances in which *composers* would think it necessary to foster a technique of impressing grooves into waxen discs, perhaps with a finger nail, and so of writing directly onto the surface of the record. They would then accomplish the purpose of getting themselves heard without reliance upon intermediaries. But this would not be a strictly *musicianly* accomplishment; for the technical intelligence, though it serves to record, has in no way determined the form of the work. Now that is just how Croce conceives the actual techniques of music and architecture and of all the arts.

The deficiencies of this analysis are glaring. Any child who studies music or drawing must divine them, and I can do no more than to put our latent criticism into explicit form.

In one particular, Croce's interpretation runs afoul of traditional usage. There are practical arts, of course: the shoemaker is an artist, if we follow Plato and Aristotle; while Croce admits none but the single aesthetic function—"art" and aesthetic experience are identical. This restriction might prove inconvenient. But the English Crocean, Collingwood, intervenes providentially, proposing the word 'craft' for the *techne* of the ancients and reserving the name of art to the loftier feat of aesthetic expression. I do not object to this revision (which is terminological), for it implies nothing as to the role of technique in the fine arts themselves. Productive labor is predominantly practical or aesthetic according to the nature of its end: aesthetic if the form itself is the end, practical if form serves a further end outside of itself. (Let us add that there is no inherent opposition between one of these aims and the other: most works of art serve more purposes than one.) Now the psychology of the aesthetic purpose being fairly obscure, it might be difficult to establish this distinction in terms of the inner direction or set of the organism; but we recognize it very easily in the *test of finality* that is applied to the work. If an artist has worked with the practical object of drawing tears from an audience, he must wait to see whether the tears are forthcoming, and judge his success accordingly. If he labors to obtain a likeness, the test lies in comparison with the model. If he makes a key to fit a lock, he can not know that he has finished until he tries it out. But if he strives for expression and beauty of form, then he reads the work back to himself or holds it up to the light and asks himself whether it truly defines his feeling—the test is the inherent perfection of form. And this test defines an aesthetic purpose, a purpose whose end is immanent. But what holds for the composite purpose holds for its parts. *Inspiration* may have a practical direction: in every mechanical invention there is a component of originality. And *skill* may have a purely aesthetic function: the routine exercises of students in art schools have no purpose but to provide something to be looked at. At the outset, then, we find reason at least to *question* one of the chief Crocean assumptions—the identity of the technical with the practical.

Technique is an ability acquired by practice, assuring dependable performance. This suggests the idea of a standard quality in the result, attainable at will—some general feature of style or attack common to an entire profession or school or to all the works of an individual; and it follows that a technical achievement is eminently communicable, teachable, imitable. It makes good sense, then, to say that either I *can* paint in the manner of Rembrandt or Manet, or I *cannot,* I *can* compose an acceptable fugue, or I *cannot.* Unfortunately, this way of speaking lends itself to the distortions of academicism, which assumes that there are certain legitimate aesthetic aims laid down beforehand. It happens that most artists go to school to men who think it desirable that certain facilities which exist already should be imparted also to them; there are practical motives, too, for making oneself able to draw a likeness or compose variations upon a theme. And I suppose this is not regrettable; I suppose it is well that the individual should not commence *de novo.* But if he shouldn't *want* to paint like Rembrandt or to utilize the resources of diatonic harmony, and if, disregarding everything known and established, he chooses an entirely novel departure, then, if only he repeats the original effort, it will crystallize in a new manner, a technique. We should not be led, then, by a word like 'ability' to think of a requirement posted ahead, limiting creative opportunity, for this comes down always to the possession of a particular skill by other men; we should think of an influence exerted from behind—the effect, that is, of past performances, actively shaping the direction of interest. The point is not trivial, for in aviation, carpentry, or typing the whole object is to measure up to a preestablished standard of performance. Artistic energy, on the other hand, is free and hence may appear to flow at random; but in fact it is channelized by conditions of which the work of the past is one, and this implies no contradiction of its liberty.

Skills are not stereotypes. A certain latitude or versatility, a generalization of specific acts performed, may be found within the strictly technical accomplishment. Yet in general it is true that by technique alone we achieve only what we have once done before. But every original work of art achieves something more— or, let us say, something different. We recognize, therefore, a motivating or inspiring factor, an impulse which springs ahead from the basis of technique. Ability as such is latent—a mere ability will never call itself into play. We look to something that can provide the *call* for the exercise of ability and we give it the name of inspiration. It is natural, as a further step, to identify inspiration with the "what," the "idea," and technique with the "execution" or "how;" but this step would lead us inevitably to the position of Benedetto Croce. It will soon be clear that inspiration and technique are *not* related as "knowing what" and "knowing how" or as "conception to be realized" and "means of realization."

The mere analysis of these terms, and of terms like 'aptitude', 'industry', 'genius', and 'mastery', raises questions of great complexity, which would carry us far afield.[2] There remains only one point which is directly pertinent to our issue. 'Technique' has as its correlative 'medium' an appropriate environmental complement. Skill is not just ability; it is ability to act in a certain way upon a physical material, apart from which its very definition is incomplete. This fact is relevant because Croce's conception of art excludes the physical product no less than the physical act. (To our confusion, it also excludes as physical what we should call sensuous quality—like color and sound. But this, we shall find, is not an accident. It is implied by what Croce has to say about medium and technique.) In this essay, because *we* can not analyze the techniques of all the arts, we may content ourselves with the vague formula of "interaction"—for the following reason. There is danger of interpreting the process of art upon the model of the plastic arts alone, where the medium, the working, and the result stand in an exceptionally clear relationship to each other—and hence of *mis*interpreting it. What, for instance, is the medium of poetry? The specifically poetical techniques are superimposed upon a broad technique acquired in infancy—speech; and this *does* involve an ability to make sounds out of air with the mouth. *Meaning*, similarly, accrues to sound only through special forms of inter-

2. As an ordinary precaution at this point, we must say that a theory of art cannot ignore what is called the "unique individuality" of every work. There is something absurdly over-simplified in the idea that a work of art can be viewed as the resultant of two factors, both general—motivation and technique. Yet these concepts will prove adequate if we see the total effort of the artist as a complex reintegrative activity, like preparing a plan of campaign, in which dozens of skills and, it may be, hundreds of suggestions are tried out, criticized, shredded, and combined. The artist's work is a product, so to speak, of his collective efforts—each of which is reducible, theoretically, to the basic terms of learning and motivation. To say that each work is irreducibly unique and also that it is in principle exhaustively analyzable—these two things are at bottom entirely consistent.

action between organism and environment. But we see already that poetry bears a different relationship to its physical medium from that of sculpture to stone.

Now we reach the decisive considerations:

1. When I find a clean blackboard or sheet of paper before me, I have an impulse to draw. As it happens, I do not "know how" to draw; but that is not the trouble. My trouble is that *I have nothing to draw*. Devoid as I am of purpose and conception, I amuse myself by sketching the features of a head. This is drawing at random, and it is characteristic of such work that I do not know beforehand how it will come out. The result will surprise me as much as anyone; and having intended nothing in particular to begin with, I am powerless to say whether it has *come out right*. My companion, who has studied drawing, works beside me; and it is obvious to anyone that where I am only puttering, he is "going somewhere." Does he copy an image already prepared in his mind? We do not know, and it is no matter; for he strokes and erases and modifies in obvious obedience to a sense of what he wants. And for this comparison it is quite unnecessary to say anything about our respective *talents*.

Art is nothing if it is not control. But we control only those of our acts whose outcome we foresee; and we foresee no result unless we have been over the ground before. It is *technique*, therefore, that gives direction to impulse and marks the difference between art and caprice.

Now it comes of the nature of *originality* that the outcome can not be *quite* foreseen. An original impulse is one we never have felt before: it *must*, therefore, lack the assurance of a developed purpose. Hence a period of searching, probation, trial and error. The painful crudity and incompetence of our first efforts repeat themselves, in a sense, with every new conception—but hardly at the original level. If we can not instantly achieve expression of an idea which supervenes upon the discipline of a lifetime, that implies no reversion to the utterly inarticulate. Accomplished mastery can never account for any masterpiece; but a masterpiece *without* the basis of mastery will never be seen.

2. It seems to us that we do sometimes generate *poetical* ideas; but here it turns out that we cannot develop them. The inspiration is stillborn, or it fizzles out in a line and a half, without renewing itself in the project for a work. How different, it may be, from philosophy, where if anyone should toss us a suggestion, instantly

it arrays itself in implications and parallels and before an hour has grown into a system.

The technique of the artist, it is thought, corresponds to the aspect of *development* in the work. Invention, which gives the theme, is peculiarly the composer's own. Exposition, elaboration, and construction reflect the technical tradition, which is formulated in "theories" or rules and transmitted by teaching. But the notions of subject and development have a purely relative standing. The seed has already a structure, and every part of that structure is complex. The subject is composite and must therefore have been *composed*, no matter with what apparent artlessness or lack of premeditation. So we should expect what we find—that the difference between a Schubert or a Burns (themselves relatively "natural" artists) and the folk material which they exploit is felt not alone in organization and power of development but in sweetness and poignancy of tone, that is, in the immediate expressive quality of the theme. Needless to say, the converse is also true: originality displays itself in the "development."

In experiments like these it is difficult to control the factor of aptitude. Thus, the reader may object that it is Schubert's *genius* that explains the superior concentration of his melodies. Yet we have no ground to assume that the makers of the popular ballads and songs were not gifted men: it is their very ignorance of professional traditions that makes it impossible to judge *what* their genius may have been. But this is my whole point.

3. "At the time when he is constructing his plots, the poet should remember to put the actual scenes as far as possible before his eyes. In this way, seeing everything with the vividness of an eye-witness as it were, he will devise what is appropriate, and be least likely to overlook incongruities."

In this passage Aristotle notices the disparity between the conditions in which the play is prepared and those in which it is received—a gap which must be bridged by an imaginative projection. Everywhere in the arts this circumstance presents a difficulty —even for a writer, who will make an effort in the morning to look at yesterday's work as if it were somebody else's. But in architecture the problem may seem nearly insuperable; for, in the first place, there is the greatest difference, aesthetically, between a building and a set of plans—the proportions which seem suitable on paper may be hideous when projected over cubic meters of space; and, of course, a building once reared can not be corrected. It appears astonishing, then, that there should be any such thing as a beautiful house. But not when we reflect that the architect has a *trained* imagination, practiced in the translation of plans into stone or steel and of physical dimensions back into pencil drawings—so that his eye automatically assesses a paper plan not for its inherent quality of design, like students who know the monuments of Europe only in photographic prints, but for its meaning in terms of architecture. The technical studies which taught him how to make what he conceives taught him to conceive what he makes.

The role of technique, in the artistic conception, is *constitutive.* It determines form, as a mere reproduction does not. It is never summoned to execute what has been shaped without its help but enters beforehand into the shaping. A pupil of Perugino could not *see* what Rembrandt saw because his vision was conditioned and confined by his habits of execution. And this truth, as I have said, is known to everyone.

Here I find it necessary to paraphrase, without comment, a chapter of the history of philosophy. It is in the spirit of romanticism to scorn the means essential to attainment. At the simplest grade of conduct this leads to futility and failure. At another level the romantic temperament shows itself sufficiently adept at tactics; but we see that it fails to incorporate the "reality principle" within its *objectives,* which remain willful, unmodifiable by reflection. And since reflection upon means can modify desire only through some reference to other interests of the personality, this implies that romantic *values* must be limited and inadequate. Now absolute idealism as a historical phenomenon is a romantic philosophy. I can only quote the analysis of historians, which reveals a connection between the theory which affirms the unconditioned primacy of spirit or will in nature and a personal temperament contemptuous of material conditions. Now Croce—sponsor of the extraordinary syllogism: art is not physical because nothing real is physical and art is real—holds that the activity of spirit is unconditioned. The survival of romantic idealism in his theory of art appears from this fact alone, that *he denies the existence of an aesthetic purpose:*

> To choose is to will: to will this and not to will that: and this and that must be before us, expressed. Practice follows, it does not precede theory: expression is free inspiration.[3]

The true artist, in fact, finds himself big with his theme, he knows

3. *Aesthetic,* p. 51.

not how: he feels the moment of birth drawing near, but he cannot will it or not will it. . . . Expression does not possess *means*, because it has not an *end;* it has intuitions of things, but it does not will and is therefore unanalyzable into the abstract components of volition, means and end.[4]

There are specialized situations in practical life where it is possible to discriminate purpose and execution. We think it necessary to repair the sink, and the plumber knows how to do it. Two men wish to reach a certain part of the city: one knows the way, and the other does not. We can speak of means to an end, assuming that an end has been adopted and that the problem of ways and means is not such as to make us reconsider it. To this there is no parallel in artistic composition.

But there is an earlier stage of the practical purpose—the stage at which it is being *formed.* It may be that the plumber's fee is prohibitive or that to reach the other end of the city would take too much time. The question is *whether* to adopt this particular course, to change it, or abandon it. This is the phase of deliberation in conduct, of which I borrow Dewey's account. (As a matter of consistent usage, the steps tentatively envisaged in deliberation, the foreseen consequences of a hypothetical choice, perhaps should not be entitled *means,* because it is just the case that an end does not yet exist.) Only to reach a decision in this matter, while the achievement of the goal lies all ahead, is to experience satisfaction, because it is passing from confusion to clarity, from the state of conflict and uncertainty to the state of knowing one's mind.

Now the process of art is not deliberative, because there are no intellectual forecasts to be made, no ulterior probabilities to be reviewed. But *like* deliberation it clarifies and integrates desire; and *like* the practical choice it incorporates knowledge beforehand—knowledge, on this plane, being only skill, the fact of having been over a similar path before. In art the phase of purpose formation is *everything.* The purpose is consummated the moment it is finally constituted. There remain no means to be chosen because there is no *ulterior* goal to be reached. The "means" went into the idea, which could not have been the same without them. Thus to say that one has an idea but lacks the ability to carry it out is to say that one has part of an idea but no idea of a work of art. Without knowledge suggestions may still abound, but they abound as fragments and

4. Ibid., pp. 51, 112.

abortions; inspiration is fitful; feeling may be powerful, but it falls short precisely of expression; ideas can never join to make a work. It is just this side of the subject that romantic theorists, though as artists they often possessed the technique they needed, tended to ignore. If I am not mistaken, Croce's aesthetic, though couched as a general theory of art, is itself the expression of a special artistic emphasis.

It is perfectly true that inspiration is spontaneous and cannot be controlled by the will. But that is true of *every* voluntary response. Imagine that after some thought I decide to leave this country and pay a visit to Mexico. In the first place, I don't know how I got this idea. I certainly didn't will it. It *came*. And I don't know why I adopt it. I know only that after holding it before me, together with its alternatives, I act. Taking thought consists in having such ideas and acting on some of them: it would be unreasonable to ask that they in turn should be the products of thought. A decision cannot be willed, since it *is* an act of will. First denying the impossible—that an aesthetic volition should will itself—Croce then denies the obvious—that an aesthetic volition exists—and gives the one as the reason for the other.

It now appears grossly inaccurate to think of a finished conception which an artist must only "execute" with the knowledge at his command.[5] Practice directly affects the artistic consciousness, the quality of inspiration; the ideas are different from what they might otherwise be. Technical incompetence stultifies expression, and imposes the penalty that one cannot *have* one's intuition before there is any question of communicating it.

Granting this, the reader may still find it strange to speak of an artistic purpose or will or to think of an artist's vision as embodying *means*. What is a purpose, he says, that is wholly self-gratifying, that is not set to accomplish something beyond itself? He is thinking of the difference between a practical purpose and an aesthetic "purpose"; whereas I am thinking of the difference between an aesthetic

5. As Maritain does in the following passage: "Clearly the more exalted the conception, the more the means run the risk of proving inadequate. Is not Cézanne an eminent example of such an inadequacy of the means in relation to the elevation of the conception? . . . He introduced a conception or a vision of superior quality—his *little sensation* as he used to say—which his means were inadequate to express. Hence his complaints of his incapacity to *realise*" (*Art and Scholasticism*, trans. J. F. Scanlon [New York: Scribners, 1930], p. 183).

purpose, which issues in a work of art, and an aesthetic whim or fantasy or craving or suggestion. The difference is that the first incorporates practice or technique; and that is what I am talking about.

II

These strictures would hold even if we conceded to Croce that the work of art proper terminates in the *idea*. It would still be true, empirically, that the idea is a fruit of practice. But we might, on that basis, have to revise and, as it were, dephysicalize our notion of practice. Piano-playing, for instance, is not the technique which is proper to the composer, who acquires his art by exercises in tonal arrangement; theoretically, it should not be impossible to become a master though one had been born without arms. Yet harmony and counterpoint have no existence save as systems of habit within individual organisms. Hence it will remain a task for psychology, pressing beyond the gross external performance, to study perception and ideation and the training to which these finer capacities submit. *Skill, inspiration, execution, conception*—all would suffer a translation onto the more rarefied psychic plane and begin to mark divisions within the spiritual domain; but places would have to be found for all. Let us observe that dualists even, who advocate an independent "soul," insist that the powers of that soul can and must develop themselves through exercise.

To acknowledge a difference between "thought" and "action" or between carnal and spiritual love is to make no ontological commitments whatsoever, since these can appear only as the result of an *analysis* of such distinctions. A behaviorist can pride himself, consistently, on being an "intellectual" worker; he can subordinate "physical" pleasures to the pleasures of the "mind"; and he can accept a distinction between the inner creative phases of art and the overt rendition, if that distinction is otherwise warranted. It is quite possible that art should be spiritual and that 'spirit' should denote a class of subtle motor responses. No doubt there are questions in the theory of art that wait upon the solution of the psychophysical problem. Of any activity that involves impressions, images, thoughts, and movements, behaviorists, dualists, parallelists will have their several interpretations; and it is hard to see how light can fall on this page of aesthetics without first illuminating the general relationship of consciousness to the brain. But the aesthetic categories of expression and execution, inspiration and technique, will certainly run athwart the categories of mind and body, no matter what these last turn out to be. 'Technical' is opposed, on the one hand, to 'nontechnical', 'primitive', 'amateurish' and, on the other hand, to 'original', 'inspired'—not to 'spiritual', 'mental', 'aesthetic'. I repeat, then, that it is possible to deny the physical character of art without prejudicing the importance of technique.

Yet it can not be easy to dismiss the narrowly "physical" act. We do not readily entertain the idea of an *essential painter*, experienced and accomplished in the fabrication of visions yet ignorant of pigments and brush. The muscular aptitude, the motor performance, is, we feel, *artistically* significant. Was it possible to *conceive* diffuse and subtle effects of atmosphere until painters had begun to mix their pigments with oil? Could anyone have dreamed the combinations of the *Appassionata* while the piano, with its dynamic range, did not exist and while the art of fingering was still in its infancy? This gives us our second topic—the role of the overt execution and of the material embodiment.

In aesthetics it is not uncommon to repair watches with meat axes. The least reflection should warn us against cutting through this subject with any set of categories intended to apply univocally to all the arts. In relation to any scheme of concepts that has yet been developed the arts still loom as a tangle and not as a system. In every art the principles are different. "Words" are not related to "thoughts" in poetry as "colors" to "thoughts" in painting or as "tones" to "thoughts" in music. Speech has not the same standing in the art of poetry that stone has in sculpture. "Means," "ends," "style," and "content," the physical, the sensory, the imaginative— each is different in meaning and function according to the art.

To think that a *dancer* prepares his work in the imagination and renders it with his body is simply foolish. The creative idea is only the impulse, alive in the legs, which prompts him to fling himself into motion; and the execution is the impulse discharging itself. Without the performance there is nothing—the work has simply not been finished. Ideas? Images? They are there. But they are there not as finished pictures to be imitated by the flesh but as anticipatory flashes, projections of movement, proprioceptive responses to actions already under way, checking or encouraging these by the sense they give of blocking or fulfillment. They are the feeling of the body on its way to one position or another.

Now many *sculptors* seem to be like the dancer in just this respect. *Poetry* and *music*, at the other extreme, *seem* (at least) to be purely inner activities. In the case of the aged Beethoven afflicted with deafness it is paradoxical to urge that he did not experience his own compositions. A group of verses, it appears, stands in complete form before the poet's mind, whose option it is to utter them or no. The proof is that the utterance, once decided upon, is easy. The problem of "execution" has been dealt with at an earlier stage, and there is no wrestle with the physical medium. At that, more than one reader will object that inner speech is not really "mental" and will refer to sensations of incipient movement in the vocal organs. But I cannot analyze these examples now. The *system* of Benedetto Croce must collapse if any *one* of the major arts does not conform to it—and painting, we shall see, is such an art.

The behavior of the artist terminates in an altered disposition of matter. If the artist's purpose is aesthetic, he alters the material according to a required value of appearance: the object will be molded so as to present a new form to sense, and the work halts when the right appearance is obtained. The effect of the physical action is to make of matter the stimulus to a new sensation, and there is no way by which sensory form can be produced save by physical labor. To prove, then, that the sensation is essential (or nonessential) is to prove that the operation is essential (or nonessential); and vice versa. It may be well now to refer once more to Croce.

It might be objected to the explanation of the physically beautiful as a simple aid to the reproduction of the internally beautiful, or expressions, that the artist creates his expressions by painting or by sculpturing, by writing or by composing, and that therefore the physically beautiful, instead of following, sometimes precedes the aesthetically beautiful. This would be a somewhat superficial mode of understanding the procedure of the artist, who never in reality makes a stroke with his brush without having previously seen it with his imagination; and if he has not seen it, he will make the stroke, not in order to externalize his expression (which does not yet exist), but as a kind of experiment and in order to have a point of departure for further meditation and internal concentration.[6]

Let us observe this painter, whom we shall suppose to be a man of unusual facilities, one who sees his subject easily. We should

6. *Aesthetic*, p. 103.

expect to find him rapt in a complacent revery, enjoying the vision
of his own making. Then, with a sigh: "But I must hasten to
record this conception before it slips away—else I shall have nothing to show for my spiritual effort. Somehow, what with these dis-
tractions, one gets so little time for art." Is that what we find?
On the contrary, everything in the expressive act impels toward
execution. For a good reason: because image and sensation are
disparate experiences. The clearest image can only *adumbrate* the
effect of a colored border curving through four feet of space; and
it is not until he stands before the finished canvas that the artist
can enjoy the experience of the work. The image is no fit object
of contemplation, except in the absence of anything better. Functionally, it is the expression of work in progress, the counterpart
of the plastic aim which wields knife and brush and paint. It has
a reference within it; it points *toward* the end result; the image is
for the work. It is the opposite of the truth to say that the *stroke*
is the "point of departure for further meditation." *Meditation* is
the point of departure—for further strokes.

Expression is achieved, according to Croce, when the stroke is
seen with the imagination. It follows that the painter has a double
task—the achievement of this experience and, secondly, the "externalization." Now there must be some criterion for this second
task, as well as for the first—and I ask, how does the painter know
when he has succeeded in the "practical" part of his work? How
can he tell that it is his authentic vision that he has externalized in
paint, to communicate to others, and not some inferior version?
Presumably, by comparison. The difficulties which beset this
notion of instituting comparisons between percepts and ideas are
extraordinary. Think only of matching colors where one color
belongs to an image—how could anyone know whether the color
in the painting was the same, or even what was meant by 'the
same'? If it should be replied that Croce does not envisage anything so literal and crude as this, I answer that it will then be impossible to avoid the conclusion that getting the right tone on the
canvas is an original and crucial aesthetic task. Again, it follows
from the idea of the double task that a man can be a great painter
and a poor craftsman, with magnificent conceptions imprisoned in
his mind for want of adequate means of externalization. This absurdity comes of misconceiving the first, or essentially artistic, act;
of supposing that the criterion of truly aesthetic achievement is the
presence of a satisfactory vision before the mind, later to be "trans-

lated" into physical materials. In opposition to this let us advance this statement: *What it means to say that I see my subject clearly, where a moment ago I did not, is that I know exactly what strokes to make.* Thus to one man his whole picture comes in a few seconds while he is walking in the fields; and he goes home happy, not because he knows how to get it rapidly and decisively when he sets to work. The image itself, if it could be studied by introspective methods, might be quite fragmentary and cloudy; but it is enough, because its direction is right. Another painter must struggle to achieve expression, and it is a matter of indifference whether we say that he can not *clarify his ideas* or that he can not *find an outlet for action.*

And now, at the risk of seeming to retract a statement which appears above, we may venture a formulation that will draw us a little nearer to Croce. Let us put the question whether a painter who is separated from his tools *must* experience artistic frustration. He loses the pleasure of beholding his conception writ large and plain—and this is a genuinely aesthetic loss. But not an aesthetic tragedy; for if by mental activity he has effected such an organization of his response system that he knows exactly what he *would* do with his brush if he had it, then he has solved the artistic problem and virtually "created" the work of art. Even in practical life, a complete plan of action is often the better part of action; but here there is the further advantage that since the actual control of the material is assured to the artist, since by our hypothesis the conquest of all difficulties is taken into the decision beforehand, there will remain no doubtful struggle to be waged, there can be no slip between resolution and performance, the possibility of defeat is precluded, the overt attack upon the environment becomes a perfunctory matter.

For the final sensation is not an ulterior satisfaction, to be realized by the artist in consequence of a series of steps. If a man is poised to shoot at a bird, to run for office, to catch a bus, we do not say that he requires *another* technique for *acting;* but there is still a distinction between the experience of willing and the final experience of victory or defeat. In an art like painting the end realizes itself progressively in the course of action: the sensory appearance streams, as it were, off the end of the brush. Success is to frustration as the relatively complete to the relatively incomplete. Motor activity is only the last stage of the self-development of the aesthetic purpose. A thorough analysis would show a complete consistency, at bottom, between these two propositions: that Beethoven "heard" his Ninth Symphony and that he did not hear it, that his purpose was consummated and that it was thwarted. In a thousand exercises his ideas had gone directly onto instruments—or into notation, which is a set of instructions for performance on instruments; and these in turn had fed his ears with sound. If he had lost his arms as well as his hearing, if he had been born without arms, it would have made no difference: he would still have had to learn how sounds are produced, to develop motor facilities within his nervous system. When we ask, then, how essential to the "work" is the sound, it is not as if we were comparing the experience of listening to music with that of recalling it in memory or reading it to oneself from a score. I don't see how one could answer *that* question about Beethoven's subjective experience in his state of deafness. The indubitable creative success lay in being assured that the composition *for* keyboard or strings was achieved, that he, Beethoven (who played the piano in solitude until the end of his life), knew how the right sounds were to be produced. Hence fulfillment of a kind, and frustration of a kind—the first undoubtedly more substantial than the second.

If now we read, "He never makes a stroke with his brush without having previously seen it with his imagination," and translate, "He never makes a stroke without first being completely ready to make the stroke," we shall make no objection. There are passages in Croce which seem to agree with this interpretation.[7] But let us emphasize the points in which our criticism remains irreconcilable with Croce:

1. In the mere activity of imagination there is an essential reference to overt production.

2. To have worked overtly with materials at least in the *past*

7. See, in the quotation on the first page of this essay, the words "movements which we have already made in little and rapidly." And see the *Aesthetic*, pp. 9–11 (a passage which I cannot square with the rest of Croce's argument): "People think that all of us ordinary men imagine and intuit countries, figures, and scenes like painters, and bodies like sculptors; save that painters and sculptors know how to paint and carve such images, while we bear them unexpressed in our souls. . . . Nothing can be more false than this view. . . . He who nourishes delusions as to the wealth of his own thoughts and images is brought back to reality, when he is obliged to cross the *Pons Asinorum* of expression. Let us say to the latter, speak; or here is a pencil, draw, express yourself."

is a condition of imaginative efficacy, since it is this which informs us of those limitations and possiblities that we cope with *now* in the *inner* activity.

3. There is no "translation" or "externalization," since the "internal" factor is already bodily action.

5
The Aesthetic Function of Language

The main problem of this paper can be stated as a paradox:

1. If the "aesthetic object" is purely sensuous, language can not be an aesthetic object, because language is not purely sensuous.

2. And the aesthetic object *is* purely sensuous; for a nonsensuous object cannot be directly perceived and enjoyed; and what is not directly perceived and enjoyed is not aesthetic.

3. But language is, or can be, an aesthetic object.

Anyone who opens a textbook of aesthetics must soon become aware that poetry and prose literature are somehow not taken in by the description given there of the aesthetic state of mind. For aesthetic experience is characterized as "perception for its own sake" or as the "self-motivated and self-gratifying exercise of perception"; while language is, as Santayana says, a "symbol for intelligence rather than a stimulus to sense"; and as a symbol for intelligence language is an instrument for dealing with things other than the symbols themselves, with a world vastly transcending the scope of immediate attention. Yet poetry, drama, and fiction are fine arts, therefore aesthetic objects, par excellence.

There are three ways of dealing with this predicament. You can deny my third proposition, that language is an aesthetic object, saying, as D. W. Prall was in one vein inclined to say, that

Read at Columbia University in 1947; revised and published in *Journal of Philosophy* 46, no. 1 (January 1949): 5–20. Reprinted with permission.

"the various arts differ very greatly as to the proportion of their value that is strictly aesthetic, music being almost purely aesthetic in essence, poetry very slightly so." Now nobody doubts that language has many extra-aesthetic and anti-aesthetic functions. But to limit the aesthetic side of poetry to its phonetic surface, as Prall did, is to leave the great body of poetic values isolated, classified neither with theoretical and practical nor with aesthetic values; it is to preclude the development of a unified theory of the fine arts. And, of course, it by no means spares us the necessity of giving some account of the class of values which have been thus set apart.

In the second place, you could deny my second proposition, that the aesthetic object is purely sensuous, maintaining with Greene, Urban, Morris, and Langer that aesthetic experience is a department of cognition and that the aesthetic object is some sort of sign, containing a reference to something beyond itself. Now it seems as if we could show that this alternative is empirically false, false to the facts about the kind of attitude which is assumed by lovers of nature and devotees of the abstract arts, who certainly seem to be absorbed in what is given to their senses. But more significant is the fact that this approach invariably winds up by reinstating the original issue. If the aesthetic object is a special kind of symbol or sign, what kind of symbol or sign is it? What is its referent and how shall we tell whether the reference to this referent is correct or incorrect? The answer, so far as we can understand it, always comes down to some such formula as that the aesthetic object is the kind of sign which does not signify anything or the kind of symbol which symbolizes itself— a long way round to immediate experience. Notions like that of the "presentational symbol" and of the "form which asserts nothing yet conveys a truth" *look* like contradictions in terms and in my opinion *are* such. These devices bear witness to the simplicity and fruitfulness of the orthodox approach which assumes it to be the hallmark of the aesthetic experience that sensory phenomena are therein divested of their sign functions.

As a third alternative you can show that language can be intelligible without indicating or referring to anything; and if you can show this, you can again deny that the aesthetic object is purely or exclusively sensuous without denying that it is directly perceived and enjoyed. As rough names for the two processes that I wish to distinguish here, I will use the terms 'meaning' and 'reference'. Our question, then, has to do with the existence and nature of nonreferential meaning.

The existence of such a process is hardly open to doubt. To begin at the level of the natural sign, I would call your attention to Winslow Homer's painting, *The Gulf Stream,* in the Metropolitan Museum. (For the present purpose it will do as well as a good picture would.) In this picture we see a man lying in an open boat at sea, surrounded by sharks; while in the distance there is the shape of a waterspout which indicates an approaching hurricane. In another paper[1] I made the point that our use of the terms 'man', 'boat', 'shark', and so on, to describe the forms in the picture, does not of itself show that we attach any meanings to these forms. But it is clear that the dramatic element in this picture, depending as it does on the quasi-anticipation of a "future" event, is not given to the sense of sight and can be apprehended only through some process of interpretation on the part of the observer. Yet the observer does not treat the forms in the picture as genuine signs; that is, he does not seriously believe in the reality of man, boat, sharks, water, or storm; does not *raise the question* of their reality; and does not respond emotionally as he would if he did. Hence these forms have a function which is somewhere between sensory stimulation on the one hand and reference or indication on the other; and our own state of mind is somewhere between pure aesthesis and cognition. A person afflicted with a kind of sensory aphasia and a person deluded into belief would each miss the sense and the value of the picture.

At the more advanced level of language or symbolic function, the point is illustrated by the art of fiction, where sentences seem to withdraw their claims to truth. Suppose we read this sentence in a novel: "On the first of March, 1820, a man stood for three hours at the portal of the Cathedral of Notre Dame." This sentence is more than ink or wind. It conveys ideas. It introduces us to a "world" full of "people" and "events." Yet it does not inform us (or misinform us) about anything in the actual world outside of the novel. The same sentence could, however, be treated as an assertion and be tested for its historical accuracy. Hence the property, informativeness or noninformativeness, is not inherent in the sentence: it depends on the attitude of the reader. The ability of language to divest itself of its reference to reality without losing its

1. See "Perception, Meaning, and the Subject Matter of Art," chapter 3 in this volume.

intelligibility is thus a specialized functon which can be assumed or discarded.

Now imagine that in place of this sentence we have a general observation on the part either of the author or of one of his characters—for example, the first sentence of *Anna Karenina:* "Happy families are all alike; every unhappy family is unhappy in its own way." Needless to say, there are important differences between this statement and the particular statement quoted above. But there is no such difference as might lead us to say that though the first can be taken as fiction, without consideration of truth, the second never can or should be taken so. If any sentence can be comprehended without being credited or rejected, so can any other sentence down to the furthest theorem of physics or economics. There is a perfect continuity, from this standpoint, between the narrative and the speculative portions of a book like *War and Peace* —though the chapters in which Tolstoy writes as a philosopher do naturally provoke the reader to an exercise of thought. Another step and we see that structures like *The Origin of Species, The Critique of Pure Reason, The Decline and Fall of the Roman Empire,* can be treated as figments of imagination, describing so many possible worlds, less pictorial than Lilliput or Erewhon but not less intelligible; though it is not to be expected that works which were not shaped primarily by artistic motives should prove to be very rewarding when taken purely as works of art. Bacon characterized the philosophies of his own time as "so many stage plays, representing worlds of their own creation after an unreal and scenic fashion." Our own point is somewhat different. *Any* philosophy, and any system of science, is a "stage play" in so far as we endeavor to understand it without caring to check up on it. The contemplative attitude embraces meanings which can be carried to any degree of depth whatsoever. The real world, displayed to us by science, figures as one spectacle among many. And when Thomas Hardy writes, "Art is concerned with seemings only," and holds it to be "the mission of art to record impressions, not convictions," we must understand that convictions *become* impressions when the sentences which record them are taken in a certain way.

So far I have been concerned only to establish the fact from which our paradox emerges: the fact that we are able to hold before our direct attention theories, systems, cities, worlds—structures so complexly elaborated in depth that sense-perception could not possibly comprehend them.

It is interesting to notice that this phenomenon could not have

presented any problem for a psychology such as Hume's. A psychology of sensations interprets the phenomena of meaning in
terms of the accrual of associated images to a sensory core. But
that an image should become an object of direct contemplation is
as easy to understand as that a sensory datum should be one: the
aesthetic attitude is, in fact, indifferent to the distinction between
imagination and sensation. The free play of fancy in accordance
with laws of association was the one thing Hume could regard as
simply obvious. He was confronted with the inverse problem to
our own: how to go forward to a description of cognitive processes
rather than how to get back from cognition to pure ideation. What
is the difference between *imagining* and *believing*, for example, that
I live in London? What is the difference between recollection and
prediction? What is *added* to a notion when it becomes a reference?
When does a word name an object and when does it merely remind
us of one? These were the difficult questions for Hume as a psychologist; and it is the inability of his method to cope with these
questions that has brought it into disrepute. It is generally believed today that there are reasons for which Hume's method in
psychology must be rejected; that an introspective psychology
cannot give an adequate account of mental processes. It cannot, for
example, adequately analyze the features of generality and par-
ticularity, precision and vagueness, in meanings or in references.
The differences in meaning among such terms as 'a mile', 'a mile and
a quarter', 'a million miles', 'a very great distance' cannot be
brought down to differences among mental images. On the other
hand, it is considered that a dynamic psychology of cognition can
attack such questions with greater success. But an apparent result
of this shift in psychological approach is the following. The fact
that a waterspout stands for a storm is to be understood in terms
of expectancies, preparatory sets, the assumption in response to
the waterspout of an attitude appropriate to a storm. The fact that
the word 'man' stands for men and the word 'shark' for sharks is
to be understood in terms of ostensive procedures or verificatory
procedures. Every such index or criterion of meaning carries with
it the idea of discursus—a displacement of attention from the given
object to an object not yet given. The analysis of meaning in the
hands of philosophers, subordinating this topic as it does to the
interests of theory of knowledge, reinforces this conception. To
understand a sentence is to know on what conditions you would
accept it as true; but to know this is to know where to go and

what to look for—it is to rehearse a line of experimentation. The possibility of an eventual, conditional, and ulterior course of action becomes the criterion of intelligibility. At this point it becomes difficult to see how it should be possible merely to enjoy the content of an idea. If the understanding of language is nothing but the implicit commitment to a procedure of ostention or of verification, then the values of language must lie in the results of that procedure. They would be such as clarity, precision, and truth (or their opposites); they could not be such as splendor, eloquence, poignancy, or wit. These values are inherent in the immediate grasp of meaning. They are subject to a critical check on a second or third reading; but they neither require nor depend on any process which goes beyond that.

Thus, while the statement, in general terms, of the fact that we can contemplate an object which is not presented but only symbolized, designated, thought of, is perhaps already paradoxical, it becomes flagrantly so on a behavioristic, or "operational," analysis of symbolization, language, or thought. For this reason I would like to make it clear, if I can, that the immanent or nonreferential function of meaning in aesthetic experience can be recognized and treated operationally. This will require several preliminary points.

1. The word 'contemplation' is imaginatively associated with sitting and with looking or listening; and it also seems to imply the existence of a contemplated object. An illiterate person, perceiving a man seated for several hours with a novel, could understand his preoccupation if he assumed either that there were interesting shapes inscribed on the pages or that there were shapes which evoked interesting mental images. But, with these two assumptions barred, what could he make of the information, "I am really absorbed in the life of a man named David Copperfield"? It would seem to him that there was nothing which *was* the "life of David Copperfield" to be absorbed *in*. Yet such a person would, after all, be equally mystified if he were told, "I am studying the life of Charles Dickens," or, "I am calculating the life expectancy of the present generation"; until perhaps it was pointed out to him that he was himself apparently engaged only in listening to spoken sounds yet was in some sense dealing with the question of other people's reading habits. The question "How can language be an aesthetic object?" is partly rooted in a psychological confusion, in the fact that we take staring as a model for all contemplation and continue to feel that contemplation *ought* to be pictorial when we

no longer suppose that to be the case with other kinds of thought. If there exists a genuine difficulty in the fact that I can contemplate David Copperfield though there be no David Copperfield and no image or picture of him, the difficulty is not peculiar to the present topic. It holds equally for the question of false assertions, which refer to something though there is nothing to which they refer. And if one presumes to settle it by invoking ideal entities to serve as the designata of our thoughts, that will still not take us a single step toward distinguishing between contemplation and reference. That distinction is psychological; it marks a difference between two kinds of response to symbols.

2. In the second place, we should take note of difficulties and limitations which mark the current behavioristic theories of interpretation. For one thing, it is difficult to identify the operational index to a given act of interpretation. When we say that a waterspout means "storm" to certain people, we judge this equally by people who are running away, people who are organizing rescue parties, people who are sending messages in the weather bureau, and by an indefinite variety of other actions. The psychologist's conception of this interpretative act is a construction from such facts as that you run away *if* you fear storms—with a good many other if's. The reference can not be identified with this act or with any finite set of such acts. A given reference is a characteristic component of a set of adjustive reactions. It is identified as a parallel change in direction of thousands of variously motivated and qualified types of response; and just what class of changes shall be regarded as a sufficient basis for imputing the reference is not an easy thing to formulate, even in the animal laboratory. This point has been emphasized by many writers.[2] Again, many references are put in evidence at most by implicit responses which would not serve us, in the present state of knowledge, to distinguish them from other references. Thus, you could not tell from the most refined description of the state of my muscles and glands as I approach the breakfast table whether I expect to have tea or coffee. Again, there is the point demonstrated by Tolman and other experimentalists: that the preparatory responses, for example, to a shock are not identical with those elicited by the shock itself. This exposes ambiguity in attempts to characterize sign-interpreta-

2. See C. L. Stevenson, *Ethics and Language* (New Haven, Conn.: Yale University Press, 1944), p. 64.

tion in terms of the display of responses "appropriate" to the signified objects. And such attempts meet a further and very formidable obstacle in the fact that we are capable of interpreting altogether unique and novel combinations of signs and of symbols, which refer to objects never encountered as direct stimuli in our past experience.

Now I believe that most of the objections you will have to the following account of nonreferential meaning will be objections that apply to the operational approach to interpretation in general and not to the attempt to clarify operationally the peculiar function of meaning in aesthetic experience.

Let us assume that the consummatory phases of behavior, in which terminal values are realized, can be accurately described; and that contemplative activity is a form of consummatory response. Let us assume, in other words, that we understand the nature of *sensuous* contemplation. The feeling-responses which are obtained when one adopts the contemplative attitude, though they may appear just alike to the naked eye, are highly variable. To put it crudely, there are subtle differences in heart-beat, respiration, circulation, and so on, which correspond to the differences among the contemplated objects; and the subjective counterpart of this fact is the enormous wealth and range of aesthetic feelings. Now if we suppose that the consummatory feeling-response is modified by associative connections established in the course of past experience and reactivated by the present stimulus, we can go on to say that the operational index of the fact that a certain shape in a painting by Winslow Homer has the meaning "storm" is the occurrence of a feeling-response appropriate to the contemplation of a storm. Potentially, there are millions of meanings attached to the surface of *The Gulf Stream*. The water can be resolved into oxygen and hydrogen; the boat can be burned; the man has perhaps a wife and children whom his death would afflict. In principle, any and all of these meanings can be taken into the experience without destroying its aesthetic character; but whether a given meaning is artistically and critically *relevant* depends on the increment of positive value that it can contribute; and whether a given meaning is *in point of fact* active in somebody's experience is to be known by the particular feeling that he has and shows or expresses. Relevant feeling-response; plus the admittedly fragmentary and eccentric flow of imagery, is also what gives the rich life to the otherwise barren act of following a page of print.

As an essential precaution here, it should be added that there
is no reason a priori why we should be able to say what the full
meaning of a work of art is; for that would be either to describe
the meaning it has for an observer, which presupposes an elaborate psychological theory that we do not possess, or to say something which has exactly the same meaning, that is, the same influence on feeling, as the work of art—and this, for various reasons,
may well be impossible. One measure of mediocrity in Homer's
Gulf Stream is the degree to which we can juggle its forms about
on the canvas without destroying its value; and another measure
is the fact that an expression like 'a lonely Negro in an open boat
at sea, in the path of a hurricane' conveys a feeling not *much* different from the feeling conveyed by the picture.

Aesthetic feeling as an index of meaning is like any other index:
it is nothing but a modification of behavior induced by previous
learning. The difference between what I have called meaning and
what I have called reference corresponds to the difference between
the *kinds* of behavior which are thus affected. The existence of a
meaning attached to an aesthetic object is to be recognized by a
change in the quality of the *contemplative* feeling-response. The
taste of an orange can bear out a prediction, or fail to bear it out;
it can satisfy an appetite or disappoint it. But to say that the
taste of an orange can itself be borne out or satisfied is surely to
make no sense whatever, even if the taste in question happens to
be an acquired one. In quite a parallel sense: the shapes in *The
Gulf Stream* are sufficient to suggest the idea of a rising storm;
and once suggested, the idea is present as a possession to be enjoyed. To ask, then, whether the idea is correct, whether it is
confirmed by the sequel or agrees with an archetype, is meaningless and irrelevant, because it ignores the nature of the act which
we take as the index of the idea.

At the root of the whole difficulty is the persistence of the ancient dichotomy, contemplation *versus* action. Once convinced
that learning is to be understood as the redirection of behavior, we
naturally turn to theoretical and practical responses as models of
learned behavior, simply because of the practical facility of discriminating responses when they are brought out into the open
field; and mental processes seem to be clearly differentiated when
we trace their implications for action and chart the courses or tendencies which they would follow if completely carried out. The
aesthetic attitude is by comparison apparently impassive, immo-

bile, static—a sort of dark night for behaviorists where anything that happens looks like anything else. For this reason I have emphasized both the practical difficulty of discriminating "references" and the theoretical possibility of discriminating "meanings." But some very eminent writers have taken a different tack. When their attention is called to the aesthetic attitude, they observe its resemblance to a case of deferred response and accordingly interpret it, not as a full-fledged action of its own kind, but as an abortive action of some other kind. Thus, a picture like *The Gulf Stream* induces us by some of its features to assume that we are dealing with a dangerous situation; but the frame of the picture, the walls of the gallery, and other circumstances cut off this inference, leaving us like some of the stupider animals in the laboratory to display a reaction which is no longer appropriate. The aesthetic emotion is a sort of abridged version of the alarm we should feel if we were present at the scene itself; and the significance of the picture lies, so to speak, in this false reference. It is impossible to mention all the valid objections to this type of theory as it applies itself to the arts: one is that we do not see how an emotion like alarm, merely by growing smaller, should become positive and pleasurable when it was negative and painful. But it is rather important to see the reason for the existence of such a theory. It is the assumption of the primacy of theory and practice based on the fact that aesthetic contemplation, as traditionally conceived, provides no foothold for the study of meanings, which do nevertheless sometimes function in that experience. It is, if I may say so, not the *fault* of the aesthetic attitude that it has its whole field before it and therefore cannot and need not go outside. It is nature's fault, or perhaps even the fault of logic; for in the last analysis when we say that aesthetic experience contains meanings but no references, we are saying something which is analytically true.[3]

3. Mr. Lucius Garvin ("The Paradox of Aesthetic Meaning," *Philosophy and Phenomenological* Research 8 [1947]: 99–106), propounding the same question that I dealt with in this paper, also offers what is apparently the same solution. "The solution proposed is as follows: What an art work means, aesthetically, is simply the feeling-response obtained from it in aesthetic contemplation." But this statement is, in my opinion, unsatisfactory.
(1) It implies that *every* art work has a meaning and thereby either denies the possibility of a response limited to sensuous quality and formal order or confers on that type of response the gratuitous designation of 'meaning'. Even if we adopt a sense of the word 'meaning' so

Let us now consider a simple empirical statement. I choose Nietzsche's remark about the relatives of a suicide: "The relatives of a suicide take it in ill part that the deceased was not more considerate of their feelings and their reputations." Some of the normal reactions to a sentence like this would be the following: you can accept it; accept it "in part"; doubt it; reject it; or hold it before your mind as a hypothesis for further examination. In every case except perhaps the last it is clear that the *understanding* of the sentence must be distinct from the act in question, if only because it is also presupposed by the other acts: to accept, reject, or doubt a sentence you must first understand it. It is also clear that the act, for instance, of *accepting* the sentence expresses this fact about the person who performs it: that his response system is geared to one order of things or events in the environment rather than another; in other words, he has an expectations about the behavior of the relatives of suicides. He has also feelings which are conditional upon the expectations: one might feel despondent if one has to accept Nietzsche's proposition and relieved if one is unable to reject it.

The case in which we "entertain" the sentence as a mere "supposition" would seem to be different; and it is this frame of mind

---

general as to make Garvin's statement acceptable, we should still be faced with the characteristic differences between decorative design and formal construction on the one hand and poetry and expressive prose on the other; and it is on the resemblance and difference between these kinds of aesthetic object that the "paradox of aesthetic meaning" rests.

(2) It obliges us to say that a piece of music *signifies* the feeling which (as one would usually say) it produces. This is as if Pavlov had said that his unconditioned stimulus—that is, food—signified salivation to the dog to whom it was given.

(3) It would compel us to say that the meaning of the forms on the canvas of *The Gulf Stream* was "apprehension," "tension," "excitement," rather than "storm," "danger," "possible catastrophe"; or that Pavlov's conditioned stimulus (the bell) meant "salivation" rather than "food" to the dog.

Feeling-response is not the meaning of a work of art. *Alteration* of feeling-response, in ways which remain to be specified by a theory of learning, is the tangible evidence (the only evidence, other than linguistic paraphrase, available to the student of aesthetic experience) that a person is thinking of something more than what he perceives; or, in other words, that certain forms are endowed for him with certain meanings.

that we are apt to identify with the understanding of the sentence, as opposed to the various degrees and kinds of assertion. Yet it is in the nature of a supposition, after all, that it is something *to be* tested. It expresses a verificatory set, a group of implicit exploratory responses which look ahead to an eventual result— though a result which is not prejudged. One is, so to speak, prepared for this *or* that in the relatives of a suicide—the presence or the absence of a certain trait. And this attitude corresponds, on the psychological side, to a definition of the meaning of the sentence as the set of testable consequences that can be deduced from it. Considered as a supposition, Nietzsche's sentence would certainly be clearer if it were modified to indicate whether we are to look *only* for resentment in the relatives of a suicide or for a mixed attitude of resentment and grief; and, again, whether it means to say that they are resentful *if* they think of their own reputations or that they *do* think of their own reputations and *are* resentful; just as, considered as an assertation, it would have a better chance of proving true if it were modified by the word 'frequently' or 'sometimes'. But any of these changes would spoil the quality of the sentence as a piece of writing. That quality is poignant, ironical, and shocking. It can be exhibited, though not duplicated, by a paraphrase: "The dead man himself, among all those affected by his deed, was presumably the most unfortunate; we might suppose, then, that his family would be overwhelmed by pity and grief; but *on the contrary* they are resentful, for they are thinking more of themselves than of him." Here the element of contrast, incongruity, which is without interest for the psychology of suicides or their relatives, is made plain. This element would be weakened and reduced by exactly those changes which would increase the theoretical value of Nietzsche's sentence. On the other hand, it would exist in that sentence if there were not a single case for which the sentence held good. It would exist in a note jotted down, perhaps, as the sketch for a play: "The relatives of a suicide *who* took it in ill part, etc." It would exist in an imaginary construction which ran counter to all the laws and facts of human psychology. There is, then, a quality of insight which is inseparable from the understanding of the sentence; which yet does not fluctuate with any shift in the weight of the evidence for its truth; and which is also distinguishable from the values characteristic of a good supposition. One is forced to assume that there must be a kind of understanding, not to be identified either with believing or with supposing, of which the criterion is the kind of feeling obtained in contemplation.

The example from Nietzsche was chosen precisely because it is *not* devoid of cognitive value; for, though probably false, it suggests that *some* relatives do *sometimes* act in the way it describes; and this is not only true but it might well be connected with some very important truths in psychology. One may therefore be tempted to conceive of its value for imagination as being that of a suggestive half truth. And so with many great passages from the world's literature of exposition and argument. You may admit that in many cases they are demonstrably false; you may admit that they frequently contradict one another; but when you are asked how in that case they can one and all be accepted as valuable, you will be tempted to reply that they are contributions—that they *contain* or *suggest* valuable truths—and to conceive their authors as collaborating on the single structure of knowledge and wisdom. This argument, I repeat, is plausible because its premise is fairly sound. These writers—Montaigne, Milton, Pascal, Swift, Goethe, Emerson, and so many others—*were* great thinkers, great moralists, contributors to science and philosophy. But as an objection to the point that there exists a distinct dimension of aesthetic meaning and an imaginative insight which corresponds to it, the argument is exposed to a crushing retort. This is simply that the greatest contribution to knowledge is in principle supersedable, whereas these passages are not to be superseded: they have a final and permanent value.

The idea that poetry as poetry is neither true nor false goes back at least to Sir Philip Sidney and perhaps to St. Thomas; and it is rather widely insisted upon today. Quite obviously, it enables us to avoid certain difficulties which arise for some critics, for instance, from the fact that Shakespeare made equally magnificent capital out of the affirmation and the denial of immortality. But it seems to lead in its own turn to consequences embarrassing to criticism. Thus, if a poem is not to be judged through an evaluation of its content, what remains but the form? We are led to the idea of an abstract poetic magic, a technical facility in the invention of rhythms or the management of vowels and consonants, which when superadded to an otherwise commonplace thought can render that thought poetical. And it is no wonder that such an interpretation of poetic value should seem to many people to be intolerably reductive. It is this dilemma which is posed for us by Professor Urban:

Shelley, we are told, is not making a statement that must be accepted by the hearer as either true or false. The question of truth or falsity does not enter. Now ... I may indeed "enjoy" these lines of Shelley merely for the music of his words, the beauty of his imagery. . . . If the hearer is enjoying the poet's utterances without any reference to their truth or falsity, he is not enjoying the poet's meaning but something else. If, on the other hand, he is really *understanding* the poet, that understanding does involve communication of meaning in which questions of truth and falsity are relevant.[4]

And it is this dilemma which is rejected by Mr. Cleanth Brooks when he says that the critic who refuses "to rank poems by their messages" is not thereby "compelled to rank them by their formal embellishments."[5]

Now I think we can see in what sense it is that a certain famous passage from *The Tempest* has the "same content" as the sentence, "Everything passes away," and in what sense it has a different content. If you will allow me to assume for the moment (what is certainly debatable) that both the passage—Prospero's speech—and its paraphrase have an empirical character, I would say that they are equivalent in the sense that they express the same reference or, if you prefer to consider it from the evidential standpoint, that any observation which confirmed or weakened the one would confirm or weaken the other. It is on this understanding of the word 'content' that Shakespeare's passage figures as a platitude with aesthetic frills and the "cloud-capp'd towers, the gorgeous palaces, the solemn temples, the great globe itself" as so many ornamental flourishes; and it is for Mr. Urban to explain how two passages which have the same "content" should be so infinitely disparate in poetic value. In other words, it is just by ignoring the existence of a distinctive aesthetic function of meaning, by assuming that the absence of a reference to reality would leave us with nothing but a sequence of meaningless sounds, that we are led inevitably to a formalistic interpretation of literary values. Before considering the alternative, we should disclaim any attempt to explain what

4. Wilbur Marshal Urban, *Language and Reality* (London: Allen & Unwin; New York: Macmillan, 1951), p. 480.
5. *The Well Wrought Urn* (New York: Harcourt, Brace, Harvest Books, 1947), p. 180.

we do not understand. Just as there is no theory of design from which we could deduce the fact that one bowl of flowers should be beautiful and another one worthless, so there is no theory of meaning which can explain why the exact combination of words in Prospero's speech should be uniquely valuable. But for our immediate purpose, which is the clarification of the word 'content' as a critical concept, there is at least the point that the poem and its paraphrase are made up of entirely different words. The component meanings are not the same. This means that the same body of meaning is *not* present to the mind in the two cases; and perhaps it is not more mysterious that two sentences which express the same proposition to be proved or disproved should have different effects upon feeling than that two such different sentences should manage to express the same proposition. In the modest paraphrase, "Even the solidest and apparently most enduring objects shall pass away," there already exist certain relationships among component meanings which are not to be found in the sentence, "All things shall pass away," from which it can be logically derived; and those relationships, which give to the one paraphrase some slight equivalence in point of emotionally appreciable content to Shakespeare's passage, constitute a difference between that passage and the other paraphrase. Thus the very features which are adventitious to the reference made by the passage are integral to its nonreferential content.

Finally, I would like to suggest the bearing of my argument on another issue of some importance. To revert to our old example, let us suppose that in an upper corner of *The Gulf Stream* there was dimly sketched in a very small area a boat laden with women and children. It seems evident that our interest would focus mainly on the apathetic Negro in the foreground lying prone in the boat, rather than on them. It is his fate and not theirs which projects the romantic thrill, just as Achilles is more important to us than all his myrmidons and just as Macbeth, whether we are for him or against him, is more important to us than Lady Macduff and her children. In practical life it would be our business to correct the distorted evaluations which result from the nearness and prominence of certain objects; to give things the value and importance which they have in themselves; to be more concerned about the women and children than about the man in the boat; and not to bother about the conflicts in the soul of Macbeth when he is every day murdering innocent people. Plato's charge against the fine arts is that they impair the integrity of our intellects and wills, induce conflict and division in the human mind, by persuading us to judgments which are at variance with those of sober reason. Just as to cultivate the illusions of perspective without intellectual criticism is to remain rooted in the childish notion that a boat in the distance is smaller than one close at hand, so poetry and painting present the issues of life in a kind of moral perspective. Anyone not a fervent nationalist and imperialist who has felt himself deeply stirred by Heine's grenadier when he declares he will let his wife and child go begging for food while he follows the Emperor on his crazy and wicked adventures and who has been troubled by the presence of an apparently treasonable element in his own soul has implicitly registered Plato's whole problem. The critics of Plato from Aristotle down have been busy inventing queer kinds of truth to ascribe to the arts in order to defend them against Plato's charge. But Plato cannot be refuted on his own ground. If factual or moral truth is the standard, some very great works will have to be condemned. At the very least we shall be faced with the issue, explicitly underwritten by Plato's critics, whether to sacrifice the impartiality and catholicity of our taste or the integrity of our scientific and moral judgment. Yet Plato, when he assumes that the arts evoke responses *antagonistic* to those approved by reason, assumes that they evoke responses of essentially the *same kind*, leading ultimately toward practical decision; and it is at this point that his aesthetic philosophy is vulnerable.

The reader of Heine's poem or of the passage in which Othello proclaims the "quality, pride, pomp, and circumstance of glorious war" has a limited number of choices. He can approve the sentiment, if he is enough of a militarist, and with it the poem. He can reject the sentiment and with it the poem. He can reject what he calls the "content" and acclaim the technical cunning which by manipulating sounds and meters knows how to make good poetry out of deplorable ideas. None of these choices fails to offend either against taste or against reason. Or he can ask himself, finally, what exactly he is committed to if he accepts the poetry, content and all. For what Heine, what Othello, is "saying" may bear a different construction from what a person "says" who expresses the evaluation—makes the claim—"War is glorious." That claim marks out a domain of morally relevant consequences: in other words, it is the whole phenomenon of war, with its glory, horror, advantage, and suffering weighed against one another, that we are presuming to judge. To base that judgment on a glimpse of one aspect is to be as irrational as Plato fears. But to *appreciate* that aspect is to be committed to no judgment whatever concerning the whole. In this mode of contemplative appreciation there is no ambivalence, no temptation, no rebellious impulse to be contented with. On the contrary, it is the doctrinaire moralist who, suppressing the honest deliverance of taste and feeling, leaves something out of his philosophy which is sooner or later to be reckoned with.

A thorough treatment of the aesthetic function of language would have to concern itself with the didactic quality in literature where and when it appears, above all in those passages which take the explicit form of a moral judgment:

> It is better to be vile than vile esteemed
> Let not ambition mock their useful toil
> Neither a borrower nor a lender be

and so on. It would have to distinguish the nonreferential meaning of such expressions from the moral reference or supposition or claim and this in turn from the acceptance or rejection of the claim.[6] If these distinctions are accurately drawn, it becomes possible to show how we may critically "accept" apparently conflicting creeds without subscribing to anything which we do not believe. Instead of endorsing either the moralistic judgment of poetry or the critical dogma which would banish didacticism from poetry as extraneous, it would develop a conception of literature as moral experience based on the apprehension of "moral meaning." Thus the justification of a purely aesthetic interpretation of the arts would be found in its ability to reconcile one with another all values which are recognized by intelligence, conscience, and taste.

6. In this essay the term 'nonreferential', qualifying term 'meaning', is not identified with 'emotive', 'dynamic', or 'expressive', and is not opposed to 'factual', 'indicative', 'descriptive'. We have seen how purely descriptive statements can be taken in such a way as to be appreciated for their meaning and make no reference to any state of affairs. On the other hand, moral propositions like those quoted above contain implicit references just in so far as the feelings which they express are (genetically) conditioned by or (normatively) based on opinions with respect to fact. For aesthetics the emphasis in *emotive meaning* must be on *meaning* rather than on *emotive*, because the emotion which is inherent in the *understanding* of a piece of didactic writing is different from the moral attitude which it expresses or produces. The second is a feeling about how people should behave; the first is a feeling taken in the contemplation of a *view* about how people should behave. I can have the first without the second.

6

The Problem
of Belief

People are influenced in their responses to works of art by the beliefs which they hold on all sorts of questions and by the ways in which the works seem to impinge upon those beliefs. It might well be an object of interest to psychologists to study these influences. Critics and aestheticians, however, find themselves raising the strange question of the "legitimacy" or "relevance" of these belief reactions.[1] Some think them improper and intrusive, while others hold them to be quite in order. The question, though not excessively clear, has been much debated; and it is possible to speak of "sides." I take one side, holding as I do the extreme view that belief and aesthetic experience are mutually irrelevant. I shall marshal some of the arguments that support this side, then state one fairly serious objection and reply to it. But, first, there are three ways in which the subject is to be limited; and I must take a few minutes to explain what they are.

1. "Belief" and "disbelief" are closely connected with problems of mimicry and illusion, psychic distance, topics in the theory of painting and of drama— in a word, with many problems in aesthetics. But I shall be considering as prime examples only lines of poetry and sentences of prose and, among those, only straight-

Originally published in *Journal of Aesthetics and Art Criticism* 13, no. 3 (March 1955): 395–407; reprinted with permission.

1. Henry Aiken, "The Aesthetic Relevance of Belief," *Journal of Aesthetics and Art Criticism* 9, no. 4 (June 1951): 301–15. "The Aesthetic Function of Language," chapter 5 in this volume.

forward statements of fact—of which, as I am not the first to remark, imaginative literature is full: "The rainbow comes and goes," "From fairest creatures we desire increase," and so on without end. In other words, I am keeping (for the most part) to propositions which *can* be believed and *are* believed or disbelieved; for here, if anywhere, belief should count. The revival of interest in our present subject which started with Mr. Richards thirty years ago, like the original statement of the problem in the philosophy of Plato, began with the observation that much poetry that we all think very fine is incredible while much that we believe to be true is mediocre or bad. And this remains for most people the central conundrum—for how can we love and enjoy what we doubt or reject? Let us remind ourselves of this paradox by recalling some beautiful lines from *Hyperion*. One of the old hierarchy of gods and Titans, now deposed by Zeus and the Olympians, speaks these consoling words to Saturn:

> So on our heels a fresh perfection treads,
> A power more strong in beauty, born of us
> And fated to excel us, as we pass
> In glory that old Darkness: nor are we
> Thereby more conquer'd, than by us the rule
> Of shapeless Chaos . . .
> . . . for 'tis the eternal law
> That first in beauty should be first in might.

I should think it a fair paraphrase to say that this asserts a constant and unending progress from lower to higher in nature. Herbert Spencer may have believed something of the sort. We do not believe anything of the sort.

2. Each of us has millions of beliefs, not one of which is left behind when we go to the theater or open a volume of poems. But no work of art will impinge on more than a few of these beliefs. "Ode to a Nightingale" does not impinge on my belief that Sirius is very large; it may, however, impinge on various beliefs about the sadness of life or the longevity of nightingales. When this happens, the belief is called out of its subliminal grotto and becomes what some would call a state of consciousness and others an active set. It grapples with the poem that aroused it and, as often as not, strangles it. (I have also heard tell of poems that slew grisly beliefs in single combat; but I have not known whether to believe these stories.) What shall we call this aroused state of the belief? I would call it

assent, or dissent, or by one of the names—like 'doubt'—that stand for equally lively states in between. Let us take assent and dissent as typical. But now we should observe that the poem need not impinge directly on the belief or the belief respond to something directly stated in the poem. The reader may dissent from some idea that is, in any of a thousand ways, "implied" by the poem. The *tone* of the poem may evoke in him the idea of a belief that he dislikes. For that matter, he can respond to a belief that he thinks is held by all who brush their hair as the poet does. The poem need not give offense for the belief to take offense. Beliefs and believers are more and less sensitive. I need only speak the phrase 'red grass', or paint some red grass, and some people will bristle with dissent, though it be hard to say just what they are dissenting from. Hence a vague, circumambient displeasure, the source of which the reader hardly knows, or a mood of diffuse but genial consent. This might be called the cognitive penumbra of the poetic experience; and I mention it only to dismiss it and return to the central statements of poetry, the direct response of the reader. If it were our task to sweep every last shred of belief from the nooks and crevices of aesthetic experience, these lurking insinuations might be of greater concern than the open clash between poet and reader; but such a labor might well be of infinite magnitude.[2] I am helped in my present resolve by this reflection: no matter how far we should penetrate the cognitive recesses of poetry, there would still subsist for us and our argument the question of assent or dissent. If belief in the manifest doctrine of the poem is not relevant, we should hardly consider relevant a belief in some elusive intimation. I can thus hope to circumscribe the entire problem by reasoning "from the stronger."

3. If a man should take exception to something that a poet says and at the same time express a dislike for the poetry, or if he should give his disagreement as a ground for his dislike, I do not know how we can separate his "cognitive" from his "aesthetic" reaction. In critical theory we are not competent experimentalists. And I do not know that we are in a position to *moralize*. Does it make good sense to ask whether beliefs, considered as psychological states,

2. Since secondary meanings—"overtones" or "connotations"—of which poet and reader are scarcely conscious, unquestionably do figure in the experience, who is to say what other occult forces may be working in the abyss? A specious case can be made for the role of unconscious beliefs simply by *argumentum ad ignorantiam*.

should influence tastes? They do; and that may well be the end of the matter! It is not clear, therefore, how we should understand such a phrase as 'the aesthetic relevance of belief'.

But beliefs, like poems, are subject to criticism. The criticism of a belief follows a standardized method, commonly termed "verification," and terminates in a verdict of 'probable' or 'improbable', 'true' or 'false'. Our snap judgments and stubborn prejudices are compelled by this method to follow the courses to which they have previously committed themselves. They come out into the open field and can be spotted for what they are. Now if the criticism of poetry also follows a method by which, it is hoped, genuine values can be distinguished from spurious ones, it should be possible to compare that method with the characteristic criticism of belief, and to determine their identity or difference in character and result. Factors in human response which, as states of mind, are imponderable and mutually inextricable become distinguishable in terms of their several commitments. In other words: even though we should be unable to say how far the *liking* for a poem depended on *agreement* with the poem, we could quite intelligibly ask whether the *criticism* of a poem coincided with the *verification* of its statements and so, in the end, whether beauty depends upon truth. I shall, at any rate, assume that the question of the place of belief in the appreciation of poetry leads us over into the question of the role of truth as a criterion of aesthetic value. Let us dwell for another minute on this point as to how the psychological and the criteriological questions are bound together.

In modern philosophy since the time of Peirce, beliefs have been treated as a class of motor dispositions. Assent and dissent are, or involve, motor sets. And these motor sets are, in the well-chosen word of Eliseo Vivas, "transitive": that is, they look beyond the present to its sequel, beyond the meaning of the poem to its truth. Hence they distract us from the values given to contemplation and set up a tension between what is seen and what is foreseen. Now I am inclined to think that aestheticians on my side of the fence have made too much of these motor attitudes. It is true that, with refined methods of study, we might find it possible and worthwhile to distinguish carefully between one kind of covert impulse and another. The suspense of music and drama is *not* the suspense of waiting for news from the hospital. The neural and muscular impulses, if investigated, would not be found to be alike. But we need not jealously guard the aesthetic experience and reprimand every faint muscle tremor of the wrong sort. Small belief reactions are harmless if they are enveloped and controlled by a dominant aesthetic set. Mention *criticism*, however, and belief can no longer remain snugly coiled, or half unfurled, in some kind of causal interaction with the enjoyment of poetry. Criticism takes belief on an open and explicit review of all that it has committed itself to, including evidence it may never yet have taken into account. And there we see it manifestly parading not only far beyond the casual aesthetic experience but beyond all those considerations which the *criticism of the poem* has found it necessary to review. The most detailed criticism of the passage I quoted from Keats will not begin to notice the major points that everyone would consider "relevant" for an evaluation of the doctrine of progress.

Now for our main points. These are not steps in consecutive argument but successive aspects of the problem that, along with others, would need to be taken into a rounded survey.

1. Whatever is believed must at least be understood; and this suggests that there is such a thing as understanding, detachable from belief. When something is said to us, we understand *before* we can assent, and to accept or reject must take further steps in search of evidence; but then it should be possible to understand without being concerned with truth or falsity. I said that when a poem impinges on a belief, the belief is aroused. But this does not always happen, and, in principle, need not happen. I should think that all of you in this room had read the lines from *Hyperion* many times before and that few of you had ever asked yourselves whether you agreed with them—and this not from any slackness of attention but from the very fullness and fineness of your preoccupation with the meaning. You were making a different use of the proposition, which became for you simply an "aesthetic object." To be pre-occupied with the aesthetic object implies no disregard of the "content" of the poem—only a disregard of one function of that content, namely, its relationship to observable fact. Someone has said that "ideas have consequences." Well, ideas have values— many besides their truth values, many even besides their aesthetic values. Gottlob Frege, in his famous essay "On Sense and Nominatum," said that "in listening to an epic, we are fascinated by the euphony of the language and *also by the sense of the sentences*. . . . Whether the name 'Odysseus' has a denotatum," he goes on, "is

therefore immaterial to us as long as we accept the poem as a work of art."[3]

Readers of poetry are capricious in their habits of dissent. We do not dissent from everything we think false but, perhaps, from statements we think *wildly* false, silly or preposterous, false on points of doctrine that we think *important*, or false, again, on petty points of information learned in school, such as that it was stout Balboa and not stout Cortez who discovered the Pacific. Poetry drugs the dragon of disbelief, who can be rearoused only by counteracting features of provocation in the poem, such as sensational error. On the other hand, if something is so obviously false that it could not take anybody in, we do not dissent; for some of us are concerned primarily that others should not believe what we think is false. But if these extra determinants are needed to make us raise the question of truth, we may at least wonder whether it is truth and falsity as such that are relevant.

Belief *adds* nothing to what is proposed. It only affirms the proposition. But a proposition first affirmed and then denied remains the same aesthetic object.

When we have once seen the understanding of the poem as something independent of belief, we begin to ask whether it does not account for everything in the experience of poetry that has been ascribed to the influence of belief. Language often *plays* upon the environment and demands, therefore, for its understanding, some attention to the environment. Someone says, "Here comes old Winston." I turn and see a dog. Instead of confirming my friend's words, this might well alter my understanding of them; then I may or may not take up the new question of truth. Critics often turn from a poet's text to discuss the things he is talking about and sound as if they were rating his lines by their truth. But if they keep coming back to the passage and turn all their observations to the clarification of its meaning, it becomes obvious that the world is being treated as an illustrated supplement to the poem, and not the other way round. We hear it said sometimes that we cannot enjoy the Greek plays as the Greeks did because we do not have the same beliefs. But those beliefs posited an environment; and that environment may have been needed to give the right shades of sense to passages in the play. How, in other words, do we know that we

3. "On Sense and Nominatum," trans. Herbert Feigl, in Feigl and Wilfrid Sellars, *Readings in Philosophical Analysis* (New York: Appleton-Century-Crofts, 1949), pp. 85–102. Quote appears on pp. 90–91.

understand the plays as the Greeks did? Before we say that believing is relevant to value, we should be sure we know what is being valued and what is being believed.

2. The understanding can encompass anything that has been found to be true, as well as much that has not. It is nothing against a proposition, considered as an idea, that it should describe the world as it is; but then it is the world described that matters to us and not the fact that it is the real world that is being described. If the real world is interesting, it is still no better than many imagined worlds. In a fine chapter on intuition in *The Realm of Spirit*, Santayana explained how "intuition . . . sublimates knowledge into vision." "Then a body of positive knowledge of fact acquires the values of fiction." Reality surrenders its ontological prerogative when it is treated as one spectacle among many; but it may gain something in return.[4]

3. Truth is not sufficient for beauty nor belief for enjoyment. Thousands of propositions that we believe to be true we also deem perfectly trivial. Truths about the human heart are no *truer*, and no more firmly believed, than truths about the human pancreas. And this suggests at once that when we have "a great truth about the heart," what makes it *great* and what makes it a truth *about the heart* are not what makes it true. Perhaps it is not the truth but

4. This point, which in spite of much discussion still lacks a proper theoretical development, has been variously adumbrated as follows: "The aesthetic experience is imaginative not in the sense that all its objects are fictitious, but in the sense that it treats them indifferently, whether they are fictitious or real; its attitude, whether towards a real object or a fictitious, is the attitude which neither asserts reality, truly or falsely, nor denies it, but merely imagines" (R. G. Collingwood, *Speculum Mentis* or *The Map of Knowledge* [Oxford : Oxford University Press, 1924]).

"Nothing that man has ever reached by the highest flights of thought or penetrated by any probing insight is inherently such that it may not become the heart and core of sense" (John Dewey, *Art as Experience* [New York: Milton, Balch, 1934]).

"The whole course of a life is raised to a present datum possessed virtually in all its details by the dramatic imagination. . . . And in that case it would be indifferent that this truth happened to be true rather than mere poetry, since it would be only as poetry that the spirit would entertain it" (Santayana, *The Realm of Spirit* [New York: Scribners, 1940]).

Then there are well-known remarks by Sidney, Goethe, Coleridge, Wordsworth, Hardy, *et al.*

what the truth is about, that is, the content of the proposition, that makes it great.

Men of letters who insist upon some version of the idea that beauty is truth would never accept as an example of their meaning the truth of the proposition, "There are no fewer than three people in this room." Their "truth" is not plain truth. Theirs is a fancy truth or, to speak more respectfully, a higher truth. But they are not unwilling to appropriate the prestige of the plain truth. And this prompts a query, which I must leave it to you to answer, about the sources of that prestige. What is so glorious about the truth? Why should a quality which all except the demented commonly attain in the greater number of their ideas be considered so precious as to increase the stature of a Milton or a Beethoven if it can be ascribed to him? Perhaps it is because of the prevalence of liars or because our propensity to error in matters of difficulty and importance creates a reactive emphasis on truth, which then spreads itself over the rest of the cognitive field. Or perhaps there is some other reason.

Again. We do not consider the fact that we believe something a good enough reason for saying it. If we did, we should be uttering stupid truths all day long. A belief, to deserve utterance, must be to the point or purpose; or it must have some quality of interest and originality. There are distinctive cognitive values in ideas over and above their truth; and these are what warrant their publication. Now, poets too are silent about most of their beliefs. And when they pick some out for expression, it is through some sense of their exceptional value. It would be foolish to think that Dante did not know that the Christian view of things was not waiting for him to set it forth, or that Milton thought that until his time the ways of God had not been justified to man. These poets knew they were original; but they did not for a minute suppose they were original thinkers. Hence it looks as if the poem existed for some other reason than to enunciate the belief it may express.

Yet, you say, these poets did believe what they wrote. What would you have? Where should a poet get his material—if not from his fancy—but from the world he believes himself to be living in? What should he write about but the things he knows? That does not mean that knowing something is a sufficient reason for writing it down. As well say that if a painter paints a tree, he must be inflamed by the conviction that there are trees.

4. Next, I should hold with those who say that truth and belief

are not *negative* conditions either of beauty or of the perception of beauty except insofar as an active dissent may disrupt the entire aesthetic consciousness. In other words, falsity is not a negative aesthetic value but an accident, like a noise in the theater, the awareness of which may displace aesthetic values, good, bad, and indifferent.

There is a famous sentence by Coleridge which has for its grammatical subject a phrase so arresting that many people stop right there. I do not claim to be the first to have reached the predicate—only an independent discoverer. "That *illusion,* contra-distinguished from *delusion,* that negative faith, which simply permits the images presented to work by their own force, without either denial or affirmation of their real existence by the judgment," said Coleridge, "is rendered impossible by their immediate neighborhood to words and facts of known and absolute truth. . . . What would otherwise have been yielded to as pleasing fiction, is repelled as revolting falsehood."

Say: "Mr. Eisenhower is aged six hundred." That is all right, according to Coleridge; that is a mere *jeu d'esprit.* But add: "—and he is President in 1954," and the whole thing becomes revolting. There is something odd in this: why should falsity be innocuous in itself and become offensive only when accompanied by truth? Didn't Coleridge see how strange it is that truth should *damage* the mixture into which it enters—as if a man who can swallow cyanide in any amount should perish in agony if you add a few proteins? I think perhaps he did. For Coleridge is not saying that the neighborhood of truth somehow makes falsity for the first time objectionable. That is not so: truth can only redeem or balance falsity. Coleridge is saying that the awareness of truth makes us aware of falsity. It converts fiction into assertion of fact; and assertion of fact can be erroneous. By a kind of psychological infection, a sentence held to be true communicates to its neighbor the cognitive concern which lies behind it; and so, if the neighboring sentence is false, creates a contrast effect on the plane of cognition. Coleridge, then, is so far on the side of us who say that dissent is an intruder on the domain of poetic experience.

But there is still something that Coleridge has overlooked: infection can be reciprocal. If fact can elbow harmless fiction into becoming something fiercer and more ambitious, why should not fiction in turn hypnotize fact so that it lapses into fiction? If we have a sentence *a,* which is neither asserted nor denied, and another sentence *b*, which is asserted, why shouldn't *a* throw its cloak of neutrality over *b*, instead of adopting *b*'s partisanship? Why should illusion be rendered *impossible* by "the neighborhood of truth" if truth itself is passing for illusion?

I think Coleridge would have accepted an example like this. We have, in a novel by Samuel Butler, the description of a wholly fantastic system of law and of medicine. That's fine; that passes. But if a naturalistic novel, or a movie, should present medical practice very largely as it is but with deviations in detail, then that—according to Coleridge—would be held erroneous and provoke objection. The touch of reality allergizes us to mere fancy. But that is not true. *The Tempest* has much in it of the world as it really is, along with its fantasy and magic. Everything fabulous has in it, as the early empiricists stoutly contended, much that is real and true. All fiction combines ideas of what is with ideas of what is not. And we swallow the composition in one gulp, without sifting its ingredients.

Coleridge has taken a mere contingency and blown it up into a principle. We are *apt* to be disturbed by what we take to be an error, just as we are apt to be distracted by something that we think may be true. And—if I am permitted an ordinary generalization not weaker than Coleridge's—we are the more apt to be disturbed if we are not entranced by a work wherein fact and fable, "truths" and "untruths", have been melted into a single vision. But if it is the power of the aesthetic idea which helps to decide whether we shall submit to the illusion or look for little cognitive blemishes, then it is hard to see how those blemishes should enter into that power or detract from it.

5. Those whom I may call the Believers, in aesthetics, have a certain burden of analysis if not proof. They will admit that people who are warmed by agreement with a poem or disturbed by disagreement are always mistaking those reactions for perceptions of value. Belief and disbelief *can* be baneful influences. The Believers, then, instead of arguing that belief is relevant should try to mark off the relevant kind of belief. But wherever they draw their line, what is to keep someone else from saying of them in their turn that they are "arbitrary," make "artificial distinctions," "emasculate art," "cushion it from reality," "reduce the significance of poetry," or erect a "phantom aesthetic state"? Everyone likes to have the advantage of seeing the subject in its concrete fullness and protesting against schematic divisions. But if at the same time you

believe that distinctions are necessary, you should be able to show why one is to be preferred to another.

Now we come to a major difficulty. I do not know that it has ever been framed as an objection to the analysis that I have been defending; but it stirs in the minds of people otherwise well disposed and makes them uneasy.

I could rephrase some of my previous remarks by starting from certain speeches in plays and novels, which proclaim opinions or express moral judgments. Settembrini and Naptha in *The Magic Mountain*, with their long arguments, make a good example; or you could think of Polonius, of Portia with her sentiments about the quality of mercy. One remarks a certain indulgence in our response to these speeches. We do not rate them by what we believe to be their truth. A false speech can be a great speech, just as an evil character can be a great character. We take these "doctrines" as so much action and character, like the bodies and physical motions of the persons in the play. We enjoy the interplay of thesis with antithesis as we do the clashing of swords in a duel. We are satisfied with the aspect recorded, the point of view. And this is not to be confused with the dialectical interest of the themes in Plato, where, though we may not reach a conclusion, we are always pressing toward a conclusion. One who sits back and admires the give-and-take in the *Protagoras* is aestheticizing the dialogue. He does not share the main concern of the author and the characters, who are interested in the truth and who stop at the point of view only because the truth of the matter, embracing so many aspects, is so hard to get at. But in Shakespeare the points of view are somehow final.

I would then go on to say that we can and to some degree do extend this same toleration to lyric poetry and to prose. Opinions become ideas, which are enjoyed simply as contents. Certain poems by Swinburne, for example, which sound as if they bespoke the poet's outlook on life—as, indeed, perhaps they did, despite his subsequent disclaimers—are an expression of "a weary pagan aestheticism" or of "a decadent sensuality." Since "weary sensuality" and the like are to be denounced or rejected and since the poems are distinguished—and distinguished *as wholes*, their philosophy and all—the critic with an ounce of logic in his head finds himself confounded. But we discover that Swinburne, in a note to the really perverse and unwholesome *Dolores*, says, "I have striven here to express that transient state of spirit through which a man may be supposed to pass, foiled in love and weary of loving, but not yet in sight of rest; seeking refuge in those 'violent delights' which 'have violent ends,' in fierce and frank sensualities . . . ," with more to the same effect. Taking the poet's cue, we find suddenly that what was a vicious sentiment becomes a histrionic moment, a picture of thought and feeling, a "speech," and a fine one. But surely we did not require instruction from the poet. His note is not decisive: it will not disarm the moralist and it did not help the intelligent Victorian reader, who took the proper attitude from the beginning, as witness his consent to the poet's "genius," despite a residual consternation.

I do not mean to suggest that drama is to be taken as exemplary for literature in general. Our ability to set a sermon, an argument, a piece of information, a cry for help in a dramatic frame shows how flexible, in principle if not in fact, is our response to language, how independent of any rigorous control by the contents presented. And if as I contended above there is an aesthetic mode of commerce with human speech, no utterance of whatever cast or complexion need be ultimately refractory to this mode.

But now comes the antagonist, who takes me up at my own words. He says: Begin with the simplest case. Imagine a person in the play. Suppose he is a slanderer. He says something about Desdemona; and what he says about Desdemona is not true. Suppose he is a trickster. He says something about Birnam Wood's coming to Dunsinane; and Birnam Wood both does and does not come. Before he can so much as characterize himself by his speech, you must know at least *some of the rest of the play*. But references in the play do not always restrict themselves to the play. Oswald Alving, the hero of *Ghosts*, goes mad at the end. How do we know this? Because he asks for the sun. "Give me the sun, mother. I want the sun. The sun. The sun." It is only because we know that he cannot have the sun that we take him for one who has lost his mind —and this is knowledge about the real world. If we were to consider speeches of ethical import, it would soon appear that they cannot characterize either, unless the audience has at least some ethical convictions, some perception of ethical truth. Cordelia is not good and Goneril is not bad unless something is good or bad. You could not detect a weary aestheticism, in Swinburne or elsewhere, you could not relish that "aspect of things," unless you had first judged it by standards of goodness and virtue.

The antagonist continues: You said, "Belief does not add anything to what is proposed." But belief has its own linguistic counterparts: usually, the declarative and categorical form of the verb. The poet, if he wished to entertain you with "ideas," was at liberty to use gerunds or subordinate "that" clauses—as diarists who are not confident of their opinions in fact do. Or he could (and sometime does) weaken the force of his verbs with 'maybe's' and 'possibly's'. If he comes right out and asserts something, he seems to be demanding assent or challenging dissent as he need not have chosen to do. But surely that does not make a difference to the aesthetic content.

The position here is rather novel. It does not say that poetry must be true or that it must be believed. On the contrary, it may be disbelieved, and be good almost for that reason. But its contents, and hence its merits, are *relative* to knowledge or at least to opinion about the truth. Hence belief and truth are "relevant."

Before replying to this objection, I would like to display something of its scope and ramifications. The following examples are in apposition with those just considered.

Frederick, the hero of *The Pirates of Penzance*, was to have been apprenticed as a child to a pilot; but his nurse, misunderstanding her instruction, brought him to a pirate, with whom he remained until the opening of the play. And Alfred Doolittle, the cockney dustman of *Pygmalion*, returns in the last act a wealthy toff, for he has been recommended to an American millionaire as the most original moralist in Great Britain. Such incidents, it might be said, are farcical just because they are so wildly improbable; and without the belief in their improbability, no farce. The point might be extended beyond farce to fantasy, and further. The shock of surrealist extravagance comes just from the intrusion of the unreal upon some natural setting, where it is not expected: it is this deliberate offense to our knowledge that makes the devices of these artists so weird. And a critic has said of the Shakespeare tragedies that "their improbability is the price of their effectiveness"; but some might insist that it is more than a price. Cognition is constitutive of the aesthetic fact.[5]

5. When we begin to deal with objects which are not propositional in form, we no longer have sure footing. We do not understand how a picture or a dramatic episode can be an "object" of belief. Hence, there is as much temerity in denying as in affirming that belief is relevant. It is only in an endeavor to meet the critical tradition on its own ground that I venture to discuss such examples.

This argument certainly gives us much to think about and opens many new opportunities for confusion. One who has assumed the burden of a universal negative, as I have in this paper, now finds it increased; for he must show, it would seem, that belief is not *in any way* relevant. In such circumstances one can "answer" the opposing case only by offering a simpler and better explanation of the facts on which it rests. Such an explanation may be sketched out as follows.

1. In plays and novels we are apt to have something assumed or identified as "reality," operating as a framework against which the beliefs and assertions of the characters mark themselves off as "appearances" or "illusions." This "reality" and this "appearance" stand to each other much as "real" objects and "mirror" objects do in a painting, both comprised within the fundamental illusion. We in the audience can identify the "real truth" of the play even when this "real truth" is really false. In a horror story you often have one character who at the beginning is a skeptic and who is instantly put down by the reader as a fool simply because he does *not* believe in black magic. Sooner or later he is confounded by the unspeakable "truth." So in serious literature: you and I may think there are many fewer things in heaven and earth than are dreamed of in Shakespeare's *Hamlet;* but we have or should have no doubt that the Ghost is "real." Jocasta, the second personage of *Oedipus the King,* by making light of oracles and their forecasts, displays an offensive "levity." This is a part of the "tragic flaw" which, in the eyes of stern classicists who believe no more in oracles than they do in leprechauns, "justifies" the terrible fate that befalls her. And, indeed, if we regard her as an enlightened, far-seeing woman, we mistake her character; but this mistake is easily avoided. So with Antigone and her projection of the Greek burial taboo into the very heavens, Isabella with her fanatical chastity, and so many others: we judge them in the framework of beliefs and values provided by the play and not by our own serious convictions. And so with the "assertions" of the poet. It does indeed make a difference that he should state and declare rather than suppose or inquire. But the *tone* of assertion, which has become associated with the verb, does not necessarily denote real assertion—any more than the mere word 'fire' or the words 'nine o'clock' must *fail* to express an assertion. The idea of an assertion is not the assertion of an idea; and it may well be that in poetry it is the idea—the bracketed, fictive "assertion"—that matters.

2. But of course I do not say that there are no serious assertions and no real truths in poetry. The "reality" of the poem may coincide with reality itself or overlap with it in any measure; and we agree with the poets and their beliefs in every manner and degree. But then truth and reality become illusion. There is no reason why the real sun, in the world outside of Ibsen's play, should not be an assumed "reality" in *Ghosts*, as much as the law of gravitation which is obeyed by the characters. It will then be the case that "truth" is a particular and special issue in the play, on a par with any other.

3. Among the terms which we apply to objects in painting and incidents of the drama are some which denote frequency, incidence, distribution, causal determination, deviation from or conformity to a rule. There are "common" wild flowers and "rare" tropical ones, "prodigious" happenings like the birth of a two-headed child and "commonplace" or "average" ones. Some events in fiction are "accidental," others "inevitable," still others "miraculous" or "magical." When such statistical and causal characters are presented as actual qualities of the aesthetic object, we must of course note them, as we note red and green, large and small, or proud and humble. And I have just argued, by implication, that we need not bring our own opinions to bear in doing so. The downfall of Oedipus is not "expected" by the protagonist; in the larger frame of the play it is, however, "predestined"; but whether the action as a whole is in the eyes of the audience "probable" or "improbable" is still another question. The underlying question of aesthetic principle is whether what *we* find artistically original, or surprising, or trite, or incredible is relative to our own serious beliefs and anticipations.

One could urge, on many strong and varied grounds, that the frequency and causality adjectives are not often useful or essential. To paint a cat with its tail where its head should be is to produce something as unusual as a Gargantua or a Caliban—but with none of the brilliance of artistic fantasy or of farce. Caliban is grotesque; is he also "unique"? Is that important? Does it make a difference how many of him there are? If men were always biting dogs, journalists would lose interest; but would it become inherently less absurd? We get used to prodigies like the two-headed child; after a while, the smallest shred of incredulity that remains in us as an echo of serious doubt disappears and with it any real surprise. But are they then less monstrous? Or were they better sights to begin with because they were extraordinary? And we get used to the Surrealists: does that deprive them of any genuine eeriness they may have achieved? Apparently, it makes a great difference *what* the event may be that is qualified as "improbable"; for what is utterly unique and unexpected may be aesthetically humdrum and trivial. We may imagine even that Calibans were as common as imbeciles; that events should normally fall out as in Gilbert's operas; or that the universe of Hieronymus Bosch should be our familiar surrounding. Men would then develop a protective imperviousness; for they could not afford to marvel at a Caliban who faced them on every street corner. But, even as things are, we must be exhorted by a Wordsworth, an Emerson, or a Rilke to the recovery of perception. And when, heeding them, we pierce the film of familiarity that has spread itself over objects, we find that roses are red and violets blue, though there be millions of them. Nothing changes its character on account of its prevalence—unless that very character, frequency or rarity, should become an object of experience (much as "universality" becomes a thing actually considered in the Keatsian lines about joy "whose hand is *ever* at his lips/Bidding adieu"); and then, as with any other character, the question of value, far from being settled, is still to be raised.

But conceding as much merit as we can to this group of critical concepts: they still do not entail the relevance of *belief* and *disbelief*. Experience provides us with most of our beliefs. It also makes things familiar or leaves them unfamiliar; and it lends them their meanings and secondary associations. That does not mean that when we evoke and utilize past experience, we are utilizing beliefs. Cross eyes, which many of us thought comical when we were young, carry the suggestion that the bearer is trying to look two ways at once. Nobody believes this. Nobody acts *as if* he believed it. It is quite enough that we should possess the "connotation." Before we adopt a strong principle of explanation like belief, we should see what can be done with a weak one like association.[6]

6. Cf. Henry Aiken, in "The Aesthetic Relevance of Belief," p. 313: "No doubt Prokofiev's *Classical Symphony* is capable of giving a certain pleasure to persons who have never heard a classical symphony. But the charm which this work has for one who is aware of the classical symphonic forms and devices lies very largely in the composer's witty play with them. To perceive this, however, is . . . to respond immediately, through anticipation and surprise, to his allusions as a felt quality of what is heard." I cannot see how any scrap of *belief* comes into this.

In my opinion, that would always suffice. And criticism confirms this opinion by a justifiable laxity in pressing the question of frequency, generality, probability; for though one can recall hundreds of passages in which critics have said "this occurs" or "that does not occur," one cannot think of any critic who ever bothered to find out whether it really does or does not.

4. I have not made these last points as convincing as, with a more thorough study of a larger number of examples, they could be made. It is enough that they should indicate the *possibility* of dispensing with the concept of belief in the aesthetics of poetry. There remains now only the very special class of statements within the poem which refer to other parts of the poem. I believe that with time for detailed consideration we should come to see that these, too, do not require the reader's assent or dissent or any perception of truth or falsity on his part. And I would leave with you as a suggestive model the idea, suitable perhaps as a cover painting for the *Saturday Evening Post*, of a front gate with the sign BEWARE THE DOG while behind the fence parades a small dachshund. I do not think that our way of judging the "falsity" of this sign is properly to be called "disbelief." But I do not mind it if you say that this last remnant of belief does figure quite significantly in the experience of poetry. For a belief whose confirmation terminates within the poem will neither destroy the psychological illusion nor compete with the judgment of aesthetic value. It will act as a minor cognitive phase within a controlling aesthetic purpose.

I come to a last word about the problem of belief in aesthetics. Those of us who offer purified conceptions of the field of aesthetics give reasons, some of which I think you must admit are plausible. But you can probably detect in us an animus which goes beyond those reasons: a desire to sweep the field clean of the trace of cognition. We do indeed have motives which prompt us to draw a sharp line between art and knowledge and to dispose as best we can of objections to the proceeding. Of these motives I may mention two. First, we believe that when aesthetic experience is freed of its entanglement with belief, everything comes out as it should; that is, works of art are seen upon reflection to take the various places in the scale of values that they have already forced mankind, by their own power, to concede to them. When beliefs are admitted as a proper element in valuation, we are not only prone to distortion of values but we are *committed* to greater distortions still, from which we are saved only by blessed inconsistency. In the second place, we believe that aesthetics is full of problems of the greatest interest, as are too the psychology of belief and the theory of knowledge. But the kind of interest which exists in these two latter disciplines has never transferred itself, along with their categories, to aesthetics; on the contrary, these categories have blocked progress and account in large part for the "dreariness" of the subject, on which a writer in *Mind* lately commented. Is it not strange that after 2500 years during which cognitive conceptions of art have dominated the field of criticism—endorsed as they are at the present time by accomplished logicians, semioticians, and epistemologists—no one has ever thought of asking whether a law of excluded middle applies to art: can there be statements in poetry which are neither "poetically true" nor "poetically false"? No one has ever thought of drawing and *following up* a distinction between artistic truth and artistic probability. No one has so much as asked whether the concept of degree of probability might not be useful in the aesthetics of the drama. Nobody speaks of inductive and deductive process in aesthetic experience. Nobody asks whether the truths of art are not known inferentially and if so, whether they rest on immediate truths. The most elementary ramifications of the problem of knowledge are ignored, for it is very properly felt that their application would be barren. 'Truth' and 'Knowledge' dignify the subject but do not illuminate it. As for belief, I could offer parallel examples. Epistemology and the psychology of belief furnish poor *models* for use in aesthetics; for these models do not yield principles and details which prove applicable in aesthetic inquiry. That is another reason for avoiding them.

7

On Defining
Metaphor

My argument proceeds by four stages, which in brief outline are as follows: in the first section I say enough about metaphor to bring out the explicit or tacit presence, in all historical explications that most of us are acquainted with, of a pair of complementary terms: similarity and difference, terms which *may*, for all I know, represent one necessary condition for the application of the term 'metaphor'. In section II, I point out that the situation created by this pair of terms is not merely unsatisfactory but intolerable, and I say something to show why. In section III, it will be made to appear that the particular trouble, so far from being peculiar to the analysis of metaphor, runs precisely parallel to others which come up in the study of major concepts in aesthetics; understanding, however, by "major concepts" not such as the concepts of beauty, aesthetic object, creativity, taste, judgment, art, and the like (although these *are*, in most points of view, the central concepts of aesthetics) but such as harmony, melody, rhythm,

Read to the Philosophy Club, San Francisco State College, May 1961. Revised and read in a symposium on Metaphor at the American Philosophical Association, Eastern Division, December 1963. A drastically cut version was published in the *Journal of Philosophy* 60, no. 21 (October 1963): 609–22. The present version is expanded from the published article, using passages from the paper delivered at the APA, copies of which were made available to the editors by Professors Mary Mothersill and John Goheen, Stanford University. Reprinted with permission of the *Journal of Philosophy*.

rhyme, composition (in painting), symmetry, order, design, and others. In characteristic and widely accepted attempts to clarify or define such concepts, there always appears a pair of complementary opposites. In the fourth and final section, I pick up a hint from something that is often said of the single most important of complementary pairs, namely the principle of unity in variety, to help me resolve, so far as I can, the special difficulties set forth in section II.

I

Simile and metaphor are often said, by writers without pretensions to theory, to be modes of comparison. And indeed it is natural to say of the poet who wrote the line "O, my luve is like a red, red rose" (or of the "person" represented in the poem by 'I' and 'my') that he compares his love to a rose. If we omit, from this verse, the single word 'like', we spoil the effect of the line but, surely, obtain a metaphor; and of this too we can say either that his love is compared to a rose or that it says his love is *like* a red, red rose. And by introducing such a word as 'like' into certain metaphoric expressions, as if misquoting: "All the world is *like* a stage," we obtain—whatever the impairment of general effect—a simile. It is, no doubt, the possibility of such conversions that has led many rhetoricians to say that a metaphor is a condensed simile and a simile an expanded metaphor. Now this point, I think, is to be rejected; for there are metaphors, even simple ones, that cannot be thus converted without circumlocutions so devious as to make the results *very* distant in meaning and effect from their originals. Yet since some points and questions apply to both of these figures alike, it may be helpful now and then to hold simile up as a sort of model for metaphor.

To begin with, let me quote the definition offered by one major dictionary (*Webster's New International*): "Metaphor: (*rhet.*) the use of a word or phrase literally denoting one object or idea in place of another, by way of suggesting a likeness or similarity between them (the ship *plows* the sea; a *volley* of oaths)."

To point out that there need not have been and probably was not any original *word* or *phrase*, in the poet's mind, that is replaced by another and that, if there had been, we could hardly ever know what it was, is to offer a merely substantive criticism. What I really want to point out here is not any blemish, but an indispensable feature of this definition. Suppose that it lacked the qualifying phrase "by way of suggesting a likeness or analogy between them." Then the conditions set down would be met by almost any slip of the tongue or pen, any improvement of diction, a good many puns and euphemisms, and many cases of deciding that you want to say something else. Hence it appears that, if we are to have a metaphor, at least a "suggested" resemblance—a likeness or analogy—between two kinds of things is essential. And this is hardly more than is implied by the idea that metaphor is a mode of comparison.

The relation of resemblance holds, if the Webster version is followed, as between *"kinds of things denoted"*; and this offers for consideration one view as to the nature of the terms of a metaphor. But rather than pin ourselves down to one defectively worded definition, we may go on to emphasize one of the two things that *all* nonelliptical definitions have in common.

The idea of a relation of resemblance between terms brought together for comparison, that is, the idea of *resemblance in difference* considered as a necessary condition for the application of the term 'metaphor', is already present in Aristotle's first remark on the subject in the *Poetics;* which in one translation reads, "A metaphor consists in calling one thing by the name of another" and in another version "the transfer of a word belonging to something else."[1] For whatever the process of transference may be, if it is a *word*— rather than a word *form* or a vocal sound—that is being transferred, then some good part of its previous literal connotation must be retained in the new use to which it is being put; and that is to say that the first term and the second term are to some extent similar or the same. If this first clause of Aristotle's were in other ways acceptable, it would have the advantage of dispensing with any such dangling qualifier as "by way of suggesting." What is now brought to mind by these translations of Aristotle is the other half of what I have called "one necessary condition." It is obvious, is it not, that what Aristotle has in mind when he speaks of "the name of *another*" or of a word belonging to *something else* is not, for example, the fact that a new frying pan on a counter in the store is, like every other, called a frying pan; or that one's son is called Nicomachus after one's father; but that the name of one thing or the word belonging to it is given to *another* not only distinct but qualitatively different thing—otherwise, no "transference."

1. See *De poetica*, at § 1457^{6}.

In Butcher's translation of the same passage, "A metaphor is the application of an alien name by transference," there is the suggestion that the difference should be considerable; and this impression would be reinforced if I quoted the rest of the sentence, including "from genus to species," and so on. But we need not rely on suggestions or implicit meanings to arrive at Aristotle's opinion, for a little later on he is led to say, "But the greatest thing of all [in the way of "diction"] is the use of metaphor. . . . It is a mark of genius, for to make good metaphors is to have an eye for similarity among dissimilars." And so we get the formula of *similarity in difference*, or a relation of resemblance holding as between disparate or even discordant things. To sum up, let me quote from the New English Dictionary: "Metaphor: The figure of speech in which the name of a descriptive term is transferred to some object different from, but analogous to, that to which it is properly applicable." And let me note further that *no* writer with whom I am acquainted, not even one of those who in recent times have explicitly contended against a "comparison" or "similarity" theory of metaphor, has failed, in his positive analysis, to stipulate something that is obviously translatable into "resemblance in difference."

Finally, let us give what meager support we can to what seems to be a unanimous interpretation; and first, as to simile. "Like his father and his grandfather before him, he lived to a ripe old age." Here is no simile, no hint of a figurative use or meaning. Although we can assume a priori the existence of innumerable differences between any person and any of his forebears, it may still seem that the trouble is "not enough difference"; while "old as Methusaleh" has at least the beginnings of a figurative standing. "My son is now about as high as a Shetland pony." Despite the odd comparison, this is literal statement. Compare with it a line from Chaucer describing a young woman: "Tall as a mast and upright as a bolt." This is hyperbole, which is a species of metaphor. It might almost seem as if, at the lower end of an axis or pole upon which degrees of difference between Much Too Little and Much Too Much were registered, one would come first to feeble and insipid similes, then to doubtful cases, and finally to expressions that, although containing such words as 'like', are not—perhaps cannot be—employed figuratively at all. An example of the first stage: "The curfew tolls the knell of parting day." Since the curfew is a bell that sounds at the end of a day and a knell is the bell that sounds at the end of a life, the comparison would seem to require no leap of imagination, or, as Aristotle would have it, no "eye"; so although this is not a bad opening line of verse, the *metaphor* in it seems to me barely discernible as such. I do not know whether to say of two other lines in the same poem, "Some village Hampden that with dauntless breast/ The little tyrant of his fields withstood," that there is any metaphor in them at all, turning on "village Hampden" and "little tyrant of his fields." Finally, in the distinctively poetical lines from the incomparable passage on the poet's blindness at the beginning of the Third Book of *Paradise Lost*— "nor sometimes forget/ Those other two equalled with me in fate/ (So were I equalled with them in renown), / Blind Thamyris and Blind Maeonides"— it seems clear to me that there is no simile or figurative mode of speech whatever; that the poet is saying simply and literally, that all three are blind and two of them more famous than the third.

At the other end of the scale, where there is "too much difference" or "not enough resemblance" to satisfy the condition for metaphor, we seem to reach, first, fantastic and laughable excess, then *catachresis*, which is the "wrenching of a word from its true significance as in a forced trope or mixed metaphor," and, finally, perfect nonsense. To skip the first immensely populous level and start with *catachresis*: Although the late Hart Crane defended some of his most nearly impenetrable images on the ground, among others, of their impenetrability, I have come to believe that he and they open themselves to you the more, the harder you work at them. But since examples of provisional unintelligibility are for our purposes as good as the real thing, I may quote first from a passage in which, addressing the Brooklyn Bridge, he says, "And like that obscure heaven of the Jews/ Thy guerdon," and then the line, "Our tongues recant like beaten weathervanes." Presumptive simile-cum-metaphor is present in both, with no question of threshold or borderline status to be settled. But how much of a step is it from either of these to an example Ryle gave of absurdity resulting from confusion of categories: "Saturday is in bed"? Seeing, especially, that if you encountered the latter in isolation you might think it had—like the phrase, in itself unintelligible, "putting the paper to bed"—a figurative meaning, you know not what? This is the prima facie plausibility that I can give to the stock requirement of "resemblance in difference." But I do not at all believe in the existence or in the possibility of any such continuum as I have just been pretending to illustrate.

II

We do not and perhaps never shall have an explicit understanding of metaphor. For no one has come up with anything faintly recognizable as a sufficient condition for the application of the term. (Not that anyone has tried; and there, as Bacon might have said, lies an argument of hope.) But suppose we find that we can express the degree of understanding we believe we *have* attained only with the help of a proviso for resemblance in difference. Now we are in a situation not of mere want and insufficiency but of indescribable muddle.

What is wrong with the requirement of resemblance in difference? It seems that we have no way of knowing when to say that it is satisfied. The problem is not just a matter of "vagueness" or of borderline cases. Let us grant, for the sake of argument, that there are statements of comparison for which no noncomparative statements can adequately substitute. It is still not clear which of these statements meet the requirement of resemblance in difference.

Perhaps it is also true that we sometimes exhibit a pretty good intuitive sense of "closeness" and "distance," of how much or how far one thing or property resembles or differs from another. When the right sort of comparison is expressed in the right sort of setting —as if I should declare to the father of a pair of nonidentical twins that each resembles the other more than he does their elder brother —such a remark will be both understood and accepted. Now, passing over the use of the same terms—'like', 'different from', 'a weak analogy', 'a superficial difference'— in *theoretical* contexts, note that in the literary criticism of poetic imagery we also find meaningful and usefully debatable remarks of the same type. We may use as an example a single general proposition, the one in which Dr. Johnson expressed a small portion of his dislike for those whom he called the metaphysical poets: "Ideas the most heterogeneous are yoked by violence together." I must leave it to you to decide whether Johnson's coinage, "the *metaphysical* poets," yokes together by violence ideas the most heterogeneous or is, as a metaphor, barely visible, or perhaps, in obedience to the grand principle of resemblance in difference, somehow combines both of these antagonistic glories in its own nature. But if one should glance at a couplet by Carew

> In her fair cheeks two pits do lie
> To bury those slain by her eye,

or recall the lines in which Donne compares a pair of separated lovers to a pair of compass points, one would seem to understand Dr. Johnson and to feel that he is right.

Maybe. But it is impossible to *show* that the terms of any metaphor are closer together or further apart than the terms of any other. It is also impossible to give, here and now, a proof of the impossibility. But I can quote, almost at random, a figurative expression no one would think of describing as metaphysically conceited and whose terms, nevertheless, are not felt to lie closer together, to resemble each other more, than those of the compass-points simile: for example, the lines toward the end of Shakespeare's sonnet 29 in which he says, "then my state / Like to the lark at break of day arising / From sullen earth, sings hymns at heaven's gate"; And I will quote—as an example of something that, perhaps *on account* of the felt distance between the terms, has prompted people to exclaim with delight, "*What* a comparison!"— a few words from Cleopatra's obituary speech on Mark Antony: "his delights / Were dolphin-like, they show'd his back above / The element they liv'd in."

The real trouble with the requirement of resemblance in difference is that the discussion of it has been so utterly primitive that we cannot say even that this or that is *the* logical fault. For all that we are told by Aristotle or any of his successors, we may say (as some have said) that the requirement is satisfied by everything whatsoever, not excluding the case of qualitatively identical particulars and not excluding "My honey is the square root of minus three." Or that it is satisfied *only* by "just the *right* kind and degree of resemblance, neither more or less, between objects *sufficiently* different and neither more nor less so." Again, not an easy criterion to *use*. Moreover, it is not hard to find cases for which the criterion seems radically inept. Two examples will suffice. First, when, toward the end of *King Lear*, someone says, "As flies to wanton boys, are we to the gods; / They kill us for their sport," we recognize a great and indubitable simile or, if you please, a simile-and-metaphor. Yet, on the likeliest interpretation of these lines, it is hard to tell the difference between them and "My son is now about as high as a Shetland pony"; for the passage from *King Lear* seems to say, quite literally, that boys do kill flies and gods do kill men for their sport. Or consider the following:

You know, my friend, with what a brave carouse
I made a second marriage in my house:
Divorced old barren Reason from my bed,
And took the daughter of the vine to spouse.

The second and third lines are, I suppose, unquestionably figurative (and very far from being bad). But what are we to do, in terms
of resemblance and difference, with the idea of kicking *Reason*
out of *bed*?

The idea of some kind of medium or balance or compromise
between resemblance and difference may be fairly ascribed to
Aristotle in his treatment of metaphor. But it would be easy to
quote almost equally distinguished authorities whose formulas for
metaphor come much closer to Leibniz's recipe for the best of all
possible worlds, that is, the maximum resemblance combined with
the greatest possible difference. And perhaps we should not overlook the clue offered by the late G. D. Birkhoff, whose system of
aesthetics revolved about the formula "M [for *aesthetic measure*
or value] is equal to O [for *order* or unity] over C [for *complexity* or variety]." Then we should say that metaphor or beauty of
metaphor is equal to resemblance over difference, and difference,
like complexity, would play a role not radically different from that
played, for instance, by the factor of distance in the inverse-square
law of gravitational attraction. While only hinting at what seems
to me to be the absurd result of this way of understanding the
resemblance-in-difference requirement, let me emphasize that here
is a third interpretation with neither better nor worse claims than
the other two; and there are many others still.

The upshot of these first two parts: Resemblance in difference
seems to be something that we cannot live without. And it certainly
is something that we cannot live with.

III

It is not only in the study of metaphor that appeals have been
made to complementary opposites as supplying criteria, principles
of explanation, or fertile suggestions. We may briefly consider one
other example; and I shall mention a number of others by name.
Balance is often thought to be a desideratum in the composition
of a painting. But since one can achieve aesthetic as well as physical
balance by leaving a rectangular canvas bare or by painting it a

uniform shade of gray, it is often said that the balance should be a balance of centrifugal forces, heterogeneous forms, or complex disposition of objects. Now, something very similar seems to be the orthodox thing to say about the rhythm of verse and, for that matter, of music, the development of a theme by repetition with variation, rhyme, harmony, the use of dissonances among consonances, and so on indefinitely.

Among renowned and classical passages on the subject, I may quote the following paragraph from Coleridge. Speaking of the imagination or (what for him amounts to the same thing) the power that yields and enters into true poetry, he writes that this power,

first put in action by the will and understanding, and retained under their irremissive, though gentle and unnoticed, control *(laxis effertur habenis)* reveals itself in the balance or reconciliation of opposite or discordant qualities: of sameness, with difference; of the general, with the concrete; the idea, with the image; the individual, with the representative; the sense of novelty and freshness, with old and familiar objects; a more than usual state of emotion, with more than usual order; judgment ever awake and steady self-possession, with enthusiasm and feeling profound or vehement; and while it blends and harmonizes the natural and the artificial, still subordinates art to nature; the manner to the matter; and our admiration of the poet to our sympathy with the poetry.[2]

It was held, I believe, by the late D. H. Parker, among others, that all of these "principles of form" could be reduced to the single principle of unity in variety. Let this be supposed true or untrue. Still, unity in variety is the single most important concept of its kind that the history of aesthetics can show. If it does not include resemblance in difference, balance, and so forth, as cases or special types of itself, then, at least, it outranks them one and all. Now, everything that I said was wrong with the idea of the resemblance of different things as employed in definitions of metaphor can be generalized to apply with equal force to the concept of unity in variety.

But let us ask why, in view of its apparent worthlessness for all theoretical and critical purposes, so many have invoked it. For its use does not represent a mere continuous tradition, but is a history of recurrences: each of the writers who use the idea—say, Hutch-

2. Samuel Taylor Coleridge, *Biographia Literaria* (Oxford: University Press, 1907) 2: 12, ll. 15–29.

eson, Kant, Coleridge, Fechner, Santayana—sounds as though it were a fresh discovery of his own.

Unity is regarded by many writers simply as the mark of a work of art, that is, of one single work of art; and some degree of variety is required to certify that the same object is so much as a work of art. Unity, as "wholeness" or "completeness," seems to enter into Aristotle's first and fullest definition of tragedy: variety, although represented only by a note or two in the same definition, is amply provided for once we come to see what are the "parts" of a tragedy and the parts of each part—Recognition, for example, Reversal, and the like.[3]

But surely, although this interpretation of unity in variety may seem to be correct, yet it is not. For Aristotle, like almost everyone since, applies these ideas only to works of art. An anthology of lyric poems, having *no* unity of subject, style, or authorship, will not be either praised for its diversity or attacked as a miscellany. It is one thing to read a poem, skip twenty pages, and read an entirely different poem; another to read the first four lines of a poem and, on reading the fifth, to realize that although you had some idea of where you were going, you now don't know where you are.

Now what real and positive use does the concept of unity in variety have in high or in common art talk?

1. "Unity in variety" gives notice that it is the *structure* of works of art or of a given work that is being considered. And it helps to fix our attention on the structural features that the writer or speaker may be alluding to. The over-all organization, or certain specific connections between specific parts of this picture or that, is usually the sort of thing it asks us to discern in the work. Let us suppose that the presence, in *Hamlet*, of so many comic and apparently digressive episodes, like the first part of the graveyard scene, should make us feel—as it has made so many French critics feel— uneasy.[4] Or, again, some critic may ascribe an "accidental" hurry-up quality to the tragic *dénouement* in the last scene of the same

3. Once, however, we get to the place where Aristotle speaks of "the imitation of a *single* complete action, with a beginning, a middle, and an end," I for one begin to feel that the requirement of wholeness now comes closer to what we have called variety.

4. Or to give a minor but realistic example of something that does make most of *us* uneasy, there is in the previous scene the remark of the grief-stricken Laertes, brother of the drowned girl, "Too much of water has thou, poor Ophelia, / And therefore I forbid my tears."

play. Then, as we are considering any such incident or episode not only in itself but with regard to its "place" in the action or design, we speak of lack of unity or of inevitability, of incongruity or of an underlying coherence. And we can, of course, fall back on any of the hundreds of almost equally general words or phrases in our lexicon that belong to the "hanging together" or "falling apart," the "sustaining," "culminating" categories that we find suitable for the occasion.

"Unity in variety" embraces all these specific connections and disconnections like a great barn. It is a general rubric beneath which they fall. It does not *denote* any class of individuals or attributes of which some of these structural characteristics are members and from which others are excluded. A term like 'unity' does not enable us to find, by some purely intellectual process, that it does or does not apply to the order of events even in the *Phèdre* of Racine, not to speak of *Tristram Shandy* or *Bleak House* or *The Brothers Karamazov*. It helps us only to decide, by a process in which the experience of the work and the effective response to it are ingredients, something that we may then express by saying that it has or lacks genuine unity.

2. Further, "unity in variety" can be and has been treated not only as a defining characteristic of art, but as a defining characteristic of art in the noblest and loftiest sense of the word, and also as a criterion of merit: a "good-making" characteristic in the sense that, with or without being itself a good quality, it confers some value upon any work in which it appears. It remains now for us to see how these suggestions concerning the role of the *idea* of unity in variety are to be applied to the notion of resemblance in difference considered as a condition for metaphor.

IV

There are three propositions now to be advanced: first, that a metaphor is by its very nature an aesthetic object; second, that metaphors are strokes, if not always works, of art; and, third, that metaphor is art in the special sense of the word that is active when it —the word—is withheld from something which, though obviously a product of human contrivance, one deems positively bad or at least devoid of aesthetic value—in other words, that metaphor belongs to the sphere of what H. L. Mencken used to call *lovely* letters.

1. All that my argument requires is that every metaphor have *an* aesthetic status and function. I believe, however, that metaphors do have a purely aesthetic standing; that is, that they exist as metaphors only for the imagination, which, at the same time, is the only faculty by which they are appreciable. If I give what must inevitably be only slight support to the latter and stronger thesis, perhaps the weaker one will be made fairly convincing.

When a metaphorical statement is put to a predominantly non-aesthetic use, the metaphor goes to sleep; it "dies," not by the slow oblivescence, on our side, of the second term and the correlative growth of a new literal meaning, but immediately, by an act of murder. This main bulwark of my first thesis is itself a theoretical proposition, requiring—in view of all the practical, scientific, and philosophical uses to which metaphors have been sacrificed—ample support. But I shall use only small-scale examples, hoping that they are representative.

a. We overhear these words exchanged between two persons: "Don't let him get your goat." "I won't." Everyone will agree that there is here, for both speakers, nothing but a literal reference to a situation of provocation and possible annoyance. And we too at this moment—although we know that there is something funny about "getting your goat" cannot, unless we are philologists, tell what the original metaphor was or even that there was one; for there are unfathomable idioms of nonfigurative kinds that creep into a language.

b. Suppose that a man of a certain age, speaking to a younger friend, should remark that he is declined into the vale of years; or perhaps, again quoting Shakespeare, that his "way of life is fallen into the sere, the yellow leaf"; and that the other should reply, "Oh, come. You are as sound as a nut and have many good years before you." We may even allow the case in which the younger man is hearing the classical text for the first time. Then he grasps the intended sense only by penetrating the figurative language and yet, as it seems to me, "looks right through" the *quondam* second term to the qualities that the other is ascribing to himself, and possesses no fleeting consciousness of metaphor.

c. A speculative biologist, reporting on his studies of termite colonies infesting houses, states that the impulse proceeding from any disturbance at the center, where the queen lies buried, to the farthest caves of the house was so rapid that a termite colony is best interpreted as a species of nervous system. Now a simple test of the merits—the "strength"—of such an analogy is of the following kind. There exists a law of specific nervous energies and also an all but infallible principle to the effect that a lesion of neural tissue is irreparable: can either of these facts about nervous systems, together with the new hypothesis, yield verifiable predictions concerning termite colonies? Whether it can or cannot, obviously, the whole point of the analogy lies in the inference to be made, the prediction of something not yet observed that is to be drawn from it. But if the analogy were in fact found to be wholly sterile, then —as with the fable of the belly and the members and, to my eccentric way of thinking, the Parable of the Cave—we are left with nothing but a comparison to be brooded upon: a comparison, in this case, weak and grotesque, with no aesthetic impact at all.

While it was still a working scientific analogy, not even a strong sense of its strangeness could contribute toward making the author's consciousness or that of his readers metaphoric; for the whole interest of the analogy is in the question, "What is to be said about termite colonies?", that is, in the question of the nature and properties of "the first term."

2. Though a metaphor is not a *work* of art, metaphor is art. Taken together with my first proposition, this means that metaphor is fine art. The joint proposition hardly requires support; or if it does, this has already been given by philosophers like Croce and Dewey and writers like Wordsworth and Emerson, who tell us that elements or snatches of poetry and original imagination are apt to appear in the prosaic utterances of common men. The American Indian who first give whiskey the name that someone else translated as "firewater," the American housewife who first called one of her neighbors a "rubberneck," may have been inspired only in that one moment—and at that to no great extent; but they *were* inspired.

3. The word 'metaphor' is approbative: it ascribes positive aesthetic value to anything to which it is applied—to about the same extent as do such words as 'art', 'poetry', and 'music'. Merely by way of rephrasing the point, we may say either that the word 'metaphor' has emotive meaning of a certain sort or that every genuine metaphor is a valuable even if sometimes tiny artistic accomplishment.

The definition of music given in one dictionary is this: "The science or art of making agreeable combinations of tones." If we ruled out every such word as 'agreeable',[5] we should leave the way open for the kitten on the keys. But if we *admit* some such word as 'agreeable', are we not committed to the idea that there is no such thing as bad music? If we are so committed, the mere meaningfulness of such an *obiter dictum* as that "the most brilliant and technically prodigious music of this century is to my mind utterly dreary" would seem to confute us. As for the word 'poetry', I need not explain why you may resolutely refrain from terming James Whitcomb Riley or Robert Service a poet and yet, although detesting the verse of the late Dylan Thomas, concede the opinion that he is a leading modern *poet*. In the concept of *art*, finally, the ambiguity we have been speaking of is obviously present.

'Metaphor', on the other hand, does not *look* like an expression with a built-in connotation of approval. It looks as if, *whatever* be the example to which we correctly apply it, we can then go on to pronounce it good or bad. This idea of a ubiquitous, exclusively descriptive meaning is demonstrably false. But the truth is not only that the element of admiration and of applause is to be found in a good half of all the explicit definitions that have been offered but that it enters insidiously, usually with devastating results, into all but the shortest explications of the idea of metaphor.

It is, however, necessary to concede three things: first, that the word 'metaphor' never has a purely or solely approbative force; second, that it is used, often enough, in such ways as to have no approbative force whatever; and, third, that we *want* and perhaps need on occasion to speak of pale and timid, grotesque or fantastic or outrageously far-fetched metaphors.

We can now tentatively draw conclusions parallel to those we have seen to apply elsewhere. "Resemblance in difference" is, first of all, a commodious framework within which multitudes of specific relationships are housed. By the same token, it is a guide to critics and readers who wish to explain or come to understand certain aspects of a passage in which a figure of speech is embedded.

We may now attempt a suitable modification of the first definition of metaphor quoted in part I: "The displacement of one term by another by way of suggesting such a resemblance or analogy

5. In another edition of the same dictionary, we find "agreeable," replaced by "pleasing, expressive, or intelligible."

as will be aesthetically moving." Or, to adapt the definition of the N. E. D.: "Metaphor: the figure of speech in which a name or descriptive term is transferred to another object different from, but analogous to, that to which it is properly applicable, so as to give life or emphasis to an idea." However we put it, it turns out that one of the implications presented in part II as a *reductio ad absurdum* is really the thing to say, namely, "the *right* kind and degree of resemblance between objects *sufficiently* different and neither more nor less so." Aristotle also was right in speaking of "an eye for similarities among dissimilars."

Many philosophers hold that "normative" terms are not to be analyzed by expressions themselves containing no normative term whatever; and there are those who have disputed this proposition. But one thing is clear; and that is that we shall never, and in principle can never, have what Mr. Richards once called a poetic thermometer, that is, a list of points the exemplification of which, in a work of art, can alone render it meritorious. It is worthwhile quoting the single passage in which this assertion is most grandly and convincingly made. It is from the *Critique of Judgment*.

THERE IS NO OBJECTIVE PRINCIPLE OF TASTE POSSIBLE
By a principle of taste I mean a principle under the condition of which we could subsume the concept of an object and thus infer, by means of syllogism, that the object is beautiful. But that is absolutely impossible. For I must immediately feel pleasure in the representation of the object, and of that I can be persuaded by no grounds of proof whatever. Although as Hume says, all critics can reason more plausibly than cooks, yet the same fate awaits them. They cannot expect the determining ground of their judgment (to be derived) from the force of the proofs, but only from the reflection of the subject upon its own proper state (of pleasure or pain), all precepts and rules being rejected. . . . But although critics can and ought to pursue their reasonings so that our judgment of taste may be corrected and extended, it is not with a view to set forth the determining ground of this kind of aesthetical judgments in a universally applicable formula, which is impossible.[6]

The moral for those who would understand the nature of metaphor is obvious. There may be defects connected with the resemblance-in-difference proviso, even when the definiendum,

6. Immanuel Kant, *Critique of Judgment*, trans. J. H. Bernard (1892; reprint ed., New York: Hafner Publishing Co., 1951), pp. 127–28.

'metaphor', is taken as a term of admiration or of approbation. But it is no defect in the proviso that it should give us no additional way of spotting or of ruling out a single candidate that is not also qualified by the power to give pleasure.

But the present analysis is not adequate; and to make it more nearly so we must provide it with an extension that comes much closer to coinciding with the extension of the term 'metaphor' itself. Let us say that it is *not* a condition of the application of the term that the thing to which it is applied should have *positive* value; all that is necessary is that it should excite, or be capable of exciting, the imagination with an effect of some novelty and of greater or less propriety. We then alter our modified definition out of the N. E. D. to read that a metaphor is such a transference of a word or phrase, normally applied to one thing, to a different but analogous object, as to register upon the aesthetic sense and evoke some response, positive or negative. We thus ensnare even the tamely figurative lines from "The First Snowfall":

> Every pine and fir and hemlock
> Wore ermine too dear for an earl

—while at the same time fencing out, for example, the application of the word *cat* to the Siamese variety.

But in our new formula, "Metaphor is the aesthetically exciting transference of a word or phrase," and so forth—which does not require that the actual or potential effect upon feeling should be for good—there is still something that may be wrong. As with the general topic of aesthetic values and judgments of value, the question of indifference is bound to come up. Can we not recognize the unequivocal metaphor in the lines just quoted from "The First Snowfall" without having so much as a sense of its tameness? And if we can, do we not understand and apply the word 'metaphor' with no sense whatever of an effect upon sensibility? Consciousness, of course, there must be; but what is it but a consciousness, not of resemblance in difference (for we have seen that this alone will not do) nor of an aesthetically qualified resemblance in difference, but simply of the presence of a metaphor? The same unwelcome conclusion seems to result from the fact that the effect upon feeling ought to be referred not to the line of verse or whatever other expression we use as our example nor to the figurative quality of the line but, presumably, to the element of resemblance in difference that helps to articulate that quality. It is this to which the element of affect should attach itself and which, *with* this value property, together with the rest of what the accepted version considers necessary, should yield a notion of metaphor.[7]

7. It *should* yield the notion of a metaphor, but in fact it does not, and I have found no definition that properly states what such a definition should state. In the course of writing this paper I have come to believe that while there are a number of interesting philosophical questions about metaphor— its role in science or philosophy, whether its influence is beneficial or pernicious—the question, What is a metaphor? is not itself a philosophic question. It seems doubtful that it is either deserving or capable of philosophical analysis. I never did believe, for one moment, in either the adequacy or the philosophical character of lexicographers' and rhetoricians' definitions; or that a philosophical treatment could terminate in a brief and handy definition of, let us say, thirteen or seventeen words that would do any but the slightest part of the work of delimitation for the sake of which we start looking for definition. But I think now that metaphor (the general concept), like the serpent girl in Keats' *Lamia*, cannot bear the mere touch of cold philosophy. This would appear, in one way, if we looked into its origin (as a crude figure of speech), its history, the company it has always kept, and the surroundings in which, almost always, it has resided. The crux of the matter lies in the nature of the concept. Of this, however, I will say only that it is a good deal less like the concept of fiction (or *a* fiction) that has been examined by philosophers such as Moore and Ryle than it is like the concept of fiction entertained by the author who plans to answer the question, What is a Novel?, by an exhaustive survey of the novel from the twelfth to the twentieth century.

PART II

Criticism

8
Cordelia Absent

Perhaps there is no valid observation about *King Lear* that does not already sprout up somewhere in the vast wilderness of Shakespeare criticism; but I do not know of any critic who has been impressed by the disappearance of Cordelia, from the stage and from Lear's lips, during the long middle portion of the play. Yet this factor of absence is immensely important. Without it, the play would lose the dimension in which some of its greatest values are spread out.

Between the end of the first scene, when she vanishes into exile, and the middle of the fourth act, Cordelia is mentioned five or six times, each time very briefly and casually. Twice she is mentioned by Lear.[1] The first of these passages (1. 4. 288–94) —

> O most small fault,
> How ugly didst thou in Cordelia show!
>
> . . . .
>
> O Lear, Lear, Lear!
> Beat at this gate that let thy folly in
> And thy dear judgment out!

Originally published in *Shakespeare Quarterly* 2, no. 3 (July 1951): 185–94. Reprinted with permission. The line references follow G. L. Kittredge, ed., *The Complete Works of Shakespeare* (Boston: Ginn & Co., 1936).

1. A third time, perhaps, in the isolated sentence, pressed between two of the Fool's speeches (1. 5. 25), "I did her wrong."

—seems to show the king beginning to change his mind. The subject is not yet too hot to be touched, for the enormity of Lear's error has not dawned on him. Scarcely a trace, in this passage, of conscience: the king is accusing himself of a mistake, not a crime. But the second reference to Cordelia (2. 4. 215–18) revokes the small contrition of the first, for it shows not the slightest abatement of Lear's displeasure. It is as if an insurrection in his thoughts had been quelled. The king's fury against his older daughters does not turn him to the thought of his youngest. With the descent of madness, displayed to us over four long scenes, Cordelia seems to be banished from his mind as once from his kingdom and his affections. In his worst and most necessitous moments he takes it for granted that he is childless. If there is a birth or rebirth of feelings such as love and guilt toward Cordelia, Shakespeare does not show it to us. The exiled daughter is, as it were, not less out of mind than out of sight.

Yet she is continuously present both to Lear's mind and our own; and the silence, the absence, are not only compatible with this visionary presence, they are the positive pledge and proof of its reality. The evidence that supports this reading is threefold.

I

There is the poetry of the later scenes, the scenes of reunion and reconciliation. Shortly before, we had a report on Lear's state of mind: safely harbored in the French camp, he will "by no means yield to see his daughter":

> *Kent.* A sovereign shame so elbows him; his own unkindness,
> That stripp'd her from his benediction, turn'd her
> To foreign casualties, gave her dear rights
> To his dog-hearted daughters—these things sting
> His mind so venomously that burning shame
> Detains him from Cordelia. (4. 3. 44–49)

But this is surely to be read back into the episodes of madness; the audience took it all along as ingrained in Lear's frenzy—of which, however, not one word gave manifest expression to it. Dimly, at the base of the spectator's emotion, the question was stirring, "What do you think now of your decision? How do you feel about Cordelia?"; and Kent's words chime in, late, with this subconscious train. The manifest burden of Lear's rages was "ingratitude"— not the acts he had committed but those he had suffered from. Always uppermost in his thoughts were the two bad daughters.

His inability to sustain the idea of their wickedness is testimony, so far, only to his enormous vanity. He cracks because he cannot bear to believe himself so discarded and deprived. In his dire comfortlessness he might have turned for solace and refuge to the image of Cordelia—even this was never so much as hinted at in the text. But to go all the way back and *change his idea*, commence the terrible review of his wrongness and injustice, expose himself to the assaults of shame, guilt, remorse—nothing could be farther from the surface of Lear's passion. Yet the audience was not deceived; it divined the torment of self-accusation; and the poet counted on its prescience. Otherwise Kent's speech would take us by surprise: it would denote a wholly unlooked-for mutation of Lear's character.

But if we did not have Kent's report, there would still be the poetry of Lear's speeches in the seventh scene of the fourth act and the third scene of the fifth. *King Lear*, we may observe in general, is a standing confutation of theoretical prejudices (Poe's and in some measure Croce's) in favor of the lyric and against the longer poem. Poe argues that a poem must express emotion; emotion cannot be long sustained; hence, a long poem is only a series of lyrics connected by passages of prose. But what if the constituent lyrics, separated from the parent frame, should pine and die? *Lear* is a play from which hardly three consecutive lines can be extracted and kept alive. No "great speeches"; no *To-morrow and to-morrow* or *To be or not to be;* nothing detachable, nothing quotable or declaimable in isolation; no slackening of dramatic pressure; everything comes from the situation and must in turn be applied to it. Passages almost unbearably intense, like "I tax you not, you elements, with unkindness./ I never gave you kingdom, call'd you children," and "What, have his daughters brought him to this pass?" are cold and dull—the poetry washes out of them—unless we are thinking of the speaker and of all that has happened to him. *Lear* is the great example of a seamless dramatic entity. Now the recognition scene in the fourth act, the imprisonment scene in the fifth, have unmistakably a quality of fulfillment—a quality that presupposes a previous demand. Lear's ecstasy is meaningless, unthinkable, without his earlier agony. But there is a strict inner relationship, in human psychology, between need and gratification: not every object is fit to meet every requirement. Love is not satisfied by eating nor hunger by scientific demonstrations; the desire for fame will not be in the least appeased by the birth of a son; one could not be rejoiced by the good fortune of a friend if one had

been intent solely on the destruction of an enemy. And the recovery of Cordelia will not so gratify a spirit suffering from hate,
disillusion, and injured pride. From the joy of the later scenes we
know what sort of pain is felt in the earlier, because this—the pain
of self-blame for the offense against love—is the one emotion to
which the other fitly responds. Let us, as the third act ends, think of
other ways, each consistent with the text, of interpreting Lear's
ordeal. He could, for all the poet tells us, have reversed his opinion
of Goneril and Regan without any change of feeling toward Cordelia: their wickedness does not prove her merit. Then he is left
without daughters, home, or land and is indeed forlorn enough to
be driven mad. Or—if we suppose that Lear has throughout been
grieving chiefly about himself—he could have some portion of his
pride restored to him by the recovery of one daughter, his kingdom, and his power. Or he could look to Cordelia, as the least
offender, for shelter and toleration—as once he did to Goneril:

> Those wicked creatures yet do look well-favor'd
> When others are more wicked; not being the worst
> Stands in some rank of praise. I'll go with thee. (2. 4. 259–61)

Every degree of revulsion, besides the greatest, is compatible with
the text. But, on any of these suppositions, the fierce joy of the king
is unexplained; the note of redemption is lost; the ache of an antecedent hunger, which is measured by the intensity with which he
feeds, is not provided for. Such a craving is, however, quite evident in the Lear to whom his daughter has been restored.

The audience is prepared for these scenes because its emotions
have been evolving in silent underlying correspondence with
Lear's—almost like two mathematicians who, given the same problem, work on it apart and announce the same solution at the same
time. We appreciate his transports only because we have taken
step by step with him in the development of his conscience. It is
the resolution of his abnormal tensions and our own that defines
as by a retrospective light (much what, as DeQuincey claimed, the
knocking at the gate does for the murder scene in *Macbeth*) the
character of what we have been enduring in the scenes of dissen-
sion, storm, and madness.

The audience considers it entirely natural for the harried king
to fall into Cordelia's arms. And it *is* natural—but only if there has
been a progression in his thoughts. For Cordelia has been away;
she has had no chance to approve herself to the king. Goneril and
Regan can reveal and condemn themselves: they give new evidence

of their natures. Cordelia remains, for Lear, exactly what she was or seemed to be. He has no experience on which to found a modification of his judgment. He cannot discover her as she is, only as she was. And he can discover himself, his own frivolity and turpitude, only as he and they had been. He must go back and convict himself of error: uproot the old Lear along with the old idea of Cordelia. This is more painful, as it is more abrupt and violent, than learning by experience. There is no medium in it between acceptance and rejection: everything is either black or white, because already fixed and accomplished. Lear cannot evolve with the course of events except by first breathing flames upon his ego and annihilating it. And it is with some such searing convulsion of judgment and attitude that the audience intercalates his ordeal, producing a continuity between the old king and the new one.

II

But this line of reasoning shows, at most, that Cordelia is in our thoughts all along, notwithstanding Shakespeare's silence. It does not show why that silence is useful or necessary, why it was chosen as a method, why it is better than an occasional breast-beating or a string of remorseful comments. I do not know that the resources of psychology and aesthetics are at all equal to this question. If Shakespeare has any standing with us as a psychologist, we should believe that there is some connection between silence and emotional force. For speech is show; and the show of feeling is, in Shakespeare, perhaps not always false but always suspect. The plays are haunted by this prepossession as by few others: it is a prime facet and exemplification of the greater theme that dominates his art—appearance and reality, the difference between *seems* and *is*. Cordelia, who does not protest too much nor even half enough, communicates her sincerity by that quality alone—as if her unwillingness to declare her love were sufficient proof of it. Hypocrisy and pretense, protestation and profession, the glib and oily art which generates plot after plot, are of course evident to the most careless reader. Not less pervasive, though less conspicuous, is the idea embedded quite casually in so many passages: that the facility of feeling is in inverse relation to its depth. Hamlet cannot profess his friendship for Horatio without a reaction of distaste; he is touched to the quick by the slightest allusion to his outward show of grief. If Shakespeare's people weep, it is albeit unused to the melting mood—the reservation underscores the tears and makes us think that the cause must be really profound. The very villains, as a part of their craft, seek an appearance of reticence, as if a straightforward denunciation of Edgar or Desdemona were bound to discredit itself. Shakespeare's apprehension in this matter is mounted upon a great tide of proverb and traditional experience. Like other intuitive divinations, it is not scientifically exact: it carries with it no statement of the conditions in which the expression of feeling is trustworthy and those in which it is not. And if we *could* frame this insight of Shakespeare's in scientific language and verify it by experiment, we should still be a long way from applying it to his own practice as a dramatist.[2] Some explanation, however, can be given for Lear's silence in this play.

Silence is negative. The fact that a man does *not* speak about some topic I pick out at random proves only, in the usual case, that he is not thinking about it. There are all sorts of things we never mention because they do not interest us; and the silence of other people on those subjects which do concern us manifests a similar ignorance, inattention, or indifference. No special cause or reason needs to be invoked. But if we have an independent reason for believing that it would be natural, in a certain situation, for a man to say something on a certain point, then his silence will "speak volumes" and will seem to us to require a cause. Consider an analogy. The absence of glowing street lamps from the middle of a pasture is nothing that needs to be explained. The *presence* of a street lamp there would provoke curiosity. But when the presence of these lights has become the rule for large cities of our acquaintance, then the blackout calls for some explanation—and finds it in the imposition of an interdict. Similarly, Freud did not think of invoking a positive force of repression to account for the forgetting of lines of poetry or algebraic formulas; for his experience did not convince him that it was natural to remember them. The forms of amnesia he did try to explain by repression were those he thought somehow singular and defiant of ordinary laws of memory. Now Cordelia is one of Lear's three daughters, "his joy", "best object,/The argument of your praise, balm of your age,/Most best, most dearest," and one whom in righteous wrath he has dismissed. Even in peaceful times it would be natural to think back to her again and again. His failure to recur to her amid the extraordinary strife within his family, in the utmost bitterness and distraction of

2. Dowden and Bradley have made suggestions toward the analysis of silence as a dramatic method. See Alwin Thaler, *Shakespere's Silences* (Cambridge, Mass.: Harvard University Press, 1929).

spirit, is something not to be expected in the ordinary course of things. But the king who turns this way and that in his disconsolate quest; who can say, "Yet have I left a daughter [Regan]"; who eats crow before Goneril; who fumes and rails in public and in private —can never,[3] by way of taunt or reproach, recrimination or petition, mention his third daughter and express, to himself or others, the least regret. Nor frankly respond to the mention of her by another:

> *Knight.* Since my young lady's going into France, sir, the fool hath much pined away.
> *Lear.* No more of that; I have noted it well. Go you and tell my daughter I would speak with her. (1.4. 79–82)

This is not neglect but avoidance. Lear is mute through an excess, not a deficiency, of feeling. His lips are sealed by force, as if the most oppressive of his sorrows had been too strong to be acknowledged and were expunged by violence from his brain. The relief of madness, which gives free rein to thoughts hitherto suppressed, does not cut the strangulating cord affixed to the idea of Cordelia; for there are crimes and griefs with the contemplation of which madness would lose its wits. As the play progresses and chance after chance is passed up for an easy expression of remorse and longing, a conviction settles down in the audience. Going by its own experience of life, it takes Lear's silence as a gag upon his feelings and evidence of their existence in an extreme degree; and decides, unknown to itself, not that he is not thinking about Cordelia but that he thinks of her too much.

If we believe that the poet could count upon the audience's presentiment of agonized repentence in Lear, we can find excellent dramatic reasons for his choice of method. For once we are mindful of the true nature of Lear's distress; it is protracted and swelled by silence to an intolerable height and resolved with a rush, like the thawing of Niagara, in the great scenes of the fourth act. Our feelings about ingratitude and hurt pride, about age and destitution, find ample discharge in the body of the play. But our feelings about love and conscience are suspended, at a place where they can only accumulate to the bursting point. The great display of vindictive rage builds up and intensifies the antagonistic tenderness by contrast, leaving it the whole stage when its time comes. To have anticipated this climax was to have reduced tension and

3. We have noted an exception. See also the last section of this article.

staggered our reactions, providing dribbles of emotion instead of a flood. The pattern of this play conforms to principles which, though not well understood, are illustrated in different contexts over and over again—as in the intense grief over sudden death which a long illness would have dissipated.

III

Not ingratitude but injustice—not Goneril's or Regan's but Lear's—is the theme of the play. Or the main theme; for the other is also real and essential. The duality of Lear's nature is expressed in a competition of groups of passions, the one group—arrogance, vanity, resentment—overt and predominant yet secondary, the other—belated love with its attendant guilts and shames—primary though latent. These do not wrestle with each other; and they do not alternate. They are interwoven; the one lies beneath the other and speaks through it as through a heavy mask. The peculiar and (to many readers) puzzling, because apparently unjustified, force of Lear's speeches to his daughters is explained by the muffled presence of this ulterior motivation, as if beneath his patent grievances throbbed the perpetual refrain: "I threw Cordelia out for you; please do not make me admit it was the crime I now know it to have been." Thus when Lear comes upon his messenger imprisoned in the stocks, his emotion—

> O, how this mother swells up toward my heart!
> Hysterica passio! Down, thou climbing sorrow!
> Thy element's below! (2. 4. 56–58)

—does not repeat the accents of outraged vanity which marked his rupture with Cordelia. And the terrifying curse with which he blasted Goneril (1.4. 297–311) when her offense was still comparatively trifling does not, in the present perspective, represent a mere continuation of the fickle and childish king. For he has new pricks and stings to goad him: he has acquired, in the meanwhile, new reasons for excess. His passion is complex, with liberal infusions from concealed sources of self-hatred and contrition. Lear, in other words, is a larger and deeper, less simplified and specialized nature than a naïve witness of these outbursts would take him for—therefore, a better hero for the play. The last point by which I would justify the present interpretation is simply that if it be true, a greater range of values is to be found in the play. Let us, therefore, pretend that it is false: I think we shall see that the complaints of certain critics turn out, on this supposition, to be sound; for Lear becomes unsympathetic to a degree which is very nearly fatal to our interest.

Tolstoy could attack the play on logical grounds:

No reader or spectator can believe that a king, however old and senile he may be, could put any faith in the words of wicked daughters with whom he had lived all their days and not trust his favorite daughter rather than curse and exile her; and therefore the reader or spectator cannot share in the feelings of the personages engaged in this unnatural scene.

The "therefore" is somewhat arbitrary. Lear is not so improbable as Tolstoy thought; but if he were improbable, it does not follow that he is not congenial to the feelings of the audience. The important thing is not that he is unnatural but that he is strange; and if there were thousands like him in the world—as there are, indeed, thousands of psychopaths—they would all be strange. For a man of eighty who is so dependent on his daughters as to require constant reassurances of their affection is pathetically foolish and weak. Lear's weaknesses do not in themselves impair his tragic quality. Maurice Maeterlinck was writing in the spirit of Aristotle when he said: "The mere presence of the sage suffices to paralyze destiny; and of this we find proof in the fact that there exists scarce a drama wherein a true sage appears; when such is the case, the event needs must halt before reaching bloodshed and tears."[4] Tragedy can do nothing with the idea of a man who is, by hypothesis, protected against error and catastrophe. And so I believe we mark Lear's original imperfection without being alienated from him on account of it. But as the play proceeds, the fault in his character reasserts itself. The flaw widens into a rent and devours the vessel. For added to his immense vanity as a father and a man is his immoderate vanity as a king. The haughty old man who brandishes his whip against the Fool, curses his daughter with sterility after a quarrel about the size of his retinue, bristles at the indignity inflicted upon his messenger (it is the insult to the king, not the injury to the servant, that matters here), calls on the gods to feel the same pity he feels for himself, and yields in madness to sadistic images of vengeance—"To have a thousand with red burning spits/

4. *Wisdom and Destiny*, trans. Alfred Sutro (New York: Dodd, Mead, 1910).

Come hizzing in upon 'em—" is monotonous in his egotism. He grows shrill and strident, harping forever on the one string. He is inclined toward pathology: the insanity is there to begin with in the mere height of his pride. The audience is disaffected: we feel ourselves to be looking on at a distance, as upon some specimen from the annals of psychiatry. We can "understand," from without; we cannot enter and participate.

A part of this objection is no doubt peculiar to modern readers but will not for that reason seem less valid to them. A hundred knights, fifty knights, twenty-five knights—try as we will to consider the meaning these terms have for Lear rather than the meaning they might have for one of us today, we cannot wholly acquiesce in the values ascribed to them; it is difficult, therefore, to take the king's predicament quite as seriously as he does himself. There is a limit to sympathy; if there were not, we could ask an audience to respond to the spectacle of an obsessed man, moving heaven and earth to recover a collar button. But the audience, while it has plenty of compassion for suffering—as for psychotics, victims of plague and earthquake, an animal in pain—does not respond dramatically to the elements in such a case: it can pity where it does not sympathize.

It is true that Lear's is not in the end a pride of power and possessions. His security, dignity, and self-esteem rest on the knowledge of being held dear by those from whom he might reasonably expect that tribute. The kingly privileges, such as adulation, flattery, a staff of retainers, are pledges of the allegiance of hearts. It is the loss not of these perquisites but of the love which willingly concedes them that he fears in his refusal, for so long, to admit that Regan can be as bad as her sister is. Throughout the first three acts his sorrow is as conspicuous as his resentment; for he is not merely reduced but bereft. And this trait of human nature forms a bridge between the barbaric British king and any democratic audience, to whom the same psychic needs are familiar in different symbols and vestments. Yet, notwithstanding this defense, the character of Lear remains severely limited. Even if he were not as touchy as he is— imperious and demanding; over-sensitive to compliments and slights; greedy for the shadow of deference above the substance (and these are the faults that can be forgiven most easily)—it would still appear, from the surface of the earlier acts, that his need to be loved is immensely greater than his capacity for loving. And this is pure egotism, which estranges the audience. "Better thou hadst not been born than not t' have pleas'd me better," he says to Cordelia. The speech is typical.

Of course, the later acts would in any case force us to correct and expand our idea of Lear; but by that time a good measure of sympathy has been withdrawn.

Only if we assume the existence of another process by which the King's mind is agitated through the course of the play, can we restore the balance between his humanity and his folly: then his febrile narcissism enriches his dramatic character and does not confine it. "I am," he says, "a man more sinned against than sinning"; but he does not altogether believe it. His derangement follows more from the consciousness of what he has done than from the knowledge of what has been done to him; the meaning of it is Cordelia.

IV

One side of Lear's character has, if I am right, to be presumed; for until a late point in the play it is not shown. Needless to say, we are given the materials to work with: we could not construct the loving father from the tyrant and megalomaniac. Nobody supposes Edmund to be gentle or pure on the strength of his being painted in just the opposite colors; and the selfish Lear does not yield an idea of the selfless one. There are the touches of pity and of generosity, the larger sense of justice which displays itself through and amid Lear's distraction; there were the incipient motions of conscience, soon to be stifled, that we have noticed before; there is a magnanimity in his very petulance, a general though distorted sense of right which has little in common with the mean language of calculation. There is the exacerbated violence and pathos of Lear's revulsion from his two daughters: nothing we have seen in either of these women explains why their defection should so wrench his mind and rankle in his breast. It is such a man, not just any man, whose inner reactions to his own misdeed we are left to supply for ourselves. Shakespeare controls our thinking; he leaves no room for conjecture; he surrounds the hidden area in Lear's mind with such unmistakable signs that there can be just one understanding of its contents. But he *dares*. He stretches his bridge of speech over a fearful gap of the unspoken and expects the audience to span this gulf along with him.

The feat is prodigious, unique. Yet it is in the poet's manner and is outstanding only in degree. I am now alluding to a feature of Shakespeare's art that has seldom been ignored, though it will probably never be defined by his critics. Human motives are not counted like beans or measured like bolts of cloth; and it would be risky to say that we experience a greater complexity of motivation in Shakespeare than in another dramatist. When Phèdre is confessing her love for her stepson, Hippolyte—

> Contre moi-même enfin j'osai me révolter:
> J'excitai mon courage a le persécuter.
> Pour bannir l'ennemi dont j'étais idolâtre,
> J'affectai les chagrins d'une injuste marâtre;
> Je pressai son exil, et mes cris éternels
> L'arrachèrent du sein et des bras paternels.

—we are afforded an extraordinary view of duplicity of character. But the woman is describing, she is not evincing, her state of mind; and the psychological elements—the infatuation, the consciousness of sin, the need to remove temptation from her sight, the pretense of hatred as a means—are laid out before us on a plane like the counters in a game of skill. Shakespeare would have suppressed some of these forces and made them work through the others: we should have recognized them by their intrusion upon the style of straightforward speech. Thus, Macbeth communicates his real thoughts, early in the play, by the question addressed to Banquo:

> Do you not hope your children shall be kings,
> When those that gave the Thane of Cawdor to me
> Promised no less to them?

—from which no person in the audience gathers that Macbeth has any real solicitude for Banquo's children. And we have the familiar passage from the murder scene in *Othello:*

> It is the cause, it is the cause, my soul.
> Let me not name it to you, you chaste stars!
> It is the cause. Yet I'll not shed her blood,
> Nor scar that whiter skin of hers than snow,
> And smooth as monumental alabaster.
> Yet she must die, else she'll betray more men.

The note tells us: "He is resolved to kill Desdemona as an act of justice. 'It is the *cause* that I must bear in mind—the guilt that calls for the punishment of death.' He will not think of his own wrongs but solely of her offence against the right."[5] Now we could half believe that Othello is sincere, conceives himself as an impartial agent of justice, and is mediating retribution rather than revenge. But, "—she'll betray more men"! We cannot at all believe, from anything we know of Othello, that he holds a Benthamite theory of punishment and would like to protect society from adulteresses. This is a wild thought thrown up for an instant by the turmoil of his passions; a pretext, a straw of justification which, in his extremity, he clutches only to throw aside. Othello is a little delirious; he is raving—but not so flagrantly as to make us aware of our diagnosis. We react simultaneously to the declared motive and to the foreshadowed disturbance, which is conveyed to us by the slight deviation in his thinking from the normal and expected pattern. But we do not analyze our intuition and see what a complexity of materials it contains. *We do not know what is being done to us.* The draught upon our experience and understanding is not paralleled elsewhere in literature. This is that "something more"—the sense of being affected to a degree which is not explained by the explicit contents of the plays—that has so dazed Shakespeare's critics and prompted them to describe his drama as an art of implication and indirection, of oblique expression and tangential reference. Cordelia's absence is only the most remarkable example of his ability to stretch these strangely disturbing fingers into regions of the heart that could not be probed by speech.

5. *Othello*, ed. G. L. Kittredge (Boston: Ginn and Co., 1936), p. 220.

9

A Poem by Frost and Some Principles of Criticism

A STAR IN A STONEBOAT
For Lincoln MacVeagh

[1]   Never tell me that not one star of all
That slip from heaven at night and softly fall
Has been picked up with stones to build a wall.

[2]   Some laborer found one faded and stone-cold,
And saving that its weight suggested gold
And tugged it from his first too certain hold,

[3]   He noticed nothing in it to remark.
He was not used to handling stars thrown dark
And lifeless from an interrupted arc.

[4]   He did not recognize in that smooth coal
The one thing palpable besides the soul
To penetrate the air in which we roll.

[5]   He did not see how like a flying thing
It brooded ant eggs, and had one large wing,
One not so large for flying in a ring,

[6]   And a long Bird of Paradise's tail
(Though these when not in use to fly and trail
It drew back in its body like a snail);

[7]   Nor know that he might move it from the spot—
The harm was done: from having been star-shot
The very nature of the soil was hot

[8]   And burning to yield flowers instead of grain,
Flowers fanned and not put out by all the rain
Poured on them by his prayers prayed in vain.

[9]   He moved it roughly with an iron bar,
He loaded an old stoneboat with the star
And not, as you might think, a flying car,

[10]   Such as even poets would admit perforce
More practical than Pegasus the horse
If it could put a star back in its course.

[11]   He dragged it through the plowed ground at a pace
But faintly reminiscent of the race
Of jostling rock in interstellar space.

[12]   It went for building stone, and I, as though
Commanded in a dream, forever go
To right the wrong that this should have been so.

[13]   Yet ask where else it could have gone as well,
I do not know—I cannot stop to tell:
He might have left it lying where it fell.

[14]   From following walls I never lift my eye,
Except at night to places in the sky
Where showers of charted meteors let fly.

[15]   Some may know what they seek in school and church,
And why they seek it there; for what I search
I must go measuring stone walls, perch on perch;

[16]   Sure that though not a star of death and birth,
So not to be compared, perhaps, in worth
To such resorts of life as Mars and Earth—

[17]   Though not, I say, a star of death and sin,
It yet has poles, and only needs a spin
To show its worldly nature and begin

[18]   To chafe and shuffle in my calloused palm
And run off in strange tangents with my arm,
As fish do with the line in first alarm.

[19]   Such as it is, it promises the prize
Of the one world complete in any size
That I am like to compass, fool or wise.

                           Robert Frost

"A Star in a Stone-Boat" is one of Frost's best poems but still very imperfect. In the first part of this essay I attempt a criticism of the poem. In the second part I turn about and review some of the terms of my criticism—the purpose being to understand the nature of the standards to which one resorts in verbalizing spontaneous reactions. The whole poem is reprinted here; and it might be well to read it entire before turning to the commentary.

I

Never tell me that not one star of all
That slip from heaven at night and softly fall
Has been picked up with stones to build a wall.

Some laborer found one faded and stone-cold,
And saving that its weight suggested gold
And tugged it from his first too certain hold,

He noticed nothing in it to remark.
He was not used to handling stars thrown dark
And lifeless from an interrupted arc.

The idea is all his own invention (the poet's or the speaker's—for the moment, it doesn't matter which); he hasn't any *reason* to think that anybody ever did any such thing. But the fancy occurs to him, and: "I insist on it. I won't have it otherwise." No sooner thought than believed. There is a lot of this gentle willfulness in Frost, a way of fondling his caprices and making a display of them. But I don't find it objectionable here, perhaps because there is not much of it. The self-consciousness is not blatant in these lines so far: the poet is rather more taken with his idea than with himself for having it. In any case, we can't say that it is a bad quality in literature unless we are ready to despise Laurence Sterne.

Perhaps we should not abandon the point without framing it a little more precisely. There is a difference between a poet who says, "I propose to imagine," and one who says, "Look at me imagining; am I not charming (or frolicsome, audacious, cunning, and so forth?" The first is as eccentric as you please, but not self-conscious. The second is self-conscious, and not as free as he thinks. The difference is manifested by the presence or absence, not of a reference to self, but of a manner of assertion which is such as to call attention to self. It is intangible, indefinable; not theoretically understood; recognized by the reader's sensibility and by that part of his understanding (commonly called "intuition") which he uses to estimate people in daily life. In this poem, our judgment wavers: the poet's ego obtrudes itself barely, if at all.

While one writer cares for his work and takes credit to himself when it is finished and another lets his craving for credit show up in the work to spoil it, there is a third writer—Sterne or, in different ways, Byron, Max Beerbohm—who is as it were conscious of his self-consciousness and makes a deliberate use of it. Then the self gets into the text as a subject and becomes art, the real self of the artist coolly controlling its maneuvers from the outside. Such writing is an "objective" as an Elgin marble, in the chief sense that matters to criticism. The real question for the critic is not whether the ego appears in the poem but how it appears: as patterned content or as intrusion. But this is also the question with any other element in the poem.

> He did not recognize in that smooth coal
> The one thing palpable besides the soul
> To penetrate the air in which we roll.

Read: "The one thing, besides the soul, which palpably does penetrate." Not: "The one palpable thing besides the soul." Conventionally, the soul is the one thing impalpable; and there would be no point in making it palpable unless Frost had some paradox to spring on the reader; but he has none. The stanza is weak. "Besides the soul" is an afterthought. The way the star penetrates the air and the way the soul does it are mechanically aggregated: there is no intimate relation between them. In other words: "Oh yes, there is one other thing which, in some sense of the word, can be said to 'penetrate' the air." The poet is using a vague duplicity in the word; he is not building a conscious simile. And why "the air *in which we roll*"? Presumably, for the rhyme. We roll with the globe, and the air rolls with us. While we roll, we are *in* the air; but we don't *roll* in the air. I am not objecting to misstatement, for there isn't any: there is a compression of two distinct images. The poet has no clear perception. It's as if he were about to write "the air in which we live" and then thinks, "But we do roll, don't we? All right, let's slip the extra thought in." (There is a better example of this crowding of ideas in the fifth stanza reproduced below.) You could, however, reply that 'roll' gives the astronomical image that he is looking for, as 'live' does not; but that is just what I object to. We are suddenly compelled by a single word to shift our perspective; and the two vague ideas which the line gives us are no substitute for one clear one.

He did not see how like a flying thing
It brooded ant eggs, and had one large wing
One not so large for flying in a ring,

And a long Bird of Paradise's tail
(Though these when not in use to fly and trail
It drew back in its body like a snail);

The star is now compared to a bird.

Nor know that he might move it from the spot—
The harm was done: from having been star-shot
The very nature of the soil was hot

And burning to yield flowers instead of grain,
Flowers fanned and not put out by all the rain
Poured on them by his prayers prayed in vain.

The first four lines are rather marvelous. The last two are violent, difficult, perhaps impossible. First, the matter of tenses. "The soil was hot and already burning to yield the flowers that were to grow and would not be put out by the rain for which he was to have (still later than the growth of the flowers but earlier than the fall of rain) prayed." Second, why "prayed *in vain*"? Because, though he gets the rain he prayed for, it doesn't put out the flowers. But we knew that already. "Prayed in vain" is redundant. Third, why should he want the flowers put out? For the grain? But why won't the grain be killed too? Finally, we notice that the heat passes not only from star to soil but from soil to flowers, which are figuratively interpreted as flames, to be "fanned" or "put out." The figure does not work out. On the one side, the rain will extinguish but will not fan a crop of flames; on the other side, it does nourish but does not, in any parallel sense, destroy flowers—certainly not without having a similar influence on grain. As the farmer prays for rain, the flames necessarily become *literal* ones, because the rain is literal; they cannot remain flowers. The figure, in other words, does not extend to the rain. The poet is trying to have the best or both terms of his comparison and ignore the inconvenient implications in each. As we bring these out, our feeling shifts, transforming our opinion of the entire metaphor. If the reader, instead of assuming that I have asked him to object in principle to "inconsistent" imagery, will concentrate on the sense of Frost's metaphor, he will experience my difficulty.

So that one doesn't know quite what to think of the fifth line. It is an effort to sustain the thought of the preceding lines. That thought is magical, in a double sense: it is contrary to fact; and it is surprising in its beauty. A mysterious law of affinity whereby the celestial body is linked with the more ardent and finer products of the soil. But all this moves easily, naturally; it is not strained and tangled, like the flower-flames and the rain.

At this point one may be inclined to plead the advantages of a careless reading. The two lines flow trippingly on the tongue and seem good enough, as long as one does not think about them too closely. Why peer into the pores, to our own discomfiture?—But it is too late to recover our inattention. We began to read closely in the hope of a greater reward—a more exact thought and keener emotion focused in the words 'fanned' and 'put out'—than the surface of the lines could offer. We can't very well back out now when our purpose has miscarried.

> He moved it roughly with an iron bar,
> He loaded an old stoneboat with the star
>
> And not, as you might think, a flying car,
>
> Such an even poets would admit perforce
> More practical than Pegasus the horse
> If it could put a star back in its course.

"He put it in a stoneboat, to drag it to the wall, and not in a flying car, which could take it back where it belongs"—that is the true substance. It carries the poem's basic contrast forward and is in keeping with the rest. But the second stanza is a most annoying example of Frost's subjectivity—the sleepy associative method by which he stumbles off and on his path. Why poets? Why Pegasus? What are they doing here? Why should poets hesitate to admit that something might be more practical than Pegasus? And why *is* the flying car more practical than Pegasus unless somebody *wants* to put the star back in its course? Has anybody suggested, incidentally, that *Pegasus* be recruited for the purpose? And why couldn't he perform just as well as the car? All this—and especially the idea of the poet's loyalty to Pegasus—is weak, sickly, dishonest sentiment; but, more, it is the clearest evidence of the aimless musing that we have noticed before; for there is no reason for the stanza but the fact that Frost, mentioning a flying car, was led to think of a flying horse.

He dragged it through the plowed ground at a pace
But faintly reminiscent of the race
Of jostling rock in interstellar space.

It went for building stone, and I, as though
Commanded in a dream, forever go
To right the wrong that this should have been so.

It is beneath the dignity of a star to be put into a wall—that is
the wrong. The real trouble starts here. The speaker tells us that
he is obsessed by this injustice. If he were quite serious, we should
think him mad; and since it is not implied that he is mad, we must
believe either that he is being playful or that there is some deeper
meaning that we have yet to find.

Yet ask where else it could have gone as well,
I do not know—I cannot stop to tell:
He might have left it lying where it fell.

These lines are on a plane at which, if it were sustained, we
could find it possible to accept the poem. They tell us of a gently
ruminating, fanciful, not too coherent or realistic mind. "Have I
been illogical? Oh well, don't bother me. I'm just rambling along."
Notice that the verses are reasonably explicit. In the stanza that
refers to Pegasus, Frost is maundering pitifully; in this one Frost
is awake and, as it were, apologetic about his sleep-walking.

From following walls I never lift my eye,
Except at night to places in the sky
Where showers of chartered meteors let fly.

Some may know what they seek in school and church,
And why they seek it there; for what I search
I must go measuring stone walls, perch on perch;

The poetry has become once more portentous, philosophic, self-
important.

Sure that though not a star of death and birth,
So not to be compared, perhaps, in worth
To such resorts of life as Mars and Earth—

Though not, I say, a star of death and sin,

The first line of these four, coming where it does, has for me that
rise which announces a solution, a climax to which the whole poem
has been moving. The note is held for three more lines, suspending
us. Then:

> It yet has poles, and only needs a spin
> To show its worldly nature and begin
>
> To chafe and shuffle in my calloused palm
> And run off in strange tangents with my arm,
> As fish do with the line in first alarm.

These are among the more delightful images in the poem. But they are not different in kind from those we have already seen. If you thought you were going to find out why he measures stone walls instead of going to school or church, you are disappointed: you learn only what you knew already, and that wasn't enough.

> Such as it is, it promises the prize
> Of the one world complete in any size
> That I am like to compass, fool or wise.

This is the last stanza and our last chance to wring a philosophic meaning from the poem. To do that we have to give a particular interpretation to the word 'compass'. There are two ways of reading it. One is literal and concrete: "This is the only world I shall ever get my hand or my arms around. Imagine, having a heavenly body right there in the palm of your hand!" This reading continues the modest imagery of the poem; it puts the stanza on a plane with the lines which come just before. But it makes "fool or wise" irrelevant, excrescent. And it fails to bear out the vague intimations of earlier stanzas: they subside into silence, like imagined whispers, and are seen in retrospect as a false alarm. If, on the other hand, we make 'compass' ambiguous and symbolic—"Man's finitude, his inability to grasp this world in which he lives, seems momentarily transcended when I hold this rock in my hand. That is why I am so impressed with the star in the stoneboat"—we read some kind of wisdom into the poem and seem to justify the earlier emphasis. But that's quite a load to be borne by the slim thought of this stanza, which turns on a rather conventional pun in the word 'compass'. I don't say the philosophy is unsound. I say it is shadowy, and barely perceptible—the reader has to supply most of it himself. And it is isolated: we have been prepared for a moral of some sort but not for this one more than another. We have to choose, then, between a thought which is small but sensuous and clear and another which is grander but pretentious and obscure. Neither of these readings will save the poem.

Frost's mind was excited at the start by the idea of something

remote, cosmic, magnetic, complete, and "worldly" thrown down
so close among bits of dead mineral broken off from the earth.
The poem is essentially a chain of images, all equal and parallel,
developing the one idea. The development is not progressive but
iterative; it is like a set of variations compared with the structure of
a sonata. It is not supposed to get anywhere; it is supposed to add
up, to delight us with a string of thoughts similar and different. The
very scheme of the stanzas, with consistent rhyming within the
tercet, seems designed to convey this parallelism. Many poems of
the seventeenth century are constructed on the same principle—a
multiplicity and variety of coordinate ideas. And this one is reasonably successful, except at a few places where the author has to
stretch lines of doubtful sense over gaps left by the collapse of his
inspiration. This writer, as his eye passes down the poem, does not
lose the exhilaration, as of a mind disporting itself in a stream of
brilliant fancies, that he felt the first time he read it. But woven into
the pattern is a subjective element, a quest, which looks as if it had
some destination, though it hasn't any. Frost is always *returning*
to his first thought; while we, when we read, "Some may know
what they seek in school and church," assume that what *he* seeks
cannot be just a star in a stoneboat and are disappointed when we
find it is nothing more. Perhaps it is not the poet's fault that we
develop these anticipations? Perhaps he can be acquitted of pretentiousness and pseudo-profundity? Let us see. When we have
once come to the end of the poem, it is easy to dispel preconceptions another time round. What we took to be the portent of the
twelfth and the fifteenth stanzas fades out of them, leaving only
a choice of words, more or less blown up by comparison with the
theme to which they are devoted. The effect, I suggest, is either
ridiculous or shocking. No longer assuming that it contains a
claim which is to be made good in the sequel, the reader finds in
"for what *I* search I must go measuring stone walls perch on perch"
a burlesque or a gaga quality, like: "You take your philosophy and
your science—I'll stick to dominoes," or like something from the
Hit Parade: "I'm just wild about me-te-o-rites;/ I can't forget
'em;/ I wanna go an' get 'em." On the other hand, he can take it
seriously; but then the eccentricity deepens; the mild hobby becomes itself a philosophy; the whim becomes fierce and fanatical;
and it is hard to avoid thinking, "This is one of Frost's *studies* of
deviation. The speaker in the poem is a case."

In other words, we cannot escape the inherent tendency of the "bigger" ideas. They will do *something* to the poem, and not something good. I can imagine just one more attempt to justify them; and that would be by insisting that the star in the stoneboat *is* just as important as Frost says it is, neither more nor less. Frost's idea belongs to the class of nature experiences taken up and magnified by the imagination: it places itself, therefore, in a respectable tradition. When Wordsworth, discovering the small celandine, "makes a stir,/ Like a sage astronomer," he elucidates his excitement by the comparison and offends no one by the exaggeration. Can it be that Frost has no greater pretensions; that his magniloquence is only what is called for by the internal quality of his experience; that by taking the philosophy as playfully and the vision as seriously as possible, we can make the subjective emphasis agree with the poetic matter? If that be true, then my last paragraph was quite unfair. But I can see it that way only for a second, after which the poet's overweening claim reinstates itself, pointing to some moral or metaphysical significance which is never revealed. I cannot escape the conviction that the poem is steeped in a meditative film which collapses when touched with a pin; and this prevents me from assuming its innocence. Every reader's feeling must make the decision; and the necessity for making it seems to indicate a dubiety in our interpretation or our reaction which is perhaps not to be overcome.

II

My criticism of the poem has constantly been using standards from logic and ethics. We must now go over the ground and ask how well these standards apply. The standards from logic are two: one which we may call truth and the other consistency. (Please note that the empirical truth or falsity is to be considered as part of the "logical" character of the poem.) In this essay we are working "up" from a poem by Robert Frost to an idea of the relation between logic and poetry. We can't hope to get very far; but if we labored hard and well enough we should expect to meet aestheticians working "down" from general principles. If we can't shake hands with them, it is because either they or we have been climbing crookedly.

The argument of the first two stanzas is highly irrational. To put it quite literally, the probability that stars have been picked up with stones to build a wall is, on any evidence the poet adduces, much smaller than he asserts it to be. Now before we had any such reference point, any such cognitive norm, from which to measure the degree of departure in the poet's thinking, I doubt that we saw very clearly what was going on. The peculiar slanting impulse in the lines did not impress itself on us; it seems less far-fetched, less conceited, than we perceived it to be after we have compared it with the normal logical process. It "places" itself by its contrast with reason. But no judgment is yielded by that contrast: we did not find in the deviation of the fancy from the probable fact a ground for praise or rejection. The judgment is left to our feelings, *once the object is viewed distinctly*. And the judgment, in this case, is not unfavorable. Since the lines are not bad, and since logic would have it that they *are* bad (that is, false, unwarranted), the critical verdict cannot be the logical one —*unless* the logical canon is imposed by force to forestall the verdict of feeling; and this is the essence of prejudice, the definition of mechanical criticism.

The poet can always escape the jurisdiction of reason by withdrawing a part of his claim.—"I'm not asserting, I'm imagining. It's true I say, 'Some laborer found one—.' But I don't care whether he really found one or not. I could as well say, 'Suppose he found one.' Then you would have nothing to which to apply your standards, 'true' and 'false'." What he cannot change or evade is the *difference* between his mental process and the rational one; but he can afford to admit the difference.[1]

But does this apology quite meet the point? After all, it *was* within the poet's power to say "maybe" or "possibly" or "what if" instead of "never tell me"; and he chose not to do it. An air of assertion *belongs* to the poem, which would otherwise not have

---

1. A poetry which cleaves to the logical line of development (and there is much less of this in existence than one would think, to judge by the language, say, of critics of Pope, who did not employ a very strict conception of "logic") will necessarily be different in quality from Frost's, but not necessarily better. It, too, awaits the verdict *after* it has been cleared by reason.

I am not sure that the logical understanding is peculiarly qualified to serve as a frame of reference for poetical thinking. We can choose our standpoint anywhere. Spinoza's quality of mind is as well set off by Caliban's as Caliban's by his; and if, like Lewis Carroll, we are accustomed to read logic or geometry with an eye for its aesthetic flavor, we could hardly do better than to measure off from romantic poetry as a fixed pole. Fantasy and unreason become the norm by which the strange qualities of mathematics are suddenly made apparent.

the capricious tone that we noticed at the start. In other words, the fallen meteor—the figment of the speaker's mind—is not the entire subject. The speaker himself, with his obsessed imagination, is part of the subject. If he did not confuse fiction with reality, we should not be either charmed or disturbed in quite the way that we are. A man who follows stone walls looking for shooting stars when there *are* shooting stars is not the same character as one who looks for them where they are not. (This is, of course, a minor characteristic compared with the value he puts on them; but it is the one we happen to be talking about.) Hence the "scientific facts" enter into the meaning of the poem, just as we recognize a lunatic on the stage by the "false" ideas—hallucinations—to which he gives utterance.

But it would be strange if this last point, which shows us nothing we had not seen in the opening stanzas, could compel us to reverse our opinion of them. It seems to me, rather, that we must stick to that opinion and counter the apparent force of the objection as follows:

A *proposition*, of which we have an example in the clause "that not one star . . . to build a wall", is true or false, well or ill confirmed, as the case may be. An *assertion* is correct or erroneous, justified or unjustified. Now the negative value, "false" or "improbable," that may attach itself to the proposition is not invested with any particular feeling tone. We may coldly consider and reject hundreds of ideas that are offered to us as mere hypotheses. It is error that moves us; and error implies assertion; without which, as we saw just above, the aspect of irrationality would simply not display itself within the poem. But what is an assertion? Normally, the *verb* carries with it the feeling of assertion, which it has acquired through its customary use as the vehicle of assertion; but this is certainly not a fixed connection. There are languages which dispense with verbs, using other forms, such as a combination of noun and adjective, to convey assertion. We do this ourselves when we cry "Fire!" or make the announcement, "Nine o'clock." Assertion is possible without the verb. On the other hand, the verb need not express assertion: for example, a novelist who tells us that "*A* killed *B*" is not asserting but feigning. We are left to wonder, then, how we know that a person is asserting something; for it is possible to utter a proposition as a surmise or speculation, without asserting it. And we may agree that perhaps we do not ever know *for certain* that an assertion has been made. There are frequent misunderstandings on this score, as when we assume that a speaker has been endorsing certain views when he has only been reporting them. An assertion is the verbal expression of a belief; and we think that a man has been making an assertion when he speaks in such a way as to lead us to infer that he believes. We judge by the whole context of the speech—perhaps by a special emphasis placed on the verb, perhaps by the earnestness of the speaker's manner. But another clue is the kind of verb prefixed to the proposition: "I assert" rather than "I suggest" or "Never tell me" rather than "Do you think?" It is obvious that we sometimes judge the degree of assertiveness by these introductory forms of speech. But it is equally plain that they are not more essential to the expression of belief than, say, a stamp of the foot or a vigorous nod of the head. And it is also true that they are not absolutely conclusive indications of belief. For we can on some occasions (and this poem, in my opinion, is one) quite correctly interpret them as extensions of the mere proposition. The speaker, in other words, instead of asserting that A is B, is voicing another proposition, this time about himself: "I assert that A is B"; and he is not necessarily asserting this second proposition. In that case, the whole sentence is, as it were, placed within a frame; and that is just what happens in "A Star in a Stone-boat." It does, indeed, make a difference that the tone and air of asseveration are conveyed to us by certain words—that the protagonist believes and does not only imagine. But this difference is to be compared to the difference between "real" objects and "mirror" objects in a painting, both comprised within the fundamental ilusion. And just as one does not reach reality by multiplying the levels of illusion, painting framework after framework around the scene (imagine a picture of a "real" audience watching a movie in which a "fictitious" stage is presented, a play within the play on the stage, and so on), so the poet, by altering his content to "I insist that I really do assert," would not pass from the idea of assertion to assertion itself but to the idea of the assertion of assertion. Having now come to what may seem to the reader a fantastic extremity in the defense of my position (and of the passage), I may concede not only that poets do make assertions but that we can, with some probability, tell from their writing whether they are doing so or not. It was only, therefore, a theoretically tenable attitude, a way of taking the poetry, that I was just now delineating. But perhaps that is the necessary and right way of reading the present lines. For who cares what Robert Frost really believes about

meteors and stone walls? Whether there is a genuine assertion in
these lines is a question that could be settled not just by what the
verses say but by such steps as writing a letter to the poet, inter-
rogating his neighbors, and so on—the results of which could not
possibly influence our critical opinion. It is the bracketed, fictive
"assertion" that matters to the reader, because the poetry could
not be the same without it.

In the whole poem one finds not a single explicit inference.
Where there is a trace of one (as in the sixteenth stanza), it involves
a suppressed premise at which one is forced to guess. Nothing, then,
is in a strict sense logically coherent or incoherent. But common
sense uses wide and vaguer notions of relevance than logic does.
Some people never stick to the point of a conversation and are
criticized accordingly, though no science has formulated standards of "sticking to the point" and they certainly would not coincide with those of logic. Again, if one praises some member of a
group for honesty, one may or may not be "implying" that the
others are thieves; and the implication here is not of any kind
recognized by logic. There are numerous examples in this poem of
such processes, remotely analogous to logical inference; and the
author offends against our sense of how such reasoning should be
conducted. The idea of the twelfth stanza, for example—"I don't
know where else it could have gone"—should have been considered before the eleventh was written. To blame the man and then
admit there was nothing better for him to do is shiftless thinking.
Yet we do not find the stanza objectionable; if we did, it would be
like disapproving of dreams because they are not cogent arguments. The poetical process here is, once again, *defined* and not
judged by its contrast with reason—this time, with the idea of a
rational connection of distinct thoughts. But, in that case, what can
be my objection to the tenth stanza? My complaint was, in the
main, that it flies off at a tangent from the course of the poem; but
don't we have to exhibit the nature of the relevance that it fails
to observe? No doubt, the right formula for this occasion is, as
I. A. Richards would say, "emotional incoherence": stanza ten is
(with emphasis) *poetically* undisciplined as even twelve is not. But
isn't that, after all, what we felt at the start; not the answer but the
question?—something that has to be accounted for through the
connection or disconnection of the thoughts in the lines?

The train of thought is, by standards of ordinary discourse,
queer. Compare: "He travelled to X and not, as you might think,

to Y, which even those who admire a third place, Z, for a certain quality (q) would admit is superior to Z in respect of another quality (r) *provided that* Z has a third quality (s) the possession of which may or may not entail the possession of r." The oddity is so great that one despairs of finding any single principle by which to justify one's dislike—and I don't think that the oddity itself is that principle. I shall have to be satisfied with arguing that the principle, whatever it be, is *not* in either a strict or a loose sense logical. For in its main outline the tenth stanza is, in fact, guilty of no transgression against reason. The fundamental connective is 'such as'— "of a kind that"—which properly introduces an embellishment, a comparison. The types of order in which thoughts arrange themselves when they are marching toward a theoretical result or a practical goal therefore disqualify themselves as standards. The mental process in this stanza is, in other words, not illogical but nonlogical. T. S. Eliot has recently ascribed an "inspired frivolity" to Milton—a "skill in extending a period by introducing imagery which tends to distract us from the real subject." Milton leaps and wanders as unaccountably as Frost does, but to good poetic purpose; and, indeed, it would not be hard to show from the history of English verse how well a purely logical irrelevance can comport with an explicit and closely knit poetic texture.

We must, then, I think, reach a certain conclusion about the series of questions I asked earlier. It seems to me still that these questions represent valid objections to the tenth stanza; but their apparent force and their real force are entirely different. In logical argument, a train of associations is subject to a judgment in terms of its degree of conformity to a general norm. Thus, if I say that a car is more practical than a horse if it can haul merchandise from a shop, I am being incoherent unless I have reason to assume (at the least) that a horse cannot haul the merchandise. Frost, therefore, would be incoherent if he were conducting an argument in this stanza. By applying the norm of rational thinking, we judge him as a reasoner. Simultaneously, we expose the slack, feeble, dreamy, erroneous impulse in the poetry. For want of a tangible aesthetic norm—a rule of order and coherence—in poetry, we have fallen back on norms from logic and common sense, for without *some* norm to fall back on, our reaction would be inexpressible. We are now in danger of assuming that the logical and the critical objections are identical—that the poet's error *consists* in his deviation from the logical, but this assumption is terribly confused. For the logical rule condemns *any* argument which departs from the route it lays down, and condemns it in advance; but whether any similarly deviant sequence of ideas is bound to be *unpoetical* is something that we do not know in advance: and in my opinion it is false.

The greatest fault we could see in the poem was the strain between its somewhat vasty philosophic pretensions and the minor, specialized experience it records. Now this could be interpreted as a *moral* blemish; and our objection would read: "He should not imply as he does that shooting stars are important, for shooting stars are *not* important. It is not well for men to go following walls instead of schools and churches; and if it is not well to do so, then it is not well to speak quite so heartily of doing so." In other words, it is the ethical attitude of the poet that annoys us; and our criticism was an expression of disapprobation, as if we were listening to repellent sentiments from a speaker on a platform.

There remains little room in which to spread out the reasons for and against accepting this interpretation. Since I am not conscious of feeling disapproval for anything Frost says in this poem, I can't believe that my criticism registers disapproval. The sources of moral feeling are manifold. When the linen manufacturer advertises his produce, "Wamsutta . . . A Way of Living," we do not react merely to the distorted evaluation; behind it there is the cold-blooded design of the advertiser—the private motive for distortion; and it is this, more than the expressed sense of values, that offends us. Similarly, the question of the poet's assertion—this time, his moral assertion—and the motives behind it would have to be brought up here again. Can we, furthermore, assume the validity of our own ethical standard? What would happen if men did base a great part of their lives, as nature poets seem to recommend, on the experience of landscape? Surely this would be better than going to *some* schools and churches; and Frost's protagonist is a sounder person than some heavyweight moralists. When you consider this —together with the fact that it is not the antecedent importance of shooting stars, but the importance which they acquire for the first time in the imaginative experience of this poem, that must figure in our evaluation—you see that we cannot simply register disagreement or disapproval, as if we had already made up our minds about this whole class of experiences. It's a new question, and we have to *discover* our opinions by hard thinking. When we get down to the business of moralizing and give serious attention to the implications of ethical ideas, we find that our judgment gets eaten into, becomes qualified by distinctions which do not seem to affect the experience or the criticism of the poetry. Thus, the unpleasant quality in this poem which can, with some license, be called bathos remains what it was, though we have just found a little more justification for Frost's ethics.

Yet I do not maintain that the poem is "amoral." Let us fall back on an analogy. Criticizing the figure of speech in the eighth stanza, I seemed to be saying that it was counterfactual. "On the one side, the rain will extinguish but will not fan a crop of flames," and so on. (Many critics, when they tell us that a certain metaphor is "inaccurate," think they mean that it is not true to fact.) But since the whole idea in the two stanzas, including these lines which I think are the best in the poem, is utterly fantastic, such an objection must be mistaken. Now, the meaning of most words, like 'fan' and 'rain', is derived from a state of fact; but the meaning survives the fact. 'Buccaneer', 'unicorn', 'ether', 'flapper' continue to give us ideas —remind us of things, which either do not any longer exist or never did. This *sense* of the word is carried with it, by a sort of inertia, into sentence structures, where it combines with the senses of other words to give a new total meaning. That meaning is the poet's perception or idea; and it is either good or bad. It would be fine if we understood, as we do not, why the several parts of the idea go together well or badly; but it is something to see that these inner relationships among component meanings are the locus of poetic value. When I seem to be talking about what rain does and what it doesn't do, I am really alluding to the reader's thought: to those implications which the presence of the word 'rain' in this verse will inevitably bring into his mind. And I am asking how that thought agrees with the connotations of the other words in the lines. I am criticizing the idea, not comparing it with fact; for if you look closely at this idea, you will see that it is not fit to be compared with fact—it is logically too muddled to be either true or false. A relationship with fact lingers in the connotation of the several words and determines their combined sense. But the combined connotation does not refer us to fact. You can, for instance, say that meteors shoot or glide; but if you speak of hopping, dancing, or bicycling meteors, you confound the reader. He is not primarily aware of falsity (meteors don't breed flowers any more than they hop or dance) but disturbed by unclarity; he doesn't know what idea he is expected to entertain; and this difficulty of his is indeed an inheritance from his knowledge and experience of fact.

Now the word 'meteor' has connotations of value as well as of fact. If the idea is serious rather than trivial or petty rather than grand, that quality is derived from the value of the *thing*. 'School' and 'church', similarly, get their respective connotations of importance from the importance of school and church. Effects of bathos, as in Baudelaire, are a function of these value qualities in the words, not annulled but utilized by the poetic context:

> Et s'introduit en roi, sans *bruit* et sans *valets*,
> Dans tous les *hôpitaux* et dans tous les *palais*.

So, in Frost's poem, the fifteenth stanza keys us for a thought which the sequel does not provide. We stumble and fall, as at a sudden declivity, and complain afterwards that the wrong sign was posted.[2] But this discordance is experienced as a quality of the poetic design. It is found in the pattern of meanings; it is just what is not found in the naked value judgment, "Fallen planets are a matter of great importance for the life of man." Our criticism of that judgment commits us, as the poem does not, to an estimate of human needs and does not commit us, as the poetry does, to an awaited grandeur of thought and feeling. Good *reasons* for the moral judgment and an adequate *fulfillment* of the pattern of meanings are not the same thing; and it is not by the same act that (in this case) we reject the one and the other. Our aesthetic response is not moralistic; yet it is not by ignoring moral values that we comprehend and judge the poetry, for these values play as experienced meanings, calling back and forth to each other, in the texture of the verse.

2. The fine lines from Baudelaire's *Le Soleil* show, of course, that "bathos" as such is neither good nor bad.

10
Critical
Communication

That questions about meaning are provisionally separable, even if finally inseparable, from questions about validity and truth, is shown by the fact that meanings can be exchanged without the corresponding convictions or decisions. What is imparted by one person to another in an act of communication is (typically) a certain idea, thought, content, meaning, or claim—not a belief, expectation, surmise, or doubt; for the last are dependent on factors, such as the checking process, which go beyond the mere understanding of the message conveyed. And there is a host of questions which have to do with this message: its simplicity or complexity, its clarity or obscurity, its tense, its mood, its modality, and so on. Now, the theory of art criticism has, I think, been seriously hampered by its headlong assault on the question of validity. We have many doctrines about the objectivity of the critical judgment but few concerning its import, or claim to objectivity, though the settlement of the first question probably depends on the clarification of the second. The following remarks are for the most part restricted to meeting such questions as: What is the content of

Read at the annual meeting of the American Society for Aesthetics, Cambridge, Mass., September 1–3, 1948. The author is indebted to Mr. Herbert Bohnert for assistance with this paper. It was first published in *Philosophical Review* 58, no. 4 (July 1949): 330–44, and has been reprinted in William Elton, ed., *Aesthetics and Language* (Oxford: Blackwell, 1954). Reprinted here with permission of the *Philosophical Review*.

the critic's argument? What claim does he transmit to us? How does he expect us to deal with this claim?

A good starting point is a theory of criticism, widely held in spite of its deficiencies, which divides the critical process into three parts. There is the value judgment or *verdict* (V): "This picture or poem is good—"; There is a particular statement or *reason* (R): "—because it has such-and-such a quality—"; and there is a general statement or *norm* (N): "—and any work which has that quality is *pro tanto* good."[1]

V has been construed, and will be construed here, as an expression of feeling—an utterance manifesting praise or blame. But among utterances of that class it is distinguished by being in some sense conditional upon R. This is only another phrasing of the commonly noted peculiarity of aesthetic feeling: that it is "embodied" in or "attached" to an aesthetic content.

R is a statement describing the content of an art work; but not every such descriptive statement is a case of R. The statement, "There are just twelve flowers in that picture" (and with it nine out of ten descriptions in Crowe and Cavalcaselle), is without critical relevance, that is, without any bearing upon V. The description of a work of art is seldom attempted for its own sake. It is controlled by some purpose, some interest; and there are many interests by which it might be controlled other than than of reaching or defending a critical judgment. The qualities which are significant in relation to one purpose—dating, attribution, archaeological reconstruction, clinical diagnosis, proving or illustrating some thesis in sociology—might be quite immaterial in relation to another. At the same time, we cannot be sure that there is any *kind* of statement about art, dictated by no matter what interest, which cannot also act as R; or, in other words, that there is any *kind* of knowledge about art which cannot influence aesthetic appreciation.

V and R, it should be said, are often combined in sentences which

1. Compare, for instance, C. J. Ducasse, *Art, the Critics, and You* (New York: Liberal Arts Press, 1944), p. 116: "The statement that a given work possesses a certain objective characteristic expresses at the same time a judgment of value if the characteristic is one that the judging person approves, or as the case may be, disapproves; and is thus one that he regards as conferring, respectively, positive or negative value on any object of the given kind that happens to possess it." See, further, pp. 117–120.

are at once normative and descriptive. If we have been told that the colors of a certain painting are garish, it would be astonishing to find that they were all very pale and unsaturated; and to this extent the critical comment conveys information. On the other hand, we might find the colors bright and intense, as expected, without being thereby forced to admit that they are garish; and this reveals the component of valuation (that is, distaste) in the critical remark. This feature of critical usage has attracted much notice and some study; but we do not discuss it here at all. We shall be concerned exclusively with the descriptive function of *R*.

Now if we ask what makes a description critically useful and relevant, the first suggestion which occurs is that it is *backed up by N*. *N* is based upon an inductive generalization which describes a relationship between some aesthetic quality and someone's or everyone's system of aesthetic response. Notice: I do not say that *N* is an inductive generalization; for in critical evaluation *N* is being used not to predict or to explain anybody's reaction to a work of art but to vindicate that reaction, perhaps to someone who does not yet share it; and in this capacity *N* is a precept, a rule, a *generalized value statement*. But the *choice* of one norm, rather than another, when that choice is challenged, will usually be given some sort of inductive justification. We return to this question in a moment. I think we shall find that a careful analysis of *N* is unnecessary, because there are considerations which permit us to dismiss it altogether.

At this point it is well to remind ourselves that there is a difference between *explaining* and *justifying* a critical response. A psychologist who should be asked "why *X* likes the object *Y*" would take *X*'s enjoyment as a datum, a fact to be explained. And if he offers as explanation the presence in *Y* of the quality *Q*, there is, explicit or latent in this causal argument, an appeal to some generalization which he has reason to think is true, such as "*X* likes any work which has that quality." But when we ask *X* as a critic "why he likes the object *Y*," we want him to give us some reason to like it too and are not concerned with the causes of what we may so far regard as his bad taste. This distinction between the genetic and the normative dimension of inquiry, though it is familiar to all and acceptable to most of us, is commonly ignored in the practice of aesthetic speculation; and the chief reason for this—other than the ambiguity of the question, Why do you like this work?—is the fact that some statements about the object will necessarily figure both in the explanation and the critical defense of any reaction to it. Thus, if I tried to explain my feeling for the line

But musical as is Apollo's lute

I should certainly mention "the pattern of u's and l's which reinforces the meaning with its own musical quality," because this quality of my sensations is doubtless among the conditions of my feeling response. And the same point would be made in any effort to convince another person of the beauty of the line. The remark which gives a reason also, in this case, states a cause. But notice that, though as criticism this comment might be very effective, it is practically worthless as explanation, because we have no phonetic or psychological laws (nor any plausible "common-sense" generalizations) from which we might derive the prediction that such a pattern of u's and l's should be pleasing to me. In fact, the formulation ("pattern of u's and l's," and so forth) is so vague that one could not tell just what general hypothesis it is that is being invoked or assumed; yet it is quite sharp enough for critical purposes. On the other hand, suppose that someone should fail to be "convinced" by my argument in favor of Milton's line. He might still readily admit that the quality which I mentioned might have something to do with *my* pleasurable reaction, given my peculiar psychology. Thus the statement which is serving both to explain and to justify is not equally effective in the two capacities; and this brings out the difference between the two paths of discussion. Coincident at the start, they diverge in the later stages. A *complete* explanation of any of my responses would have to include certain propositions about my nervous system, which would be irrelevant in any critical argument. And a critically relevant observation about some configuration in the art object might be useless for explaining a given experience, if only because the experience did not yet contain that configuration.[2]

2. I should like to add that when we speak of "justifying" or "giving reasons" for our critical judgments, we refer to something which patently does go on in the world and which is patently different from the causal explanation of tastes and preferences. We are not begging any question as to whether the critical judgment can "really" be justified, that is, established on an objective basis. Even if there were no truth or falsity in criticism, ther would still be agreement and disagreement; and

Now it would not be strange if, among the dangers of ambiguity to which the description of art, like the rest of human speech, is exposed, there should be some which derive from the double purpose—critical and psychological—to which such description is often being put. And this is, as we shall see, the case.

The necessity for sound inductive generalizations in any attempt at aesthetic explanation is granted. We may now consider, very briefly, the parallel role in normative criticism which has been assigned to N. Let us limit our attention to those metacritical theories which *deny* a function in criticism to N. I divide these into two kinds, those which attack existing standards and those which attack the very notion of a critical standard.

1. It is said that we know of no law which governs human tastes and preferences, no quality shared by any two works of art that makes those works attractive or repellent. The point might be debated; but it is more important to notice what it assumes. It assumes that if N *were* based on a sound induction, it would be (together with R) a real ground for the acceptance of V. In other words, it would be reasonable to accept V on the strength of the quality Q if it could be shown that works which possess Q tend to be pleasing. It follows that criticism is being held back by the miserable state of aesthetic science. This raises an issue too large to be canvassed here. Most of us believe that the idea of progress applies to science, does not apply to art, applies, in some unusual and not very clear sense, to philosophy. What about criticism? Are there "discoveries" and "contributions" in this field? It is reasonable to expect better evaluations of art after a thousand years of investigation than before? The question is not a simple one: it admits of different answers on different interpretations. But I do think that some critical judgments have been and are every day being "proved" as well as in the nature of the case they ever can be proved. I think we have already numerous passages which are not to be corrected or improved upon. And if this opinion is right, then it could not be the case that the validation of critical judgments waits upon the discovery of aesthetic laws. Let us suppose even that we *had* some law which stated that a certain color combina-

there would be argument which arises out of disagreement and attempts to resolve it. Hence, at least there exists the purely "phenomenological" task of elucidating the import and intention of words like 'insight', 'acumen', 'obtuseness', 'bad taste', all of which have a real currency in criticism.

tion, a certain melodic sequence, a certain type of dramatic hero has everywhere and always a positive emotional effect. To the extent to which this law holds, there is of course that much less disagreement in criticism; but there is no better method for resolving disagreement. We are not more fully convinced in our own judgment because we know its explanation; and we cannot hope to convince an imaginary opponent by appealing to this explanation, which by hypothesis does not hold for him.

2. The more radical arguments against critical standards are spread out in the pages of Croce, Dewey, Richards, Prall, and the great romantic critics before them. They need not be repeated here. In one way or another they all attempt to expose the absurdity of presuming to judge a work of art, the very excuse for whose existence lies in its *difference* from everything that has gone before, by its degree of *resemblance* to something that has gone before; and on close inspection they create at least a very strong doubt as to whether a standard of success or failure in art is either necessary or possible. But it seems to me that they fail to provide a positive interpretation of criticism. Consider the following remarks by William James on the criticism of Herbert Spencer: "In all his dealings with the art products of mankind he manifests the same curious dryness and mechanical literality of judgment. . . . Turner's painting he finds untrue in that the earth-region is habitually as bright in tone as the air-region. Moreover, Turner scatters his detail too evenly. In Greek statues the hair is falsely treated. Renaissance painting is spoiled by unreal illumination. Venetian Gothic sins by meaningless ornamentation." And so on. We should most of us agree with James that this is bad criticism. But *all* criticism is similar to this in that it cites, as reasons for praising or condemning a work, one or more of its qualities. If Spencer's reasons are descriptively true, how can we frame our objection to them except in some such terms that "unreal illumination does not make a picture bad," that is, by attacking his standards? What constitutes the relevance of a reason but its correlation with a norm? It is astonishing to notice how many writers, formally committed to an opposition to legal procedure in criticism, *seem* to relapse into a reliance upon standards whenever they give reasons for their critical judgments. The appearance is inevitable; for as long as we have no alternative interpretation of the import and function of R, we must assume *either* that R is perfectly arbitrary *or* that it presupposes and depends on some general claim.

With these preliminaries, we can examine a passage of criticism. This is Ludwig Goldscheider on *The Burial of Count Orgaz:*

Like the contour of a violently rising and falling wave is the outline of the four illuminated figures in the foreground: steeply upwards and downwards about the grey monk on the left, in mutually inclined curves about the yellow of the two saints, and again steeply upwards and downwards about . . . the priest on the right. The depth of the wave indicates the optical center; the double curve of the saints' yellow garments is carried by the greyish white of the shroud down still farther; in this lowest depth rests the bluish-grey armor of the knight.³

This passage—which, we may suppose, was written to justify a favorable judgment on the painting—conveys to us the idea of a certain quality which, if we believe the critic, we should expect to find in a certain painting by El Greco. And we do find it: we can verify its presence by perception. In other words, there is a quality in the picture which agrees with the quality which we "have in mind"—which we have been led to think of by the critic's language. But the same quality ("a steeply rising and falling curve," and so on) would be found in any of a hundred lines one could draw on the board in three minutes. It could not be the critic's purpose to inform us of the presence of a quality as banal and obvious as this. It seems reasonable to suppose that the critic is thinking of another quality, no idea of which is transmitted to us by his language, which he *sees* and which by his use of language he *gets us to see.* This quality is, of course, a wavelike contour; but it is not the quality designated by the expression 'wavelike contour'. Any object which has this quality will have a wavelike contour; but it is not true that any object which has a wavelike contour will have this quality. At the same time, the expression 'wavelike contour' *excludes* a great many things: if anything is a wavelike contour, it is not a color, it is not a mass, it is not a straight line. Now the critic, besides imparting to us the idea of a wavelike contour, gives us directions for perceiving and does this *by means* of the idea he imparts to us, which narrows down the field of possible visual orientations and guides us in the discrimination of details, the organization of parts, the grouping of discrete

3. Ludwig Goldscheider, *El Greco* (London: Phaidon Press, 1949), p. 13.

objects into patterns. It is as if we found both an oyster and a pearl when we had been looking for a seashell because we had been told it was valuable. It *is* valuable, but not because it is a seashell.

I may be stretching usage by the senses I am about to assign to certain words, but it seems that the critic's *meaning* is "filled in," "rounded out," or "completed" by the act of perception, which is performed not to judge the truth of his description but, in a certain sense, to *unedrstand* it. And if *communication* is a process by which a mental content is transmitted by symbols from one person to another, then we can say that it is a function of criticism to bring about communication at the level of the senses, that is, to induce a sameness of vision, of experienced content. If this is accomplished, it may or may not be followed by agreement, or what is called "communion"—a community of feeling which expresses itself in identical value judgments.

There is a contrast, therefore, between critical communication and what I may call normal or ordinary communication. In ordinary communication, symbols tend to acquire a footing relatively independent of sense perception. It is, of course, doubtful whether the interpretation of symbols is at any time completely unaffected by the environmental context. But there is a difference of degree between, say, an exchange of glances which, though it means "Shall we go home?" at one time and place, would mean something very different at another—between this and formal science, whose vocabulary and syntax have relatively fixed connotations. With a passage of scientific prose before us, we may be dependent on experience for the definition of certain simple terms, as also for the confirmation of assertions; but we are not dependent on experience for the interpretation of compound expressions. If we are, this exposes semantic defects in the passage—obscurity, vagueness, ambiguity, or incompleteness. (Thus: "Paranoia is marked by a profound egocentricity and deep-seated feeling of insecurity"— the kind of statement which makes every student think he has the disease—is suitable for easy comparison of notes among clinicians and all who know how to recognize the difference between paranoia and other conditions; but it does not explicitly set forth the criteria which they employ.) Statements about immediate experience, made in ordinary communication, are no exception. If a theory requires that a certain flame should be blue, then we have to report whether it is or is not blue—regardless of shades or variations which may be of enormous importance aesthetically. We are bound to the letters of our words. Compare with this something like the following:

"The expression on her face was delightful."

"What was delightful about it?"

"Didn't you see that smile?"

The speaker does not mean that there is something delightful about smiles as such; but he cannot be accused of not stating his meaning clearly, because the clarity of his language must be judged in relation to his purpose, which in this case is the *evaluation* of the immediate experience; and for that purpose the reference to the smile will be sufficient if it gets people to feel that they are "talking about the same thing." There is understanding and misunderstanding on this level; there are marks by which the existence of one or the other can be known; and these are means by which misunderstanding can be eliminated. But these phenomena are not identical with those that take the same names in the study of ordinary communication.

Reading criticism, otherwise than in the presence, or with direct recollection, of the objects discussed, is a blank and senseless employment—a fact which is concealed from us by the cooperation, in our reading, of many noncritical purposes for which the information offered by the critic is material and useful. There is not in all the world's criticism a single purely descriptive statement concerning which one is prepared to say beforehand, "If it is true, I shall like that work so much the better"—and *this* fact is concealed by the play of memory, which gives the critic's language a quite different, more specific, meaning that it has an ordinary communication. The point is not at all similar to that made by writers who maintain that value judgments have no objective basis because the reasons given to support them are not logically derivable from the value judgments themselves. I do not ask that R be related *logically* to V. In ethical argument you have someone say, "Yes, I would condemn that policy if it really did cause a wave of suicides, as you maintain." Suppose that the two clauses are here only psychologically related—still, this is what you never have in criticism. *The truth of R never adds the slightest weight to V*, because R does not designate any quality the perception of which might induce us to assent to V. But if it is not R, or what it designates, that makes V acceptable, then R cannot possibly require the support of N. The critic is not committed to the general claim that the quality named *Q* is valuable, because he never makes the particular claim that a work is good in virtue of the presence of *Q*.

But he, or his readers, can easily be misled into *thinking* that he has made such a claim. You have, perhaps, a conflict of opinion about the merits of a poem; and one writer defends his judgment by mentioning vowel sounds, metrical variations, consistent or inconsistent imagery. Another critic, taking this language at its face value in ordinary communication, points out that "by those standards" one would have to condemn famous passages in *Hamlet* or *Lear* and raise some admittedly bad poems to a high place. He may even attempt what he calls an "experiment" and, to show that his opponents' grounds are irrelevant, construct a travesty of the original poem in which its plot or its meter or its vowels and consonants, or whatever other qualities have been cited with approval, are held constant while the rest of the work is changed. This procedure, which takes up hundreds of the pages of our best modern critics, is a waste of time and space; for it is the critic abandoning his own function to pose as a scientist—to assume, in other words, that criticism explains experiences instead of clarifying and altering them. If he saw that the *meaning* of a word like 'assonance'—the quality which it leads our perception to discriminate in one poem or another—is in critical usage never twice the same, he would see no point in "testing" any generalization about the relationship between assonance and poetic value.

Some of the foregoing remarks will have reminded you of certain doctrines with which they were not intended to agree. The fact that criticism does not actually designate the qualities to which it somehow directs our attention has been a ground of complaint by some writers, who tell us that our present critical vocabulary is woefully inadequate.[4] This proposition clearly looks to an eventual improvement in the language of criticism. The same point, in a stronger form and with a different moral, is familiar to readers of Bergson and Croce, who say that it is impossible by means of concepts to "grasp the essence" of the artistic fact; and this position has seemed to many people to display the ultimate futility of critical analysis. I think that by returning to the passage I quoted from Goldscheider about the painting by El Greco we can differentiate the present point of view from both of these. Imagine, then, that

4. See D. W. Prall, *Aesthetic Analysis* (New York: Crowell, 1936), p. 201.

the painting should be projected onto a graph with intersecting coordinates. It would then be possible to write complicated mathematical expressions which would enable another person who knew the system to construct for himself as close an approximation to the exact outlines of the El Greco as we might desire. Would this be an advance toward precision in criticism? Could we say that we had devised a more specific terminology for drawing and painting? I think not, for the most refined concept remains a concept; there is no vanishing point at which it becomes a percept. It is the idea *of* a quality, it is not the quality itself. To render a critical verdict we should still have to perceive the quality; but Goldscheider's passage already shows it to us as clearly as language can. The idea of a new and better means of communication presupposes the absence of the sensory contents we are talking about; but criticism always assumes the presence of these contents to both parties; and it is upon this assumption that the vagueness or precision of a critical statement must be judged. Any further illustration of this point will have to be rough and hasty. For the last twenty or thirty years the "correct" thing to say about the metaphysical poets has been this: They think with their senses and feel with their brains. One hardly knows how to verify such a dictum: as a psychological observation it is exceedingly obscure. But it does not follow that it is not acute criticism; for it increases our awareness of the difference between the experience of Tennyson and the experience of Donne. Many words—like 'subtlety', 'variety', 'complexity', 'intensity'—which in ordinary communication are among the vaguest in the language have been used to convey sharp critical perceptions. And many expressions which have a clear independent meaning are vague and fuzzy when taken in relation to the content of a work of art. An examination of the ways in which the language of concepts mediates between perception and perception is clearly called for, though it is far too difficult to be attempted here.

We have also just seen reason to doubt that any aesthetic quality is ultimately ineffable. 'What can be said' and 'what cannot be said' are phrases which take their meaning from the purpose for which we are speaking. The aesthetics of obscurantism, in its insistence upon the incommunicability of the art object, has never made it clear what purpose or demand is to be served by communication. If we devised a system of concepts by which a work of art could be virtually reproduced at a distance by the use of language alone, what human intention would be furthered? We saw that *criticism* would not be improved: in the way in which criticism strives to "grasp" the work of art, we could grasp it no better then than now. The scientific *explanation* of aesthetic experiences would not be accomplished by a mere change of descriptive terminology. There remains only the *aesthetic* motive in talking about art. Now if we set it up as a condition of communicability that our language should *afford* the experience which it purports to describe, we shall of course reach the conclusion that art is incommunicable. But by that criterion all reality is unintelligible and ineffable, just as Bergson maintains. Such a demand upon thought and language is not only preposterous in that its fulfillment is logically impossible; it is also baneful, because it obscures the actual and very large influence of concepts upon the process of perception (by which, I must repeat, I mean something more than the ordinary *reference* of language to qualities of experience). Every part of the psychology of perception and attention provides us with examples of how unverbalized apperceptive reactions are engrained in the content and structure of the perceptual field. We can also learn from psychology how perception is affected by verbal cues and instructions. What remains unstudied is the play of critical comment in society at large; but we have, each of us in his own experience, instances of differential emphasis and selective grouping which have been brought about through the concepts imparted to us by the writings of critics.

I have perhaps overstressed the role of the critic as teacher, that is, as one who affords *new* perceptions and with them new values. There is such a thing as discovering a community of perception and feeling which already exists; and this can be a very pleasant experience. But it often happens that there are qualities in a work of art which are, so to speak, neither perceived nor ignored but felt or endured in a manner of which Leibniz has given the classical description. Suppose it is only a feeling of monotony, a slight oppressiveness, which comes to us from the style of some writer. A critic then refers to his "piled-up clauses, endless sentences, repetitious diction." This remark shifts the focus of our attention and brings certain qualities which had been blurred and marginal into distinct consciousness. When, with a sense of illumination we say "Yes, that's it exactly," we are really giving expression to the *change* which has taken place in our aesthetic apprehension. The postcritical experience is the true commentary on the precritical one. The same thing happens when, after listening to Debussy, we study the chords that can be formed on the basis of the whole-tone scale and then return to Debussy. New feelings are given which bear some resemblance to the old. There is no objection in these cases to our saying that we have been made to "understand" why we liked (or disliked) the work. But such understanding, which is the legitimate fruit of criticism, is nothing but a second moment of aesthetic experience, a retrial of experienced values. It should not be confused with the psychological study which seeks to know the causes of our feelings.

NOTE

In this article I have tried only to mark out the direction in which, as I believe, the exact nature of criticism should be sought. The task has been largely negative: it is necessary to correct preconceptions, obliterate false trails. There remain questions of two main kinds. Just to establish the adequacy of my analysis, there would have to be a detailed examination of critical phenomena, which present in the gross a fearful complexity. For example, I have paid almost no attention to large-scale or summary judgments—evaluations of artists, schools, or periods. One could quote brief statements about Shakespeare's qualities as a poet or Wagner's as a composer which seem to be full of insight; yet it would be hard to explain what these statements do to our "perception"—if that word can be used as a synonym for our appreciation of an artist's work as a whole.

But if the analysis is so far correct, it raises a hundred new questions. Two of these—rather, two sides of one large question—are especially important. What is the semantical relationship between the language of criticism and the qualities of the critic's or the reader's experience? I have argued that this relationship is not designation (though I do not deny that there *is* a relationship of designation between the critic's language and *some* qualities of a work of art). But neither is it denotation: the critic does not *point* to the qualities he has in mind. The ostensive function of language will explain the exhibition of *parts* or *details* of an art object but not the exhibition of abstract *qualities;* and it is the latter which is predominant in criticism. The only positive suggestion made in this paper can be restated as follows. To say that the critic "picks out" a quality in the work of art is to say that if there did exist a designation for that quality, then the designation which the critic employs would be what Morris calls an analytic implicate of that designation. (Thus, 'blue' is an analytic implicate of an expression '$H_3B_5S_2$' which designates a certain point on the color solid.) This definition is clearly not sufficient to characterize the critic's method; but, more, the antecedent of the *definiens* is doubtful in meaning. A study of terms like 'Rembrandt's chiaroscuro', 'the blank verse of *The Tempest*', and so forth, would probably result in the introduction of an idea analogous to that of the proper name (or of Russell's "definite description") but with this difference: that the entity uniquely named or labeled by this type of expression is not an object but a quality.

If we put the question on the psychological plane, it reads as follows: How is it that (a) we can "know what we like" in a work of art without (b) knowing what "causes" our enjoyment? I presume that criticism enlightens us as to (a) and that (b) would be provided by a psychological explanation; also that (a) is often true when (b) is not.

Contrary to Ducasse[5] and some other writers, I cannot see that the critic has any competence as a self-psychologist, a specialist in the explanation of his own responses. There is no other field in which we admit the existence of such scientific insight, unbridled by experimental controls and unsupported by valid general theory, and I do not think we can admit it here. (For that reason I held that critical insight, which does exist, cannot be identified with scientific understanding.) The truth is that, in the present stone age of aesthetic inquiry, we have not even the vaguest idea of the form that a "law of art appreciation" would take. Consider, "It is as a *colorist* that Titian excels"; interpret this as a causal hypothesis, for example, "Titian's colors give pleasure"; and overlook incidental difficulties, such as whether 'color' means tone or the hue (as opposed to the brightness and the saturation) of a tone. Superficially, this is similar to many low-grade hypotheses in psychology: "We owe the *color* of the object to the retinal rods and cones." "It is the *brightness* and not the color that infuriates a bull." "Highly *saturated* colors give pleasure to American schoolboys." But the difference is that we do not know what test conditions are marked out by the first proposition. Would it be relevant, as a test of its truth, to display the colors of a painting by Titian, in a series of small rectangular areas, to a group of subjects in the laboratory? I cannot believe this to be part of what is meant by a person who affirms this hypothesis. He is committed to no such test.

Anyone with a smattering of Gestalt psychology now interposes that the colors are, of course, pleasing *in* their context, not out of it.

5. *Art, the Critics, and You*, p. 117.

One has some trouble in understanding how in that case one could know that it is the *colors* that are pleasing. We may believe in studying the properties of wholes; but it is hard to see what scientific formulation can be given to the idea that a quality should have a certain function (that is, a causal relationship to the responses of an observer) in one and only one whole. Yet it appears to be the case with the color scheme in any painting by Titian.

We can be relieved of these difficulties simply by admitting our ignorance and confusion; but there is no such escape when we turn to criticism. For it *is* as a colorist that Titian excels—this is a fairly unanimous value judgment, and we should be able to analyze its meaning. (I should not, however, want the issue to turn on this particular example. Simpler and clearer judgments could be cited.) Now when our attention is called, by a critic, to a certain quality, we respond to that quality *in its context*. The context is never specified, as it would have to be in any scientific theory, but always assumed. Every descriptive statement affects our perception of— and our feeling for—the work as a whole. One might say, then, that we agree with the critic if and when he gets us to like the work about as well or as badly as he does. But this is clearly not enough. For he exerts his influence always through a specific discrimination. Art criticism is analytical, discriminating. It concerns itself less with over-all values than with merits and faults in specified respects. It is the quality and not the work that is good or bad; or, if you like, the work is good or bad "on account of" its qualities. Thus, we may agree with his judgment but reject the critic's grounds (I have shown that the "grounds" to which he is really appealing are not the same as those which he explicitly states or designates); and when we do this, we are saying that the qualities which he admires are not those which we admire. But then we must know what we admire: we are somehow aware of the special attachment of our feelings to certain abstract qualities rather than to others. Without this, we could never reject a reason given for a value judgment with which we agree—we could never be dissatisfied with descriptive evaluation. There must therefore exist an analyzing, sifting, shredding process within perception which corresponds to the conceptual distinctness of our references to "strong form but weak color," "powerful images but slovenly meter," and so on.

This process is mysterious; but we can get useful hints from two quarters. Artists and art teachers are constantly "experimenting" in their own way. "Such a bright green at this point is jarring." "Shouldn't you add more detail to the large space on the right?" We can compare two wholes in a single respect and mark the difference in the registration upon our feelings. Implicit comparisons of this kind, with shifting tone of feeling, are what are involved in the isolation of qualities from the work, at least in *some* critical judgments. I am afraid that as psychology, as an attempt to discover the causes of our feelings, this is primitive procedure; but as a mere analysis of what is meant by the praise and blame accorded to special qualities, it is not without value.

If, in the second place, we could discover what we mean by the difference between the "object" and the "cause" of an emotion, *outside* the field of aesthetics; if we could see both the distinction and the connection between two such judgments as "I hate his cheek" and "It is his cheek that inspires hatred in me"; if we knew what happens when a man says, "Now I know why I have always disliked him—it is his pretense of humility," there would be a valuable application to the analysis of critical judgments.

11

'Pretentious' as an Aesthetic Predicate

I can do little more in this paper than, first, to say what I think the importance of the subject is and, second, to point out what I think are the main difficulties of the subject.

The chief general problem about pretentiousness in art raises itself in this way:

1. 'Pretentious' and 'unpretentious' are words of common occurrence in the intuitive criticism of the arts. And critics, it would seem, have every right to the use of these adjectives. That is to say: these terms do sometimes apply to works of art, if only by extension from their primary social and ethical meanings. Suppose someone has said that a certain work, of sculpture or of fiction, is pretentious. The meaningfulness of such a judgment would seem to be indicated by the fact that we may very well disagree with it. I should think there would be little argument about some of Victor Hugo's prose, certain parts of Thomas Wolfe, some of O'Neill's plays, a good part of Maxwell Anderson, a number of other writers that one might mention; the paintings of Benjamin Robert Haydon; *Wellington's Victory*, by Beethoven; certain large-scale orchestral works by composers like Bruckner, Sibelius, and Shostakovich. I should think people would find themselves agreeing that such works are pretentious. But a well-known critic has spoken of

Read to the Society for Aesthetics, Western Division, Berkeley, 1952, under the title " 'Pretentious' as a Critical Adjective." A typed copy of this paper was made available to the editors by Professor Mary Mothersill.

"the pretentious and bombastic large-scale works of composers like Franck and Brahms." I do not entirely agree with this opinion. On the other hand, in my opinion there is much that is merely pretentious in the writing, both poetry and prose, of T. S. Eliot, and little that is not merely pretentious in the writing of Ezra Pound; but these are not the accepted judgments. The possibility of such disagreement suggests that there is a considerable vagueness and elusiveness in the idea of an artistic pretension; but it also seems to show that there *is* some quality, or some range of qualities, which is so much like a certain unpleasant trait in human character and in social behavior that the same name is properly given to it.

2. Yet, it is hard to see how a work of art can be pretentious. For the term involves the idea of a claim that is not made good. There are two parts to this idea and both are necessary: there must be a claim, and it must be unwarranted. But poems and statues do not state themselves twice over. They do not first say what they are and then show or fail to show that they are what they say. They act all at once and as wholes, putting nothing forward, keeping nothing in reserve. An English philosopher once remarked of the so-called "sense-datum" in perception that it has "all its goods in the shop-window." So does the work of art. The "promise" and the "performance" are identical; but where that is the case, there is neither promise nor performance—there is only the single fact. In an obvious and easy sense of the word one may discover pretensions in a work, say, on philosophy of history—if it announces that it is going to reveal the fundamental laws of history and then fails to do so. There is room for both the claim and the fiasco within the covers of a single book. A similar discrepancy may exist between the preface to a play and the play itself. But the play proper, once it gets started, never pats itself on the back; nor does it make announcements of what it supposes itself to be accomplishing. So how can one decide whether it either claims or deserves such acclamation? How can it be pretentious?

The word 'pretentious' seems to fit the work of art; but the articulated meaning of the word does not seem to fit the *nature* of the work of art, when that in its turn is analyzed and articulated. There is the main problem that is to be considered here.

Before pursuing it any further, I would like to say something about its scope. 'Pretentious' is related closely not only to such terms of rhetoric and criticism as 'pompous', 'bombastic', 'inflated', 'swollen', but also to 'insincere', 'affected', 'false'. 'Insincerity' in turn has been thought (for instance, by such writers as Bosanquet and Katharine Gilbert) to be a synonym for ugliness; and ugliness is by far, despite current neglect, still the greatest and most difficult problem of aesthetics. I must say that I do not see how 'ugly' can be only a synonym for 'insincere'; but even if it were, neither 'insincere' nor 'pretentious' could possibly provide an analysis of 'ugly' while these terms themselves remain even less articulate than the notion of ugliness. That is one reason why I consider that a good analysis of 'pretentious', if it ever were forthcoming, might be of some use to aesthetics. Let us notice one thing more. The present topic is also closely linked with that whole vein of thought in criticism which presumes to compare what an artist has done with what he is supposed to have been trying to do. Recent strictures on the famous "criterion of the artist's intention" are probably well-deserved; yet they do not quash that sense, so often given by bad art, of the presence of the substitute and the counterfeit, qualities whose identification seems to presuppose a knowledge of the original and the authentic. When in a poem we think we see "the will trying to do the work of the imagination," it is certainly not the case that we know what the imagination would have done if *it* had been active and in control of the situation. We simply do not know this. But then what do we mean by saying that the will was *trying* to do this thing which is utterly unknown and has never existed? And when we think we see an artist "straining", by every manner of hint and allusion, portentous tone, or shrieking emphasis, for an effect of deep meaning or grandiose utterance, we are confronted with the same dilemma.

This being the extent and these being some of the ramifications of the subject, I think I may be excused for limiting the following remarks to the one aspect that has been touched upon already.

No doubt there are as many kinds of pretentiousness as there are kinds of claim or pretension; and there are cognitive pretensions, moral, social, political, legal, and so on. Starting from a cognitive pretension like the one in my first example (about the laws of history), we can probably get closer to art by considering certain examples of theoretical thinking where the claim and the performance are not separated but run together. Suppose we have a pamphlet on how to mend socks which begins, "The key concepts on which this whole subject rests are *needle, thread,* and *hole.*" The claim here is not explicit. It is made simply by the use of the phrases "key concepts" and "whole subject" which, on account of their previous history, have a weight and dignity which suggest that the treatise to follow is comparable in difficulty at least to the higher algebra. But the reader may have a different opinion; so he will feel that the author is giving himself airs of importance. We could not instantly analyze this effect into distinct elements, the high claim and the low degree of achievement; but with a little time and care we could do so; there can be no doubt that both elements are present. When we do not attempt such analysis, we remain vaguely cognizant of something we would call a pretentious "tone."

Or consider a passage like this, by a contemporary critic of the arts:

Why did Braque paint these lines . . . which seem to divide the area into little space cells? There is no apparent reason, except the urge to follow freely the subconscious dynamics of visual fundamentals.

This is sciolism, or the pretension to knowledge that one does not have—in this case a knowledge of the psychology of art. The truth is that the author is in a position to say only, "why did Braque paint these lines? Because he wanted to." But big words are more impressive—or so he seems to think.

As a third (and last) example of this quasi-aesthetic pretentiousness, where there is a knowledge claim that does not declare itself as such but makes itself known through the tone, consider this passage from T. S. Eliot:

Keats wanted to write an epic, and he found, as might be expected, that the time had not arrived at which another English epic, comparable in grandeur to *Paradise Lost*, could be written. . . . Milton made a great epic impossible for succeeding generations; Shakespeare made a great poetic drama impossible. . . . For a long time after an epic poet like Milton, or a dramatic poet like Shakespeare, nothing can be done. Yet the effort must be repeatedly made; for we can never know in advance when the moment is approaching at which a new epic, or a new drama, will be possible.[1]

In this passage I think there is a special difficulty. It is (or seems to me to be) ineffably vain and affected. This quality apparently cannot consist in anything but the fact that the writer, really know-

1. ["Milton II," in *On Poetry and Poets* (New York: Farrar, Straus, and Cudahy, 1957), p. 170.—ED.]

ing only that no great drama *was* written after Shakespeare and no great epic after Milton, lays claim, by his *could*'s and *could not*'s, to an immense secret knowledge of laws of art production; which is such, in fact, as the whole human race does not possess and perhaps never will. Now I said that pretentiousness always involves an unwarranted claim; but the converse is certainly not true. One could not say that every honest error, fallacious inference, or unfounded truth claim contained a personal presumption. The determinism of Spinoza—to pick an example from a field in which the human intellect scarcely ever restrains itself from running wild —went far beyond anything that the author had a logical right to affirm; yet the very passages in Spinoza which most confidently proclaim this doctrine have nothing of an immodest or pretentious tone about them. So that to explain the effect of Eliot's remark one goes back and looks for something beyond the sciolism; but that might not be such an easy thing to find. It is a strange double truth that some avowed and outright knowledge claims, which moreover seems to us unwarranted, do *not* sound pretentious; and that some other claims, which are far from having been avowed, do.

But the general point which deserves emphasis here is this: It should be evident from these last examples that *any kind of pretentiousness* can take on a quasi-aesthetic quality and evoke immediate feeling responses. This, moreover, is in agreement with general considerations in aesthetics, which teach us that anything whatsoever can become an aesthetic object. It belongs also under the particular heading, devised and sustained by writers like Shaftesbury, Goethe, Ruskin, and William James, of The Sheer Ugliness of Vice.

The grounds on which we decide that a claim has been made and that it is warranted or unwarranted are, as it were, collapsible: we take them in and react to them without always knowing quite clearly what they are: indeed, it is much easier to make the judgment of insincerity or pretentiousness than to justify it.

Still, if one is interested in reaching a conception of pretentiousness in art, one should try to avoid the complications that are presented by examples which also involve some knowledge claim, personal arrogance, or pretension of the ego. We should, in other words, look for the meaning of a pure feeling claim—a claim solely to aesthetic significance. Many cases of this can be found in works of music, abstract painting, or lyric poetry which are devoid of all other pretensions; and I present two beautiful examples.

A. S. M. Hutchinson's novel, *If Winter Comes*, has a first chapter in which some of the characters are introduced. The second chapter begins:

Thus, by easy means of the garrulous Hapgood, appear persons, places, institutions; lives, homes, activities; the web and the tangle and the amenities of a minute fragment of human existence. Life. An odd business. Into life we come, mysteriously arrived, are set on our feet and on we go: functioning more or less ineffectively, passing through permutations and combinations; meeting the successive events, shocks, surprises of hours, days, years; becoming engulfed, submerged, foundered by them; all of us on the same adventure yet retaining nevertheless each his own individuality, as swimmers carrying each his undetachable burden through the dark, enormous and cavernous seas. Mysterious journey! Uncharted, unknown, and finally—but there is no finality! Mysterious and stunning sequel—not end—to the mysterious and tremendous adventure! Finally, of this portion, death, disappearance,—gone! Astounding development! Mysterious and hapless arrival, tremendous and mysterious passage, mysterious and alarming departure. No escaping it; no volition to enter it or avoid; no prospect of defeating it or solving it. Odd affair! Mysterious and baffling conundrum to be mixed up in! . . . Life!

After this even Thomas Wolfe is a little tame.

Oh, he thought that he could tell her all that could be told, that youth could know, that any man had ever known about night and time and darkness, and about the city's dark and secret heart, and what lay buried in the dark and secret heart of all America.

The interesting thing about such efforts, of course, is the element of unconscious parody. Not only are they reminiscent of certain great passages of literature; but they all recall certain impulses or half-born ideas that we have no doubt all had and which, if they were not forcibly restrained, would have issued in lyrics as dreadful as these. It is no wonder that aestheticians should have believed—though I think mistakenly—in the existence of some antecedent datum or raw matter for art, some *thing to be expressed*, which by capable artists is expressed well and by poor ones unsuccessfully.

At the start it was said, in effect, that we need to discover two things—or else dismiss the use of the word 'pretentious' in criticism as mere licentiousness: first, what the claim is that the work of art can make; and, second, what the grounds are on which the claim is decided. We need, so to speak, to find room within the art object for these two things. The trouble is, as I have implied already but perhaps not made perfectly plain, that we cannot go *outside*, as we do when we make such remarks of ordinary life as, "He claims to have found a cure for cancer, but we can prove that it doesn't cure," or, "He acts as if he were a man of great wealth; but I happen to know that he is penniless." By contrast with cases like these, the place in which we are to find the claim "exposed" is exactly the place in which we find the claim "made"—that is, in the work of art itself. Now it becomes natural to suggest that the two factors which make up the pretentiousness are to be looked for *within* the work of art; that they are to be found in the relationship of part to part or in the relationship of part to whole, or, finally, in the relationship of some quality to the rest of the work. Let us use the word 'element' to denote anything that is either a part or a quality. Now according to the present suggestion: some element in the work creates an expectancy (this is the pretension) which the rest of the work does not live up to (this is the failure).

I am afraid that this (though an interesting aesthetic phenomenon in its own right) will not do as an explication of pretentiousness. First of all, the conditions can be met without pretentiousness. A thing can be a disappointment without being a sham. A splendid introduction to a musical work, arousing the highest expectations of accomplishment in the sequel, remains a splendid introduction when the work has fizzled out. A good first act in a bad play remains that much of a success when the play is over. Aesthetic quality, if at all genuine to begin with, remains genuine to the end, no matter what rubbish it may lead into or be surrounded by. There are people, indeed, who say that *Measure for Measure* is a failure as a play because it fails in its last two acts to bear out the sombre tone of the earlier acts; but nobody questions the merit of the first half. In the second place, you can have pretentiousness even though the stated conditions are not met. For a work can be pretentious throughout. Or without being wholly pretentious, it can be permeated, like certain expressionist paintings, with an exaggerated emotionalism, a note of excess, a facile overemphasis. It is not easy to separate the expectancy and the satisfaction. But perhaps also, so far as this phenomenon is concerned, they do not exist. Perhaps there is only one feeling or one judgment which is simultaneously a perception of claim and of failure. I will touch on this point again before the end.

Yet I think we are on the right track when we discuss the question in terms of elements and wholes. I would now like to make three brief points. First, we can recognize a feeling claim when we do not experience a feeling. This calls for a good deal of explanation; but I do not have time for more than an example. Suppose that I utter the word 'eternal' before you now. I should not think that anybody in the room was particularly moved. Yet there are few contexts into which this word can enter without carrying a sort of inert feeling charge—one which it has, of course, accumulated through its history and usage. It is a word, so to speak, of high denomination: it bears a strong potential of grandiloquence as it lies there in the dictionary. So with 'life', 'death', 'time', and many other words, phrases, and stylistic qualities that one could mention. Now our actual feelings (and this is my second point) may sometimes be touched by fragments—a shred of color, the sound of a syllable, a word, a phrase, or a sentence. But we are also, in the normal aesthetic situation, responding or failing to respond to the concrete wholes of which those fragments are qualities or details. Elements of high positive denomination, gravity, or voltage can be absorbed and canceled in such wholes; and if the effect of the whole is negative, a positive element within it can fail to arouse any actual feeling. But we continue to recognize the feeling *tendency* of the minutest element in the whole: this does register upon us. We may sometimes experience this tendency as a demand that is being made upon us. That is what happens to me when I see or read a play by Christopher Fry: I feel that it is up to me to live up to the occasion. I have this feeling, of course, on account of the poetically charged verbiage. The tones and accents and isolated phrases, if laid end to end, would form a fairly exalted feeling plateau. But since there is no real poetry in the play as a whole or in any extended passage taken as a whole, and hence no "actual feeling" of the kind that is given by poetry, one feels that the mood of exaltation is unwarranted. Or to take a simpler and less controversial example: In a single issue of a weekly magazine I noticed not less than five passages with the word 'eternal': "Great literature deals with the eternal tragic dilemmas of the human spirit." "It is the eternal business of tragedy . . . ," and so on. These sentences, *as wholes*, seem rather stale and tired: their actual feeling value is negative or indifferent. But we cannot ignore the "big" stuff out of which they were made. So we say that the authors were "trying" to be eloquent and impressive and that they succeeded only in being pretentious.

The origins of what I have called the feeling charge or potential of elements which enter into a whole are probably diverse. Loud sounds, large scale, and full orchestration may acquire their charge from the innate responsiveness of the ear or the imagination. But other qualities, and perhaps these too, may have acquired a strong feeling tendency from their resemblance to *really* great artistic qualities or from the use which has been made of them in previous works which have been successful as wholes. In this case we sometimes say that the artist is trying to exploit the prestige value of the accomplishment of his predecessors.

It will perhaps now be granted that we have succeeded in locating, though by no means with extreme precision, one of the two things we were looking for, namely, the claim which the work of art is capable of making. (This "claim" is a *disposition* that we recognize, in some of the elements of a work which as a whole does not move us, to the evocation of high or intense feeling.) What about the other? Where is it that the work lives up to, or falls short of, its pretensions? A partial answer is implied in what I have said already. In a word: *elsewhere*—that is, in other parts or in the effect of the whole. I should think this answer was not wholly wrong. An emphatic tone plus a trivial meaning, a dull idea couched in words which are individually of large import, an elaborate development of worthless material—these are fair examples of what critics mean by pretentiousness.

Yet there is an important qualification to be made. In a truly pretentious work, the pretentiousness is the main and perhaps the sole aesthetic effect. Not seldom it takes up all the space and leaves no room for the perception of anything that is merely poor or mediocre. Let us imagine that upon some weak and incompetent landscape painting there should be superimposed on one side a heroic theatrical figure, badly imitated from the Italian Baroque, who is drawing a curtain and pointing to the scenery in the picture. One would say: much ado about very little. But this, I suggest, is what is *not* typical of pretentious art. One gets no such opportunity to note humble incompetence and compare it with what is elsewhere claimed for it. Instead one is conscious of ambition and display throughout. Now if we are to make *this* phenomenon congruous with the customary sense of the term 'pretentious', we shall have to show how a single quality can have a double function, how it can embody two facts, how a double judgment should be true of it—how, for instance, a flourish of instruments, the gesture of a figure in a painting, can be at once grandiose and (at the same time) empty. Without attempting to show this, I would like to say that I believe it can be shown. For in the case of a highly derivative work, while remaining unmoved by its contents, one notes in them in another direction the endeavor to borrow great and established values. And this is a second fact. But perhaps the relationship is even more intimate. It may be that the existence of a claim to value, as we understood that a few minutes ago, has as a sort of reverse side the absence of authentic value. Pretensions, therefore, would preclude fulfillment simply by pre-empting its field; and we would say that one does not have to add to the idea of a pretension the term 'poor' or 'empty', since it will be entailed by it anyhow.

I fear that this point will have to remain obscure; but in the time remaining I will try to elucidate it somewhat by means of an analogy. 'Pretentious' is a term primarily of social ethics; and wherever else it may be used, it has been borrowed from that sphere. The use of the term in moral discourse can be illustrated by a case like this. If a man wears a colored ribbon across his chest, he seems to be informing us that he is an ambassador. If he is in fact not an ambassador, we shall consider him a fraud—even if there is no calculated intent to deceive but perhaps only the unconscious desire to assume the prerogatives of a certain rank.

The ambassador himself is of course not considered pretentious when he wears his ribbon. The claim is there, all right; but it happens to be warranted.

Ethical criticism, however, operates at many different levels; and someone may come along to raise a question about the manners of castes and ranks. Why should ambassadors wear a special dress? Are they not thereby laying claim to something over and above that specialized function which is signalized by the clerk's eyeshade or the white coat of the pharmacist? And what is this thing to which they are laying claim but social superiority with attendant privileges? Can such a presumption ever be warranted? Ethics, in short, when it considers things in their widest context, may discover that there are some claims which are absolutely and not conditionally inadmissible: which nothing—no merit, accomplishment, status, or character—could ever make good. If I am overbearing, I am not to be chastened only for acting like a lord; for that is a way in which a lord should not act; and if it belongs to the rank to have the right to act that way, then there shouldn't be any lords. People who say of this or that man, "Who does he think he is?"

seem to imply that if he *were* somebody important, his arrogance or conceited manner would be justified. And the implication has this much sense: there are limited, conditional rights and duties in the world, varying with circumstances. The drum major can without rudeness place himself at the head of the procession when the same act would be insufferable on the part of anyone else. In such cases as these people act or think *as if* they were something or somebody; and the justice of their claim is exactly proportional to its truth. But rudeness and conceit are faults in anybody; and it is not hard to see how such a fault would define itself in the behavior of the greatest man in the world. It would define itself in his social relationships, where he is on one plane with a host of equals. The man of genius lapses into his human role when he is dealing with another human being. There he is as one facing another and can only treat that other well or badly. (His skills and acumens, his accomplishments, his record of leadership are so much dead weight, of no use for the purpose. Moral virtue itself—the only basis on which one person can be considered humanly superior to another— cannot figure as a reason for a claim to superiority; for that virtue is precisely what is now in question and is to be proved all over again.) You cannot (whoever you are) talk to a criminal or a child without presuming the one status, the common subjection to the laws of courtesy and reciprocity. That is why a smug man of genius looks exactly like a smug head waiter: the trait is being measured along a social dimension, where the different things *for which* one or the other may be giving himself credit are simply not counted. Or, to revert for a second to the first of my earlier examples, there is a way of saying, "I have discovered the laws of history," which could not be justified even if one *had* discovered the laws of history. In short, though the two words have a common stem, there is no essential connection between *pretensions* and *pretenses*. And so a second person need not know what one is pretending to be in order to identify a pretension of the ego.

Now if in art there are certain qualities of an overwhelming brashness and assertiveness; if these qualities are flatly and absolutely unpleasant; and if they can be compared to the rudeness or ruthlessness of certain actions in practical life—then it should be unnecessary to ask what sort of beauty they are a claim *to* and whether that beauty is actually to be found in them.

It may be just worth saying, finally, that pretentious art, though it cannot be too severely criticized on aesthetic grounds, probably does not deserve any moral rebuke. An aesthetic pretension need not entail or reveal any other pretension whatsoever. Those of us who do not produce works of art do not incur censure. It is hard to see how those who try and fail should be accounted criminals only for doing what the rest of us would almost certainly do if we tried.

12
Superlatives

"Dickens is the greatest of English novelists and one of the three greatest of all novelists."

Judgments which, like this one that I quote, say that a work or an author is the greatest or best in its class may be called superlatives. Besides the problems encountered in the analysis of critical judgments in general, superlatives present certain peculiar difficulties, and some of these I wish to discuss.

On first consideration there is something very dubious and suspect about superlatives. They seem peculiarly inane, and the disputes which they engender, singularly sterile. Superlatives spring from moods of extravagance, and even at the moment when we pronounce something to be "the very best," we hardly take ourselves seriously or are convinced that we are not talking nonsense.[1] We wrangle about such questions to be sure, but no one expects either to persuade or to be persuaded. It is a bandying of aesthetic reactions which ends as it began, with each sticking to his

---

Read at the University of California, Los Angeles, in May 1954. A copy of this paper was made available to the editors by Professor Mary Mothersill.

1. Superlatives have a way of breeding superlatives. 'Matchless sublimity' leads to 'incomparable splendor' and this to 'unique nobility'. And so whole books are made. Read, for instance, any volume of criticism written by the poet Swinburne. "This is a barbarous business of greatest this and supreme that that Swinburne and others practise" (*Further Letters of Gerard Manley Hopkins* [London: Oxford, 1938], letter to A. W. M. Baillie, 20 May 1880).

own opinion. Indeed it is difficult to imagine what it would be to give a serious and systematic defense of a superlative. Good books have been written about the absolute merits of writers and artists, and there are good books which compare artists with one another. But a book devoted to showing that some poet is the best or the worst could hardly be anything but pure gush or pure invective. May we say then that superlatives belong to the controversial periphery of criticism and that they can never claim status as forms of responsible judgment? Surely not; such a ruling would be much too strong, for we think at once of counter-instances. For example, it is my own serious opinion that Dickens *is* the greatest English novelist, and I cannot help thinking that this judgment is sound in the way a critical judgment may be sound, and if sound then it cannot be either inane or groundless. This is the situation that calls for analysis: we feel intuitively that there is something specious about superlatives, and yet it is very difficult to believe that they are radically indefensible. In the following discussion I shall try to account for both these impressions and to show the extent to which each is justified.

I

It is sometimes objected vaguely that superlatives are "meaningless," but this does not accord with our ordinary ways of thinking and speaking. Quite the contrary; it sounds very odd to say that a sentence like "Shakespeare is the greatest English poet" is without sense. The notion of the "greatest" or "best" is not intuitively obscure or puzzling and may be defined without any technical difficulty. Without prejudice to any of the major issues of value theory, we may say that "This is good" is an expression of admiration. And "This is better than that," whatever else it may be, is an expression of preference. "This is the best" expresses the fact that the speaker prefers this to all other candidates. The superlative has a sense which is continuous with the sense of comparative and absolute judgments. Therefore, while there are many problems having to do with the meaning of aesthetic judgments in general, there are no grounds for discriminating against superlatives in particular.

Where then does the difficulty lie? Perhaps it has to do with the problem of justifying or supporting judgments of this kind. The question then would be: Can there be any good reasons for holding something or other to be the greatest or the best? Let us agree once more to limit the range of this question by granting that ordinary judgments of good and bad can be and often are supported by good and solid reasons. Such an assumption is neither artificial nor question-begging. Tastes may be hard to justify; and criticism is certainly no science; but the solidity of appreciative criticism at its best is hardly open to question. No one who has really entered into disputes about tastes, that is, read or practiced criticism, can have failed to find them occasionally profitable, whether or not they be theoreticaly resolvable. But it is just in this context, that is, in comparison with debates about the absolute merits of an author or work, that arguments about who or what is really the best seem fatuous and lacking in substance.

Now since superlatives are a subclass of comparative judgments, we may consider whether there is not some generic weakness which they inherit. Let us consider some of the arguments which have been advanced in the effort to show that while absolute judgments are legitimate, comparative judgments are not. Most familiar perhaps is the claim that comparative judgments are baseless because different works of art are fundamentally incommensurable. But can we really believe this? Isn't it as certain as anything can be in this subject that if Dickens is good he is better than Edgar Wallace, since Wallace is bad? And notice that no one objects to this. People who raise a cry of "incommensurable magnitudes" if you presume to compare Dickens with Balzac are quite content to let you say that Dickens is better than Wallace, and that his novels are more valuable than an ugly old beer mug. But what is the difference? It is simply that Dickens and Balzac are somewhat comparable in value. But to compare Dickens with his immediate peers is surely not different in *principle*. It is only a closer decision and therefore all the more critically intelligent and worth making. I do not wish to suggest that there are no difficulties involved in the conception of commensurability; there are. But if these are to be dealt with successfully, they must be seen in relation to such obvious elements of practical criticism as those I have mentioned.

A second objection rests on the contention that comparative judgment presupposes that we have techniques for the quantitative measurement of aesthetic value; but (it is argued) we do not have such techniques, and therefore comparative judgments are pretentious and empty. In reply to this objection it must be admitted that a good many of our judgments of comparative value are phrased in quasi-quantitative terms and that if we were challenged to give some interpretation of these we should be quite unable to do so. But our manner of speaking in such cases is the result of carelessness. Notions of rank and of magnitude were impressed on our imagination by early experiences of heights and weights, amounts of food, speeding cars, and orders of authority. When we turn from these objects to experiences of quality and value, we slackly transfer our notions of quantity: this is not even figurative thinking but simply the path of least effort. We hear "tremendously good jokes" and attend "infinitely moving performances." We say that one author is "much" greater than another or even "ten times as great." Perhaps you have had, as I have, the experience of reading a play by Molière with pleasure yet with a sense of disappointment. Fame and reputation are measurable magnitudes; and so one had come to expect that a "great" comedy, on which a thousand chapters had been written, should be at least a thousand times more hilarious than a good Broadway farce. Distorted notions of greatness thus enter the mind by natural channels. It is not to be supposed that a literal meaning can be found in every such use of the terminology of comparison. We cannot assume before analysis that the most innocuous concept of rank (as "first-rate," "third-rate," "tenth-rate") corresponds to anything in the aesthetic situation—much less that there are "measurable distances" which separate mediocre authors from "vastly" greater ones.

If it seemed worthwhile, we could delete all vague and metaphorical suggestions of quantity from our judgments of comparative value and resolve to restrict ourselves to saying that one thing is better or worse than another. These concepts may be vague and subject to misuse, but we regard them as unimpeachable. And if some works or art are better than others and can be shown to be so (which no one doubts), then there are no grounds for skepticism about superlatives. Some works are better than any others of their class for reasons that are there to be discovered and announced.

II

At least part of the difficulty with superlatives arises not from any inherent peculiarities but rather from certain more or less accidental characteristics. We are likely, for example, to be rather unguarded and irresponsible in pronouncing such judgments. Talk is cheap; and people may say what they please when there is noth-

ing to be lost by doing so. There must be at least twenty slow
movements that one has called the greatest of all, each time disregarding the other nineteen simply because one was not then
listening to them. To reflect on what we have said and heard in
company is enough to account for our impression that opinions
about supreme greatness are not worth much. Moreover, we have
no great incentive to be responsible about superlatives. Our interest
in this sort of question has few external supports. Who cares what
the greatest work of art in the world may be; and why should anyone care? Absolute judgments are compelled from us by individual
experiences; if we never express them, we should be making them
all the same. Comparative judgments must be ventured by collec-
tors, critics, anyone who is asked to recommend a movie to a
friend. But we are not forced to think of all novelists or all painters
together. When we are asked to say what three books we would
take to a desert island, we know that this is only a game. There is a
motive for the discussion of the *summum bonum* in ethics; for
this, once defined, can be set up ahead of us as an ideal; but there
is no such preconception of an artistic greatness toward which
an artist or anyone else might steer. It is no wonder that questions
of supremacy should remain a theme for idle discourse.

A more important fact, and one which affects all questions of
comparative value, is this: that we are often not sure of our preferences. If the works we are asked to compare are unfamiliar, or if
we have never thought of comparing them before, we are apt to be
unsure. Just as you may say of a work newly confronted, "I don't
know whether I like it or not," so, given two definite likings, you
may not be able to extract a preference from them; for comparison
is a new situation.[2] After a moment's thought or renewed examination you may know what you prefer to what else. But there is
no guarantee that this will happen. It may be that a thorough
understanding and appreciation of two works may leave you still
undecided as to which to prefer. And this may happen when the
question is one of supreme preference. We may be unable to say
which poet is the "greatest" because we find that we have no preference as between Homer and Shakespeare.

2. The balancing of defects and merits in a poem, to reach a judgment of value "on the whole," involves some kind of neural integration.
That is one reason why one may, for a time, not "know" what one likes.
But two aesthetic reactions must, similarly, be integrated before a
preference can emerge.

When a person is indecisive or indifferent with respect to a question of preference, he may express this feeling (or perhaps attempt to conceal it) by raising the question of commensurability. Being unable to decide whether Homer is better than Shakespeare, he may ask: "How can you compare them?" "How is it possible to speak of any single poet as 'the greatest'?" It is hard to know what to make of such questions, because, as was noted in the preceding section, the people who ask them are not usually consistent. The man who finds it improper to ask whether Homer is better than Shakespeare may be willing to say without hesitation that Homer is better than Marlowe and Shakespeare better than Hesiod. Of course we must admit the possibility that there is no single highest place, that the highest place is, so to speak, a plateau. Indeed it may be that there is an inherent upper limit to artistic greatness and that this limit has been reached any number of times already. But if this were the case, we should have no reason to think it absurd to speak of "the highest place."

There is a further point which bears on the general question of preference. Works of art are related to each other as better and worse, but they are reciprocally diverse in value as in other respects. A great tragedy is certainly better than a mild joke; but that is not the only difference between them and may not be the most important one. They differ in *quality*, and whatever the success of future logicians and psychologists in defining degrees of merit, it is likely that there will remain a qualitative residuum. "The world of values" might be compared (inadequately, to be sure) to a space in which bodies as different as clouds and marbles, spread out irregularly in all directions, execute the oddest configurations. The universal eccentricity of shape and texture and motion does not keep them from being one and all at relative distances from a single baseline; it only contingently hampers the comparison and measurement of those distances. But these essentially comparable distances need not be a major or interesting feature of the supposed universe. So, too, there are more interesting things to be said about a group of poets than that one, Byron, ranks somewhere "between" two others, Milton and Swinburne.

I suspect that, in the natural hostility of men of letters to the notion of a strict order of merit, a strong factor is the feeling that the kind of value is more important than the degree or amount. Now this feeling will be increased if very great men should be the objects of comparison. Suppose that the greatest masters of some art are clustered close together in our estimation. Then to say that one is greater than the rest will seem to some people not only futile but invidious. In fact, 'second in rank' will sound like 'second-rate'—as if a positive derogation were implied.[3]

In summary: Superlative judgments are continuous with comparative judgments and with respect to questions of meaning and justification present no peculiar difficulty. They may be well founded and correct in whatever sense value judgments are well founded and correct. We are likely to view superlatives with suspicion (a) because they are used carelessly and seem relatively unimportant, (b) because we are often undecided about our preferences including our supreme preferences, (c) because we are often more concerned with qualitative differences in works of art than we are with their comparative value.

III

Good criticism is not solely a matter of correct judgment. This is required, to be sure. A work of art must possess the merits ascribed to it and what is said to be superior must be found to be so. But beyond this, criticism should be *fruitful*, should lead us back to the aesthetic object with sharper perceptions and a deeper understanding. Now judgments of comparative value, for reasons I shall presently examine, may be correct without being fruitful, and superlatives are peculiarly liable to this defect. Let us consider what is involved in giving reasons in support of a comparative judgment, taking as our model the so-called absolute judgment. In the case of the latter, the reasons which we provide analyze the object which is judged. They are statements of fact; they describe or interpret qualities that the senses have discovered in the work of art. The aesthetic experience, which is like a swift pulsation, becomes shredded into moments of perception and feeling; for criticism is a discursive procedure, which takes things up seriatim. The critic's reasons are, however, *connected* by way of direct reference with the handiwork of the artist: in other words, when we talk about art, we are thinking about art. They are also connected with the critic's sensibility; for it is his purpose in writing or speaking to bring out not just anything that he may have noticed

3. Dylan Thomas, having been asked by a member of one of his audiences who the greatest living poet was, replied, "What is this—a contest?" In this one remark, by a man who no doubt has definite opinions as to who were the foremost poets of his day, lies the entire complex of apprehensions that have just been reviewed.

but whatever it is in the work that he takes to be particularly good or bad. So we may say that the critic's reasons are in direct relation with his sense of what is enjoyable. Aestheticians have tried to clarify this double relationship; and we need not go over the ground. In the paradigm *A is good because it is x and y*, the minor clause is an "aesthetic reason" inasmuch as it stands in certain relations both to aesthetic quality and to feeling.

Now suppose that a man has *compared* two objects and decided that *A is better than B*. We might think that, to support his judgment, he should make some statement of comparative quality, such as that *A has more of x and y and less of the unpleasant quality z.* (I shall call statements like this one "comparative reasons.") Suppose, for example, that he likes a picture by Lautrec because of the sharpness of contour in the profiles. If there is another picture that he thinks is better still, should he not extend his original reason, that is, show that the second has *more* of what made the first picture good? This cannot be right; it sounds odd to say that the second picture must have still sharper contours, if only because we know that a man may prefer to a Lautrec some painting which contains no faces or contours at all. And yet we continue to feel that the critic should discover something of the kind; some point in which the two pictures are related as more and less, to correspond with the preference that has been expressed. And so, perhaps, we retreat to higher levels of abstraction and cite such phrases as 'a tighter metrical scheme', a 'stricter control of sensuous imagery', 'a more forceful characterization', or 'a greater seriousness'.—But I think that it can be shown that our entire preconception in this matter has been mistaken.

No work of art that is better than another need be *more* than that other in any further respect. Pitch, tempo, sharpness, brightness, and a good many other qualities certainly exist in degree; and there are critical observations which take advantage of the fact. "A little more red on this check." "A slower pace in the slow movement would have been better." "Bring this shoulder forward and set the wall farther back." These remarks have clear comparative meanings. But they do not express a preference for *more of what is already found good.* On the contrary, to suggest "more red" is exactly like suggesting a spot of green in place of red. This is especially clear when the original quality has been judged positively bad and, again, when a slight change of quality makes a great difference in value. One often invokes concepts of degree in any known dimension as a way of indicating the *right* quality, any alternative to which would be *wrong*. This is like advising someone to move over a few inches so as not to fall off a cliff.

If the terminology of comparison can be thus employed in behalf of some judgment of sheer merit, it is also true that comparative valuations are supported by notations of the sheer presence or absence of certain qualities. Even if a few degrees of some quality should be found correlated with degrees of value, as when the performance of a piece of music gets worse and worse the more it "drags," that would have no general import. A 'tighter metrical scheme' would still connote superiority just in that one instance, when the two qualities are being compared. If a still tighter scheme, which might well be a dreadful error, be placed on the other side, then 'looser' becomes the term of praise.

To find comparative reasons for comparative judgments is always, or almost always, impossible. It is also unnecessary. For consider: When we examine a single object critically, we sometimes find that our judgment changes from "dull" to "interesting" or from "bad" to "good." If such a *reversal* can be effected by noncomparative criticism, then surely by the same means we can come to think something "exciting" that before was only "interesting." The enjoyment changes in degree without any perception or statement of degree in the object. And when a work is found exciting, it may be preferred to something to which it was not preferred before. Comparisons instigate us to a double effort of perception, by which the "real" qualities in each object are brought to light. And we reach such conclusions as that *A is better than B because A is l, m, and n, while B is r, s, and t.* This is the typical mode of expression for judgments of comparison. Consider the following examples:

Sober as is the ceiling of the Sistine Chapel, its view of man still retains a youthful hope of redemption, but the Last Judgment is hopeless, sinister, vengeful. The power of the ceiling has turned to vehemence, the movement to strain, the sorrow to bitterness. However great the Last Judgment, it has not the clarity or the universality of the ceiling.[7]

Kreisler's tone . . . is silken, his technique and intonation clean,

7. Everard M. Upjohn, Paul S. Wingert, and Jane Gaston Mahler, eds., *History of World Art* (Oxford: Oxford University Press, 1949).

his phrasing simple and in good taste; but his playing is without the vitality and sparkle and style that are in Szigeti's performance.[8]

It appears now that the judgment of comparative value, which expresses a preference for one work over another, is justified by a conjunction of statements about qualities. This is exactly what we should expect from considering the kind of experience that is involved, namely, an experience first of one thing and then of another. There is no such thing as an aesthetic experience of "moreness," upon which a composite judgment of value could be based. And no aesthetic quality stretches across two objects to yield a joint or blended verdict.

If 'better' has a greater force than 'good', then, that must come just from the fact that two sets of absolute qualities have been criticized and at least two reasons given. But it follows from this that there will be something in the justification of a comparative— namely, the conjunction itself—that does not connote an aesthetic quality, and does not express an aesthetic enjoyment of its own; in short, that is not an "aesthetic reason." The only aesthetic reasons are the component ones, which are just what would be said to support the judgment "good" or "bad." Comparatives are removed by a step from the experience of art: one has a new thing to say when one says that *A is better than B;* but one has no new datum to base it on. We should therefore expect to find criticism which is comparative rather thin and pallid—merely "opinionated"—save insofar as it gets substance from the absolute perceptions on which it rests.

Comparisons, however, considered as mental acts, are propaedeutically significant even at the first level of criticism. Many fresh individual perceptions and, with them, new absolute judgments are drawn from comparisons in which objects serve each other as foils, making us aware of qualities in each which we ought, in principle, to have seen without their juxtaposition. We know Balzac better for having compared him with Stendhal· we come to a new and finer opinion of his merits. Though the reasons given for a preference can be resolved into statements of absolute quality, it does not follow that only the same absolute reasons will be found in the comparative situation that would have been found otherwise.

8. Bernard H. Haggin, *Music on Records* (New York: Alfred A. Knopf, 1941).

I do not go so far as to admit that a comparison, conscious or latent, is a factor in aesthetic pleasure. We find critics, who have been struck by some effect in poetry, casting about for inferior phrasings that the poet might have used, just to make the reader feel the edge of the phrase he did use. They *first* see, *then* look for ways of making others see. This suggests that the comparison is only a device, an aid to perception, which can then do without it, and not an essential thing in the experience. But it is interesting in itself, and useful in the study of superlatives, to see how often comparisons are instituted and controlled by the desire to reach judgments of absolute merit. Objects are not plucked out of the air that we may decide what is better than what else. And critics do not, like psychologists, care to establish systematic rank orders for the members of certain classes. Apart from rivalries and jealousies and other practical motives, two works will be selected for comparison because someone thinks that by likeness and contrast each can throw a light on the other.

This possibility of embodying new absolute perceptions in the comparative judgment gives it a redeeming weight and body.

IV

If preferences are not supported by comparative reasons, supreme preferences are not supported by superlative reasons. There are no aesthetic qualities which exist in supreme degree in the greatest works: indeed nothing is altered in the work or in our opinion of it by the fact that there are other works too. We discover the highest merits in the same way that we discover minimal merits; though to *call* them the highest merits is to presume that we have examined many other works. Hence there is no special brand of critical reasoning that is addressed to the justification of superlatives. They are justified simply by a series of comparisons, which in turn rest on the inspection of individual works. That is all, and it is enough.

The superlative, like the comparative, is without roots of its own in the aesthetic earth. But, unlike the comparative, it can claim little incidental utility in improving our primary perceptions. One does not see more in an object for comparing it with a host. Not that it is of no use, in judging a work of art, to know a great many others; but this utilization of "background" is quite a different thing from the successive comparisons to which we are prompted by the pressure of the superlative. Moreover, the term 'best' has a baneful disposition. It sends us hunting through the annals of art for examples which might challenge its inherently general claim. We pick up name after name and try them out as possible exceptions. If the genre or class is a large one, this of course spreads our thinking flat and leaves no time for criticism. What is the sense of starting a minute comparison in points of detail when the assertion, on the face of it, is that one work is superior to *all* others? And so superlatives do not make for good criticism. Yet this must be qualified: sometimes the superlative judgment proceeds from a comparison of two works whose rivals have been eliminated by previous comparisons. In that case critical argument can be mature and rational; and, since the discussion of great works is naturally rewarding, this can be the mostinteresting kind of criticism.

In conclusion: I have tried to account for the rather mixed feelings we have about superlatives. I have defended them as fundamentally warrantable judgments and have argued that those who question their status invoke a notion of "incommensurability" which is at the very least confused. My account of reasons which justify a preference has been designed to show that superlatives have the weakness but not the strength of comparatives, and to suggest why it is that, despite their legitimacy, superlatives are customarily shallow and barren. In calling attention to the limitations of the superlative, I do not wish to leave the final impression that it is useless or trivial. Such judgments are after all important. Supreme value is conceded to some artists by consent; and social arrangements rest on this concession. Whole journals and whole courses are devoted to the greatest men while lesser authors are merely "surveyed." We do not argue about Shakespeare's standing not because it is not arguable but because it is agreed upon. If a new figure such as Joyce or Picasso should come to the fore, the verdict of criticism becomes a thing of some consequence. Practical decisions follow from it. We have, in principle, the same kind of reason for spending great energy or great amounts of money on the study of a great author that we have for bothering to read a good one.

PART III

*Ethics and
Moral Psychology*

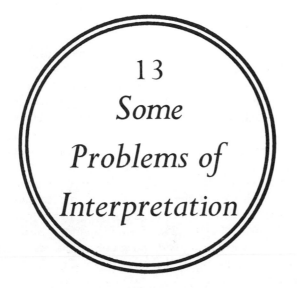

13

Some
Problems of
Interpretation

INTRODUCTION

The study of human thought embraces at least these three kinds of
work: (*a*) interpretation, (*b*) explanation, and (*c*) criticism or
evaluation.

a. Always we have before us a speech, a book, a monument, a
record of thought or action. This text must be understood. Sometimes, as when we read a newspaper article in our own language
or as when specialists discourse in a technical terminology, the
understanding presents no difficulty. But sometimes it is necessary
to expound, translate, paraphrase, decipher, condense, or summarize, in short, "explain the true meaning"; and those who do this,
though they may bear such other titles as editor, translator, or
textual critic, are one and all interpreters.

b. Every text has a background in personal psychology, literary
or scientific tradition, social history, the national class membership
of its author; and there are those who interest themselves in investigating relationships between this text and elements in this
background. This kind of study is termed "genetic" and sometimes
also "contextual"; and it is here mainly, of course, that the various
doctrines about the causation of ideas—psychoanalysis, historical

---

Read at the Aspen Conference on Chinese Thought, 1952, under the
title "Aspects of Intercultural Communication." Revised and published in Arthur Wright, ed., *Studies in Chinese Thought* (Chicago:
University of Chicago Press, 1953). Here reprinted with permission.

materialism, sociology of knowledge, history of ideas—endeavor to apply themselves.

We may describe it as the ideal of genetic study to explain ideas through their causes. But, for any purpose I hope to accomplish in this paper, it will be unnecessary to insist upon a very strict conception of causal explanation. Any example of loose and general relevance between a work of the mind and various items in its background (such as might be found almost anywhere in Parrington or in Van Wyck Brooks) will serve us well enough.

c. Clearly it is part of the study of ideas to determine not just their contents and their antecedents but their truth or falsity, aesthetic merits, general significance for human life, special values and disvalues. This is criticism; and those considerations which have, for a critic, some bearing on the value of an idea may be called its "domain of verification."

This threefold division, not of labors but of kinds of labor, is the tritest but still the most useful framework for the study of ideas that one could propose.

Among these three processes interpretation certainly does not hold the final or sovereign position; on the contrary, we interpret a text for the sake of the criticism or the explanation which, we assume, is to follow. But interpretation is, by all odds, the central part of the study of ideas and the one on which everything else depends; for it would seem that we can neither criticize nor explain without first understanding what it is we are speaking about.

The lines between interpretation and explanation, between interpretation and evaluation, are thus speciously clear: interpretation comes first; explanation comes later and goes backward to causes; evaluation comes later and goes forward to reasons. But in truth the case is not so simple. The earliest phase may be in certain ways dependent on the later ones; the fields merge, or overlap, or variously partake in each other. In contemporary thought (for example, Mannheim's) it is suggested that even genesis and validity are not such distinct dimensions as had been previously assumed. This paper will, in fact, consider only such problems of interpretation as have been created by the mutual entrenchment of these processes on each other, the indistinctness of the lines of division between them. We may expect to discover a situation of which the following analogy provides a sketch. Psychologists divide the response system into three parts: a receptive process, a connective process, and an effective process—we look, then we think, then we act. But on closer examination it appears that each phase has all three phases within itself. In "looking," for example, the position of the eyeballs produces sensory signals which determine perpetual readjustments of the eyeballs. So with "thinking," which incorporates subtle sensory and motor processes. So with "walking," which incorporates sensory and associative processes. It is convenient to retain the rough division of phases for the description of human responses on the gross scale; the finer analysis does not conflict with this scheme. So, I would suggest, the rough demarcation of the idea from its causes on the one hand, its validating reasons on the other, will sustain itself on one level, notwithstanding the minute interconnections which may reveal themselves on others.

A problem *in* interpretation is one which reflects some doubt as to the meaning of a text: it is the sort of problem with which interpreters are faced. What is it the poet means just here? How shall this Chinese phrase be rendered in English? Of these two strains of thought, which is predominant in this author? Does he mean this seriously, or is he being sarcastic? These are examples of the ways in which problems in interpretation tend to couch themselves.

A problem *of* interpretation is (or will be so understood here: I do not recommend the general observance of this distinction between 'in' and 'of') the sort of problem which confronts the semanticist, logician, or student of general linguistics who wishes to understand the interpretative process. Interpretation, as we have noted, is not always problematical; and, even if it were never so, people would still raise questions about the nature of interpretation. But it will be convenient for us to assume that a problem of interpretation has some special connection with the *doubts* of the interpreter; it is, in other words, a question about the proper method of solving some class of problems in interpretation. Such questions belong, therefore, to the methodology of the interpretative disciplines; and, in contrast to the examples listed above, we may cite such questions as these: What degree of equivalence, as between a translation and its original, it is reasonable to demand or to hope for? How do we judge such equivalence? What, in other words, is a relatively "faithful" translation? Does a text have a single meaning, fixed by the author, which it is necessary to ascertain? How shall we know when we have reached this meaning?

How, if at all, can a knowledge of the tradition to which a work belongs clarify the contents of that work?

Problems of interpretation are not foisted upon honest scholars by a set of scheming methodologists. Practicing interpreters seem to be impelled, by the material in their hands, to the development of some theory or principle of method; one could examine a roster of eminent interpreters without finding one name that was not identified with some conception of interpretative procedure.

But though the interpreter is inevitably led over into questions of method, it is another question whether he can ever find his way out of them and still another whether it will have profited him to have been for a time so beguiled. And we have to ask: What value would the solution of some problem of interpretation have for the practice of any craft? Could we "apply" it, with increased prospect of success, to the interpreter's problems as they come along? Or would it leave him where he was, dependent for his achievement not on any conception of method but on his intuition, experience, and skill?

It would be easier to frame an answer to such questions if we could point to some outstanding problem of interpretation the solution to which was known. We could then see whether this solution had some lesson or implication for the practice of interpreters. But the truth is that the art of interpretation has by far outstripped the theory of interpretation. We have, for instance, accurate translations; we do not have any clear conception of the meaning of accuracy in translation. It is therefore hard to say whether such a conception, if we did have one, could or should make life simpler for the translator. In default of such an ability to demonstrate the pertinence of methodology, I can only give voice to the *opinion*, which does however seem to me to be plausible, that no method, and no theory of interpretation, will ever relieve the interpreter of the need to settle his problems by the use of nice judgment in the individual case. At the present time, certainly, methodology can do no more for him than to make him aware of the kinds of decision he has to make and the sorts of factor which enter into his decisions. I attempt no more in this paper than to mention some of these sorts and these kinds.

In presenting some issues in the theory of interpretation to the reader of this volume, I have to make one further assumption: that the differences between one language and another, one intellectual tradition and another, are not such as to prevent some of the same problems from arising for the interpreter of each. Distance is always a matter of degree. Chinese thought and language are no doubt different from English; but Joyce's thought and language are different from those of Pound and of Yeats, who are also different from each other. There must be some works of ancient Chinese art which are clearer, or more accessible, to American students of that subject than are the most recondite contemporary poets to their best students. If one insisted that every difficulty in interpreting Chinese were uniquely characteristic of that field, one would not know where to stop short of saying that there were no general problems of interpretation, recurring in two or more places; and that would seem to be absurd. It is more reasonable to postulate a certain continuity among differences in thought and language, assuming that, while indeed there are problems peculiar to each subject, there are also some which repeat themselves everywhere.

INTERPRETATION AND EXPLANATION

Let us then suppose it may prove to have some slight relevance to oriental studies to consider closely the situation in which we find ourselves when we read a passage from a work relatively near to us in time and space. I am thinking of a single sentence from Thoreau's essay on "Resistance to Civil Government": "That government is best which governs least," together with some of the remarks which follow: "This government never of itself furthered any enterprise, but by the alacrity with which it got out of its way. *It* does not keep the country free. *It* does not settle the West. *It* does not educate . . . ," and so on. A doctrine is stated here. This doctrine belongs to the field of abstract political theory. It was taken up, as we know, by persons called philosophical anarchists, as being similar to their own tenets. Philosophical anarchism is a theory with a universal reference; that is, it is meant to apply to human society as such, regardless of special conditions. If Thoreau's views are an example of such a theory, they will naturally provoke a *criticism* of a very general type. Abstract considerations of human nature and social organization will be in order; so will particular questions about any society we may care to think of. We shall feel it entirely proper to ask, for instance, what would happen to the life of modern cities if they were to have no government at all or only a very weak one. And if Thoreau's views, so interpreted, are to be *explained*, we must ask ourselves how a doctrine of anarchism could have sprung from the soil of mid-nineteenth-century New England.

How did Thoreau come to think as he did? It is sometimes

pointed out that his mentality was a product of the primitive American Republic, with its expanding frontier, its pioneer spirit, its predominantly agrarian society, its Jeffersonian politics reflecting the interests of that society, its laissez faire capitalism operative in some degree both in practice and in theory. I do not propose to consider the adequacy of such explanations, that is, the ability of the specified conditions to account for the individual thought of Thoreau. But there is no paradox whatever in the fact that conditions as limited and specialized as these should give rise to a political doctrine bearing the stamp of those conditions, yet universal in its intended scope and reference—any more than in the fact that certain cosmological theories in Greece should have reflected the structure of the city-state yet should have been theories about the world and not about the city-state.

Yet, in Thoreau's case, an investigation of his background will surely make us begin to wonder whether our original interpretation of his ideas was correct—whether they are indeed quite such an abstract and general version of anarchist philosophy as we thought. As it happens, the purely literary context is sufficient to modify our opinion, for Thoreau says: "To speak practically and as a citizen, unlike those who call themselves no-government men, I ask for, not at once no government, but *at once* a better government." But the external context also has a bearing, for the conditions of nineteenth-century America not only influenced Thoreau to think as he did but were also borne in mind by him as he wrote; he counted on his readers to bear the same conditions in mind and insert his thoughts, as it were, into that setting. Some of the conditions of his thought were, in short, also objects of reference in his thinking. In that case his meaning becomes more particularized than the meaning of the words as they stand on the page. His libertarian principles were asserted, in view of some of the experienced benefits of individualism, against a government which supported slavery and imperialism; and whether they were also intended as general principles of political theory is a question that cannot be judged apart from that special reference. The Mexican War—one of the two great immediate evils in the eyes of Thoreau—was one in which the role of government was secondary to that of the sturdy individualist. The slaveholder also professed himself an advocate of weak central government. Phrases about "strong government" and "weak government" do not discriminate between such positions and that of Thoreau—who would, perhaps, have hailed any strong federal government which had undertaken to abolish slavery. It is, of course, possible for a writer to be inconsistent, confused, and careless about the implications of his words, or (in any of a dozen senses) "not really mean what he says." But we wonder whether Thoreau can have been oblivious of such discordances as those I have just noted; and we come, perhaps, to propose to ourselves an interpretation which trims the meaning of some of his words. "That government is best, at least in some times and places, which interferes as little as possible with some activities, which I could specify, of some kinds of men, whom I could name."

There is, at any rate, an option here for the interpreter of Thoreau. The circumstances of his time may set a man thinking and instigate him to the promulgation of a universal doctrine. On the other hand, those same circumstances, taken as a setting for that doctrine, may curtail its intended significance and application. The point is that this option has been created, and indeed enforced upon the interpreter, by contextual knowledge; so that background factors which seem at first to have a purely genetic significance turn out to be engrossed in the very text whose "origins" we thought we were exploring. It is not difficult to show, in general terms, how this comes about. When two people who are engaged in communication have common objects in their environment—as a husband and wife may have their dog and as Thoreau and his readers had the basic issues and institutions of their time and country—they can rely on the awareness of these objects to supply a larger or smaller part of the ideas which they are exchanging and do not need to have the exact meaning embodied in their speech. One can say, "The animal is sick," meaning specifically this dog; and Thoreau can say, "That government is best which governs least," meaning just that certain functions of the American government should be restricted in certain ways. When one can really count on the presence of these surrounding circumstances to fill out or specify one's meaning, one's speech is not so vague or ambiguous as it might seem to a person who had only the speech before him. But later times are apt to be in just that position and, in order to understand what was said, must try to reconstruct the situation of the writer. The need for this effort, and its usefulness to the interpreter, will vary according to the document or the passage. Scientific treatises tend to disclose themselves pretty fully to one who understands merely the language in which they are

written; and the context of a scientific doctrine is something superadded to its content. But anyone who, though not at all puzzled
by the language of political writings in the seventeenth century,
has felt himself to be in the dark as to their import until he could
know just what persons and parties they were written against,
what those persons and parties stood for, with what or whom the
authors in turn affiliated themselves, and so forth, will not question
the merits of contextualism as a philosophy of interpretation.

But these merits can be exaggerated and can become a source
of confusion. When the historian Taine said that "to comprehend
a work of art, an artist, a group of artists, we must represent to
ourselves with exactitude the general state of the spirit and cus-
toms of the time to which they belong," he was taking the verb
'to comprehend' in two ways: first, in the way in which we speak
of comprehending the Northern Lights or the growth of population, that is, to explain through its causes; second, in the way we
speak of understanding Stravinsky's music or a poem by Rimbaud,
that is, to know what it says or contains. The program called for
the causal explanation of literature, in keeping with the deterministic assumption of Taine that works of the mind were "products,
like sugar or vitriol"; and it is, indeed, for his failure to provide
sufficient explanations that Taine is usually criticized. But the program sought for itself the extra credit of being the means of clarifying literature and of providing canons of interpretation. Now
we have conceded, or even insisted, that historical knowledge can
illuminate literature. But this—an incident or a by-product of the
historian's mission—should not obscure the difference between
the nature of a thing and its causes, the meaning of a text and its
background. A writer can refer to things which do not form part
of his own background at all: historical research may be largely
wasted if we are trying to clarify this part of his meaning. And,
conversely, circumstances which have had a material influence on
the formation of his personality may be unknown to him or, if
known, not even remotely alluded to in his writing.[1] The historian

1. Of course there are many moot cases. A famous one is the question
whether we can say there is an "unconscious" allusion to an Oedipus
complex in *Hamlet*—granted that we have any reason to attribute an
Oedipus complex to the author and to suppose that it was a genetic
factor in the creation of the play. But, to bring out the difference between meaning and background, we should look to the clear-cut case:
an Oedipus complex might have played a part in turning a man away

is interested primarily in things which do not enter into the sense of a passage; the interpreter, primarily in things which are not found among its antecedents. Many texts (e.g., treatises on the stars) show no overlapping whatever between meaning and background; and our attention is called to entirely different things when we investigate one and the other. When we do touch upon background factors which are significant also for interpretation, we are taking them two ways over: first, as related existentially to a person's thought and, second, as part of what he is thinking about. The same *fact* belongs to two classes, but this does not mean that the classes are not distinct.[2]

Any given portion of historical context will have unequal values as applied to the purposes of interpretation and explanation. Thus I should think that the general history of Thoreau's time is rather more useful to us in clarifying his position than in showing why he took it; while psychogenetic factors, if they were known, might have a different kind of utility.

A slack historicity in interpretative criticism, contenting itself with some formula about the "need to see every work in its place in the tradition," ignores its own controlling motives. When the over-all purpose is interpretative, history will function as a moment within that broad intention. The interpreter will make short excursions into the historical background, selecting items for notice through an implicit sense of their relevance to the meaning of his text. When the aim is basically historical, quite a different

---

from his father's occupation to the study, say, of geology; it has, therefore, causal or genetic significance; but it will probably not show up, even in the faintest way, as an object of reference in the work on geology.

2. A short and pointed example may be useful here. When, in Victor Hugo, a Spanish grandee, who with some of his fellows is about to be executed in the presence of the king, refuses to take his hat off and remarks—

> "Oui, nos têtes, O roi,
> Ont le droit de tomber couvertes devant toi!"—

and a footnote tells us, "A Spanish nobleman had the traditional right of standing with his head covered before the king," we admit that the historical fact is helpful, without it the play on words, on which the whole effect of the lines depends, would be lost. But does it have to be a *fact*? Might it not as well have been a legend, or an invention of Hugo's, so long as the *idea* of such a traditional right somehow gets framed for consideration by the audience along with the explicit sense of the lines?

emphasis is shown; and certain questions in interpretation will be raised as minor incidents in the prosecution of that aim.

Establishing the general principle of contextual relevance does nothing to simplify the problems of the interpreter; it simply exposes areas in which there are decisions for him to make. Contextual relevance has its limits, beyond which the genetic method becomes either useless or baneful to the interpreter. And let us say, first of all, that there are limits to the plasticity of the text.

What sort of context could compel us to interpret Thoreau as advocating absolute government? What kind or amount of external evidence would force us to read "that government is best which governs least" as meaning "that government is best which governs most"? Suppose we found Thoreau, elsewhere in his life or in his writing, admiring contemporaneous absolute monarchies or dictatorships. We would say that he had changed his mind, that he contradicted himself, or that he was ambivalent in his political attitudes. We would say that there were "conflicting strains of thought" in his work. We would say that he was speaking of different things (as Marxists speak of a *provisional* dictatorship and an *eventual* anarchy). We would say any of these things before conceding that the right interpretation of the passage in the text was the reverse of the apparent one. There is something fixed and rigid about the words and their public usage, though there is something else that is not rigid but variable with the complementary context. The purely linguistic content has a gist which contextual study can modify but which cannot be twisted at liberty into any shape proposed.

A Japanese colleague with whom I once shared an office would sometimes enter when I was there and say, "Please don't make trouble." I could easily interpret this: "Please do not trouble yourself on my account." One could hardly—apart from codes in which, by secret agreement, familiar words are given wholly arbitrary meanings—encounter a greater reversal of the apparent meaning by the true meaning, a greater difference between what a man "says" and what he "means." And, since I was able to effect the reversal by knowledge of the speaker's character and probable intention, it becomes tempting to say that the true sense is what the author intends. But one then forgets that the words as uttered, in their common public American connotation, did after all lend themselves to the "correct" interpretation; the probable intention did fit in, however awkwardly, with the words as spoken. Scholars working on literary texts which have for the most part public conventional meanings find special choices posed for them among possible alternatives (that is, readings which fit the text); and in these circumstances they may declare, for good reasons or bad, that the author's sense is the true or decisive one. But lifting this out of situation and framing it as a naked rule of interpretation, which might apply automatically to any case, they convey the preposterous suggestion that an author who had written "Cats eat mice" could by his own say-so make it mean "Three two's are six." This is to overlook the need for the dovetailing of internal and external evidence, the weighing of kinds of evidence one against another. The recognition of this need will reduce any overweening claim for the "uses of history" and provide in its degree the justification for those who say that, life being short, they wish to get what they can from art and philosophy, directly confronted.

There is a principle of diminishing returns in the application of knowledge. Appreciative understanding does not grow in exact correspondence to the growth of contextual information; and the interpreter must know when and where to stop—he must separate the extrinsic facts which help to reveal the sense from those which encrust and conceal it. Let us consider an extreme example. One of Balzac's heroes, prowling through an antiquary's shop, scans object after object with reflections similar to these: "A salt cellar from Cellini's workshop carried him back to the Renaissance at its height, to the time when there was no restraint on art or morals, when torture was the sport of sovereigns; and from their councils, churchmen with courtesans' arms about them issued decrees of chastity for simple priests."

This manner of engrossing the context of a work in its meaning is a perpetual temptation to the historically minded; but—apart from Balzac's particular errors of fact and of taste—it is really *un*historical, since it assigns a meaning which could not have been shared by the artist and his contemporaries, who, being at no distance from themselves, had no way of enjoying the pathos of distance.

Like a stone or a flower, in which the naturalist sees whole volumes of natural history written out, a work of art can "speak" to the historian of anything which, however remotely, has entered into its composition. It is not improper to speak of the "meaning" an object possesses in virtue of its relations to other things; but this is certainly not the same as the thought contained in and conveyed by works of the human mind. In the example from Balzac the mistake is obvious, since a work by Cellini makes no statement about the "Renaissance luxury" of which it was a product. If one could always draw as sharp a line, the discipline of interpretation would be less taxing than it is. But when, for example, we think we see a whole system of Christian theology in the *Disputà* of Raphael, we may be thinking of historical elements in the painter's background which lead up to and more or less explain the presence of certain visual forms on the wall; or we may be apprehending further and higher ranges of significance, of which the visual forms have been set down as vehicles. In all probability, we are doing something of each. The artist has rendered a conception of theology, to which the history of that subject is the only clue but which is nonetheless present in the painting. But he has not put into the painting everything which pedantry can spell out of it, down to the last letter of every work by St. Augustine of St. Jerome. It is surely very difficult to decide what "belongs" and what does not; but such decisions must be ventured, lest, on the one hand, such a work seem poorer to us than it is or, on the other, we confuse our appreciation of our own historical knowledge with an appreciation of the work we are interpreting.

INTERPRETATION AND EVALUATION

It would seem that interpretation should be complete before criticism can so much as get started. Yet it is easy to show that criticism can function as a moment within the interpretative process. We need only consider a remark as common, among interpreters, as this: "If he meant what he seems to be saying here, he would not only be wrong but inexcusably so. But we know from the rest of his work that he is an intelligent man. He could not have committed an error like this. He must mean something else." The argument here is complicated, employing different sorts of premises; but one of the reasons for rejecting a certain hypothesis as to the author's view is the interpreter's own opinion of the absurdity of that view. Such a rebound from criticism to interpretation could be illustrated in divers ways. A first guess as to the sense of the text starts us thinking about the truth of that text, so interpreted; and the result of that appraisal sends us back to the text for a surer understanding. Criticism is then resumed from this new interpretation. Following the suggestion of the last section, we could, then, reach a view of the functions of interpreter and critic which might be epitomized in the phrase, "Broad difference in principle; minute interrelations in practice."

The ravings and maunderings of mental patients have, it is said, a "meaning" for the student of psychology, as do other worthless products of the human mind—advertisements, convention speeches, and the like. And so also the poorest or most ordinary products of the Chinese mind may attract the interest of the Sinologist, for whom they have a "value," symptomatic or documentary. One understands very well, for instance, why a historian should feel impelled to study astrology, a subject in which he personally cannot take any stock. The sterner devotees of an objective scholarship, who say it is not their business to say what they think about other people's ideas but only to say what those are and how they came to be what they are, have a good deal of reason on their side. Anyone who countenances a general distinction between interpretation and criticism must admit that the latter can, ideally, be dispensed with. No criterion of value is assumed merely in selecting a thing for study. The Four Gospels, the dialogues of Plato, and the Confucian writings, which must seem to any impartial reader to be documents of great intrinsic interest and merit, have also been thought to be such by thousands or millions of Europeans and Chinese; and this historical importance, which they share with poor stuff like the works of Hitler and of Alfred Rosenberg, is enough to recommend them to the historian.

Yet one supposes, after all, that one motive for studying China is the appreciation, perhaps the appropriation, of its positive achievements, in science, art, philosophy, and government. But this presupposes a principle of selection, an ability to tell the difference between what is valid and what is spurious or indifferent. In the end it is difficult, and not particularly desirable, for men to refrain from criticism.

The assertion of the right to criticize is, however, hedged about with epistemological problems of such depth and intricacy as to have defied solution from the time of Protagoras to the present day. Some of these can be couched in a perfectly general form. They show up, without noticeable variation, in the philosophy of science as well as in ethics and aesthetics or in comparative religion as well as in political theory; and they are exemplified just as well by a difference of opinion arising between two colleagues working side by side in the same laboratory as by the difference in outlook between a dervish and a mathematical statistician. But others seem to present themselves with a peculiar force in the criticism, say, of art or of moral philosophy; or they appear as obstacles to the criticism, in particular, of distant cultures. A scholar who would not, on account of the difference in sex or station, hesitate to criticize the opinions of his wife or his congressman would consider it madness in himself to presume to evaluate the beliefs of the Hopi or the ethics of an ancient Chinese thinker. And this not merely for contingent reasons—the relative lack of information and concrete insight into a foreign body of thought, the need for exceptional caution in procedure—but for fundamental ones, such as a sense of the unfairness in the act of judging a body of thought by norms of cognition which it does not itself recognize, a fear of the distortion which would seem to be inherent in the imposition of one's own categories of truth and value upon one who had never dreamed of such categories.

The student is caught between the need, and the very nearly irresistible impulse, to determine the validity of the ideas he is examining and the objections which tell so powerfully against any attempt on his part to do so. I could not hope, in the space of this article or in a dozen like it, to resolve such an impasse. But our subject is interpretation; and I would like to point out that there is a mutual exacerbation of the critic's troubles and the interpreter's when we shift their responsibilities one onto the other. The result is a vaguely desperate feeling about the inaccessibility of foreign modes of thought, a feeling which prevents the truly troublesome questions of epistemology from ever being clearly posed.

I. A. Richards, in *Mencius on the Mind*, asks:

Can we in attempting to understand and translate a work which belongs to a very different tradition from our own do more than read our own conceptions into it? ... Can we maintain two systems of thinking in our minds without reciprocal infection and yet in some way mediate between them? And does not such mediation require yet a third system of thought general enough and comprehensive enough to include them both? And how are we to prevent this third system from being only our own familiar, established tradition of thinking rigged out in some fresh terminology or other disguise?[3]

3. *Mencius on the Mind: Experiments in Multiple Definition* (London: K. Paul, Trench, Trubner & Co., 1932), p. 86.

It will be noted that the question has to do solely with the understanding of the foreign work. Yet, particularly in the third sentence, it is stated in a way which reminds us of those who feel that, to avoid lapsing into a complete relativism, it is necessary to find a neutral and impersonal set of standards for *deciding* between our own views and those of people who disagree with us. In other words, the question is modeled upon a problem of epistemology.

Let us suppose we had two human minds that were, to begin with, as different as possible in all their manifold expressions. How could one of these undertake first to understand and then to evaluate by its own lights the contributions of the other while still doing them complete justice?

For convenience we might confine the question to ideas about nature. There is a point often made about the basic concepts of the natural sciences which I think also holds for those ordinary concepts which are represented by the vocabulary of a language. It is a commonplace of logic textbooks that basic concepts in a science are to be rated by their heuristic value—as productive and useful, or sterile and obstructive, rather than as true or false. Thus the concept "mammal," which groups the whale and the bat together with cats, rodents, and so forth, and separates them from the fishes and the birds, is not in any way truer than the ideas of sea, air, and land animals, but is better, in ways that I need not explain, as a foundation for zoölogy. But the propositions in which such concepts, good ones or poor ones, occur will be true or false. Thus, if you have perversely chosen to call the whale a fish, then to say that all fish lay eggs will be false.[4]

Now the concepts represented by the average man's vocabulary —dog, cat, sit, stand, walk, red, green, blue, and so on—constitute, like the concepts of natural science, a grouping and selection of the phenomena of nature. The formation of those concepts is not, as in the case of the sciences, dictated by or responsible to explicit goals of predictability, system, and order. Yet there is a general resemblance in the fact that our ordinary concepts were influenced in their growth by practical needs, by emotional and aesthetic factors, by motives of convenience, simplicity, utility, and by accidents of all kinds; that no one set of them has any kind of exclusive legitimacy; on the contrary, that many different sets may exist

4. See M. R. Cohen and Ernest Nagel, *An Introduction to Logic and Scientific Method* (London: Routledge; New York: Harcourt, Brace, 1940), pp. 223–24.

side by side without logical conflict. Thus, to make up an example at random, we might well imagine that some group of people should have no concept corresponding to the English 'shadow'. It is hard to believe that any people living under the sun should not sometimes have noticed shadows; but recalling the fact that in some painting no shadows are found at all while in the works of the painter Braque the side of the pitcher which is turned from the light, instead of modeling into the third dimension, becomes a flat area of dark color contrasting with the lighter side, we can well understand that shadows might to some people seem not interesting or important enough to deserve a separate name as a class. Perhaps they are comprehended together with other things under the word for "dark spot." Now imagine further that someone should attempt a translation into such a language of an English text containing the word 'shadow'. Such a person, to be competent, would have to be a bilinguist; and this means that he knows the meaning of a word like 'shadow', as well as the words in his own language, through seeing its use in dozens of literary contexts, its application to hundreds of experiences in daily life, its definition in the English dictionary by means of other English terms the meaning of which he already knows. In other words, he knows the range of objects which this word denotes; and he knows it is not the same as that of his word for "dark spot"; so he is able to say, "We have no exact equivalent for the English 'shadow'." His ability to say this presumes an understanding of the English word. The ability to speak about the difficulties of translation, about the perils of crossing the gap between an ancient author and ourselves, presumes an achieved identification of the interpreter with the mental process of the subject, a vantage point from which he can belabor distorted readings. No "third system" of concepts is either possible or necessary. He will perhaps in a roundabout fashion and using many words attempt a construction of the concept "shadow" out of the concepts his language already possesses. If instead of "shadow" you will think of psychological or religious concepts or think of the translation of metaphors and puns from a language as close to ours as German, you will readily admit that the position just described is one in which translators really do find themselves. Now it seems to me that the real difficulty of communication, and the real danger of distortion, exists at this level of exchange of concepts. To say that two people "live in different worlds" is to say, very largely, that the world is carved up and organized differently by their respective systems of concepts; and to say that one "imposes" his own categories on the other is to say that he assumes for the other's concepts meanings which are readiest at hand and most familiar to him in his own thought and language. There then often follows a glib "appraisal" in terms of truth or falsity. But it does not follow from this that, if one *had* achieved precise understanding of the other mentality in its own terms, one would *still* be in no position to evaluate its ideas. One thing is to understand the word 'shadow', to learn the extent of the limits of the idea, to overcome the strangeness of having to pick out a class of phenomena never before noticed as a class. But to be able then to judge the truth of propositions concerning shadows, their causes and effects, their increase or diminution with various kinds of lighting, is a matter of plain experimental verification, of which in principle any human being is capable.

I have been trying to meet an objection to intercultural criticism which stems from a confusion between communication and judgment. No doubt there exist more sophisticated and formidable objections. It may, for instance, be urged against the foregoing paragraphs that "concepts" and "propositions" are not so easy to keep separate, since a given concept, say, of human nature may reflect or incorporate a whole battery of previous convictions. But even if the foregoing analysis were wholly acceptable, it still is restricted to ideas of natural science, both the understanding and the appraisal of which are—by comparison with art, politics, religion, and metaphysics—exceptionally plain and simple. Since the meaning and validity of ethical judgments are as such in dispute among professional moralists, there is a double risk and temerity involved in the evaluation of alien systems of ethics. Such difficulties I must leave undiscussed, but with the suggestion that to clear up problems of interpretation first and take up problems of judgment later would probably be a useful procedure everywhere.

14

Natural

Pride and

Natural Shame

You can reasonably take pride in strength, beauty, or intelligence; but you cannot reasonably be ashamed of the corresponding defects.

I

There is a "pride" which is *identical* with the possession of a certain gift—like the proud bearing of the race horse, which is nothing but vitality itself, or like the pride which the birds take in flight. Pride is immanent in the prance of health and of intelligence, as in the employment of any talent or skill. More, the exercise of a natural faculty can be censured as a piece of insolence: the mere enjoyment of the body or the mind takes you across the limits of what someone, rightly or wrongly, considers your proper sphere. To kick up your heels in exuberance is to fling sand in somebody's eyes. To wear bright clothes in the vicinity of a funeral is to offend the mourners—who may resent the very existence of a healthy person as an insult to the dead. The frolics of Panurge and of Pantagruel—entirely apart from the state of mind which shamelessly extols them—are an outrage to the god or man who, in Spinoza's phrase, "rejoices in our want of power." Living is an affirmation and can be taken as an affront.

Such pride might nevertheless be reasonable; but such pride is hardly pride. To pride yourself on a quality means something

Philosophy and Phenomenological Research 10, no. 1 (September 1949): 1–24. Reprinted with permission.

more than just to have that quality: it implies at least a reflection upon it. A good posture, for instance, is a pleasure in itself; but to *know* that your posture is good is a distinct, a superadded, pleasure; and this consciousness betrays itself, by a slight change, in the posture itself. (Pride is a "swelling." The proud man "swaggers" or "struts." He is "bursting" with pride. And so forth.) So also to be beautiful is to exercise the power of attraction. Beauty brings admiration, and admiration pleases. But to be proud *of* one's attractiveness (or one's riches, one's birth) is still another thing. On this basis Hume distinguished between pride and joy. To have or to get some thing which you desire is joy. But in pride there is something more—the recognition, the thought: "I have this thing." There is a reference to self and to the attainments of self. Pride is the reflex sentiment which accrues with the consciousness of what is already an advantage.

Now, what are the qualities of which we are proud? They are qualities, first, which are considered desirable; and there is no quality deemed desirable the possession of which cannot be a source of pride.[1] But in the second place it might seem to us that they are qualities by which we win, or believe that we win, social admiration or approval. On this view we are at bottom proud of nothing but a certain standing in the eyes of others. But this social thesis must be rejected, for the following reasons.

It is one thing to receive from society one's standard of good and evil, which determines what is approved even to oneself, and another thing to crave the approval of society. An approved good is one thing; the good of approval, another. No one will deny that the approbation of one's kind is an important object of desire and, in

---

1. "Every valuable quality of the mind, whether of the imagination, judgment, memory, or disposition; wit, good sense, learning, courage, justice, integrity; all these are the causes of pride, and their opposites of humility. Nor are these passions confined to the mind, but extend their view to the body likewise. A man may be proud of his beauty, strength, agility, good mien, address in dancing, riding, fencing, and of his dexterity in any manual business or manufacture. But this is not all. The passion, looking further, comprehends whatsoever objects are in the least allied or related to us. Our country, family, children, relations, riches, houses, gardens, horses, dogs, clothes; any of these may become a cause either of pride or of humility."—Hume. There is only one thing to be added: that the *opposites* of all these qualities and relationships could also become objects of pride if the notion of what constitutes a "valuable quality" shifted sufficiently.

consequence, a source of pride; that it figures to the exclusion of everything else in the love of eminence, rank, decorations, social status; or that this motive may be inextricably mixed with any pride of achievement whatsoever. But a normal person wishes to be esteemed for those attributes which he esteems. The artist and the scientist demand applause on their own strict terms. The shallowness of those who exult in empty praise is inexpressible, for they have sacrificed every other standard and have no longer a conception of what it is good to be honored *for*. Besides, there are people who, having proudly rejected the toleration of society in behalf of some notion of good, are supported in their intransigence by no one but a few dead authors, who cannot make their pleasure or displeasure felt. If the social thesis is to maintain itself, then, it must fall back on the prior influence of society on the very standard of value. It must assume that every taste and desire, from the love of money to the love of music, is created purely by the application of social sanctions; more, that the objects of taste and desire (and of conscience and emotion) *still*, in some definable sense, symbolize approval and disapproval and derive their whole value from what they symbolize. Here, of course, it is supported by a selection of the available facts, because some people have no reason for believing or valuing anything except that it is believed or valued by somebody else and, if they go to the stake, do so because they would rather defy the ruler than disobey a deceased parent. But (to establish only the minimal point) it is impossible to concede that we are primordially sensitive to nothing but the reactions of those around us. If there are natural desires which convention cannot eradicate, there may be latent but ineradicable standards of what is desirable. One thinks, for example, of a woman who "accepts" but violates the code which prescribes permanent virginity for unmarried women. Since she has done what she thinks undesirable, she is ashamed; but since she has done what in spite of herself she may "think" desirable, she is proud—as Héloise was. Even if such an instinctive basis for judgments of value, skulking beneath the conventions, be denied, there is still the rational plane above them: and the rationalist, who *thinks out* his criticism of society and its standards of good and right, may well be proud of himself and of what are, according to his lights, his virtues and achievements. This shows that we are proud when we have what we value, whether society agrees with us or not. And this point is independent of any theory which should hold that there are radically individualistic values, totally uninfluenced by the existence of a social environment.

We can also dispose of the closely related question of *comparative* advantages. We do not doubt that it is gratifying to be first in the competition—wealthiest, handsomest, foremost in anything. Some societies encourage such comparison by distributing their rewards on a competitive basis, as for example in athletics. But that does not mean that one may not equally reflect with pleasure on absolute qualities, such as agility, and on qualities, moreover, which many people have, such as health.[2]

The definition of pride, then, has three parts. There is (1) a quality which (2) is approved (or considered desirable) and (3) is judged to belong to oneself. A word about (3). Even if there were something logically peculiar about judgments one makes concerning oneself, if they did not have the same standing as judgments we make about other people, if they were not formulated and tested by the same procedures that another person uses when he makes a judgment about us, still this sort of peculiarity would have no relevance for any of the issues to be discussed below. Those issues would be illustrated just as well by the fact that you have a good batting average or a long bibliography, which anyone else can see as well as you can, as by the fact that you have a warm heart, which, according to some philosophers, you can know when other people either cannot or do not know about it. The fact that one is both the subject and the object of all judgments concerning oneself does introduce exceptional opportunities for error and distortion. Because a certain quality, such as genius or popularity, is considered valuable, I am tempted to impute it to myself when I do not in fact possess it. And because a certain quality, such as blondness or horsemanship, happens to belong to me, I am disposed to value it much too highly. Hence, innumerable varieties of "false" pride (as well as "false" modesty, "false" humility, and so on). Yet we need not, after all, go to examples of judgments concerning self to discover motives which give rise to illusion: there are forces in the self which distort our perception of many other objects than

2. I do not agree with Hume, who says that "goods, which are common to all mankind, and have become familiar to us by custom, give us little satisfaction." See the whole passage in *Treatise*, vol. 2, part 1, chap. 6. Pride, for Hume as for Hobbes, is *essentially* emulous and invidious.

the self. We deceive ourselves about many things besides ourselves
—and for reasons which are, for a theory of cognition if not for a
minute psychology of judgment, essentially similar.[3]

Pride, from the psychological standpoint, is pleasure taken in
the possession of some quality that one deems valuable—and there
is the clue to the position of this paper. A *genuine* and *reasonable*
pride, from the ethical standpoint, will depend on a comprehensive
and just sense of values.

Now "gifts" are not the basis of pride that "achievements" are.

At first sight it does not seem difficult to distinguish between
gifts and achievements. Achievements are the result of purpose and
effort. I am in no way responsible for the good looks I may have
inherited from my mother or the vigor transmitted by my father;
so I am said to "deserve no credit" for them. Yet it must be the
intention of this remark not to deprive me of all credit whatsoever
but to insist only that such credit should be *less* than the credit
accorded for traits of character or acts of will, and should be
different in quality, as honor, reverence, and admiration are different one from another. For, in a more radical sense of the word
'gift', is not everything in the end a gift? Who gave me talent or
kindness or heart, magnanimity, courage, the capacity for self-
discipline and self-development? Not I myself. The aptitude for

3. The concept of the *ego* seems to contain, first, the normal or regular
set of values in its totality; second, a special set of values which can be
described as the need to associate the first set (more exactly, the positive values in the first set) with oneself; and third, the set of judgments
which either do or do not predicate those values of oneself. (Each of
the three variables is determined by factors both of heredity and of life
experience.) By specifying constants under each head and introducing a
few notions of relationship from general psychology, it should be possible to derive from these terms all the ego concepts, like modesty,
vanity, complacency, self-love, self-reproach, self-pity, and so on—
except for those which, like conceit, smugness, arrogance, self-abasement, seem to belong as much to ethics as to psychology and involve
the application of moral norms by the observer—and to construct a
priori models for any typical state of the ego. This would also seem
to be a suitable conceptual base for an empirical theory of the ego, that
is, a set of laws which, with particular statements of fact, would yield
the whole range of ego phenomena. Needless to say, we do not envisage
the rapid success of such a project, since (to mention only the most
obvious impediment) our scheme presupposes that whole idea of self
which is built up from the earliest perception of body and surrounding
world. Yet it should be of heuristic value to recognize that the mysterious ego dissolves on inspection into a system of functions.

learning is not learned, the ability to acquire is not acquired. My acts are dependent on my will as my stature, for instance, is not. But my will—what is that dependent on? Some people are endowed with the desire for improvement as others with beauty or strength of body; and one is not at bottom more praiseworthy than the other *if it is a question of ultimate responsibility for what one is and does.* It is true that my character has been more deeply affected than my appearance has by decisions which I have taken in the past; but does that explain why it should be more seriously praised or blamed? Does a scoundrel become more lovable if we find out that his character was inherited? It is true, again, that the world is interested not in promise but in performance, and that an element of striving and practice is bound to enter into performance. But beauty and force of body are precisely the exceptions (or nearly so), the cases where the finished performance is turned out effortlessly; and it is hard to see why that should be held against them.[4]

Here we hit upon what is really meant when we discriminate, as moralists, between natural advantages and moral achievements. We mean that certain qualities are humanly more valuable than certain others. We are venturing a judgment in ethics and not in genetics. The will is praiseworthy and blameworthy where the torso is not, not because it had something more to do with creating itself but because the will is the will and the torso the torso. Just as we put taste and musicianship above mere tone in a singer and ability above glamor in an actress, so size and strength and physical charm are inferior to wisdom and moral perfection; and we are not really interested in distinctions of origin as between these things—

4. The "natural advantages" are, in fact, the "god-like" qualities which people envy more than they praise. But god-like too are moderation, serenity, poise, the "health of the soul," every quality which makes for happiness. And I draw no distinction in this essay between these latter and the further catalogue of "social" virtues, like justice and generosity; for that would be to recapitulate the argument of the *Republic* and raise the whole question about the identity of the right and the good. I assume here that the kind of person one is most disposed to honor would be the kind of person one would care most to be; in other words, that there is genuine inconsistency or conflict between values when one is *grateful* and *reverential* toward Socrates, Christ, or Lenin but *envious* of Napoleon or Rockefeller. The notion that we are indebted to the greatest of men for having *sacrificed their own good* is an interesting commentary on our own conception of good; but it finds no support in the teaching of those men themselves.

though such distinctions can of course be made. We are not the less grateful to Mozart for the prominence of the congenital factor in his ability; and if there were a man who acted wisely and justly on instinct alone, we should not withhold a jot of praise. If a woman, on the other hand, is known to have acquired her beauty by hard labor, we do not think any the better of her for it; because the attribute of beauty is consistent with her proving a bane both to herself and to everyone she may know. Some credit, it is true, is given to people who have won their health back by their own efforts or made their own money by arduous toil. But that is because industry and effort are, as it happens, valuable qualities on their own part. Between a man born crooked and one who achieves crookedness there is really nothing to choose.

I shall continue for convenience to refer to qualities like beauty and strength as "gifts" and to qualities like wisdom as "achievements." Gifts, then, are not the basis of pride that achievements are. For pride should be proportioned to the real value of the things of which we are proud. The pride taken in qualities of our own must run parallel to the respect which we should feel for the same qualities in another person, and this respect must in turn correspond to the actual worth of those qualities. You would expect, then, that people who preen themselves on trivial accomplishments (as the boarding-house keeper on her "respectability") should also worship false gods and make heroes out of crooners and prize-fighters. There lies the danger, for any actor or athlete or aviator, of accepting the homage of the crowd. He will soon begin to accept their judgment, and then he is lost. It goes, as we say, to his head.

By the same token, pride which is just and proportionate to the quality or act is reasonable. Now there exist both general and particular objections to this statement. It can be said either (1) that there can be no justification for any sort of pride, or (2) that pride in the so-called natural advantages cannot be justified.

1. The substance of this argument is simply that a reasonable person will give himself very little opportunity for reflection upon what he is or has or has done but will be devoted to purposes and tasks which remain. In other words, he will be "objective," outward-directed; and this comports very badly with pride. But this again is a question of where and when and how much. It can hardly be expected that a person intelligent enough to be sensitive to any merit in anybody should be ignorant of its existence in himself,

that while he must be conscious beforehand of what he wants to attain, he should not know when he has attained it. Self-approbation, the pleasure of reflecting upon what one has already accomplished, reinforces the incentive to acts of the same kind; and while it would be wrong to rest on one's laurels, or trade on credit issued long before, it is hardly better to plunge ahead without a stock-taking. So we find that Aristotle sanctions pride in his "magnificent man" (endowing him even with a slightly ridiculous pomposity) and that Lenin, a tolerably objective personality, could be subjective enough to indulge in a moral review of his life. Spinoza, on the other hand, seems to disparage pride; but that is because he defined it to begin with as "*over*-estimation of oneself by reason of self-love." What Spinoza calls "self-satisfaction," which is "pleasure arising from the contemplation of oneself and of one's power of action," is "the greatest good for which we can hope"—and "self-satisfaction" is of course exactly what I mean by pride.

The defense will be clinched if we can show that a just pride is not opposed to humility. Humility consists in knowing one's limitations as pride consists in knowing one's merits or, as Spinoza would say, one's power. But the knowledge of both is comprehended in the act of knowing one's place. I know my place: I am a distinguished statesman or scientist. But I know my place: I am one life among millions; I am neither omnipotent nor all-important; I am hedged about by a myriad of rights; my discoveries in physics do not entitle me to trample on anyone, to sit at the head of the table, to speak first or longest or loudest. No conceivable human attainment can override the finitude of individuality, that is to say, cancel the rights which every other person enjoys merely in virtue of being human.[5] The "humility of truly great men" is probably something of a fiction; but there is no *reason* why a great man should not also be great in humility—understand his total position as he understands his position in science or government or art.

As a matter of fact, we have been speaking so far only about modesty. Humility goes beneath modesty; for modesty and its opposite, arrogance, are related to the sphere of rights and of claims. Modesty is knowing your place in relation to other men's rights—to their right to breathe, their right to assistance, their

5. Jefferson on the Negroes: "But whatever be their degree of talent it is no measure of their rights. Because Sir Isaac Newton was superior to others in understanding he was not therefore lord of the person or property of others."

right to courtesies and attentions. But humility is knowing your place in relation to their thoughts and affections. Now there cannot exist such a thing as a claim to another man's solicitude or love. One is entitled to consideration, one is never *entitled* to love. The nature of the benefit is such that it comes necessarily as a favor, a free-will offering, a gift of grace; and the appropriate feeling is gratitude. A reasonable person, therefore, conscious of his complete dependence upon other people for this necessity of life, will be conscious of his unworthiness; and he will betray this in the humility with which he approaches those who have it in their power to confer their affection or to withhold.[6]

When Hume says, "It is impossible a man can at the same time be both proud and humble," he is confusing humility with shame. Humility is not the opposite but the complement of pride. Modesty and humility are based on the recognition of inherent and inevitable limitations, whilst shame is an experience of weakness and inferiority. The first is an active withdrawal of pretensions seen to be groundless, while the second is a passive admission of pain, failure, impotence, or vice. You could be proud and humble, like Isaac Newton, through perceiving at once that you had advanced knowledge and that you had not advanced it very far. But you could not be proud and ashamed of the same book unless it contained both truths and errors, merits and avoidable faults.

Pride, then, is consistent with humility. We may even take pride *in* humility, as an achievement of no little difficulty. And this establishes the legitimacy of pride.

2. But we must still ask whether it is permissible to experience pride in thoughts such as these: I am attractive to men—I am exceptionally powerful—I have more than my share of cleverness. We must admit that to allow oneself even a slight pleasure in such reflections is a course beset by the danger of excess—the excess of vanity, of truculence, of conceit. But where there are aberrations, there must be a norm; and the norm in the case of beautiful people or strong people or clever people is *confidence*. But confidence is something desirable, and what is desirable cannot be wrong.

A woman has begun to *plume* herself on her beauty—when? When she is blind to the necessity of other qualities besides; when she acquires a contempt for ugliness; when she considers herself entitled to privileges; when she forgets what a small part of the

6. See Note I at the end of this article.

self the appearance is; when she overvalues superficial admiration and sacrifices the affection which is due only to qualities of mind and heart. Such women are unbearable, and unfortunate,

> for such,
> Being made beautiful overmuch,
> Consider beauty a sufficient end,
> Lose natural kindness and maybe
> The heart-revealing intimacy
> That chooses right, and never find a friend.

But there are women who combine beauty and confidence with humility and show deference to experience and achievement.

The consciousness of strength of body may lead to swagger and the traits of the bully. But it is compatible with gentleness and humility. Pride of physique is at its best when it is functionally related to services and achievements. The strong man, like the skilled man, is grateful for his ability to be useful when called upon and for the place in the estimation of others which that ability confers upon him.

Intelligence which is overproud of itself belies itself: to be conceited on the score of intelligence is to exhibit a want of it. This quality belongs anyhow in a special category, because of all things it is the easiest to be proud of when you have it not. But suppose you have it—who cares? Intelligence is supposed to display itself in results and even the best results are, as we have shown, limited. Nothing is more disagreeable than the smirk of a superior intelligence, addicted to comparisons of itself with other minds instead of being devoted to positive and objective conclusions, and hardly anything more revolting than a congress of able men at which everyone backs his own insight because it is his own. Yet intelligence is intelligence; and that exhilaration, that confidence, which we feel when we know that we see things clearly or do things well is something that cannot properly be decried.[7]

The proposition that every human being has an ego is probably not necessary (logically true). For, even if we ignored the evidence from psychopathology on disintegration or loss of the ego functions, it seems possible to imagine a man, otherwise normal, who should have no need to acquire a good opinion of himself and no feelings which were conditional on that opinion; and it is a matter of fact that some people have "small" egos (a small de-

7. See Note II at the end of this article.

gree of preoccupation with themselves) compared with others. Whether the extirpation of the ego would be psychologically feasible or morally desirable—this is a different question. And the "conquest of pride" is still another. The destruction of self-consciousness would take humility with it as surely as pride, for humility presupposes the existence of an ego. Let us therefore ignore the question of eliminating the ego with all its feelings, positive and negative, and concentrate on the question of destroying pride. It is religion that provides the evidence on this point, for it is religion that presumes not to control or to normalize but to banish the feeling of pride. When, in one of the *Little Flowers of St. Francis* (not an entirely credible record of the Saint's life or words), we read: "forasmuch as those holy eyes have beheld among sinners none more vile, more imperfect, nor a greater sinner than I, therefore since He hath found no viler creature on earth to accomplish the marvellous work He intendeth, He hath chosen me to confound the nobility, the majesty, the might, the beauty, and the wisdom of the world: in order to manifest that every virtue and every good thing cometh from Him the Creator," we see that the humility is artificial, groundless, false: there is no good reason to think that St. Francis was as vile as anybody on earth. But the pride is concrete, definite, immense—and immensely dangerous: it is founded not only on the actual position of leadership in society which Francis had achieved but on the presumption of a divine endorsement for his particular mission. In Morton Wishengrad's *Chassidic Tale* a certain Rabbi Eliezer is made to say: "I have a greater love for the wicked man who knows he is wicked than for the righteous man who knows he is righteous. The first one is truthful and the Lord loves the truth. The second one falsifies, since no human being is exempt from sin and the Lord hates untruth."[8] This, again, distorts truth in the interest of a strained humility: it confuses the man who knows how righteous he is with the man who thinks he is more righteous than he is. It takes back what it grants: it assumes that one can be in error concerning that which one knows. On this reasoning there would be no difference between smugness and self-respect; and any degree of satisfaction with self, no matter how solidly supported, would be sinful. Yet the very quality which is pronounced wrong is also seen to be

8. Quoted from a review by Daniel Bell of M. Wishengrad, *The Eternal Light*, in *Commentary*, November 1947.

inevitable. The discipline of the ego, when conceived with ascetic immoderation, is like any other discipline when similarly conceived. It cannot achieve its object—the extinction of pride or of desire as the case may be. But by refusing to countenance a just pride or a legitimate desire it can forestall the existence of either. It is a notorious fact that obnoxiously complacent or self-righteous people are among those who have obscure reasons for feeling dissatisfied with themselves. Here the ego has been distorted by natural causes. The deliberate attempt to thwart or suppress the cravings of the ego leads, in its own way, just as surely to queer forms of egotism.

II

The analysis of shame runs parallel to the analysis of pride. Shame is the feeling that comes with consciousness of faults, weaknesses, disadvantages—that is, of qualities deemed undesirable. Most of these qualities, like deformity, ugliness, and vice, already entail suffering by their very nature, so that shame is a misery heaped upon miseries. To be ignorant, awkward, poor, impotent or undersized or bald, criminal, homosexual, member of a disgraced family or an oppressed race—these are in their various ways concrete liabilities; and to reflect upon them, insofar as one accepts the standard which discredits them, is to suffer a constraint upon confidence and freedom of action.

This reflexive character of shame must be re-emphasized. Take as an example the feeling of loneliness. This feeling is not always disinterested. What you might want of other people when you think you would like to see them is not their company so much as the assurance that you can have their company if you want it—that somebody is willing to kill his time with you. You want to flatter yourself with the thought: "I have friends." Loneliness would not be crushing if it did not induce the reflection that nobody cares for you, that you are abandoned. It is this reflection which makes you feel really small. (The intensity of this feeling depends, of course, on the strength of the ego-requirement which has been created by the previous life history. A proud ego, secure in the belief in its social eligibility, can face periods of solitude or desertion without loss of confidence.) But such a value existing in the ego presupposes the existence of a genuine and disinterested loneliness. You could not think it a compliment to yourself to be sought out by other people unless the friendship and company of other people were first considered valuable. And they are considered valuable because we have social needs. It is not the ego that creates these needs. The ego *superimposes* itself upon these needs —and others like them—and defines itself in relation to them.

Pride and shame have been defined as feelings, and that is what they are in the isolated act of reflection. But reflection is continual, so that the momentary reactions establish themselves as dispositions, affect the structure of personality and modify the life pattern. That is why we can characterize individuals as overbearing, craven, or diffident; and that is why pride can be a permanent blessing and shame an enduring curse.

The qualities of which we are ashamed will vary according to the standard of value. The standard is derived, of course, in a very great measure from the group and has been impressed on us through social sanctions. Moreover, even more than in the case of pride, the feeling of shame is bound up with the idea of publicity. We feel ourselves disgraced by those qualities which evoke the contempt and aversion of others. For instance: sexual inversion, which might otherwise be regarded as (at worst) a handicap, becomes a source of anguish through the fact that it evokes derision and blame. It is hard to exaggerate the degree to which we fear disfavor and are therefore ashamed of the things which bring it upon us. So that Spinoza could incorporate that element in the very definition of shame: "Shame is pain accompanied by the idea of some action of our own which we imagine others to blame." Our difference with Spinoza is only terminological: we must allow for the existence of an autonomous conscience, for the fact that a man may feel himself disgraced by something that is unworthy in his own eyes and apart from any judgment but his own. It would take us very long to analyze the reciprocal play of conscience and public opinion even in a single example, like Conrad's Lord Jim. But it is useful to notice the illusion that is usually involved in the idea of disgrace. We have a tendency to overrate certain qualities because they are ours, instead of rating ourselves according to the qualities, and to impute the complementary error to others. I imagine that people admire me for qualities which in fact they have hardly noticed and do not think very much of. So too, judging by the intensity of my own shame, I imagine a degree of opprobrium which exists in no mind but my own. I am ashamed of my stature, my income, my accent, my clothes, when nobody,

in fact, holds them against me and when I would not blame anybody else for the same things. People are more considerate than we
think: they do not concentrate upon single qualities but take them
into reckoning with other things. Besides, they do not bother
about us as much as we suppose: it is a false pride, a form of egotism, which persuades us that they have no way of spending their
time but in condemning us. Just as I can look at distinguished men
quite coolly and critically while I imagine that everyone must be
impressed by my own least attainment, so a scandal in which a
friend of mine is embroiled leaves my regard for him unaffected
while I imagine (Dostoevsky's example) that the world is pointing
fingers at a pimple on my nose. When we see public opinion for
what it is, it turns out to be a smaller thing, for good or for ill,
than what our fantasy projected. And (though the subject requires
a much closer discussion) this seems to point to the existence of
sources of shame independent of society. For if we can stigmatize
ourselves more severely than others do and impute that judgment
to them, if (in Spinoza's terms) we can "imagine others to blame
us" more harshly than they do, there must be a spontaneous and
factitious element in our sense of disgrace.

An element of comparison enters into what we regard as our
disabilities: income and height and status might rarely become
objects of shame without it. In itself there is nothing good or bad
about being exceptional: the question is whether you deviate in a
direction of which you and others approve. The *very* tall man is
regarded not with respect but with curiosity. His painful self-
consciousness would of course disappear in a community of people
like himself; for then the difference would be gone, and it is the
difference, not the height, that discomfits him. But it would disappear also in a world in which men looked at him as they look at
geniuses and not as they look at freaks. In a community of hunch-
backs no hunchback would be ill at ease, both because he would
not stand out and because the standard would be different.

But there are absolute liabilities as well as comparative ones.

Now we can discuss the thesis which I have advanced concerning shame. An immanent penalty attaches to anything that we call
a disadvantage, a penalty which, like the pain of deformity, it may
be impossible to throw off. But shame is the farthest weakness,
psychological in type, which the *consciousness* of our disabilities
involves. Now it is just as natural to be ashamed of our weaknesses
as it is to be proud of our strengths; but that does not mean that

it is equally reasonable. On the contrary, it is as reasonable to seek the cure of this secondary malady as it is, say, to consult a doctor about the first.

The following points are made chiefly by way of supporting this last proposition. They are considerations, relevant for an evaluation of shame. They are not, as they may seem to be, primarily proposed as practical "remedies," counsels, exhortations, or cheering reflections. The impression of moral optimism which the reader may draw from them is not intended. A person subject to any of the liabilities mentioned above is not merely ashamed. His reaction is endorsed by his opinion: he says to himself, "This thing is shameful." It is to this conscious judgment, this faculty of valuation, which is accessible to argument even when the shame feelings are not, that these remarks are addressed.

The influence of shame is counteracted by estimating any weakness (assumed to be insurmountable) at its actual importance, that is, by the development of an accurate sense of values. If anything at all be shameful, illness is not as shameful as cowardice nor cowardice as shameful as malice—which is only to say that some things as not as *bad* as others. The decisive consideration, be it noted, is not the deterministic excuse: "It is not my fault that I am feeble, inept, or ugly; I couldn't help it; it was visited upon me," but the moral judgment: "Ugliness is no disgrace, or but a small one; it is I, after all, who suffer from it, and I give no ground of complaint to anyone else; there remains virtually the whole field of action in which I can still win credit." We surround the source of shame with sources of pride and objects of ambition, which may well-nigh overwhelm it. We bring our emotions into correspondence with the actual balance of assets and liabilities. We dispel the illusion of centrality which shame tried to create for its object. We try to see our weaknesses as they are, in relation to everything that is desirable or the reverse, and not in the magnified form in which shame presents them. Needless to say, this is very different from *forgetfulness*, which simply tries to seal off the source of discomfiture, leaving the fundamental value judgment uncorrected. And it is different from *consolation*, which also accepts without criticism the proposition advanced by shame—that the qualities which I lack are the most desirable things in the world—and strives to discover substitutes and compensations, a weak balm for the wound to which no radical treatment has been given.

There are important sources of shame that can be cleared out entirely by this treatment. Social upstarts long for the speech and manners of the class above and are ashamed of their own, though it might be difficult to show that the one were at all superior to the other. The weakness here is not a real weakness; it is not such as a reasonable mind would inevitably pronounce undesirable; it is contingent totally upon the "level of aspiration"; and a good sense of values would resolve it.

So there are weaknesses which, since they are created by estimation, will disappear when the estimation is corrected; and with the weakness goes the shame in the weakness. But there are other weaknesses that are not created by estimation: estimation must, on the contrary, take account of them as real. Though we should not, in our feelings, *exaggerate* these weaknesses, yet they remain; and with them, it appears, a modicum of shame. An accurate sense of values does not abolish it, for it does not abolish its source. Yet it is as unreasonable to tolerate the sear of shame upon the spirit as it is to permit a wound to fester in the body. There is not such a thing as a right amount of shame, as there is a right kind and amount of pride. *Every* shame, however circumscribed, must go. This leads us to our main consideration.

It has hitherto been unnecessary to invoke the distinction between what is *desired* and what is *considered desirable*. An impartial judgment seems to be seated within us, which pronounces on the general value and rightness of things. This we call the moral standard or *attitude* (identical with the "sentiment" in Hume). The term 'attitude' suggests that it is ultimately volitional and affective. The judgment is not impartial in the sense of being a deliverance of pure reason: it is impartial in the sense that it operates in relative independence of what may happen to be our personal desires. Thus I may desire wealth above everything else; but I shall not have the brass to maintain that money is the greatest good (much less *money for me*). And I may be perfectly sincere in this concession. At the same time, the independence of desire and attitude is not absolute—it is obvious that the desire for wealth influences the moral attitude and is influenced by it. One thing more: the attitude is not *necessarily* more "reasonable" than the desire. *Either* may be reasonable or unreasonable, depending on the considerations upon which it is based. People who are relatively sane in their personal morality not infrequently hold wild and prejudiced moral or social standards.

Now the attitude and the desire should be made to agree.

Moralists usually conceive this as a one-way process, a capitulation on the part of desire; but it might in fact imply a concession on either side. Sexual desire is a notoriously difficult thing to regulate according to a standard of what is proper; but if the standard is total abstinence, then the standard might be wrong. In any case, standard and desire must be integrated, so that our normal interests may have the backing of our total judgment. But I wonder whether there is not a class of exceptions, a class of cases where there should exist an explicit separation between the object of approval and the direction of desire. In the case of a remediable ill, like jaundice, the subjective urge to get rid of it is in full agreement with the objective judgment, that health is better than disease. But take the man with a hump. He should not be expected to suffer a distortion of judgment. His standard will be the same as our own: deformity is undesirable. But his *desire?* So long as straightness remains a good for him, he will be consumed with longing and shame; he will develop a hatred for his very life; he will experience the most futile and desperate of all wishes—the wish to be reborn. There is no alternative but a total redirection of wish: privately and subjectively, normality must cease to be his standard. And when you lack what you do not want, there is no shame.

For the situation, albeit more serious, is not entirely different from those which we meet in normal life, for example, when circumstances force me to relinquish the vocation on which I have set my heart. Every choice, even the most trivial, compels us to forswear the unattainable, to accept the reality, to desire those things which with available means can be obtained. A special philosophy of handicaps must commence with the insight that *misfortunes*—which are never contemplated, never chosen or rejected, but imposed on us from without—do not belong to a completely different category from those *conditions* which we face in action and which enforce retreat, compromise, revision of plan. The difference lies in the order in which things confront us. If you begin by wanting (A) to be both a good musician and a good chemist and are led to see that you can hope to attain (B) real proficiency in only one, then B and not A is your goal and your good. If the same result is produced suddenly and violently by an accident to your bowing arm, then you are passive to begin with; the choice is made, or at least shaped, for you without your consent; the readjustment is sharper and, conceivably, more painful; but the *elements* of the psychological situation and of the

moral issue—barring, of course, the factor of traumatic sudden-
ness itself—are identical with the other case; and this identity can
be ignored only through our failure to acknowledge the relative
rigidity of many of the ordinary conditions of life.

The evil of deformity is not a simple evil. It is not the pain alone,
nor the pang of comparison, nor the unwantedness, nor the fear of
it, nor the sexual impasse, but all of these, with their psychic in-
volutions, that surcharge the countenance with the marks of a
permanent crucifixion. Yet there have been cripples whose minds
were utterly straight; and we observe that if misfortune comes late
enough, when the mind is mature, the mind can remain untwisted
in spite of it. If there is one natural injustice more hideous than
the rest, it is the fate by which afflictions are heaped on children,
whose spirit is too weak to cope with them, so that the paralysis
of fear and of shame becomes fixed and incurable.

We must now deal with the quality of unintelligence as a reason
for shame. Mental disabilities do not present an exception to anything I have written; and it may seem needless even to treat them
as a special case. No matter who you are, there are more things you
cannot do than you can: what Shakespeare and what Newton did
not know and could not say filled volumes, even in their own times.
Scientists and artists are not embarrassed by the infinite scorn of
their ineptitudes; and most of us behave just as reasonably when it
is a question of particular disabilities. When you find that you are
slow at mathematics, you take that as a reason not to become a
mathematician—and nothing more. A merciful arrangement in our
natures makes it the rule (though not an invariable one) that people
become interested in things they are good at and lose interest in
things at which they fail. It is not otherwise with special qualities
like wit, cunning, literary taste, or, for that matter, the ability to
speak French, the lack of which may be a material and social handicap in a given time and place. Everyone knows that such deficiencies can be galling; and everyone knows someone who is perfectly
accommodated to them.

But what if you are good at nothing? Many people who are not
intelligent enough to keep up with the class or group in which they
find themselves are quite intelligent enough to perceive their own
backwardness; and such discoveries are a source of feelings of
bitterness and inferiority. For intellectual gifts, though valuable in
themselves, have more than an intrinsic value: they stand for eco-
nomic success, admission to certain circles, friendship with certain

people, and bulk large therefore in the estimate of one's own personality. Hardly anybody is more pathetic than the college student whose perceptive intelligence outstrips his productive powers, so that while he appreciates gifted people, he is not appreciated by them in return. True, there are those, perhaps the great majority, who find that their social environment does not emphasize mental qualifications, and—since shame can exist only when we fail to live up to a standard of our own election—they can be stupid and know they are stupid without being crest-fallen because, like everyone else around them, they honor stupidity. But in this case the penalty for peace of mind is an error—the failure to recognize that intelligence is a good thing.

It is time to ask what intelligence and stupidity are. Let us consider a definition long accepted by psychologists and subjected to criticism only in recent years. Intelligence is the ability to learn— an aptitude distinguished in point of generality from the aptitude for lawn tennis or languages. If this is intelligence, it is certainly possible to know that you lack it, by carefully observing and comparing your own and other people's learning performances.

What it means to be good at nothing, then, is that there is a general quality of slowness in your acquisition of knowledge and skills. But you can make yourself *good* at many things all the same, with sufficient incentive and force of will. Now, a man who by working twice as hard as other people has made himself only a little better than they is not going to feel downcast about the inferiority of his mind. The lack of "intelligence," a factor of native endowment, is seen and felt as a special handicap on a plane with those we have discussed already, to be treated morally and technically as they are treated. In the developed personality, which knows many things and harbors many interests, the perception of an incapacity for rapid assimilation counts as a single trait, for which the proper kind of allowance has to be made—not as an overwhelming and insuperable stigma.

In other words, it is intelligence as achievement and not as capacity that poses the only serious problem. The flower of the natural intelligence is the developed understanding. It is this, and not a few degrees of difference in IQ, that creates the qualitative gulf between one man and another. Between genius and mediocrity (a distinction of capacities) the difference may be great; but between enlightenment and confusion (a distinction in point of attainment) the difference is as night and day. A good head is an asset in the pursuit of understanding; but understanding is the end and justification of intelligence. And this, the *result* of experience and learning—not the *ability* to learn—is, on the whole, what people mean when they describe their acquaintances as intelligent or stupid. Henry Ford, with his great congenital endowment, could have acquired an understanding of human nature and society superior to that of many people who would, justifiably, describe his actual outlook as "unintelligent." Now if, given any problem or point of controversy, there are two classes of people, those who admit their lack of understanding and those who do not, then the second kind will never be ashamed of their stupidity—so they do not give us any question to discuss. But the first kind should not be ashamed, because they are not stupid but at worst merely ignorant. And ignorance is not inherently wrong: if it were, we should all of us be *infinitely* embarrassed all of the time. Ignorance of this or that might be wrong at this time or that—when the practical situation impresses upon us the obligation to know a specific thing. But the obligation to know cannot exist for me if I lack the ability to know; and if I have that ability, the reasonable thing is to start learning.

I am aware that my treatment of this topic has been absurdly schematic. But I believe that the scheme, as a scheme, is adequate: it covers the alternatives which seem to exist in all those cases where people are ashamed of their own minds.

So much for the natural disadvantages. They are evil; and they are, by hypothesis, fixed. But the shame and disgrace of them are just as evil; and though equally natural are not, or not always, equally fixed. It might seem that pride and shame involved each other and could not be separated without a convenient but dishonest shift in the standard of value. If you are justly proud of a certain quality because you think it good, how can you *not* be ashamed to lose it unless you resort for the occasion to an attitude of sour grapes: "After all, it isn't really any good"? Superficially, this question is logical; but it ignores the intervention of the practical effort. On the same assumption it would be inconsistent to enjoy the use of money while you have it unless you were prepared to moan for it when you do not. If health is good, illness is evil: a man in his right senses accepts both these judgments, whether he is well or ill. But if health is something to be proud of, it does not follow that illness is something to be ashamed of. Between pride and shame it is the practical will that interposes itself, not to register the static judgment, "X is good" or "X is evil" but to *make* of X as little of an evil as may be.[9]

But now, is there *nothing* of which we can justifiably be ashamed? Not cowardice, nor dishonor, not incompetence or moral failure? No act of will and no trait of character? (Shame obviously merges here with remorse or the sense of guilt.) It seems almost implied in the preceding pages, where we maintained, e.g., that ugliness is nothing to be ashamed of, that there must be other things which indeed are shameful. But these things fall within the scope of effort and control, so that they seem to call for resolutions bearing upon the future rather than for reproaches based upon the past.

A man will never be ashamed of anything he has done unless he accepts a certain standard of rectitude. The feeling of shame, therefore, can *bear witness* to an uncorrupted conscience; and such a man, as Spinoza says, is better than one who is both wicked and shameless. But the feeling cannot be sanctioned just because it

9. It is unfortunately necessary, because of its extensive ramifications, to leave this point for the present largely unproved. In one of Hume's essays, "The Sceptic," there is a brief but devastating critique of the classical theory of the affects. I quote a few sentences: "Another defect of those refined reflections which philosophy suggests to us is that commonly they cannot diminish or extinguish our vicious passions without diminishing or extinguishing such as are virtuous, and rendering the mind totally indifferent and inactive. . . . In vain do we hope to direct their influence only to one side. . . . When we destroy the nerves, we extinguish the sense of pleasure, together with that of pain, in the human body." Now, I believe that every one of the following propositions, which are entailed by Hume's remark, is false: (1) To overcome the *fear of dying* is to extinguish the *will to live* and leave no incentive for avoiding death or danger. (2) If nothing is *blame*worthy, nothing is *praise*worthy: one cannot experience feelings of gratitude or admiration without being subject to feelings of indignation and resentment. (3) To *love* is to be exposed to *jealousy* and to *grief*. (4) One cannot *rejoice* in good fortune without *sorrowing* over bad. These propositions, and many others like them, which run parallel to the negation of our thesis concerning pride and shame, are false; but Hume's predecessors did not show why. Stoicism accepted them, and argued that the common *objects* of the positive and negative emotions are "indifferent": for this philosophy the choice is between sensibility and insensibility. Spinoza rejected them, but (in my opinion) with no clear justification. Modern psychology must sooner or later reinstate the distinction between the active and the passive affects, providing it with a clearer and solider basis than the classical philosophers did.

testifies to something good: the question is whether it accomplishes anything good. Shame and repentance in themselves are painful and to that extent bad. But painful things, like medicine, can sometimes lead to what is good. Can this be said of shame?

Everything that can be accomplished by a passion, says Spinoza, can be accomplished better by reason. But this, as he admits, hardly meets the issue; for if we were *perfectly* reasonable, we should not have erred to begin with, and the very question would not exist. The question for us is, granted that we *have* been cowardly or stupid or malicious, whether shame can serve any useful purpose.

It will never do to argue that just as pride of achievement encourages us toward further exertion, so to dwell upon our failures is to produce a revulsion toward good. I am afraid that there is no "law of effect" which operates in this manner; for if there were, it would follow that to *cultivate* the sense of guilt, to brood over our infirmities, would be tantamount to improvement; but this, on the contrary, is morbidity. Despondency is *weakness*; it reduces the power to act; it confirms us only in despondency, in loathing of self; it indicates no direction in which effort may move: and by its own intolerable weight, by the need we feel to get rid of it, it prompts us, if not to sheer escape in liquor and drugs, then to irrelevant acts of atonement—self-flagellation, breast-beating, the voluntary incurrence of punishment.

On the other hand, it is impossible to dispense with what I have called *reflection*; for it is the reflection upon a fault that enables us to analyze it, and analysis is the first step in treatment. One who, in the interest of moral reconstruction, should ignore his failures and imperfections, would be like a fool: his resolutions are fatuous because they take no cognizance of his problem. We could not endorse a program to abolish the habit of self-contemplation; for though there is no correction merely in looking upon oneself and cursing one's fate (or one's character), there will certainly be no correction without it. A positive morality does not forget the past, but recalls it to consider it; and reflection, in my special sense, is an indispensable phase of moral reflection in the general sense. But we cannot reflect upon errors without exposing ourselves to the attack of shame. Suppose that I let my tongue wag last night and said certain things about *Y*—which I regret. A reasonable person would not regret them because he would not have uttered them; but *I*, for whom it is a question of *becoming* reasonable, have something to reckon with. How should I change unless there were something which I deplore? Yet regret by itself effects nothing: what is more familiar than that we repeat what we have regretted? Shame and regret are literally helpless, for they are concentrated upon what we can do nothing about, on the past. Hence, they are "passive," incompatible with action. But if we *go on* from such feelings to weigh and measure, chart and explore—if, that is, they can instigate us to consideration of the future— then guilt and remorse will be replaced by a purpose, a resolution, one test of whose efficiency is precisely the degree to which the penalty of conscience has been surmounted. Shame, then, is seen as a *price* we may have to pay for our weaknesses and the attempt to cope with them; and morbidity, or the tendency to linger in self-reproach, is the evidence of the failure of that attempt, of the inability to act.

Are there not, finally, vices—just as there are bodily defects— that are incurable? Experience sometimes proves to us that we cannot hope to control certain irregularities of behavior and temper; and we conclude, at a certain age, that we are doomed to cowardice, to laziness, to futility.

Uncontrollable vices border, by definition, on pathology—the pathology of the will and of action. What we mean by a pathological trait is an undesirable trait that defies voluntary control. Every vice and every fault can be represented as an erroneous decision engrained in disposition. Now erroneous decisions are normally subject to review, so that we are not absolutely *fated* to repeat them. But it is the distinction of the "neurosis," or pathological vice, that the circumstances which gave rise to it are not accessible for review. The original motives, with their environmental causes, are buried in the unconscious; and the erroneous decision, once enacted, will bear in relation to the conscious will the character of a compulsion: we are impelled to act, as it seems, not by a voluntary choice but through *force majeure*.

True, it is never to be finally assumed, without a certificate from a physician, that a given trait is neurotic; for there exists the Freudian "preconscious," by which many of our acts are controlled. For thirty years one has hesitated, and felt a slight anxiety, before depositing a nickel in a telephone box. Only to stop and ask the reason for this would be to recall the poverty of one's youth and to see that that condition exists no longer. The motive was unconscious, but it is eminently accessible to consciousness, without the help of any special technique. There are people whose lives are pinched and bitten merely for want of a critical and reflective habit in their conduct, and to them we should recommend the Socratic rather than the Freudian method of self-knowledge. But when this whole area is accounted for, there remain the genuinely invincible perversities. And let us remember that to most men today, as to all of mankind before this century, no form of therapy is available.

I raise this topic not for its own sake but because it seems to stand as the final objection to any general criticism one can bring against shame. To be afflicted with uncontrollable vices is, *inevitably*, to be consumed with shame: indeed, the narcissistic ego formations of which exaggerated prides and exaggerated shames are the double manifestation are themselves, frequently, not to be controlled even by individuals who may be aware and critical of them. What can "reason" possibly have to say about this?

The question reaches into the foundations of ethics and is too formidable to be properly treated here. There is this one point:

We cannot admit that what is not to be altered is not to be condemned. Any analysis of moral judgments must accept as a datum the fact that "Cancer is evil" is a significant judgment, even though it expresses a helpless wish and proposes no course of action. (Such judgments are, in fact, presupposed by all those judgments which do express a resolve or an exhortation, for example, "It would be well to spend more money on cancer research.") By the same token, Spinoza makes good sense when he says that shame, pity, grief, remorse, and so forth, are evil.

But if it *were* necessary to show, for every moral judgment, that it embodies or expresses a practical decision, then we might point out that feelings of guilt and shame are constantly being produced, encouraged, and confirmed by people who *approve* of them. The moral issue could therefore be said to deal not with irremediable passions already existing but with those which are yet to be produced.

NOTE I

Both the Greek "moderation" and the Christian "humility" can be interpreted in terms of knowing one's place, if we allow for differences in conceiving the place of mankind in the universe. "Moderation," of which the opposite is *hybris*, pride, was by Aristotle's time a purely ethical conception; but it had a religious origin, which was in turn the projection of a social requirement. The fragments of Anaximander apply the idea of metes and bounds to the very elements: the cosmos itself is a system which subsists only by a kind of mutual restraint. The fate of Tantalus and of Niobe teaches us how men should comport themselves in relation to the powers that rule the world. Prosperity and power are dangerous, since they encroach upon the prerogatives of divinity. Happiness itself is somewhat too godlike and has a Nemesis appointed to dog it. (Jehovah, similarly, could not abide the tower of Babel, which threatened his privacy and supremacy.) Crimes, in particular, are reserved for the gods, who undertake to punish any poaching on this preserve. The gods, however, though they are immortal, are finite. They are subject to limitations of their own. There is an essential proportion between their nature and ours; and, accordingly, there is a middle sphere in which men are allowed to flourish. We are asked only to bring our ambitions into correspondence with our modest status and capacities; and if we are commanded to *think as mortals*, we are allowed to think at least as mortals. Now there can have been but few opportunities in Greek life for a man to trespass upon the "domain of the gods." Impiety no doubt was one, that is, the omission of any sacrifice or observance that was due them; but no one was likely to join the gods for dinner, to compare her beauty to Aphrodite's, to challenge Artemis to a foot-race or Zeus to an exhibition of fireworks. There are, however, a thousand ways in which presumption can offend against one's *neighbor*. I feel, then, that the legends project a set of social demands. How the wicked or dangerous man came to be conceived as the "uppity" individual, how the wrong was identified with the immoderate, the unlimited—to explain this would require a thorough study of Greek society. But this conception, which persists in the great ethical systems, has not even today exhausted its usefulness.

Christianity assumes that man is both vile and insignificant—dependent utterly, like an infant, upon a Father, whose value and power are incommensurate with his own, being infinite; and he is encouraged to regard himself as a worm. One phase of Christian doctrine insists even that there can be no such thing as merit, that no virtue whatsoever entitles a man to the slightest consideration. No depth of self-abasement, clearly, will be sufficient to express this relationship: it is impossible to be too humble. Now the effect of exercises in humility, like the effect of other exercises, is not confined to the situation which gave rise to them; and this doctrine seems to have produced some of the most unpretentious people in the world, men and women who claimed nothing for themselves from other people any more than from God. As an example of modest and unheroic self-effacement I cite the poet and priest George Herbert. But if "nature," according to the proverb, is difficult to expel, it is even harder to eliminate the "self." The self has a way of crawling back into the picture: it can even be found wielding the charm which is intended to exorcise it. I can vaunt myself as the chief of sinners. I can contend for the laurel of unworthiness. St. Augustine treats us to an exhibition of grovelling that must fairly have sickened an honest Deity; for a wise God will surely appreciate that there must be a limit to the claims even of the Infinite.[10] Now it can be argued (and has been argued, I think, by Rebecca West) that Augustine was not primarily an egotist. His intellect is too vast and too impartial; he speaks for mankind and not solely for himself. But it can hardly be urged that he was distinguished for *humility*. Manifestly, he makes claims upon the consideration of God even in the act of renouncing them. He seems to see himself already in the position which he occupies in the *Disputà*—can anyone imagine him waking without a shock, say, in Purgatory? Augustine deems *man* unworthy but not himself: his conception of grace has no counterpart in his innermost attitude.

The pride of individuals, then, can invert itself and adopt the

10. If it were certain that God exists and that He is infinite and perfect, it would still be hard to relish the spectacle of absolute submission. For on any premises, even pantheistic ones, there is still such a thing as otherness. The individual is separate, he is not absorbed by the Whole. He has a judgment, a mind, a will of his own. Not even an infinite being can logically exact a total abnegation of these proud faculties; and there is something preferable to the author of the *Imitation* (the most perfect example of Christian humility) in the spectacle of Job, who treats with the Almighty as an inferior indeed but one who retains the dignity and independence of a man. Not that a perfectly abject humility is the worst of the religious vices. For in postulating God in the first place, and His commandments, and His rewards and penalties; and in claiming, as he does so often, the sanction of God for his purposes, his animosities, his laws, man does after all exercise his own judgment and will—but a judgment and will that are arbitrary, unteachable, refractory to the discipline of fact. Judged by an objective standard, he is arrogant and unsubmissive in his very humility—even if there were no heretic and reformer to testify by their ashes or the stripes on their backs. And in the last analysis it is this presumption, circumscribing its deference and submission, that constitutes the menace of religion.

channel of Christian humility. But Christianity, like Judaism and other theistic creeds, is also committed, as an institution, to a special form of pride, which its apologists regard as a glorious asset. God may not be indulgent, but He is not indifferent. He made everything for us, and He takes an interest in the least event of our lives. His infinite Love strives to embrace us and is perpetually foiled by His infinite Justice. It is obvious that a life which is singled out for a solicitude of these dimensions will be invested wth a great sense of importance. This is the "grandeur of man," complementing his "wretchedness"; and herein lies the pride which man enjoys on taking the theistic view. His role in nature is after all central, after all immense. Unworthy and helpless before the Lord, it is still flattering to him to be the object of such ministrations. Religious man is like a child who craves attention above everything else and would rather receive it in the form of punishment than not to receive it at all.

Here we are naturally confronted by such questions as whether human dignity, and a sense of the meaningfulness of life, are dependent upon the family type of relationship which theism extends to the universe. Is it exalting, and at the same time chastening, to regard ourselves as the children of a Father, to be rebuked, forgiven, condemned, or saved by Him? Does it degrade us from that height, and lift us from that depth, to believe that we have risen from the slime and have not fallen out of favor? Does it render man complacent, and also insignificant, to consider that there is nothing "higher" than himself? Is there no greatness, and no wretchedness, save in relation to a paternal will? Is the nursery the only deeply satisfying model of the universe? Must we be reluctant to grow up and make our way in a world in which we are responsible only to ourselves and to one another?

I do not discuss these questions, for I am interested not in the pride and humility of "man" in relation to "his" place in the cosmos but in the pride and humility of *men* in relation to one another. It may be that certain attitudes are incumbent on the species the moment it adopts a certain conception of its cosmic role. But what limits us fundamentally, as individuals, is not God or the gods or nature but *other men*, with their rights and pretensions and the need that we have of them. I seriously question the value of the humility which comes with the reflection that one is but a man: I think it more important to realize that one is but *one* man. So that the humility which I defined above, though it is closer in most respects to the Greek than to the Christian outlook, is closer still to the Chinese—if we can suppose that the polite tradition of self-disparagement which persists in their speech reflects what is now or was once a living practice.

NOTE II

"Pride of intellect" is a sin which divinities must naturally reprobate, since their very existence is endangered by it; but it frequently assumes forms in which mortals can properly be disgusted if not terrified by it too. The claims of intelligence can easily be excessive. Yet whenever we point out that intelligence is encroaching on a sphere where it has not yet demonstrated its competence, we are paradoxically accusing it of unintelligence, since the standard by which any form of pride is judged to be warranted or unwarranted is the standard of reasonableness. The paradox disappears if we make it clear that we are talking about specialized intellectual attainments and of the claims that can be made on the strength of them. There is a false pride which is proper to the theoretical intellect. Its name is error. Error is presumption, because ideally it is always possible to know when you do not know something, to limit your claim according to the weight of the evidence in hand. There is a false pride whose name is confusion, which is the mark of the specialist who does not know that he is a specialist and who extrapolates the criteria which are applicable only within his narrow field. (The classical examples are the mathematician who wanted to know what a certain poem "proved" and the famous argument of the dancing master in Molière.) There is a false pride corresponding to every field in which claims are advanced and evaluated. (Thus when Croce speaks of the "not very great brain of the philosopher Bacon" and when T. S. Eliot refers to Hobbes as an "extraordinary little upstart," they are supercilious if not insolent. If we said that *Croce* had no very great brain and that *Eliot* was a little upstart, we should be much less in contempt of court, simply because our claims are more nearly warranted. The subjective feeling with which the claims are advanced may be the same in all cases; but the objective qualities of the several claims, when submitted to the norms of judgment, prove to be different.) Each form of exaggerated pride is corrected by mind, that is, by a better judgment, if it is corrected at all. And the pride which exaggerates the role of mind within the whole framework of life and society can be chastened only by the practical reason, which is the comprehensive tribunal to which all values must be brought. This faculty is charged with the criticism of its own claims.

It is evident from the foregoing examples that I have not, in the present note, limited the meaning of intellectual pride to the *reflection within the ego* of an attainment or claim of the intellect. I have followed a usage according to which the arrogant individual is "overweening," i.e., one who does what he should not. But if we place our emphasis (as through most of this paper) on a man's reaction to his judgment of his own merits (in this case, pride *of* intellect, in the stricter sense), the moral does not change: it is intelligence which checks the presumption of the ego, permits a due pride and fosters intellectual humility.

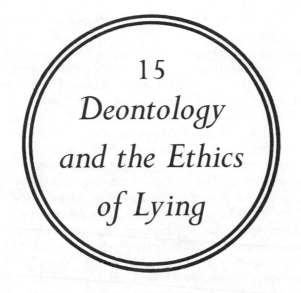

15

Deontology and the Ethics of Lying

INTRODUCTION

Three positions, on three distinct questions in ethics, having been held by a number of the same persons, have become loosely associated. The three are run together in a single sentence of Sidgwick's, which refers to those who believe that "we have the power of *seeing clearly* that certain *kinds* of actions are right and wrong *in themselves,* apart from their consequences."[1]

It is the *intuitionists* who claim that there are ethical propositions whose truth we can "see clearly," that is, know by direct intuition; some of these philosophers (not all) holding that among these self-evident truths are some which affirm that certain actions are right or wrong. Their opponents are the ethical *empiricists.*

Those who say, with emphasis, that actions are or can be right and wrong "in themselves" and "apart from their consequences" are the *deontologists.* Their opponents, who believe that actions can be justified only by consequences or by ends, are the sponsors of a *teleological* ethics; and among these the most are the *utilitarians.*

Someone ought to show whether these two issues are logically independent. It is obvious that if acts are right or wrong solely in virtue of consequences, then no act can be "self-evidently" right

Philosophy and Phenomenological Research 24, no. 4 (June 1964): 463–80. Reprinted with permission.

1. Henry Sidgwick, *The Methods of Ethics* (London: Macmillan, 1907), p. 200. The italics are mine.

or wrong, since the connection between an act and its consequences is not self-evident.[2] Hence a utilitarian cannot believe
that there are intuitions of *right* and of *wrong*. But it is not clear
that an empiricist, who rejects the notion of intuition in ethics,
must hold that no form of conduct is *intrinsically* right or wrong.
It just so happens that no empiricist—none, at least, since the
eighteenth century—does. I do not see that an emotivist, a subjectivist, or a relativist *must* deny that actions can be right or
wrong in themselves. These schools have their own conceptions of
intrinsic good, for example, "pleasant," or "desired for its own
sake." They also believe that actions may be *good* or *bad* in themselves. They have, also, conceptions of right and wrong; and
though these are often connected with the notion of "leading to
good or to evil," they are also very frequently connected with the
notion of sentiment or approbation in an impartial observer. Now
if such an observer can approve or disapprove an action for what
it is, rather than for what it leads to, then we should have the concept of intrinsic right within an ethics of approbation. But even if
such an ethics should be indefensible, we should still have a problem, in the psychology of moral judgment, as to the object of a
normal person's approbation and repugnance; and some of us, who
are not provided with intuitions in matters of psychology or ethics
either, may well feel that when an act is praised or condemned, it
is not always and wholly on account of its motives or its probable
consequences or any other relationships.

The third question—suggested in the Sidgwick sentence, by the
word 'kind'—cannot be stated both briefly and precisely: it is
large and vague and, probably, manifold. Are there general and
abstract principles in ethics which hold for *all* cases of a specified
kind? A person might claim that we can know by direct insight
that an action is intrinsically right or wrong, apart from its consequences; but that we can know this only in the individual case,
considered as a unique and concrete whole. (I confess that I do
not see much sense in such a position, which says there are axioms
that are true of only one thing—or of all things which are *exactly*
like that in all respects; but I believe that it has been held.) On the
other hand, one who should believe neither in necessary truths nor
in intrinsic right and wrong can still be a legalist and a moral tax-

2. The notion of an "intended consequence," engrained in the act, is
obviously a different case.

onomist; for he can believe that *experience* shows there are certain rules of morality, certain kinds of action that are always right or always wrong. But again, it is those who are both intuitionists and deontologists who place the greatest stress upon the validity of general principles. Nowadays this outlook takes a modified form. The moralist believes he can generalize, not with respect to the rightness of a whole class of actions, but with respect to its "partial" rightness. Kant seems to have held that lying, for example, is not only intrinsically and necessarily, but *absolutely* wrong: impermissible in all circumstances and no matter what else the act which is the lie may be. And Sidgwick, though he rejected this Kantian doctrine, still discussed no other issue in the ethics of veracity. Intuitionists of our own day are not so strict. They believe there may be circumstances in which lying is justified. But they insist that in a lie there is an element of wrongness; a non-teleological wrong-tending characteristic; in Mr. Broad's terms, a self-evident evil; in Mr. Ewing's, something which must be outweighed by countervailing elements of rightness if the lie is to be justified. It is always regrettable that one should have to lie—all the more so, perhaps, if the coercion is a strictly moral one. Veracity is, in Ross's terms, a "prima facie duty"; and a lie is, I suppose, a prima facie wrong. We have, then, a generalization which is supposed to hold a priori for a whole class of components in certain forms of conduct.

Our own interest, in this paper, is in the question of intrinsic right and wrong; but we take up only a limited aspect of that question. We need not ask whether anything can be known with certainty to be wrong; not even whether anything can be known to be wrong; not even whether certain acts *are* wrong. It will be enough if we can come to understanding *what* it is that is judged wrong, by some people at least, when certain acts are pronounced wrong. I shall sometimes use the predicate 'wrong', but always with the willingness that a longer phrase, like 'what in this situation is felt to be wrong', should be substituted for it.

For reasons which need not be specified in detail, lying and breach of promise are regarded as having a preeminent illustrative value in deontological ethics. Other acts and courses of action sometimes "look" wrong, apart from any conscious consideration of consequences on the part of the judge. Moses thought it "unfitting" to clip the corners of one's beard or that a kid should be seethed in its own mother's milk. In fact, as Bentham pointed out, nothing is commoner than that men should condemn an act without knowing what harm there is in it. But these two, the lie and the breach of promise, are thought to carry their stigmata upon their faces in some peculiarly conspicuous way and, if they are wrong, to be wrong because of what they are. Now promises and breaches of promise have been ably discussed by a number of writers. We therefore address ourselves to the ethics of the lie. We shall try to analyze its structure to see what there may be in it that is inherently offensive. By this means we hope to provide a test of the concept of prima facie wrongness, so prominent in contemporary deontology.[3]

Lying

In the following analysis of the lie, I shall keep to those points that have some connection with issues in ethics.

A lie is a statement made by one who does not believe it with the intention that someone else shall be led to believe it.

This definition leaves open the possibility that a person should be lying, even though he says what is true: for example, a man who does not know that his watch is one hour slow says, "It is ten o'clock," thinking that it is nine. He gives what he thinks is the wrong time; but it happens to be the right time. The dictionary definition—"a falsehood uttered or acted for the purpose of deception"—rules out this awkward possibility but has, I believe, other things the matter with it. Any short definition will leave some queer possibilities open. The differences among customary definitions are not very material for the ethics of lying.

3. Compare W. D. Ross, *Foundations of Ethics* (Oxford: Oxford University Press, 1939), p. 134: "In considering the problem of a conflict of duties which arises when for instance we ask ourselves whether we ought to tell a particular lie or break a particular promise when we think that a balance of good consequences will arise from our doing so, I had said that our answer will sometimes be 'yes' and sometimes be 'no' so that we cannot maintain with Kant that it is *always* wrong to tell a lie or break a promise. I had added that there are certain moral principles that remain always true, *e.g.*, that there is always a *prima facie* obligation to tell the truth or keep a promise, so that telling the truth or keeping a promise always tends as such to be right, even though in particular cases this tendency may be overborne by some other tendency which the act may have in virtue of some other virtue under which it falls, such as failing to produce a great advantage for some one else."

The essential parts of the lie, according to our definition, are three. (1) A statement—and we may or may not wish to divide this again into two parts, a proposition and an utterance. (2) A disbelief or a lack of belief on the part of the speaker. (3) An intention on the part of the speaker. Since (1) and (2) are obvious, I shall elaborate only on (3).

The intention is essential. If the speaker does not intend to make someone believe what he himself does not believe, he is not lying. Examples: (a) A *mistaken* utterance is not as such a lie. (b) The deliberate utterance of a statement that the speaker *knows* to be false need not be a lie. "There is a camel in my closet." This is not a lie if the person addressed is one whom the speaker believes intelligent and informed. (c) *Poets* do not often lie, even when they say what they know is false; for they do not often wish or expect to be believed. Plato, who tries to show that poetry is false, if not mendacious, touches only on what is relatively credible in Homer and the other poets; not on any of the real whoppers which Lucian was to list later on—one-eyed giants, caves of the winds, men turned into swine. These were not "dangerous" untruths; for they would not be believed.

Since the author of the lie wants to be believed, he will have some opinions beforehand about the people he is speaking to and will shape his lie accordingly. This means that the element of intention interlocks, causally, if not logically, with the other two elements in the lie, as they do with each other. For example, the liar will not only have reason for not believing his own words, but will have some opinion as to their "inherent credibility," that is, their plausibility relative to the general information that he thinks is available to the members of his audience. If the listener is believed to be very foolish or very ignorant, the inherent credibility of the lie need not be great. And since, among the supposed grounds of the listener's credence, there is a certain opinion about the speaker and the likelihood of his telling the truth, there will enter into the speaker's intention an opinion about *that* opinion: he will reckon upon what he believes to be the other man's opinion of him.

Thus there appears another, decidedly complex, element which, though it may not belong to the definition of the lie, is always present: a set of estimates by the speaker, apart from his main opinion of the statement he makes, of the existing evidence for that statement, the probability of the statement upon various portions of that evidence, the listener's mentality and cognitive situation. Liars, dupes, and cognitive situations are of many different kinds; and so the combination of elements within the lie can be very numerous.

Now, what *is* the liar's intention? I believe we have to say that what is common to every lie is the wish to make someone believe something—the same motive that so often prompts us to tell the truth. We should beware of ascribing a stronger intention to the liar, for example, the "wish to deceive." One can lie without wishing to deceive. A man who tells a creditor that he has no money on his person wants the other to believe what he says, not to be mistaken in what he is led to believe: it might suit this man very well, in fact, if he *had* no money just then and could say so truthfully. On the other hand, it can be the liar's intention to produce an *erroneous* belief—for example, about a future point of attack in time of war. But the "wish to deceive" is stronger still. That phrase implies that deception is the end and suggests, therefore, that a man would look about at random for a false story to perpetrate upon others. Such a motive, or something like it, is to be found in the April Fool's Day joke, where the joker indeed does not care what it is that he gets the other to believe, so long as it is false—for he wishes "to deceive." If there were a devil who enjoyed the thought of our being in perpetual error, he would be regularly governed by a will to deceive. But it is obvious that we should be letting too many people off if we said that no one is a liar who does not wish to deceive.

A liar, if successful, does deceive. And if he is unsuccessful, the observer will naturally be tempted to say that he was "trying to deceive." But that is only an example of a common mistake which, though not serious in ordinary speech, is fatal to the precise analysis of motives. Some general class to which either the object or the result of an action belongs is made to sound like the object of the action. If *A* wants to get the upper hand of *B* and *C*, we say he desires power; and that is objectionable, because there may well exist for some men a general object, power, which is different from the generalized description of a number of objects.

But though deception is not always the liar's aim, it cannot very well be absent from his consciousness. He knows that if his lie succeeds, the victim will be deceived. For not only does he not *believe* what he says; but in saying it, he is naturally aware of the proposition and therefore aware of his own opinion. And since he knows too what his intention is, he knows that he is trying to make someone believe what *he* thinks false or doubtful. (The name for this state of mind is 'duplicity'.) Therefore, even though he is not *trying* to deceive, he is *willing* that his action should deceive.

Since there is bound to be a considerable vagueness in our conception of the lie, there will be many doubtful cases. (a) If the *statement* is very vague, it can hardly be the subject of a definite lie. A celebrated case, formerly pending in the courts, turned upon the question whether a man can lie in saying that he did not "follow the Communist line." But there are vaguer statements still; and though we could accuse their authors of some kind of imposture, we could not accuse them of lying. Besides, the usage of the word 'lie' restricts the subject of the lie to questions of information in a fairly narrow sense; it does not permit us to speak of lying about matters of theory. Suppose that a scientist, who is to be the referee in a bet on the laws of motion, has been bribed to distort the truth. I do not think we would say he was lying; but if he were supposed to be reporting scientific *opinion* about the laws of motion, we should call it a lie. Yet usage is capricious; and if an adult were to tell a child that the world was full of demons, without believing it himself, we should probably call that a lie. Other types of statement could be mentioned which can only questionably figure in lies. (b) *Belief* and *disbelief* are strong or weak and also vary in a good many other ways. If a speaker thinks it very probable that a proposition, *p*, is true but intentionally communicates to another a degree of confidence slightly greater than his own, the question of mendacity may well be doubtful. (c) And the *intention* may be strong or weak, definite or indefinite. The large and irregular fringe which surrounds the concept of intention is, as a matter of fact, the source of most of our uncertainties in judging the veracity of others. An advertiser who "boosts" his product beyond its merits, knowing that everyone expects him to exaggerate and that no one will believe what he says, is probably not to be called a liar. But an advertiser who makes a false claim for his product in the hope that, though *most* will not believe him, *some* people may, is a liar. And an advertiser who makes exorbitant claims in the hope of creating, through suggestion, a partial or subconscious belief in the consumer is a borderline liar. A writer of fables who, though he knows that in a large population some people will think his stories true, does not care to prevent or correct this error is certainly no liar; since he lacks any positive intention of producing belief.

The intention is not to be defined wholly in terms of the speaker's beliefs about other people; there is also the strength of the *wish* to produce belief; and this is a source of further vagueness in the concept of the lie. We may imagine various cases: a pathetic wish to produce belief without any hope of fulfillment—this is often strong enough to cause a man to say what he knows is not true; a "pathological lie," produced perhaps by the need to boast; a person who does not mind if others are deceived and might be pleased if they were, but is not trying very hard to make them believe what he says.

Another doubtful liar is the person so nearly demented as to think that everyone will believe him when there is not the slightest chance that anyone will.

It would not be difficult to point out many other series in which lies can be placed so that they grade off from strict conformity to the definition to clear nonconformity. Suppose there is a report in the paper which I believe to be inaccurate. I say to another man, "The paper says . . . ," believing that he will trust the newspaper report. There is no doubt of my intention to make him believe something which I do not believe. But is it a lie?

Ordinarily, a lie will have a motive beyond the desire to make someone believe it: the production of a belief is only a step toward a further end. This motive may be strong or weak, and it may be of any of a million kinds: to steal a watch, to help a friend, to escape censure, to win applause, to adorn a tale.

It is a question of some importance for the ethics of lying whether *every* lie does not have such an ulterior end. For the moment, we shall only imagine what a motiveless—or "gratuitous"— lie would be. It would be either: (1) a lie told for the sake of its immediate object, namely that another man shall believe this or that—a lie whose entire motive force, in other words, must be supplied by its engrained intention; or (2) a case of "lying for lying's sake." In (2) the immediate object is nearly the same as in (1). But the lie is not told for the sake of this object. The "wish to deceive" is involved; and the important thing is the trick, the fact that the other is deceived by means of the lie I tell him: it would not do at all for him to acquire the same belief by any other means. The chief examples would seem to be jokes. But these can be supported by motives such as malice or the desire to exhibit power over another person's mind. And in this connection it would seem wise for us, though we cannot provide a recipe for detecting impurities in an ostensibly gratuitous lie, to draw a rough distinction. Not every *supporting* goal is an *ulterior* goal. One might kill two birds with a stone which one would not have taken the trouble to throw at either and yet not be aiming at either "for the sake of the other." And a man who thinks he has a *good* story to tell, by which the sense of wonder is aroused, might lie when he would not do so otherwise; but it is not perfectly clear that he has an ulterior end or what that might be. Now one cannot say offhand whether malice or any of a thousand other motives which may contribute to the act of lying are merely supporting motives or also ulterior designs. This is to be settled only by psychological analysis in each individual case.

We shall soon want to ask whether any lie is intrinsically worse than any other lie; and, as a step to this, I raise the question whether any lie is "greater" than any other lie.

We may be and often are uncertain whether to call something a lie. We are liable to this uncertainty on account of the very great vagueness in the concept "lie" and the many inconsistencies in the common usage of the word 'lie'. Examples of vagueness and inconsistency have been given in a previous section. Any vagueness or inconsistency in the terms which name the "parts" of the lie will make the concept itself vague or inconsistent; and there is much of both in every one of these terms. So there are many moot cases, of many different kinds—near lies, partial lies, lies that are only questionably lies; and these are not academic possibilities, but frequently arise to vex the judgment in practical life. To the extent to which the concept is vague and inconsistent, we may say that lying is "a matter of degree."

But if the boundaries of the notion waver or are indistinct, this does not mean that the notion is quantitative. You may not be able to say readily whether you have spent the winter in the desert, since "winter" and "desert" have vague boundaries; yet there is not and cannot be such a thing as a degree or an amount of "spending the winter in the desert." And *lies* do not exist in amount or in degree; in other words, lying is not a magnitude, in any accepted sense of that word. No real lie—that is, a lie in which the statement, speaker's disbelief, and speaker's intention are clear-cut and determinate—is more of a lie than any real lie. In Iago's lie to Othello, Hitler's lie about the Reichstag fire, and the lie of a host to a guest for whom he has prepared a surprise party, the principle of the lie is the same.

It would be easy, though hardly worthwhile, to explain what people mean by a "big lie." If the subject of the lies is an important one, if the consequences of believing it are believed to be dire, and if the lie is (in one's own opinion) inherently implausible, though with a certain chance of being believed by some, one is apt to call it a big lie. There are people who, though they would not believe without evidence that a certain statesman cheats at cards, will believe you if you tell them that he changes himself periodically into a werewolf; and it is to such a mentality that the "big lie" is addressed. By a small lie, on the other hand, we seem to mean a morally trivial one. But neither the "big" lie nor the "small" lie of popular speech occupies any position on a scale of mendacity, because there is not and cannot be any such scale.

If this is granted, one of the crucial questions for deontological ethics immediately suggests itself. Can the same "natural" quality possess different intrinsic moral stringencies in different instances and contexts? Beyond a doubt, some lies are morally worse than others, depending on subject matter, motive, consequence, and so on. But can one lie be *intrinsically* worse than another, granted that each fully conforms to definition? Can one lie have one weight in one conflict of obligations and another lie another weight in another such conflict? It would seem that those deontologists who believe there are principles of partial obligation and that these are, moreover, axioms, should deny this possibility and proclaim a "constancy principle" for component obligations; since an axiom is not an axiom unless it holds (to say the least) for more cases than one.

I am inclined to believe, further, that this constant value, if it exists, must be equal to the intrinsic value of the *least* serious lie. I cannot prove this proposition, because there is no such thing as a "bare" lie, whose value could first be gauged in isolation and then traced through the various determinate acts of lying. The definition of the lie is, to be sure, not a blank form: it specifies characteristics which every lie must possess. But the definition *is* abstract and general. Every lie is, as it were, more than a lie: it is a lie told *to* a certain person *about* a certain thing *from* such and such motives *with* such and such probable results. Now if acts can be intrinsically right and wrong, these particularities may very well contribute to the intrinsic moral value *of the act*, since some of them (at least) qualify the act internally. But then the intrinsic value of an act of lying need not come wholly from the fact that it is an act of lying. And if that is true, we may not know what part of the value is to be ascribed to the lie.

Yet it seems probable, for the following reasons, that no lie can be intrinsically worse than the least serious lie. When we experience conflicts of obligation, with the obligation not to lie as one component, the strength of that component can be small or great. We are sometimes extremely reluctant to lie and at other times make very little of it. Now if the scruple against lying is a strong one, we need strong reasons to override it, psychologically, or to justify the lie ethically. But in the average white lie ("you are looking better today"), the motive *for* lying is often a very weak one, yet sufficient to overcome a qualm about lying; while, just as often, though not always, it is when there is much to be gained and little lost that we are disturbed at the thought of lying. Consider the case of deliberately concealing from a sick woman the fact that her daughter has been killed in an auto accident. Here (we suppose) the probable gain is palpable, but the seriousness of lying is proportionately great—most people would think very carefully before deciding to perpetrate the lie. Now if we abstract from the possible negative consequences of lying, as the deontologists would have us do, and consider only the woman's "right to know the truth," we shall find ourselves in this situation. If the lie were in itself morally trivial or innocuous, we can still hope to explain why the act of lying should be a serious thing on this particular occasion, to be outweighed, if at all, only by extremely grave considerations of the woman's life or health. For besides the abstract right of a human being to know the truth, there is her right to be informed about things that concern her closely (a right, incidentally, of which she might be deprived by other expedients than lying), her right to grieve, to participate, to assume responsibility—in a word, to know *the truth about her very own daughter*. Indeed, some of the very circumstances which prompt us to lie, for example, the woman's affection for her daughter, prompts us also to consider this lie a morally serious act. But if we were to take our notion of the intrinsic wrongness of lying from cases in which, as in this one, lying seems to be a serious matter, how shall we explain the loss of this seriousness in the so-called white lie? Only by assuming that the wrongness of lying is *outweighed* by certain moral advantages. But these advantages would have to be tremendous; whereas, as I have already pointed out, it is in pre-cisely those cases where we worry least about lying that the stakes are apt to be slight or negligible.

THE ETHICS OF LYING

Now, the least moral value that we can attribute to any clear-cut specimen of a lie is certainly a very slight one. This is a fact which must certainly embarrass the deontologist, in his customary capacity as an intuitionist holding it as "self-evident" that lying is prima facie wrong or, in other words, that to tell the truth is a component obligation in any situation. The intuitionists have always been unsuccessful in their attempts to show by what method these component obligations can be compounded, or balanced against each other, to yield a concrete obligation. But now we see a further weakness in their position. Their intention was to show that the components of an act retain a constant gravity as they pass from one moral context into another; for unless they can do this, they will be unable to claim possession of an axiom. But if the gravity is extremely small, then when they come to the cases where lying *appears* to be an important matter, they will be forced to analyze the components of the act each into *its* components, searching in each case for the shred of obligation that must always attend a given subcomponent. This may well be a futile, never-ending quest. It is, moreover, contrary to one of their most explicit claims; for they claim we know the gravity of *lying* and *promise-breaking* as such and have, in situations calling for moral choice, to make up our minds only about the force of these obligations *relatively* to others which arise in the circumstances.

In these straits what can a deontologist say or do? It will be help-ful to consider some (not all) of the possibilities open to him.

1. He can assail our definition (and that means, in effect, all ordinary or dictionary definitions) of the lie.

Now this definition already permits the partial or total exclusion of many kinds of statement that Mark Twain and other popular writers have regarded as lies. For example, the words "She is not at home," delivered by a servant or relative at the door, have become a mere euphemism for indisposition or disinclination. Since the author of the message knows that the recipient will interpret it as a polite way of saying, "It is inconvenient for me to see you now," there is no intention of making him believe something that she (the author) does not believe. We could not, therefore, on the strength of these "polite lies," say that there are lies which are in themselves innocuous; for a polite lie is often not a lie at all. But it would be absurd for the deontologist to attempt to decree, by definition, that no white, venial, or noble lie should be considered a lie. That would put him in the position of incorporating the ethical element in the definition of 'lie' and of saying, in effect, "Every deception that is prima facie wrong is prima facie wrong." No, he is in the position of having to provide his own, ethically neutral definition of lying. But then he will find that his principle, whatever it be, will gain and lose weight rapidly as it shifts from one moral situation to another.

2. He can reject the "constancy" principle (the idea that where the nature of a thing is the same, its intrinsic moral value is the same), replacing it with the proposition that lies can possess *different* intrinsic moral characters according to the situation in which they find themselves embedded. He would then maintain that we have an intuitive knowledge of right and wrong in each individual situation. He could even retain his notion of "component obligation," looking for support to aesthetics and to Gestalt psychology. For he would argue that as a certain line in a painting, which would be ugly or distressing in another composition, nevertheless makes its particular analyzable contribution to this one, so a lie which would be innocent apart from its present setting(for example, what its motive is, what it is about, to whom it is being told) makes the action more sickening than it would be otherwise. For example: (a) I say this picture is by Degas when I believe it to be an imitation. That is a venial sin, so far. (b) I sell this picture for more than it is worth, without misrepresenting it. That may be wrong; but there are those who will say that I have my rights as a trader. (c) I am able to sell this picture at a ridiculously high price by representing it as a Degas. That is an outrageous swindle.

The deontologist, however, is now in this position: What other writers say we feel or deem or surmise to be right or wrong he says we know with certainty to be right or wrong. Having surrendered the claim to any intuitive knowledge of *general* ethical truths, he has nothing left but an extra emphasis to add to the analysis of individual ethical judgments. I feel quite certain, moreover, from my knowledge of Prichard and Ross and Ewing, that they would *not* be willing to abandon the constancy principle.

3. The deontologist still has two points to make, not so much by way of escape from his predicament as by way of rebuttal.

He can declare that we have said nothing that tells against the idea of the intrinsic wrongness of an action; we have attacked only the notion that this wrongness can be known with certainty.

And he can point out that we have questioned only his ability to know *how* wrong a given act of lying is. We have argued, in effect, that the degree of prima facie wrongness is highly variable. It is still possible, consistently with this argument, that there should be an axiom to the effect that lying is prima facie wrong.

These are fairly strong points. The first I think is, in a sense, true. The second will now be examined.

By an exercise of ingenuity we could perhaps uncover some few cases where a lie seems to make a positive contribution to the action that is being considered. The deception of the guest of honor is not an unfortunate condition for the surprise party but a part of the fun, which the victim himself will share. But such examples are hardly worth analyzing. The deontologists are overwhelmingly right in thinking that lies, though their moral disvalue may be so slight as to approach zero, never go over to the other side. They tell in one direction only. They can be excused or justified, according to what the motives, ends, or consequences are. There may be "necessary lies," as Plato thought, lies that should be told. But one can hardly imagine anyone saying, "Though the action was on the whole a base one, it was at least partly redeemed by its mendaciousness." Lies are to be justified; they do not justify.[4]

It is held by at least one important school of thought in ethics that human impulses have a prima facie validity. If it is felt that a certain impulse should be restrained, some reason must be given why it should not discharge itself. Though it may be wrong of me to spend the day in bed, it is up to you to show me why. Bentham and Russell have extended this even to impulses of cruelty: the wrongness lies in the injury to the victim and not in the satisfaction of the impulse. Whether this be true or not I cannot say. But lying

---

4. As far as I know, this point is exempt from relativistic strictures. I have never heard of any action in which lying was regarded as a virtue. Spartan boys were taught to be skillful liars; but this instruction seems to have had a strictly technical purpose. The ability to lie would be useful on certain occasions, as in dealing with enemies of the state; it does not follow that one who lied to parents or magistrates was not condemned. American boys, for that matter, are sometimes taught to lie in business by fathers who would consider it a prime offense if they lied to *them*.

is certainly different. There it is the normal thing to demand a reason *for* lying, not a reason why one should not tell a lie. "Other things equal," lying is wrong; so far we see reason to agree with the deontologists in their insistence on this—though, I should add, we see no reason to believe that this principle is "self-evident."

And since, as Moore showed so convincingly in the fifth chapter of *Principia Ethica*, actions of any given kind are apt to have boundlessly variable consequences, it looks as if the uniform (prima facie) wrongness of lying were due not to consequences but to something inherent in the act—to one of its components or to its structure. Hence the "first" point of the deontologist, of the two alluded to just above, seems to be supported.

But we observe now that where the offense is small enough, the concept of *moral* wrongness seems to become inapplicable, just as it does in the violation of some petty rules of etiquette. I once remarked to a class in ethics, in the course of a substantially true story, that I had lived a year in the city of Rochester, in a house with a front lawn. None of this was true; but I intended that the students should believe it; and they did. I corrected the lie before the hour was over. My purpose in telling it was to illustrate a point in the ethics of lying; and I thought I could do so effectively only by first "victimizing" the class. But suppose I had had no such noble purpose. Suppose, indeed, that someone who happened to know I was lying saw *no* purpose at all in the lie. It would seem to him, I believe, not that the lie was wrong but that it was queer. He would wonder what the motive, and not what the justification, was. And in ignorance of any such motive, he would speculate on the possibility that there was something "wrong" with me. For 'wrong' is not used exclusively in the moral sense and in application to action. In fact, as soon as my friend saw something definitely wrong in my lie, he would be apt to discard the hypothesis that I was "wrong in the head."

A lie whose motive is unknown always prompts a query about the liar, as the simple act of telling the truth does not or need not do. It will be worth our while, therefore, to pay some attention to certain aspects of the psychology of lying.

People who say what they believe to be truth call for no explanation in terms of *special* motives. There is a natural transition between believing something and thinking it, between thinking it and saying it to oneself, between saying it to oneself and saying it aloud in response to a question. Questions are "stimuli" to the expression of opinions. When one is asked for the time of day, one thinks of what time it is—not of what time it is not. And those peculiar natures who "will not give you the right time of day" are still widely separate from people who go to the trouble of giving you the *wrong* time.

There is another natural transition from saying what one thinks to saying it with the intention of making another man believe it. The wish, without ulterior motive, to make others believe what one believes oneself seems to me to be of relatively rare occurrence; for teaching and indoctrination have many purposes—"use values" —beyond the sheer desire that the pupil shall believe what one holds to be the truth. And one is perhaps less often interested in the correspondent's state of mind than in "getting him to admit that I was right." Yet another man's ignorance is, after all, a challenge. And a man who *disagrees* with your opinion is, as it were, a standing contradiction of that opinion. The effort to convince is, in such a case, not easily distinguished from the defense of the belief or the examination of its merits; and to secure the other's assent is not unlike placing a seal of assurance upon the belief. The zeal of argument, though often influenced by extraneous motives, such as the desire to "win," can arise by an easy extension of the cognitive interest itself.

The desire to make someone believe what one does *not* oneself believe is devoid of all such inherent motive force. There is no impromptu expression of opinion. The thought that has been naturally prompted by the question is suppressed, to be replaced by another thought deliberately devised for a purpose. And it is impossible to understand why, without ulterior purpose, anyone should wish another to believe a proposition, p, when he himself thinks that p is false.

I do not think, then, that there is anyone who would "as soon lie as eat." To be sure, in a full psychology of lying, we should need to guard this generalization against potential counterexamples. For, as we remember from an earlier section of this paper, it needs only a slight supporting motive, for example, playfulness or spite, to make someone lie with apparent spontaneity. And there are many people to whom lying has become "second nature": it is virtually the definition of a pathological liar that he lies without expectation of gain. And yet it is no accident that, quite apart from the moral sense of the word, lying is identified with "crooked" thinking; and veracity follows the "straight" course. When a man lies, it is obviously sensible to ask what he expects to get out of it; some motive is needed to explain why he does not say what he thinks—even if that motive be an unconscious "hatred of the light" stemming from traumas in infancy or a repressed fear of divulging certain mental contents. But it is absurd to ask why a man who thinks that today is Tuesday should say that today is Tuesday.

I shall not enter upon the question of the guilt or fear that is sometimes presupposed by the recourse to lying. These motives are exceptionally interesting for ethical analysis and contribute very largely to the impression of crooked personality that we receive from chronic liars. But, considered as ulterior motives for lying, they are in one class with the desire for practical advantages, with the wish to shine in others' eyes, and indeed with many good motives.

It is true that the impulse to lie can have an apparently naive and spontaneous character; for many complex and even perverse urges, containing conflicts within themselves, will seem primary and positive in relation to other motives which may come along to oppose them. Suppose that I have thought of an excellent story which happens to be largely false. And suppose that (as often happens) I can gain the interest, hence the later admiration, of a listener only by passing it off as something that really happened. Now it would seem that I am dominated, above all, by the wish to tell the story in such a way that it will be believed. I do not suppress any impulse of truth-speaking or even a thought of the truth. For it was the story that I thought of first. My knowledge of the truth together with any scruples I may have will, if they are active, operate as a restraint upon the cardinal impulse, the lie; it is not the lie that inhibits honesty. But it is to be noticed here that the motive power for lying is furnished by the desire to shine or to please other people; these motives utilize lying as a means. And they must be strong enough to break through the agent's sense of the truth; for unless this sense of the truth is moderately active, we have a case of imagination or hallucination, not of lying. I repeat: the internal components of the lie, taken together, do not account for the act of lying; in other words, there is probably no such thing as a "gratuitous" lie, having as its object only the production of a belief that is not the agent's own. And in the normal case there is a positive tension between this act and some really spontaneous impulses of human nature.

One conclusion that emerges from our psychological excursion is that the extrinsic motive—the fourth element enumerated in the second section of this essay—is much more closely interwoven with the lie itself than is usually supposed. Without it the lie is "incomplete": we do not understand its human function, as we do understand the function of professing and defending beliefs. This has also a bearing upon ethics; for it is probable that the motive does not merely increase the wickedness of the lie, or (if it is a good motive) balance it, but is from the start part of what is judged when we judge the lie. But on this topic we cannot expatiate here.

The main thing that has, I believe, become comprehensible is the negative aura that must attend every lie. In the first place, I would point out that there is nothing in the least surprising about the fact that there is nothing glorious about lying, that it has no intrinsic rightness in it. To reach out and plant a false idea in another man's mind—can this be a prima facie duty? We are a long way from having demonstrated the existence of a duty to make anyone *believe* anything—much less make him believe what we do not believe ourselves. It certainly requires no power of "intuition" in the human mind to be able to see that walking in the manner of a vaudeville contortionist is not a duty. Rather, the utilitarians are so far in the right here: lying can be good as a means, therefore right, and perhaps a duty if the actual or probable consequences are good ones.

But there is also an inherent stigma, a negative quality, which corresponds to the psychological nature of the lie. A man who lies in a sense opposes himself: he denies what he affirms or affirms what he denies. And this is no wrestle of legitimate natural impulses, for there *is* no autonomous impulse to lie. The ethical demand for some redeeming motive or consequence corresponds to the need for psychological explanation. Why should I wish anyone to believe that I lived in Rochester when I know that I didn't? This, while motives remain unknown, has the aspect of inexplicable perversity. It is "wrong" in the same sense in which microcephaly is wrong; it is the wrong state of character to be in. One lie does not necessarily bespeak a crooked mind or life. A strong and straightforward purpose can "swamp" the incidental dodges and devices it employs: if one lures a child from the edge of a cliff by saying (falsely) "I have candy," the means employed, though unquestionably devious, are as if submerged in the integrity of the purpose. But there is an absolute need for a knowledge of that purpose before the normality—much more than morality—of the lie can be known.

The reader will excuse a certain artificiality in this discussion, in consideration of the fact that in an endeavor to meet the deontologists on their own ground I have restricted myself to the question, "What is wrong with lying *in itself?*" To say even that truth is good and useful and error dangerous and that lying breeds error and impedes truth would be to draw in questions of consequences; whereas deontology must discover the moral value of the lie in its internal components: (1) the statement, (2) the speaker's disbelief, (3) the intention, or (4) some relationship among these components. And it is to be noted that of these the third, intention, draws some part of its moral value from the goodness or badness of its end; for how can it be bad or wrong deliberately to disseminate error, unless error is in some way bad? I have, however, been able to find a relationship of incongruity if not of diametric opposition between (1), (2), and (3)—especially (2) and (3)—above, which accounts for some part of the negative feeling we have about lying. And so far as this does account for it, the ethics of lying cannot be wholly utilitarian.

But it is still another thing to concede the intrinsic *moral* wrongness of the lie, as against merely *some* kind of inherent disvalue. It is much less noteworthy that the man who lures his child from the edge of a cliff uses a regrettable expedient than that this same expedient swells up monstrously when a man bears false witness against his neighbor. (I do not speak of luring the child *to* the edge of the cliff and over, because in that instance the wickedness of the *lie* dwindles by comparison with the motive and result.) In slandering a neighbor, we are apt to harm him; but we can do that also on occasion by telling the truth. When we slander him, his and the moralist's attention are apt to focus on the *falsity* of the charge, which seems almost as grave an offense as the damage that will be done. The deontologist is not wrong in calling attention to this stress in our moral judgments. But in explaining the world of difference that exists between calling my neighbor an arsonist when he is really a fireman and calling him blond when he is really dark, extra determinants must be sought in the variable features of the lie itself—for example, in the difference between one false statement and another.

To sum up, then, as regards the main ethical points, they are two. (1) Through an analysis of the structure of the lie, the claim to the perception of an inherent, even if partial, moral wrongness is whittled down until we reach the threshold of morality and *perhaps* plunge beneath: it makes little difference whether we say that there must always be at least a *slight* moral wrongness or say that the wrongness is not moral at all. (2) But the rights and wrongs of lying cannot easily (if at all) be assimilated totally to an ethics of ends and consequences. This is because the act is sophisticated and internally involved from the very beginning: not initially naive and therefore indifferent until experience shows predominantly good or evil results. Of itself it tends *downward* in the ethical scale. But consistently with the point of (1) above, I go so far as to exhibit in it only (a) some inherent *disvalue* and (b) a character that is probably *symptomatic* of further disvalue and of moral delinquency.

Now if we still think there is something inherently wrong with *lies*—something tangible and weighty that lends itself to analysis only along deontological lines—the thing is to go to the individual case and, notably, to the "bad" case, and see whether the specific values of the factors internal to the situation (statement, intention, motive, character and rights of the person addressed) do not, as well as actual and probable consequences, contribute something to the specific moral quality. I have no doubt that it will often be found difficult or impossible to eliminate these in favor of results. But I confess that I do not see that there can be any positive *general* conclusion to be drawn.

16
Ethical
and Aesthetic
Criticism

The esthetic attitude is directed upon what Prall has called the 'esthetic surface'; and in this it stands in contrast with that commoner concern which takes what is presented as sign of or clue to something further; else it stands in contrast with those evaluations which are determined by reference to the ends of action. Again, it stands in contrast with attention to and any appreciation of the utilities of things which are not values realizable in presentation of the object having them but find their fruition in the experience of something else.

C. I. Lewis

Ulterior judgment, practical and moral, will inevitably color every perception given to a rational creature. To say that such simultaneous human reactions do not affect aesthetic feeling is to walk the tight rope of artificial distinctions. A tripartite division of the soul, laid down by the psychologist, will not prevent all the elements present in experience from affecting the beauty, charm and perfection of the objects about which imagination may play, or from rendering them now wholly gracious and beautiful, now trivial and vile.

Santayana

You can never draw the line between aesthetic criticism and moral and social criticism; you cannot draw the line between criticism and metaphysics; you start with literary criticism, and however rigorous an

---

Read at the Berkeley Aesthetics Group in the spring of 1953 and at Michigan State University in the fall of 1953. Copies of this paper were made available to the editors by Professor Arnold Koslow, City University of New York, and by Professor John Goheen, Stanford University.

aesthete you may be, you are over the frontier onto something else sooner or later. The best you can do is to accept these conditions and know what you are doing when you do it.

T. S. Eliot

The venerable problem of "the relations between art and life" resembles nothing so much as the mass of intricately intercopulating snakes once seen by one of the English essayists on a walking trip in the country. One should consider it an achievement to have extricated, from such a snarl, a single determinable issue; and that is what I shall be trying to accomplish in this paper. But such an attempted breakdown of the famous problem requires the use of abstract and simplified concepts; and it is not to be hoped that the result will seem adequate to the warm, living, and malodorous subject matter. It should seem, rather, like a schematic construction—to be justified, if at all, as providing an entrance to that subject matter for analytic intelligence.

Specifically, we are to resolve the broad question about art and life into three parts: one about the nature of the *object* in aesthetic experience; one about the attitude of the *judge;* and one about the descriptive-or-normative character of the judging *process.* Our final position will be derivative from the answers given to these three questions.

Our present interest is further limited by the desire to mediate among the authors quoted above, of whom Mr. Lewis seems opposed to Santayana and Eliot, who seem on the whole to agree with each other. And our subject will restrict itself still further as we proceed.

ETHICAL CRITICISM

The greater part of all the art criticism that has ever been written has been moralistic in tone or content; often vehemently moralistic, dealing quite freely in adjectives like 'noble' and 'exalted' or 'base', 'vile', 'corrupt', 'sordid', and 'vicious'. A nearly unanimous practice like this on the part of critics could not very well be based on a complete misconception of their calling. It makes us hesitate to say that works of art are something wholly "amoral" and in principle exempt from the type of stricture so commonly applied to them. And it makes us feel that an opinion like the one quoted from Professor Lewis, even if plausible, even if (as I think it is) quite sound, does not do entire justice to aesthetic experience. On the other hand, there is no reason to accept every critic's language at its moral face value. Ethics has, among other things, to decide what the proper objects of moral judgment are: the whole discussion of "free will and responsibility"—to take a single example—arises from the fact that people moralize about certain acts which other people think are not to be moralized about, or moralize in a *way* that others think unsuitable. The criticism of art can of course be "unjust," as the criticism of action so often is. But besides that we must say that the very presumption in offering a judgment of art upon ethical grounds may, in a given case, be unwarranted. Let us suppose that I have drawn some marks on a sheet of paper which, though quite without merit, are wholly innocuous—"nonmoral" if anything in creation is nonmoral. Now suppose that I frame this object, exhibit it, and receive a certain amount of credit. Sooner or later somebody will denounce it as a fraud; that is, it will become the object of attacks which, though they really belong to the ethics of publishing and exhibiting, seem to be directed against the "work of art." How can a drawing which is morally indifferent when it lies on a table become morally objectionable when it hangs on a wall? Yet it is no far cry from this artificial example of intrusion by ethics on the province of taste to the confusions daily exhibited by critics in their work.

If, in contrast with such impertinence, there are genuine and proper tasks for an ethical critic, these would seem to correspond to whatever we take to be the moral functions of art. But those are endless in number and miscellaneous in type. A poet is denounced for writing about flowers in time of war—though you might read the poem and find not only nothing wrong but nothing which as a moralist you can judge. A novelist is blamed for treating living persons who might be identified and embarrassed. The production of a play involves a drain on the resources of the community; and there are those who say it should make up for this by rendering a commensurate service—art for art's sake is a luxury which society cannot afford. The writers of pulp fiction and of movie scripts have, it is said, an influence on the public mind: more notable, however, than any *effect* they may have on their audience is the fact that they *cater* to more or less inglorious appetites already installed in the public breast; and we have various ways of thinking about the trades which pander to the several desires of men. Each of these cases represents some "function" that a work of art can have in its social context and, accordingly, also some kind of judgment that a moralist could pass on it. It is obvious that the various sorts of morality and immorality, attributed by these judgments, are very different one from another. But I would say also that all *these* moral functions, selected here for notice, are adventitious to the content of the work of art and hence do not tell us what it is we understand by an ethical evaluation of that content. Let us examine only one of them. To judge the moral value of a poem by the effect it is likely to have on the character and conduct of its audience[1] is to place it in a class with acts which, like smoking or crossing the street in traffic, take all or most of their moral quality from actual or probable consequences. Speaking is an act which may sometimes be rated in this way—as when we spread false stories about acquaintances or say hello to a friend who for some reason wishes to remain unrecognized. A good speech, by this way of reckoning, is one that does good or that we have reason to think will do good. But when we are asked to consider the "morality" of a sermon, a political speech, or a didactic poem, we certainly do not consider first of all how it will affect those who listen to it. We consider first what it advocates: we ask what position the author takes. We think we can form an opinion of the contents. We believe that, by and large (and with exceptions in the case of children's reading, and so on), *good* literature will have good effects on people, if any sort of literature does; thereby assuming that the goodness of the work is to be determined independently of those effects. I call "adventitious" any function of the work of art the judgment of which is based in any part on the act of presenting that work (speaking out loud, publishing, performing) or on the cost of that presentation, or on its potential aftereffects—on anything, in fact, but what the work is or says. And by a narrowly "proper" ethical judgment, as to the nature of which we are shortly to inquire, I mean one that judges the object itself and tells us whether *that* is good or bad. But before investigating such judgments, we must say something about the object to be judged.

1. See, for example, Mortimer Adler, *Art and Prudence* (New York: Longmans, Green, 1937), p. 346: "But if it is a moral judgment, it means that the work of art judged to be good is so judged because its effects upon character and conduct are judged to be beneficial. Hence to judge a work of art upon moral grounds, we must first know the influence of the work upon men."

DIDACTICISM

If the criticism of literature were found to be necessarily an ethical one, it would not follow that the criticism of pots and pans, or of music, must be so too. But if a purely aesthetic criticism of literature were a legitimate and feasible thing, this should also be true of any other art. Literature is the *strong case* of moral involvement among the fine arts; so that if the literary work can, in any situation, relinquish its moral function, we may be reasonably sure that any other aesthetic object can do so.

The strong case of moral involvement among works of literature is the didactic poem or essay. If this were found to be susceptible of a purely aesthetic interpretation, the conclusion should hold a fortiori for any other kind of literature.

These seem to me to be good reasons for confining our attention to didactic art. But there are others. That the moral values that are held by poets manage to express themselves in poetry which is not explicitly didactic is not to be doubted. But the ways in which these values are conveyed to us by the poetry are often devious and subtle. To take an exceptionally simple example, in the line

France, mother of arts, of arms, and of men

we seem to have arts, arms, and men arrayed all on one plane, as if equally worthy of celebration. The poem does not say, yet we cannot be sure that it does not somehow "imply," that one is as good as another; and we may imagine a reader who should be disturbed by what he takes to be the underlying moral assumption. A rash moralist will not be deterred in his judgment of the poem by the elusiveness of its moral content; but a conscientious ethical critic will find no ready handle for his evaluation. But this, as I said, is a relatively simple case: to step into the atmosphere of Milton's *Ode on the Morning of Christ's Nativity* is to find oneself in a coherent moral universe without necessarily being able to grasp a single proposition that one could agree or disagree with. Such verses are commonly responded to with indeterminate moral enthusiasm or with repugnance; but it is not easy (I do not mean that it is impossible) to see how they could be rationally evaluated and "accepted" or "rejected."

It is essential, for a cogent examination of ethical criticism, to pass over, as simply too difficult for immediate treatment, all these modes of indirection and presupposition— parable, allegory, satire, and so on—in order to find something which, because it presents the moral conviction in a tangible form, admits of straightforward appraisal. This requirement is met by the ordinary didactic poem. One is aware of the fact that many critics who assign a moral function to poetry nevertheless disavow the old-fashioned belief that literature should teach or exhort to action. But for that reason they are unable to make it clear just what the moral function of the poem is supposed to be, and have to resort to high-sounding but evasive phrases. Though there may be an ethical art which is not didactic, yet didacticism is typically ethical in quality; and a moral interpretation of poetry should concern itself *at least* with this mode of direct moralizing, which has contributed so many masterpieces to literature.

We may say that a poem is didactic if (a) it features, in their customary places, any of the regular ethical terms, such as 'good', 'evil', 'right', 'wrong', as in Sophocles' passage which begins

> Of all the foul growths current in the world
> The worst is money

or (b) is cast in the imperative mood,[2] as in Sophocles' line

> Accept what life God gives and ask no longer span

or (c) assembles descriptive propositions in such a way as clearly to point to a moral conclusion, as in the remark: "He is a great practical joker but resents the slightest jest made at his own expense," where a condemnation is clearly intended. And see the poem of Blake quoted later on.

Whether a poem is *didactic* (or moral in *quality*) depends, then, on what it says; the meaning one finds in it; the particular cast of its contents. Preaching and teaching are modes of literary expression, like narrative, lyric, and drama: any one of these is marked off from another in ways that can be recognized by anyone who understands the language. A poem consisting wholly of lines like "the sky is blue, the grass is green" has no message, no moral content. Poetry can be elusively didactic, as we have seen; but this is still a question of discoverable ranges of meaning and is always to be settled merely by interpreting the text.

But whether a poem has an *ethical role* (or a moral *function*)

2. I do not assume that every imperative expresses a moral judgment. But I assume that some moral judgments express themselves as imperatives.

depends not alone on what it says but on the way in which it is taken, the purpose that happens to be afoot; the context of mental consideration into which it enters. Language has no ethical role unless it is related either to a state of moral belief or to a process of deliberation in some person or other. And language neither automatically indicates such a state or process in the writer nor compels one in the reader. I write down on this page the words, "Go to the ant, thou sluggard." This is didactic and is understood as such by every reader. But it is working here as an illustration of a point in aesthetic theory. In a dramatic context, while retaining its present meaning, it might work in such a way as to stamp the speaker as a plagiarist or a bore. The possible roles are endless. One becomes aware of the difference between these and the strictly ethical function simply by asking what one does if one wishes to know whether it is well to go to the ant. How does this maxim of thrift and prudence comport with the advice to consider the lilies of the field? And which of these is to be preferred to the other?

The point is the more worth stressing because it has been obscured in contemporary critical theory. We find critics quoting poems which are hortatory in tone and content and saying, "See, *some* poems at least have ulterior ends." Here in one breath is a statement of what the poem contains and a statement about how it must be used; but the two are always separable. Poems do not have ends, and do not lack them either; only a person can have an end or can have omitted to adopt one. And the presence of a didactic meaning in the mind is not sufficient to provide anyone with an end. I admit that, just as it would be hard to read a passage in which every other sentence began with *hence* without supposing that the author had been performing inferences and without performing them oneself, so it is hard to read some passages in Dante without supposing that the poet had both a belief and a purpose. I do not deny that some poets have been moralists in the strictest sense. But I do not concede that the use or the understanding of a form of words, no matter what, is enough to *make* a moralist of the poet or the reader. And I do, as a matter of fact, doubt that the poet who said

> Avoid the reeking herd,
> Shun the polluted flock

wished anyone, or intended himself, to avoid the reeking herd or shun the polluted flock. If one is unable to see how these lines should not function as moral precept, it is because one does not understand what other roles may be played by moral ideas: one does not, for instance—though understanding very well how the side of a mountain can be an object of interest for one who is neither a geologist nor a surveyor—see how a "side" of a moral question can be an attractive thing, in itself and apart from its merits as a solution to that question.

A didactic poem, in virtue of its content, is always *fit* for ethical criticism, as not every piece of writing is. And if ethical criticism results in a perception of ethical value, it is permissible to say that the poem "has" that value whether or not any concern for that kind of value happens to be afoot at the moment—just as it "is" either true or false that ghosts once "did squeak and gibber in the streets of Rome," even though we usually take this line in the play as pure fiction, which is being neither asserted nor denied. In other words, we should be saying that the poem would be seen to have such a value if someone did criticize it ethically. But it is implied in the point of view of this paper that this value will not be the same as one which is perceived through a different method of evaluation. Thus I should think that the following stanzas of Herbert and the poem of Blake both have (or *may* have) positive aesthetic value.

> Beware of lust: it doth pollute and foul
> Whom God in Baptisme washt with His own blood.
> It blots the lesson written in thy soul;
> The holy lines cannot be understood.
>> How dare those eyes upon a Bible look
>> Much lesse towards God, whose lust is all their book?
>
> Abstain wholly, or wed. Thy bounteous Lord
> Allows thee choise of paths: take no by-wayes;
> But gladly welcome what he doth afford;
> Not grudging, that thy lust hath bounds and staies.
>> Continence hath his joy: weigh both; and so
>> If rottennesse have more, let heaven go.
>>> George Herbert—from "The Church-Porch"
>
> I went to the Garden of Love,
> And saw what I never had seen:
> A Chapel was built in the midst,
> Where I used to play on the green.
>
> And the gates of this Chapel were shut,
> And 'Thou shalt not' writ over the door;

So I turned to the Garden of Love
That so many sweet flowers bore;

And I saw it was filled with graves,
And tomb-stones where flowers should be,
And priests in black gowns were walking their rounds,
And binding with briars my joys and desires.
                    William Blake—"The Garden of Love"

And, without begging any question as to the kind or kinds of "inconsistency" that may subsist as between ethical propositions, I should think they could not both have positive ethical value. But this means that either poem might have, in the opinion of any given reader, both a positive and a negative value; and it is not possible for such apparently "opposed" values to be determined by a single judgment. But if, in ascribing one value to a poem, we were deciding an ethical issue, while in ascribing another value we had confined our thought to a mere aspect of that issue, the two values would not be opposed at all, since they would not be of the same type.

The Aesthetic Assimilation of Didactic Content

If didactic content can be put to some of the uses mentioned above, it certainly can be put to an aesthetic use; and for this there are only two conditions, one positive and one negative. The didactic utterance must be understood; and this lends to the experience of reading an inalienable moral quality—one could not ignore the specific moral significance of 'should', 'should not', 'right', 'wrong', and other terms that may appear in the poem and still claim to have grasped the object that was presented by the poet. But the moral understanding must be its own justification: it cannot be subordinated, as a mere first stage, to the sort of concern which is shown by those who look to the poem as a guide in the conduct of life.

Every moment of experience faces two ways: it is the end of one series of events in time and the beginning of another. Besides that, experiences are commonly *treated*, by the human subject, as relatively final or relatively introductory and transitional. When we listen to ethical advice or read maxims in the Book of Proverbs, we lean, normally, toward the second of these attitudes of mind. We read for "profit"—to read for pleasure is to show no respect for the authors of moral thought, who expect us either to act as they say or to think upon what they say and then to act—and the literary experience is only the commencement of a chain of thoughts or motions which has an objective quite different from that experience itself. But the same point could, after all, be made about sense-perception, which is normally only a preface to motor behavior; and yet it is orthodox doctrine in aesthetics to say that colors, shapes, and sounds can be enjoyed for themselves. Now the present interpretation of moral literature as aesthetic experience has only this one thesis: that the moral understanding—and not only the color sense or the sense of hearing—can be called by certain objects into a kind of free play. We then give ourselves over to the reception of moral ideas. These being *moral* ideas, our experience will not be morally toneless and neutral: it involves an interest in something more than rhythms and phonetic harmonies. But since these are only moral *ideas*, our experience will take in something less than what would be needed to establish moral truth. This middle position between sensory enjoyment and ethical deliberation does, I think, describe the consciousness of the average playgoer or reader of poetry, who feels that his sympathies and antipathies are indeed engaged by the poem but does not believe he is being called upon to deliberate, choose, and act.

These remarks lead us to the single emendation we would propose to the views quoted from C. I. Lewis at the start of this article. To say that the aesthetic attitude "stands in contrast with those evaluations which are determined by reference to the ends of action" is strictly correct. But this position may unfortunately confuse itself with either of two others: (a) that art should not preach; or (b) that when poetry does preach, it cannot be aesthetically assimilated. We have then the "antididactic" standpoint, a critical doctrine which restricts the admissible content of art, forming the precise converse of the "prodidacticism" (briefly touched on above) which, while restoring that content (though perhaps with some prejudice to the legitimacy of "pure" poetry), leaves aesthetic experience unlimited in its function.

When we read, "Go to the ant," we do in a sense consider an action and may even envisage the "end" of the action, which in this particular case is plainly set forth a little later in the text. And if the words we are criticizing deal with action and end, our evaluation must refer to them. It is only the question of whether to *make* that end our own or to approve it as another's that may well be absent from consideration: if so, the evaluation is not ethical in type. This point deserves a further elucidation.

EVALUATION

A special advantage of the didactic poem, as an example of ethical quality in art, is that it can be treated as a judgment rather than as a deed. If we grant that a poem is subject to moral judgment, is it like a lie or an act of cowardice, which is condemned or defended; or is it like a tract in defense of lying, which is judged ethically sound or unsound? The line between judgment and action might not be an easy one to draw: actions have judgments among their causes; and judgments become acts again when they are expressed—people have been sent to jail for their judgments. Still one would suppose that if an act of expressing a judgment can be immoral, there must be something behind the act—namely, the judgment itself—which was simply mistaken. Now we find that poems expressing values of various kinds have often been termed moral or immoral; indeed, the adjectives of praise and abuse listed earlier in this essay apply rather better to what people do than to what they think; so that the question stated just above cannot be prejudged. But a didactic poem is at least a judgment; and it offers us the chance to criticize it as an opinion before we try it as a culprit.

Now since didactic poetry belongs to the class of utterances which advocate courses of action, whatever method we use customarily for deciding whether a sermon is a good sermon, an editorial opinion is well or ill conceived, a piece of advice is sound or dangerous, will also be followed in the ethical criticism of didactic verse. And I would describe that method somewhat as follows:

1. We fix the speaker's meaning in our minds—try to understand what it is he proposes.

2. We see what reasons can be given for and against his proposals.

These reasons are in the nature of propositions describing the consequences of the speaker's message. But *not* "consequences" in the sense of effects to be apprehended from the uttering (printing, circulating) of the poem or sermon. And, on the whole, probably not the "consequences" that can be logically deduced from the idea proposed. But, chiefly, those consequences that *would* follow *if* people were to act in the way they are being urged to act. It is these "consequences," mentally foreseen as the result of a meditated course of action, that are so often confused with the effects upon the audience of speaking or reciting certain words.

3. We try to decide whether these reasons are true. This may involve a complicated routine.

4. We weigh the reasons pro and con and try to decide how much support they give to the point of view expressed. (Various more or less conflicting accounts have been given of this weighing process.)

5. We find ourselves in agreement or disagreement with the said point of view. And according to our decision, so obtained, we *characterize* the ethical content—as "vicious nonsense," "good sound sense," or what not. This judgment represents an opinion as to that moral function which is "proper" to the poem and which is to be contrasted with all those adventitious relationships that we agreed to dismiss from consideration.

The reader may quarrel with this account of ethical evaluation. He may wish to add, qualify, or obliterate some point. I do not need to insist on every detail. But I must and do insist on certain generalities: (a) The criticism comes, and may well last some time, *after* the reception of the poem. (b) It also envisages certain matters which would arise, if at all, not only after the poem had been read but after someone had acted in the manner prescribed. (c) In still other ways (for example, verification of reasons under 3) it takes account of circumstances which lie beyond the poem, though not necessarily in time but in some ideal dimension. (d) Such criticism is discursive in essence, comprising a whole series of steps or stages within itself.

Nobody needs to be told that our *moral reactions* to poetry and other forms of speech do not always subject themselves to such a painful trial. For one thing, we have often made up our minds, before reading the poem, on the matters agitated in the poem and can respond to the moral content as speedily as to a thunderclap. ("Edification" consists in the discovery of a pat agreement between the poem and what the reader believes already.) For another thing, we do not always have minds to make up: we can go on kindergarten maxims when we are "inspired" or "revolted" by moralistic verse. We are already moral beings when we enter the theater or open a book. And we are apt to fancy ourselves as finished moral beings: nothing could be further from the minds of those critics who say, "it is the business of plays to recommend virtue and discountenance vice," than the notion that *they* stand in need of instruction from *poets*. All the usual conditions of moral response to a poem are *previous* to the reading of the poem, immediate in their rebound, and heedless of any correction of which they may stand in need.

But the same things could be said of human opinion in general, which is commonly instantaneous in discharge and vociferous in tone; and just insofar as these things are true, no criticism is possible of scientific, religious, or moral ideas—but only a swapping of reactions on common themes. The process of evaluation which I have endeavored to describe does not by any means represent a set of stages through which our feelings go in their formation but an ordeal to which they would have to submit if they were challenged and wished to defend themselves: it represents the grounds on which the moral acceptability of the poem ideally and ultimately rests. Why should the critic's moral sense be superior to the poet's, or vice versa, unless there were these ulterior grounds to which to repair for mediation of their conflict? I do not seek to show, against extreme relativists, that there is an objective moral truth but only that *if* there is such a truth, it must be found by a line of thought which takes in something more than the sheer meaning of moral propositions and the reactions provoked by that meaning.

CRITICISM AS NORMATIVE

It is only a step from these reflections to the requisite commentary of Santayana (see the passage quoted at the head of this article). Much might be said in explication of the idea that criticism, ethical and aesthetic, is a normative procedure; but all we are bound to note at this place is, first, that as regards the work of art, the critic is concerned with its value and not alone with its nature and causes; and, second, that as regards any *opinion* about the value of the work of art, no critic will regard it as being for his purpose fixed, final, and beyond review—if he did, the question of his own agreement with this opinion would not be relevant. As Santayana put it once, "It is just the function of ethics [and, we add, of aesthetic criticism] to revise *prima facie* judgments." Now it is customary for psychologists in their textbooks to provide separate chapters for Thinking, Feeling, Motivation, and so on. A strange practice, when you consider that nearly all our thinking is to some degree wishful and that there are perhaps few wishes which have not been influenced by cognition; yet anyone who on this ground alone accused the psychologist of drawing "artificial distinctions" would be a fool. And if these psychological distinctions can be defended, then perhaps it is defensible too for someone to distinguish, within the response of an organism encountering a work of art, aesthetic and practical components. But this whole question of psychology is beside the point; for our responses to art, when critically considered, are considered as committing us (*for the future*) to one or another line of investigation, by which they are to be ratified or invalidated. One of these roads takes us back to the poem, and back and back again, toward a sharper and more complete realization. The other takes us beyond the poem toward the act of choice, over all those considerations which have a bearing on choice. The aesthetic-moral judgment from which we may have started thus proves to be forked: its branches are visibly distinct once it gets out into the open field. What conceals this divergence from us, for a time, is the uncritical self—the lazy and turbid original nature which seeks neither moral nor aesthetic instruction but wishes only to proclaim itself.

Our criticism of Santayana is thus based mainly on what he has overlooked—namely, the difference between aesthetic psychology and critical procedure. But the passage from Eliot is wrong in what it says. You do not "start" as a rigorous aesthete and find yourself "getting into" ethics and metaphysics. You begin as a primitive aesthete, moralist, historian, scientist, and so on—the "whole man" that so many critics like to imagine themselves as being, with his several capacities, as it were, in solution—and find yourself adopting specialized roles the more seriously concerned you are to settle particular questions.[4]

It is so obvious that judgment purifies and does not muddy itself as it becomes disciplined and responsible that one is forced to wonder how anybody could think the opposite; and I would like to offer a partial explanation. It was T. S. Eliot who said of the great poet and novelist: "He [Thomas Hardy] seems to me to have written as nearly for the sake of 'self-expression' as a man well

---

4. Of course, Eliot may be interpreted as saying there is an *irresistible inclination* on the part of literary critics to trifle with moral problems. This, alas, is true.

Both passages are hopelessly confused in their details. For example, Eliot says "you cannot draw a line" and then says that you are bound to cross the line; while Santayana, just by using the phrase "ulterior judgment," is drawing the very distinction he describes as artificial.

can; and the self which he had to express does not strike me as a particularly wholesome or edifying matter of communication." It was Eliot who said of the great philosopher: "Thomas Hobbes was one of those impertinent little upstarts whom the chaotic motions of the Renaissance tossed into an eminence which they scarcely deserved and have never lost." And it is Eliot who quotes the glorious lines from Chapman beginning "A man to join himself with the Universe" and comments: "A man does not join himself with the Universe so long as he has anything better to join himself with"—adding a few more words equally sophisticated and fatuous. Now if you are interested in emitting flip reactions and striking fancy moral poses, *of course* it will seem to you that aesthetic criticism and moral criticism cannot be separated. For both will issue from obscure recesses in the breast, where messy complexes of feeling and emotion mingle with one another and fight and procreate and give off weird and tangled growths. But it would seem to be just exactly the office of criticism, advancing beyond this level at which so many of us find ourselves at the start, to clarify vision, thought, and feeling.

Those who proceed by intuition in ethics, politics, and metaphysics very curiously but still quite naturally do not give that method its full rights in the one sphere where it is really competent: the judgment of art. If you think you can taste the quality of a society or a government, if you rate philosophical systems by the sense of smell, if you stretch forth "antennae" to feel out the defects in modern civilization, then "thinking" will not seem to you to be very different from aesthetic appreciation. The intuition of the modern critic, as applied to the study of nature and society, is not strictly intuitive; it embodies inferential processes within itself and is different from reason only in disregarding the full commitment of empirical and of ethical judgment. It is, in fact, a shrewd but half-hearted kind of reasoning. But to bring vague moral prejudices to bear on painting or poetry does not take us *very far* beyond immediate experience. So that when discursive thought, with its responsibility to the further implications of ideas, collapses into what literary men call "perception," it finds a loosely expanded "aesthetic judgment" coming to meet it half way. And at this point in the circuit one might be forgiven for thinking that aesthetics was ethics and ethics aesthetics. It is only when either discipline is pressed to its extreme limit that their mutual distinctness can be seen. To gain or recover a sense for the strict labor of aesthetic perception and comprehension, one must first know how severe are the obligations of ethical thought.

Aesthetic Criticism

Of all that lurks unexamined at the edges of this article and of all the serious objections that can be brought against what it contains, I can take up only a single point; and that is a difficulty which cannot well be ignored. "How then *do* you tell the difference between good moral poetry and bad? What is the positive nature of this 'aesthetic judgment' whose purity you are so eager to defend?"

The question might justifiably be turned aside; for it assumes that ethical judgment is somehow easier than aesthetic judgment and only if the last is a species of the former do we have a palpable basis for criticism; but that is extremely dubious. I should think that some moral problems, never having been solved at all, were harder than some aesthetic questions, on which multitudes of men have agreed; and that some problems about merit in art were so hard that neither ethical standards nor any other have helped to settle them. People (we might also retort) do not judge linoleum patterns moralistically and yet are able to decide, to their own satisfaction, that one is better than another; how is this?

But it may be well to offer an answer which, if brief and sketchy, is at least slightly constructive. Any issue of moral ideas may be an aesthetic object. But a didactic poem is a work of *art*— which means that ethical material is not merely utilized but is worked into a structure. Now there are structures built of other than ethical materials; and there it is common enough for critics to employ such criteria as "unity" and "coherence." Without analyzing these terms or the ways in which they are applied, we may recognize that elements within a structure sometimes seem intrusive, disruptive, or discordant with the whole. So may it be too if these elements are moral significances and if the structure is a didactic one. Thus when Satan, in *Paradise Lost*, speaks of himself as having been

> glorious once above thy sphere;
> Till pride and worse ambition pulled me down,
> Warring in Heaven against Heaven's matchless king

I seem to see, in words like 'worse' and 'matchless', a sly encroachment of Milton's values upon Satan's proper character. Or if the reader does not agree with my view of these lines, he will perhaps not deny that some of the moralizing in this poem is hauled in by the heels, as if to seize the chance to plug in behalf of the true doctrines, when story and character require something else; and the effect is one of *falsetto*.

Moral elements may jar with one another, or with the nonmoral elements in the poem. But "harmony" and "coherence" are not the only structural criteria; and structural criteria are not the only ones we have. When we have stopped trying to evaluate moral ideas depthwise—that is, in terms of their connections with action and eventual result—there remains every manner of consideration concerning their inner qualities and their relations one with another; and though this, as an abstract principle, does not take us far in handling all the strange phenomena of poetry—the loathsomeness of certain poems which present perfectly correct and approved sentiments, the moral resonance and vibration of some poems which seem to have no moral content whatever, the nobility of "evil" ideas (as in Baudelaire), the dreariness of "good" ones (as in Longfellow)—still it should encourage analytical attacks upon these fastnesses, counteracting the prepossession that the critic is helpless when he ceases to be a moralist.

Appendixes

Appendix A:
Analytical
Philosophy and
the Study of Art

There can be no doubt that the revival of analysis in this century has had valuable effects upon some of the main branches of philosophy. Many problems in epistemology, logic, and ethics have been treated with an almost unexampled rigor. New lines of inquiry have been opened up and pursued with patience and care. A good deal of light has been shed on some philosophical ideas that have been obscure for centuries. And conservative philosophers, who resist some of the more comprehensive claims made by the logical analysts, have been forced to examine and restate their positions.

Against this record of accomplishment must be set the fact that analytic philosophers often have a restricted range of interests and apply themselves only to matters that already have a high technical status. Many rich and fruitful problems of psychology, ethics, social and religious philosophy which are eminently susceptible of analytic treatment are handled today by phenomenologists, existentialists, Marxists, and schools of theology. There exists something of a cleavage in philosophy between the practitioners of

---

This section consists of excerpts from pages 5–6, 14–28, 39–41, and 43–46 of *Analytical Philosophy and the Study of Art: A Report to the Rockefeller Foundation,* a monograph, multigraphed and distributed by the Rockefeller Foundation, April 1950. Excerpting done by Mary Mothersill. Reprinted with permission. Copies of the full report are available from the Rockefeller Foundation.

exact method and the students of humane subjects. Aesthetics is one field which has so far not benefited by the contemporary development of analysis.

. . . .

Critics, historians, editors, teachers normally absorbed in the primary problems of interpretation frequently turn aside and write or lecture on the tools of their trades. There are excellent reasons why they should do so. At certain stages in the development of any subject, problems of method become compelling. Some of the narrower specialties have, to be sure, attained a stable footing. The "science of bibliography" is relatively well defined; etymology, iconology, and certain parts of musicology are channels in which scholarship can move ahead without much self-questioning. (At that, we have many articles and volumes on methods of textual criticism, principles of emendation, and so forth.) But the status of the larger questions remains obscure. There is, for instance, a difference between the interpretation of an obsolete word in Shakespeare and the interpretation of a character in Shakespeare. These two questions are theoretically of the same type; yet the first can usually be determined with accuracy, while the second commonly leads to ontological and epistemological entanglements, as we shall see later. —Besides these internal incentives for the discussion of method, there are others which are provided by conflicts of teaching method and teaching aim. Scholars usually believe in the importance of their own lines of work and advocate their diffusion throughout the curriculum—or the nation. Our arts departments are governed very largely by technical historians, who draw up requirements which do not agree very well with the intellectual proclivities of students. These specialists are challenged by social and cultural historians, who again have quarrels within their own family. Meanwhile, the very premises of the historical approach are questioned by moralistic critics or by the advocates of a "pure" criticism. An interest in the methods of criticism, the relations between history and criticism, and cognate questions is fostered incessantly by these controversies over educational policy.

For these and other reasons, a secondary literature dealing with the problems of the art studies has arisen and grown to enormous proportions. Language associations have devoted whole meetings and whole issues of their proceedings to debates over method.

Many volumes devoted wholly to questions of method appear each year; and in most primary works of scholarship we find either a separate essay or a passing opinion about "the sociological approach to literature," "methods of art interpretation," "the importance of the history of ideas for the appreciation of literature," and similar topics. As for criticism, not a month or a week passes without articles on "the role of the critic" or "the function of criticism" being written by scholars, critics, or literary men. Books about "the principles of criticism" have been a well-established genre since the eighteenth century.[1]

This body of writing contains every degree of thoughtfulness, adequacy, insight, and suggestiveness, according to the author and the chapter or page that we happen to examine. I have, however, to express an opinion as to its encompassing limitations—without taking all the space that would be needed to substantiate my opinion. These writers are engaged in philosophical analysis. There is no particular reason why philosophizing should not be done, and done well, by people who have not taken their degrees in philosophy; and we find, in fact, that the most interesting work of the type we are considring has been done by art historians or critics rather than by professional philosophers. Yet these men, trained in responsibility to their own primary crafts, are unaware of the responsibilities of analysis and tend, as analysts, to be slack, casual, amateurish, and informal.

We may first consider an example. In the context of an interpretation of Shakespeare's characters, the distinguished German scholar, Schücking, enunciates the following principle:

If we fix our attention on the manifestation of his character from the very beginning of the play, we shall be better able to recognize it than by investigating minutely what Hamlet was *before* the events related in the play. This point of view, which is taken, e.g., by Kuno Fischer, Bradley, etc., must be regarded as quite erroneous if only for the reason that it always comes perilously near confounding art and reality. Only what has been present in the poet's consciousness can be adduced for the purpose of explaining artistic creations. In the case of an imagined figure we cannot

1. And books *about* books about the principles of criticism, for example, M. H. Abrams, *The Mirror and the Lamp* (Oxford: Oxford University Press, 1953); Walter J. Bate, *From Classic to Romantic* (Cambridge, Mass.: Harvard University Press, 1949); S. H. Monk, *The Sublime* (New York: Modern Language Association of America, 1935).

speak of its past unless the poet himself does so. To attempt its reconstruction from the given facts is ridiculous. As well might we look under the frame of the picture for a continuation of the scene represented on the canvas. Hence it is amazing that even a great and serious critic like Dowden should think it worth while to reflect on the probability of Hamlet's having been influenced by the fact that during the reign of the strong-willed elder Hamlet his introspective son was not compelled to take an active part in affairs. This would be an ingenious inference in the case of a real person, but it is comical if we are dealing with a fictitious character, whose nature can obviously not be determined by such reflections.[2]

This passage would not serve our purpose if it were chosen as an example of *poor* thinking on its particular subject. There is always a degree of confusion prevalent among the general run in any profession; and one could make out a case against any class of scholars by confining one's attention to the more muddled specimens of the class. But there is an important difference between the unclear ideas of individuals and the unclarified *status* of certain concepts. The latter is what interests us throughout this report; and Schücking's passage is cited as a good, plausible, even brilliant example of its kind.

It is obvious that Schücking, in this passage, is not interpreting Shakespeare but stating a rule of method for the interpretation of Shakespeare; also, that this rule of method is philosophical, since it involves a distinction between art and reality. How seriously is the author committed to the implications of his rule of method? A close textual critic like Kittredge can infer that Hamlet must have been speaking with some of his "friends among the King's counsellors"—though the fact is not stated in the text—because he seems to know about his approaching trip to England in the third act although the King does not announce it to him until the fourth.[3] In other words, Kittredge explains an apparent inconsistency in the play by invoking an assumed event that is not in the play. In another place, the same critic declares that Macbeth's speech in act 5, scene 3—"I have lived long enough. My way of life"—though it contains no mention of Duncan, implicitly alludes

2. Levin Ludwig Schücking, *Character Problems in Shakespeare's Plays* (Gloucester, Mass.: Peter Smith, 1949), p. 158.

3. See *Hamlet,* in William Shakespeare, *Complete Works,* ed. G. I. Kittredge (Boston: Ginn & Co., 1936), p. 247.

to Duncan.[4] Kittredge's interpolations and extrapolations are less speculative, less extensive, than those of a psychoanalytic critic like Ernest Jones, who goes all the way back to Hamlet's infancy; they may be better justified, on the textual evidence, than Jones's; but they are *similar* to Jones's in attempting to reconstruct the absent phases of an "imagined figure." Does Schücking mean to say that *all* such attempts are necessarily ridiculous? If so, we would point out that such inferences do not rest upon any "confusion between art and reality." For when we reconstruct the past or the future of a fictitious figure, we are talking about a fictitious past and a fictitious future. What is precluded, in the case of the literary work, is the *verification*, for example, of Hamlet's past by documents, memories, interrogation of witnesses, and so on, not the imaginary existence of such a past, which may be more or less directly suggested by the text. Of course, these reconstructions are of unequal merit; some are indeed absurd, as Schücking says; but there must be other principles, which Schücking does not mention, by which we discriminate among them—for instance, a principle of aesthetic relevance.

The point of view expressed by Schücking has become a fashionable critical cliché. But I do not know of any really careful examination of the issue. It is no clearer, no better understood, today than when Maurice Morgann, in the eighteenth century, brashly advanced the thesis that "in Dramatic Composition, the Impression is the Fact."

It has not been my purpose to refute Schücking's ideas, but to show that his attitude toward the question of method that he raises in passing in somewhat cavalier. A similar attitude toward the substantive question of character of plot in *Hamlet* would be regarded by him and his colleagues as disgraceful. Yet this attitude is, in my judgment, typical of the critic or scholar turned philosopher. His reflections upon method are struck off as by-products of his daily occupation. They contain a mixture of considerations of different type or level. The shop talk of the craftsman is confused with the theory of the craft, which is a branch of the theory of knowledge. It seldom happens that a course on Evidence in law school, which discusses (for instance) the admissibility of certain types of testimony, should identify itself with the "theory of evidence," which is another name for logic; or that a book on "methods of historical

4. See *Macbeth*, in ibid., p. 218.

research" should mix up questions about the authenticity of documents with questions about the nature of historical knowledge. Yet such confusions are customary in the theory of art study. Broad remarks about the fundamental purpose of criticism, narrow rules of thumb which have been useful to the author in his work, a few objections to prevailing practices among contemporaries, a few intelligent suggestions as to paths of thought that deserve to be opened up, some ideas of theses that belong *in* the field rather than in an essay about it, some inconclusive examples (often minutely analyzed) which are supposed to prove general principles about the distinction between creativity and criticism or the relation of art and knowledge or the bearing of historical erudition upon critical judgment—all these are scrambled together with a fine disregard for logical order and coherence. It is as if a treatise on scientific method should have something to say, within a single chapter, on: (a) deduction and induction; (b) how to set up laboratory apparatus; (c) whether fruitful hypotheses are apt to occur in dreams; (d) why ESP has not been proved scientifically; (e) science and religion; and so on. Without belittling any of these questions, it should be obvious to us that, mingled in this fashion, none of them could be followed out very far.

The same topics, in the hands of persons trained in logical analysis, could be treated with unexampled clarity and rigor. For logical analysis, however, the danger lies in lack of familiarity with the concrete subject matter and its problems, leading to an excessive abstractness. Even today there are some good ideas in theoretical aesthetics which are ignored by critics and historians because of their forbidding dryness, their apparent lack of relevance to practical pursuits. A thorough acquaintance with the rich though incoherent reflections of men working in the mines are the corrective to this philosophical remoteness.

.   .   .   .

It is certainly true that no philosophical analysis can devise methods which it imposes on a science from the outside. Every idea of method must come from the study of methods already employed in the field. But those methods which have led to the best results in one part of the field may be unrecognized, or may be merely implicit, or may be mixed up with barren methods, in the rest of the field. An explicit formulation of method, then, can lead to a greater awareness of direction and aim; it can eliminate waste activity; it can increase the general efficiency of research. Such an influence of philosophy upon science is perhaps imperceptible at the present time, for the simple reason that a highly efficient "hypothetico-deductive-experimental" method has become institutionalized in the natural sciences: it is ingrained in the working habits even of those scientists who have never taken a course in logic. But if we were living in the time of Bacon and Descartes, when the very idea of science was in a state of confusion, such a question as whether science concerns itself with efficient or final causes would be rather momentous for the future of science. And in the science of psychology today, the methodological principles of the structuralist, behaviorist, Gestalt, and psychoanalytic schools —which are really philosophical theses of a vague and primitive type—are clearly bound up with the kinds of work that are being done.

We can at once draw a conclusion for the theory and practice of criticism. A good theory of criticism should not and could not reform critical practice from the ground up. But by separating out, from the welter of reactions that pass for criticism, those lines of thought which have proved fruitful, and by explaining their tendency, it can encourage harder and sharper attacks in the same directions.

The greater the degree of disorder in any subject matter, the more significant becomes the question of method. A considerable emphasis upon method may be a symptom of distress and stagnation, but it may also very well be the only possible cure. Now, by any reasonable standard, the humane sciences are today in a state of disorder. We have already remarked that the more strictly pedantic types of historical scholarship stand in no particular need of methodological scrutiny. A student who is to occupy himself with tracing the source of certain spellings in a group of old manuscripts can, after one course in card catalogues, handle any question that will ever occur to him. Critical and historical *ideas* about literature and the arts, which are of much greater amount to the human race, are another matter: it is these which present the picture of confusion. I may illustrate by discussing a group of contemporary works that have certain qualities in common.

I am thinking of books like Rosamund Tuve, *Elizabethan and Metaphysical Imagery;* Moody E. Prior, *The Language of Tragedy;* E. M. W. Tillyard, *Poetry Direct and Oblique;* Maud Bodkin, *Archetypal Patterns in Poetry;* Chard Powers Smith, *Pattern and*

Variation in Poetry; William Empson, *Seven Types of Ambiguity;* and Kenneth Burke, *A Grammar of Motives.*[5] Comparable works by students of music and the plastic arts could be mentioned.

Each of these works displays powers of critical appreciation, as the reader can tell by noticing what happens to his own reading of poetry under their influence. Most of them also contain historical information, more or less general, more or less novel: Miss Tuve, for example, demonstrates the influence of Ramus's logic on the poetry of the seventeenth century. But over and above its collection of facts and insights, each work is built around a theory, a hypothesis, a general idea. In one case, it is a distinction between "intellectual" and "sensuous" imagery; in another a conception of varieties of multiple meaning; in a third, the thesis that the diction of tragic drama is, "essentially" and not "superficially," connected with the tragic structure and idea. I have classed these works together because of the presence in each of this theoretical element together with the commoner critical and historical motives.

Now in even the most backward of the sciences, general ideas like these would quickly find a place in a continuous movement of research. They would attach themselves to earlier ideas as corollaries, generalizations, revisions, or refutations. They would be taken up by later writers and, if found to have any merit, would be built upon—explored, re-tested, applied to new and related subjects. A careless reader of literary journals might imagine that the present works have a similar role within a framework of their own. There is, indeed, an appearance of continuity and progress. All the authors criticize some of their predecessors and express indebtedness to others. Their own ideas are minutely examined in the re-

5. Rosamond Tuve, *Elizabethan and Metaphysical Imagery* (Chicago: University of Chicago Press, 1947); Moody E. Prior, *The Language of Tragedy* (New York: Columbia University Press, 1947); E. M. W. Tillyard, *Poetry Direct and Oblique* (London: Chatto, 1934); Maud Bodkin, *Archetypal Patterns in Poetry* (Oxford: Oxford University Press, 1948); Chard Powers Smith, *Pattern and Variation in Poetry* (New York: Charles Scribner's Sons, 1932); William Empson, *Seven Types of Ambiguity* (London: Chatto & Windus, 1947); and Kenneth Burke, *A Grammar of Motives* (New York: Prentice-Hall, 1945). Each of these works displays powers of critical appreciation, as the reader can tell by noticing what happens to his own reading of poetry under their influence. Each work is built around a theory, a hypothesis, a general idea.

views and subsequently referred to in doctoral theses. One writer acts upon another as a stimulant or a provocation. There are flurries of discussion which resemble the explicit work of evaluation that goes on in the sciences. But when the smoke blows away, nothing solid remains: there is no real advance toward truth. Factual study, in art history, at least makes progress toward quantitative accumulation; but literary theory makes no progress toward greater objectivity, precision, generality, or comprehensiveness. Ideas, instead of being incorporated within a persistent intellectual effort where other ideas can be mounted upon them, fall into a miscellaneous "tradition" where they affect each other by invisible shoves and electric shocks. No work has had a greater influence on recent aesthetic thinking than Empson's *Seven Types of Ambiguity*. Yet among all its fervent admirers I doubt that one person could be found who could say what the seven types are, how one type is different from another, why there are just seven types, or how these "types of ambiguity" are related to the study of mental processes or to the theory of ambiguity in logic. Empson's book, to be sure, retains all its value as a critical study. But no such theoretical apparatus was required for that purpose; in fact, there is *no* reason for a theory like Empson's unless it is meant to be taken seriously as a theory.

Certain qualifications should, perhaps, be allowed. One might point to a few areas in which art theory seems to be moving ahead and, on the other hand, to periods when the sciences themselves seem to proceed by a succession of fashions and emphases. One might also find it strange that the foregoing criticism should come from the camp of *philosophy*, the status of whose problems is dubious indeed. But it is even more important to understand the point of view from which this criticism is being made. It would clearly be wrong to attempt to discourage the appearance of books like those mentioned above—rich works with manifold values, straddling several departments of thought. A humanist is, almost by definition, one who seeks balance and a rounded view and is *not* interested in intensive inquiry leading to definite "results"; and many humanistic works of the past exhibit a play of intelligence upon many topics without systematically cultivating any one. One may go further and, with Howard Mumford Jones, deplore an excessive emphasis upon the *study* of art at the expense of those values of enjoyment which are sought by the average cultured person. One may even admit, going beyond Mr. Jones, that the arts themselves can have only a limited role in the outlook and life of the professional, business, or working man: arts and letters are "specialties" when compared with experience in general. And, as a final concession to those who may object to the argument of this section, let us make it clear that the specifically *critical* effort is probably not to be judged by any canons of scientific progress. To set up the positivist ideal of "getting somewhere" for the criticism of art is to impose an aim foreign to its nature—though, we must add, an aim which many critics seem to accept when they talk about each other's works.

Yet none of these points impeaches the desirability of intellectual progress. They do not make it less regrettable that scholarship should be divided between pedantry which is exact and objective and theory which is nebulous and transient. The themes and issues of the authors named above (and of many others like them) are the really exciting matter of the humanities. It is these authors themselves, incidentally, who set up their theoretical objectives: if we were talking about straight biography, appreciation, or historical reconstruction, all of the present strictures would be beside the point. Now if we ask why interesting and important projects like these have accomplished so little, the answer is fairly simple. These writers, with no lack either of brilliance or of care, are irresponsible because there is no clear-cut subject or method to which they can be responsible. Their thinking, in spite of reciprocal influences, is strictly individual. Any of the strands interwoven in their work would, if followed out, lead over into psychology or general linguistics or aesthetics or logic, whither the authors are by no means concerned to follow them. Thus, Miss Tuve's distinction between "intellectual" and "sensuous" images, though it belongs to psychology, has no benefit of psychological analysis and would be completely obscure to any student of psychology. It is quite sufficiently clear for her various nontheoretical purposes, historical and critical; but it cannot be of any use for a theory of imagery. Mr. Tillyard's categories, "direct" and "oblique," make no sense whatever to a student of symbolism, though they serve well enough to convey the particular critical opinions of the author. The hybridity of these works is at the very opposite pole from a genuine synthesis of methods or subject matters; instead of infusing one discipline with the explicit principles of another, they exemplify a general unclarity as to the requirements of *any* method.[6] They subsist at an undifferentiated foetal stage of inquiry, where any of numerous tendencies, if encouraged, would result in something that could be called fish or flesh or good red herring.

Returning now to the question that was asked at the beginning of this section,[7] I believe we can answer it in the affirmative. In an unfortunate situation we can always prescribe genius as a remedy; and for all I know, the theory of art may tomorrow take an immense stride through the efforts of some brilliant person. But if we are looking for a humbler practical recipe, we must return to our diagnosis. The path of literary and art theory is clogged by an unconscious competition of purposes, each maiming or hindering the others. A critique of methods, producing an awareness of the commitments of each, might not of itself generate brilliant new attacks upon the old problems; but it is a sine qua non.

. . . .

There has long existed, in many quarters, a fairly well justified feeling about the ineptness of philosophers who tread upon the aesthetic domain. "Why," asked William James—and many people have repeated the query—, "does the *Aesthetik* of every German philosopher seem to the artist an abomination of desolation?" We here touch upon another difficult question, really demanding prolonged analysis. What are the *non-analytic* qualifications of the analyst? What, for instance, should be his degree of competence as a critic? How good a judge of art must he be if he is to have a good philosophy of art? There could be numerous answers, each presupposing its own conception of the relations among the art studies. An artist might dislike a system of aesthetics simply because it is not a work of art; but it does not seem reasonable to charge aesthetics with the responsibility of being beautiful. James forgot to ask whether his "artist," rather than his "German philosopher," might not be at fault. A work of intellectual genius like Kant's *Critique of Aesthetic Judgment*, abounding in profound implications for the understanding of the arts, has been ignored by

6. Always excepting the more concrete and nontheoretical objectives. Miss Tuve understands the requirements of historical research. Mr. Empson knows how to go about criticizing a poem.

7. We must now ask whether a good analysis [that] sets itself to interpret the concepts and methods of the aesthetic disciplines would have useful implications for the actual conduct of those disciplines.

men of letters (except for Schiller and Coleridge), but they ignore it to their own loss. Again, philosophers and psychologists have been blamed for evincing bad taste in their critical reactions and choice of examples, though it is not shown that this deficiency really impairs their analyses. Again, many an *Aesthetik* of the sort that William James had in mind is *philosophically* inept to begin with: apart from annoying the artist, it botches its own program and offends against sound criteria of analysis; it can therefore hardly serve as evidence for the mutual hostility of art and philosophy. Thus we see that many different things—his literary style, the modishness of his tastes and tone, the adequacy of his analysis —might be meant by the "competence" of the philosopher. Critically distinguished and fascinating books by Malraux, Sartre, Ortega y Gasset, full of startling intuitions and tasteful examples, seem to me to throw no particle of light on any aesthetic problem; while there are stuffy monographs by obscure Ph.D.s which successfully pursue the clarification of some aesthetic concept. Yet there are other cases—certain works on aesthetics by American philosophers—where one cannot help feeling that the analysis has been spoiled by sheer lack of critical sophistication or of genuine responsiveness to art.

These remarks serve to show merely that the question of the general competence of the philosopher is not a simple one. The one positive suggestion that I think may be of some use here is the following. An analysis is usually tested against the "denotation" of the concept that is being analyzed. Thus, a good analysis of the concept 'justice' would not result in a definition that excluded from the meaning of the term flagrant cases of what people would call "justice" and included flagrant cases of "injustice." It follows that the analyst must be at least aware of the chief specific values that are denoted by the term or idea he is analyzing. Now among the important concepts of the art studies are some which have arisen in the process of critical evaluation and which therefore denote values as well as facts. The analyst should know these values. He should know, for example, that Tennyson is considered a skillful manipulator of verse rhythms and phonetic harmonies, and why he is so considered—if he wishes to clarify the critical use of the term 'technique'. If he studies the methods employed by psychologists to determine the taste of the average American movie fan, it may not be necessary for him, the analyst, either to share these tastes or to reject them; for he is concerned with descriptive studies of aesthetic reactions. But if, as often happens, he tries to explain what is meant by 'good color' in the criticism of painting by means of examples drawn from the *worst* colorists, then (at the very least) he confuses his treatment of a normative concept by raising distracting controversies at the primary level.

A similar point could be made about the analysis of the problems of art history. One who is unfamiliar with common distinctions of style, school, period, and so forth, is certainly not fit to philosophize about the knowledge embodied therein.

An analyst should therefore be a sensitive and well informed person.

At the same time, it is doubtful whether the analyst needs to have *all* the sensitivity and delicate discrimination of the practising critic or all the information of the historian. What is more likely is that in the course of his work he should reach particular junctures where his present taste or knowledge needs to be either checked or extended. There is, for example, in the case of certain poems, no degree of understanding or clarity of interpretation so perfect that it cannot be questioned or improved. The specialist, who gives his whole time to questions of that order, is the right man to go to for confirmation or criticism.

.   .   .   .

It is possible to suspend all interest in the normative problem of taste and still have a vast and almost unexplored field left for the analysis of criticism. Instead of asking, "What is aesthetic value?" "Can one know whether a work of art is beautiful?" "How do you tell whether a piece of criticism is sound?" we can ask, "What do people mean when they call someone a good or a poor critic?" "What is involved or implied in the act of *thinking* that a work of art is ugly?" and so on. This has the advantage of enabling us to clarify many features of critical usage *before* committing ourselves to some controversial normative theory in aesthetics. At the same time, this mode of study does not lie wholly within the province of a mere psychology of critical reactions; for, without being interested primarily in the question of the validity of critical utterances, we are still less concerned with the description of miscellaneous tastes and preferences. Take as an example the use of the comparative adjectives 'better' and 'worse' in criticism. Psychology would have to interest itself not only in the fact that people say, "The Empire State Building is higher than the Woolworth,"

"Lincoln was a greater man than Washington," "Beethoven's third symphony is greater than his second," but also in such remarks as "Beethoven's third symphony is greater than the Sistine Chapel," which may seem to verge upon the nonsense of "Green is darker than middle C." A phenomenological approach has to ask what kinds of comparison have sense and what sorts of sense they have; it is therefore corrective and clarificatory rather than descriptive of ordinary usage; but it need not go so far as to decide *whether* one work is greater than another nor even tell how such a question can be decided. . . .

Critics are called "responsible" and "irresponsible," presumably upon some sort of warrant, by other critics. One frequently "suspends judgment" on the merits of a new musical work, on the ground of not knowing it well enough, or accuses oneself of "rash" judgment later on—much as one may decide that one had mis-calculated the probability of a future event on the evidence that had been available. Some critics are "prejudiced": there are "ideo-logical intrusions" upon the "proper domain" of criticism. Critical statements may be relatively "clear" or "obscure," "vague" or "precise." Judgments of "negative" value are commonplace, just as in ethics, and have given rise to controversies about the nature of ugliness among authors like Croce, Bosanquet, and Santayana; but these analyses are by no means as careful or accurate as the work that has been done on falsity and the function of negation in epistemology. We have already alluded to the problem of com-parative value. Another problem, out of many that could be chosen, is the use of the term 'insight' in criticism. A judgment like "Rembrandt is great not only for his skillful drawing but for his marvelous handling of light and dark" would probably be accepted by everyone; but few people will feel indebted to its author. It is an obtuse perception; and the question comes up as to what we mean when we feel that a critical perception is not only "true" but keen and original: this question has its counterparts in the philosophy of science and the philosophy of art.

. . . .

After all that has been written on [the] subject [of history and criticism] it may seem both needless and presumptuous to propose a new study unless one can point to remarkable new insights that have not so far been utilized. But the truth is that revolutionary thoughts about the methods of art history and art criticism are needed much less than is a comprehensive, methodical, and orderly survey, written from the standpoint of general theory of knowledge. This need not, perhaps, introduce any idea which has not already been stated or suggested; but it should attempt to get some coherence into the subject. The present literature is a collection of more or less incisive *obiter dicta,* each supported by its own small group of examples. The student, passing from one writer to another, finds himself attracted by one persuasive argument only to be drawn with equal force, in an apparently opposite direction, by another plausible presentation. It is very easy, for instance, to agree with Professor Bush when he says that "if a work of art is not a self-sufficient entity and does not make its essential impact without biographical aids, there is something wrong with it"; equally tempting to subscribe to Miss Tuve's idea that "meanings of elements or motifs in poems . . . are clarified by knowledge those elements have carried before the poem was written and, as we think, 'outside' it." Yet it must be the case either that one of these statements is false or that they are at bottom consistent though they appear not to be. I do not know of any serious attempt to bring the parts of the whole problem into systematic relation; and in default of such attempts, the theory of the subject remains heterogeneous and confused.

. . . .

It would be very helpful for the study of aesthetic criticism to have something that might be called a *general* theory of criticism, that is, an attempt to distinguish and explain the "creative" and the "critical" aspects of empirical science, technology, ethics, logic, and natural philosophy.

. . . .

What is a true and what is a false interpretation of literature? One might ask a similar question about music criticism, since there too one finds long-standing differences of opinion about the plain contents of musical works (often couched in terms of disagreement with the "interpretation" of some performer). But over and above such dubieties of content as it may share with any other object of art, the literary work presents difficulties to its interpreter through its being a structure of symbols with conventional meanings attached to them. What it "says" or does not say is, apparently, quite intangible by comparison with the elements and structure of a sculptured bust or a few bars of music. There is at first sight something nebulous about the status of a poem which is supposed to consist partly of definite letters or sounds, partly of ideas which those letters or sounds convey to the mind of a reader familiar with a certain language. When a concrete difference of interpretation arises, one is not sure about the location of the final court of appeal. Empson, for instance, is a critic who makes us see things in poetry that we had not seen before. Unfortunately, some of the things he makes us see are simply not there to be seen. Empson has been blamed for hyper-ingenuity—reading meanings into poetry that the poets did not intend. As a sort of parody on his more arbitrary interpretations, one might devise an example like the following. A line from Swinburne's *Hymn to Proserpine*—

> Thou hast conquered, O pale Galilean; the world has
> grown grey from thy breath;

is clearly addressed to the Man of Galilee and refers to the triumph of Christianity. But if I read "Galilean" as "a follower of Galileo, a natural scientist" and suppose that Swinburne is also alluding to the industrial revolution, I get a "complex" and "ambiguous" reading of the line, which may or may not have its merits. Yet such an interpretation would certainly be erroneous. Where and how does one draw the line between the legitimate efforts of Empson to draw out the implications of poetry of which the poets themselves may not have been fully aware and his fantastic attributions of meanings which are simply not warranted by the texts?

· · · · · · · · · · · · · · · · · · · ·

Kittredge and Stoll are two critics who reject the "diseased-will" theory of Hamlet's character. In his edition of Hamlet, Kittredge writes the following note to the speech (act 2, scene 2) "O, what a rogue and peasant slave am I!"

Hamlet rages against himself for stupid inactivity—not for hesitation or weakness of will. He has done nothing to avenge his father and seems incapable of doing anything. Why? Not, surely, because he is a coward! Yet even *that*, he exclaims, with bitter irony, is possible: otherwise he must have killed his uncle long ago. Thus he relieves his excitement by railing until, at the end of the soliloquy, he grows calm and expresses in the plainest language what the matter really is: *he needs evidence*. He must not kill a man on the word of an apparition, and thus far no other testimony has been procurable.

Stoll writes:

And by the second soliloquy, about Fortinbras . . . Shakespeare shows more clearly than elsewhere, not as has been thought, that Hamlet is of a procrastinating nature, but that his "tardiness" is not a sin or a disease, not a taint in the blood or a clot on the brain, but simply, as he and the ghost both say, a case of "forgetting," in other words, remissness, neglect, or "almost blunted purposes."[8]

And again Mr. Stoll says that Hamlet is "like the other Elizabethan revengers . . . melancholy, but not diseased or really de-ranged."

Now I believe there is a material issue between these men and their opponents; but the issue *as stated* is not wholly material. For how much difference is there, *in meaning*, between 'inactivity' and 'hesitation', 'procrastination' and 'neglect', 'melancholy' and 'de-rangement'? between neurotic vacillation and mere brooding on the suspicion of one's own cowardice? Do these descriptions exclude each other? Don't they rather overlap? Must we choose between alternatives stacked up against each other like so many fog banks: Is there first of all a question of the truth of description or of the clarity and sharpness of description? If, as Stoll says in another place, "the audience were accustomed to the revenger beating about the bush but reproaching himself for it," then the audience was accustomed to something unquestionably *similar* in certain respects to what was later going to interest Freud. If delay was nothing but a dramatic convention, then the drama made a convention of indecisiveness. Yonder Hamlet is indeed very much like a "camel," a "weasel," a "shale," and "introvert" and a "man of action." If we have trouble deciding which he *is*, that may be not Hamlet's fault but the fault of the concepts with which we try to snare him.

8. Elmer Edgar Stoll, *Art and Artifice in Shakespeare* (Cambridge: Cambridge University Press, 1933), p. 99.

1. Weltbilder

Romanticism: something thrilling is going on somewhere else in the world.

Religion: something thrilling is going on somewhere out of the world.

Mysticism: something thrilling is going on right here and now.

Realism: nothing thrilling is going on.

. . . .

2. Obscurity

Can an obscure and difficult work be good and great? If so, is this (a) only "insofar as" it is *not* obscure but clear; (b) only to be so judged if and when a merely provisional obscurity has been surmounted thanks to exegesis and patient attention; (c) perhaps *on account of* a strangeness, suggestiveness, or mysteriousness which could have been secured by no other means ("poetry is best appreciated when only generally and not perfectly understood"—Coleridge); (d) because the obscurity functions as a *price* to be paid—the "defect of the qualities" of the work?

This section consists of notes excerpted from letters to the author's friends; made available to the editors by Professors Mary Mothersill and John Goheen, Stanford University.

To offer two definite opinions on minor aspects of the question: (1) It would seem that clarity and intelligibility can be at most necessary or negative conditions of merit, since there are so many perfectly clear but hopelessly mediocre works. (2) To call a work obscure is to imply not that it is incomprehensible but rather that one does not know whether it be so or not. Now a major theme of one party in the critical response to modern art has been the idea that whether or not experimental writers ultimately make sense, they have no right to be so hard on the reader who wishes to follow them. But this is obviously a different thing from the critical evaluation which presupposes that impediments to understanding have already been topped or penetrated and the content of the work reached.

. . : . . . .

3. LETTER, MARCH 1960.

You would think there couldn't be a lovelier passage of ten or fifteen words in prose than Bacon's on strangeness: "There is no very great beauty but hath some strangeness in the proportion." (Have I got it right?) But yes there is, I came across it only yesterday:

Obscurity in affection of words and indigested conceits, is pedantical and childish; but where it shroudeth itself in the heart of his subject, uttered with fitness of figure and expressive epithets, with that darkness will I still labour to be shadowed.

Don't you think that last clause, with its abrupt break at the start and the marvelous new rhythm in it, is wondrous moving?

It's by George Chapman, the author of Chapman's well-known and widely used Homer—from the "Epistel Dedicatory" to Ovid's *Banquet of Sense,* or so says my authority. Naturally, it's in aesthetics, on the same topic as Bacon, and in agreement with him. If a still more beautiful piece of writing should turn up somewhere, it will turn out also to be treating the same theme to the same effect.

Now here's a *rebus* for you. I've only the faintest idea what it's all about. And not the least idea *what* "that darkness" is or who or what shroudeth what where is whose subject. And I have no intention of going to Widener to see whether any light can be gleaned from the context. Now: Do you think that *this* passage itself can be intended to illustrate the darkness it is talking about? Or without having been so intended that it does? And if so, successfully? Do you, with your limitless resources and the vast research facilities surrounding you—cyclotrata, heavy-water faucets, and so on—kindly do this piece of study for me and tell me the answers.

.   .   .   .

4. HENRY JAMES: ON ADMIRING ONE'S OWN IDEAS [LETTER, 1961]

Years ago I read a piece by the late Desmond MacCarthy telling of walks he had taken many years before with Henry James. One passage was very fine; but I have forgotten the wording and shall no doubt spoil it in transcription. The great novelist and the young critic would discuss this subject and that and exchange opinions on an equal footing. But every now and then MacCarthy would become aware of a pause on the part of his companion, feel a light touch on his arm and understand the message: "Wait, wait now. Just a moment or two and we shall both of us have the privilege of hearing what 'Henry James' has to say about this matter." Then it would come, the deliverance which Henry James considered so well worth waiting for as to interrupt himself in reverent expectancy.

Henry James has given much evidence also in his critical writing and his letters of the extraordinary respect in which he held this "Henry James" who dwelt within him. This may seem a bit egocentric.

But Henry James, after all, *was* Henry James and had, as a critic, sense enough to understand just how good was the intelligence that was his. Had I been he, I too would have waited breathlessly to hear what I had to say.

I have elsewhere described how it feels to read a paper to a professional audience and then watch the members rise one after the other and, with the air of exposing an entirely new aspect of the problem, point out that A is B, just as if the whole paper had not been concerned to show as carefully as might be that A was not B. But something else I have not described, something that I may now fitly call the Henry James phenomenon, first observing that the individuals in whom we remark this phenomenon are not

Henry James but, for instance, . . . these people [who] do not contradict you and ignore your whole argument but in a tolerant and, above all, thoughtful manner say: "That was all right, Isenberg. I'm not sure I don't agree with you. Yes. There's something in what you say." They hesitate; they look off into the distance; their eyes are fixed on remote horizons; they endorse your position but have something larger and more important in mind. And you understand their meaning at once.

It is not that they do not entirely agree. It is not that they see objections or hold reservations. It is not that they think the subject should be done in a different way; not even that they believe there is a lot more to it than you have touched upon. All these doubts and provisos are certainly in their minds; but that is not the meaning of the tone and manner. What, without knowing it, they are thinking, is this: "I'm not sure that I shall ever get around to interesting myself in your problem—I have so many graver concerns. And if I do get around to it, I am not sure what I shall say. Maybe I shall come out on your side—I do not know that you are wrong. But if I *should* decide to write on your topic, as at the moment your paper makes me think I may, that is what will *count*, don't you see? You are not a bad fellow, Isenberg. You are even useful: you can give a man an idea or two. But you are peripheral, and incidental to the main thing, which is what *I* may decide to write."

Now I am like these people. I have acted like them again and again. I do not consider myself, or my ideas, more important than other people and what they may think or believe; but when it comes to "Arnold Isenberg" and *his* ideas, I sink into silent worship. Is there anything wrong with this?

No. Even if I know and concede that another man is better than I and does what is better than I can do, it must still, naturally and properly, be my task to think of what *I* can do.

But yes, there is something wrong. For when the other man has just taken the floor for an hour and has reported what it has taken him weeks or months to think out, and when I am speaking to him about his speech, you might suppose that I should forget for a while what I can or intend to do. You might suppose that I should not instantly blot him into the general landscape but should center even my own continuing interest in his subject in him and his treatment of it.

. . . .

5. A Note on Virginia Woolf

"But all I can say is that, when lapsing into that stream which people call, so oddly, consciousness. . . ."

Virginia Woolf

A misprint? Surely. Virginia Woolf could not have said that people *oddly* call it consciousness. She would have known that it *is* consciousness and can only oddly be called anything else. No, it is the printer's fault, and what Virginia Woolf wrote was, "when lapsing into that consciousness which people call, so oddly, a stream."

But wait: she didn't write that either. For Virginia Woolf would never have said "lapsing into consciousness." As well might she have described one of her characters as "falling awake." I am certain now that her printer was a wholly incompetent fellow.

Are not reviews of current literature a perpetual illustration of the difficulty of judgment? "This great book," "this worthless book," the same book is called by both names. Praise and blame alike mean nothing. No, delightful as the pastime of measuring may be, it is the most futile of all occupations, and to submit to the decrees of the measurers the most servile of attitudes. So long as you write what you wish to write, that is all that matters; and whether it matters for ages or only for hours, nobody can say. But to sacrifice a hair of the head of your vision, a shade of its colour, in deference to some . . . professor with a measuring rod up his sleeve, is the most abject treachery.

Virginia Woolf, *A Room of One's Own*

It was, I believe, Virginia Woolf who first made up the invaluable word 'middlebrow'—explaining at the same time that, though she liked highbrows and was especially fond of lowbrows, she could not bear the middlebrows at all. A highbrow, as I remember, is "a man or woman of thoroughbred intelligence who rides his mind at a gallop across country in pursuit of an idea." A lowbrow does the same thing in pursuit of a living. Fine images, redolent of fine old English folkways: one must, nevertheless, carp at this way of classifying people. It is not just that one would like to introduce further shades of difference, remembering as one does persons of one's acquaintance who ought to be called lower highbrows or upper lowbrows, and recalling still other people—Aristotle, say, or Shakespeare—for whom 'highbrow' seems much too weak a word. But there are so many men and women who do not fit into Virginia Woolf's scheme at all! She forgets that there are foreheads that shoot up straight in the middle but slant down villainously low on both sides and others, perhaps, which squint unevenly through their whole length. There is the man, for instance, who would never leave his seat to ride after any idea unless it happens to be about dental surgery but will follow like a demon any idea that touches on that subject. The magazines in his waiting room are appalling: is he a highbrow? What about the great physicist who picks up his politics from some lowbrow columnist and his aesthetics from the comic strips? And what, on the other hand, about Goethe or about Mr. W. H. Auden—a man who will peck at philosophic or scientific ideas until they give him just the few grains he needs to start his imagination off but has not the slightest interest in coming to understand them in their own terms? Are these great amateurs, these adepts of universal intelligence, to be termed veritable huntsmen of ideas?

We shall have to worry a bit in particular about the specialists. Just because they dominate the sciences and professions, and may soon dominate the world, is no reason to exclude them from a classification; for two wrongs do not make a right. But let us for the moment forget them. Let us entertain an alternative definition of 'highbrow', one which I think Virginia Woolf might not have rejected. A highbrow is a specialist in general critical intelligence —and if this forces us to exclude certain great painters or musicians or even novelists, so it will have to be. Now the average highbrow, so understood, will not only have critical intelligence but will have and express his views about it—as Virginia Woolf does in the passage with which I began this complaint. It is inevitable: no critic fails to think about the principles of criticism. It behooves us, then, to see what a representative critic, and highbrow, may have to say about criticism, that is to say, about her own intimate mental essence.

Judgment, begins Virginia Woolf, is difficult; and the reviews of current literature prove it.

This is much like saying that since the late Mr. Voliva of Zion City maintained that the earth was flat, the question is really most perplexing. How can she think that because opinions disagree, it cannot be the case that some are not only right but easily seen to be right? One is prepared to consider almost any statement that can be made about judgment—that it is difficult or absurd or that it doesn't exist at all. But one cannot accept as evidence for such a statement the fact that children do not like Proust; and it makes no difference if the children happen to write for the *Times*.

But Virginia Woolf goes on: "Praise and blame alike mean nothing." Now when she says this, she *forgets*. She forgets that in every one of her critical essays she doles out praise and blame—and can all this mean nothing? She forgets that in this very paragraph she is praising some things and blaming others.

But let us not throw her practice up to her. *It does not follow* from the fact, if it is a fact, that judgment is difficult that it should be impossible, or "meaningless"—this is the more essential point. On the contrary, if judgment were difficult, it would follow that it was possible and meaningful.

But suppose that Virginia Woolf were so far right—there is still the next sentence. Here she glides over from judgment, or praise and blame, to the "pastime of measuring," as if everyone who denounced a book, or hailed it, were rating it on a scale. Surely we can say "good" or "bad" without saying "good by 2.157 degrees above the indifference point" or "bad by seven degrees below zero." And it is almost incredible that a sentence which is so hard on measuring should pronounce it the *most* futile of occupations. This is much as if some mystic who held that all mathematical reasoning was vicious should declare that he could prove it with ruler and compass.

But now Virginia Woolf performs a shift that will astonish even us who have followed her so far. She begins to speak like a composition teacher who, having received no poems from his class that will bear a second's inspection, still feels that versifying is a good exercise for the students; or again like one who, believing that the very badness of his papers stems from the false effort to imitate great writers, wishes to recommend a certain sincerity to his group. "Never mind whether you write like Keats. That's not the idea. The main thing is that you put down what *you* see and feel." Has this any connection with what has gone before? Yes. If you think that the critic is by nature a measurer, a grader, a rule-maker and rule-imposer, you must advise the writer to ignore criticism. But we have seen that it is only an assumption of Virginia Woolf's that the critic must be such.

And now, finally, can she tell the writer that he should not care if he writes *badly*, that it is no matter to him if some elements of his "vision" are rotten or false? Can it be such abject treachery to reconsider, to correct a fault? And what if, even, the fault had been pointed out by Professor X?

So reasons one of the best minds of our time, competent alike at writing and at judging. Is this dreadful, chaotic thinking really redeemed by the prose garnishes—a spot of intensity, a spot of aggression, a sideswipe at Professor X—which make this a "live" and "nervous" prose, such as Professor X cannot boast? Consider how extreme these phrases are. 'Mean nothing'. 'Most futile of occupations'. 'Submit to the decrees'. 'Most servile of attitudes'. 'All that matters'. 'Sacrifice a hair of the head'. 'Abject treachery'. No, this hysterical prose cannot make up for any fault: it is itself in need of some virtue to balance it.

I think I am aware of some of the good impulses behind this bad writing. Virginia Woolf, when she started this passage, had just been prophesying. She had foretold a time when women, if given their chance, would become good writers. By a natural association of ideas she then found herself meditating the question, "Yes, but will they ever be as good as men?" A really interesting question of comparison, one might suppose, reaching as it does far down into the obscure relationships among sex, culture, and creativity. But Virginia Woolf seems to be afraid of what the answer be; at any rate, she reacts rather strongly. She pours scorn upon the question itself, insisting that it is merely invidious. Her position is one that will *always* be taken by those who, like the composition teacher, wish to think upon the matter of comparative values just so far and no more. It is a sort of perennial moment in criticism, representing an attempt to reconcile conflicting motives ill understood: the wish to limit one's praise and the wish not to disparage or discourage. Everyone takes this view at times, and nobody sticks to it long. Certainly, one should be pleased that Mrs. Woolf wrote *Mrs. Dalloway* and should not point out that *Mrs. Dalloway* is not *Hamlet*. But one is not pleased at Mrs. Glynn's having written *Three Weeks;* and one knows perfectly well that *Three Weeks* is not as good as *Mrs. Dalloway*. Yet the principle of not sacrificing one's vision does not permit us to distinguish between these two cases.

The whole question is immensely deep, far-reaching, prolific. No one has ever thought it through; and Virginia Woolf does not handle it worse than most. But could one say that she was *galloping* after the idea she so dimly describes in this passage? No, the highbrow fails us just when we might expect her to be of use. We conclude, perhaps not prematurely, that the critical intelligence cannot be understood by the specialist in general critical intelligence; and we turn, in desperation if not in hope, to—the professional student. Here, among these Ph.D.s, with all their poor taste and bad style and less than thorough breeding, we might find a few who, having *studied* the critical intelligence and whether or not they *possess* so very much of it, would form a counterpart to the dental surgeon and a contrast to the dilettante. And we do indeed encounter a certain dialectical expertness, a familiarity with all the lines of thought to which the topic lends itself. Any good graduate student in philosophy can at least see at once what is wrong with the efforts of a Woolf. I wish I could say more, so as to turn my back on the Woolfs and their kind of thinking forever. But, alas, they *tell* us nothing, these specialists, they settle nothing. I do not know from them whether judgment, after all, is really difficult or not: I only know that it is very difficult to judge among them and their doctrines. This is the baffling peculiarity (or one peculiarity) of the problems of philosophy. They are only the themes of the general critical intelligence, raised to a certain degree of exactness in formulation and followed up with a certain degree of thoroughness. And we have to insist that just because they interest all men, or all intelligent men, it does not follow that they can be treated properly by any highbrow who chooses to take a fling at them. One must ride one's mind at a gallop in pursuit of them, year after year. In the end one may be able to preen oneself, as much as any technician, on the skill one has acquired. But one would like to be able to point to some one of one's fellows who has really caught up with the idea he was chasing—and that is not yet to be seen.

. . . .

6. A NOTE ON PAUL VALÉRY [UNDATED MANUSCRIPT]

Much talk about the mind. The mysterious process of analyzing the mysterious process called the mind. The difficult delights of this process—of either of these processes.

He's always claiming that he's thinking. "I have sometimes tried to observe in myself and to pursue into the region of concrete thought the mysterious effect that a clear night and the presence of stars generally has on men." He pursues this to no effect for about a page and a half—not a very hard pursuit. Even if he had as many thoughts as he claimed, there would be no room for them: the space all goes to the claim.

He would read a book on arithmetic and decide it was better than Victor Hugo. He would publish this verdict and astound other French writers, who would not have read the book.

"Women," he wrote in his youth,

are graceful little animals who have the perverse ability to turn to themselves the attention of too many minds. They are put at the summit of the altars of art, and our elegant psychologists know better, alas, how to note down their bitch-like sulkings, their cat-like clawings than to analyze the difficult brain of an Ampere, of a Delacroix, of an Edgar Poe.

There you have it—all of it.

He said, "My verse has had no direct interest for me except as it has suggested a great many reflections on the poet. How often have I lost myself in the analysis of those operations, so difficult to define, to disentangle, to render clear and distinct!"

Comment: He's lying.

. . . .

7. That Boorish Men Are neither Innocent nor Simple
[Undated Fragment]

Just because you are stupid, small-minded, and ignorant, that does not immunize you to the finer depravities nor strip you of the subtler reaction mechanisms. Devious guilts and envies, tangled repressions and defenses, breed and multiply in you all the same. When I follow you to your office, your suburban home—wherein no Proustian, no Freudian, note ever has sounded—I marvel at the involvements with which I am soon confronted. You reject a good money-saving suggestion because it came from one of your subordinates. You derive an obscure pleasure from the disparagement of culture. Are these emotions worthy of an authentic troglodyte? I was prepared for a forthright greed beneath a mask of respectability. I did not count on these insidious methods of increasing one's self-regard. You are crude, all right; nevertheless, you are complex. Your humanity gave you that maze of a soul; and your stupidity does not relieve you of it. You will never be simple and nice like a beast. I tell you there is no salvation in unintelligence; if there were, I'd immediately have my frontal lobes removed. Ignorance does not protect us from complications: it only prevents us from so much as trying to resolve them.

. . . .

8. That You Cannot Help without Hurting
[Undated Fragment]

Let it be only a young actress who asks your opinion of her performance. You cannot help her to correct it without criticizing the thing as it stands. And this is to attack the only self she possesses, the present self. She will be grateful—later, when she is no longer the person who was attacked. Criticism is surgery: it heals by cutting.

But if you cannot help without hurting, it doesn't follow that to hurt is to help. Criticism is one thing: murder is another; and it is murder when, to make yourself feel big, you try to make another man small. The spirit in which the criticism is offered is *always* divined; and when the spirit is seen to be homicidal, the criticism never helps.

No higher compliment you pay to another than, in the right spirit, to tell him an unpleasant truth about himself. For this implies that he can stand the truth about himself. For this implies that he can stand the truth and benefit by it—a much greater quality than the one which, by your criticism, you have denied to him.

. . . .

9

One of his correspondents having asked him what he thought of Bacon and of Descartes, Spinoza replied that they seemed not to have understood the three things most essential for a man to know: the nature of God, of the human mind, and of *error*. Why error, rather than truth? Because there's more of it, obviously. Error! To know this thing is to know man.

. . . .

10

When you are about to die, living people will seem to be engaged in things remote and of no concern to you and to be ignorant of that matter which concerns you most. You will feel yourself separated from the living and drawn to those with whom you can now communicate because they will have been through this thing themselves. That is when you will recover intimacy with your dead.

. . . .

11. RELIGIOUS PEOPLE [UNDATED]

When we hold religious people to a higher accountability than others, we take them at their own pretensions and implicitly subscribe to their creed. "He prays to the Holy Trinity and then goes out and robs the poor." It is as if we saw a special incongruity; as if we felt that one who prays to the Holy Trinity should, in all consistency, be better than one who does not. But the truth is that we should expect less of religious people, because their human frailty is shown already in their being religious people.

"There is practically nothing that men do not prefer to God. A tiresome detail of business, an occupation utterly pernicious to health, the employment of time in ways one does not dare to mention. Anything rather than God."—Fenelon.

Anything rather than nothing.

. . . .

12. TO TEACH IS TO LEARN TO BE ATTENTIVE [UNDATED]

When you look at something closely—any object of nature, any piece of music, poetry, or painting, any topic in philosophy or science—it starts "unfolding" and reveals its "inner nature," that is, its finer and more particular structure. So casual and perfunctory is our customary gaze that it misses the essential discriminations and relationships. But so long as these do not disclose themselves, we cannot even suspect their existence. Therefore there seldom exists a powerful counter-incentive to the normal indolence of the mind and the senses. For this reason we must be thankful to those practical circumstances which enforce upon us an exceptional attentiveness. Teaching is one of these. It is to teaching—to the necessity of preparing lecture notes and examinations—that one owes one's perception of the structure of Plato's *Republic* and of *Peter Quince at the Clavier*. It is as if a "G-man," a salaried agent of the FBI, should be given this assignment: to detect code messages or subversive sentiments in some of the more recondite modern poets. Because his professional mission forces him to read so carefully, the poems open out before him as they have for no one and show him their overwhelming secret beauty.

* * * * * * * * * * * * * * * * * * *

13 (Undated)

In Shelley occurs the word *daedal*. This is not the kind of word whose meaning you can pick up on the street. Yet it is hard to imagine Shelley consulting a dictionary.

* * * * * * * * * * * * * * * * * * *

14

A heart for these times must be a heart that revels in battle. We who do not have such hearts are disqualified for the one form of happiness permitted by the times.

* * * * * * * * * * * * * * * * * * *

15

There is a pleasure in relief from pain. But no one is long grateful for being, merely, unbedevilled—blissful as he may once, in the bad days, have imagined this freedom from suffering to be. Good health and good fortune take on a gray prosy aspect as the misery which beautified them by contrast recedes into the past. We squat in our deliverance as of right and, with arms calmly folded, begin bellowing for happiness.

* * * * * * * * * * * * * * * * * * *

16

Q. Can the soul resign itself to the soul when the soul is sick?
A. An incurably sick soul is something to which the soul should

be resigned, as to an incurably sick body. But a sick soul is a soul
that finds resignation difficult.

. . . .

17

Shaw's characters, they say, have no "flesh and blood," only
"ideas." But even if flesh and blood are better than ideas, still
Shaw's characters are better than Lawrence's; because Shaw *gives*
them ideas while Lawrence only *says* that his characters have flesh
and blood.

. . . .

18

How can one contemplate save with enthusiasm
The magical talents and virtues of protoplasm?
A "jelly-like substance," it constantly flows
Into new forms and features, an oyster, a rose,
A mammoth, an ostrich, a beetle, a whore,
A Shakespeare, a Hitler, a saint, or a bore.
It sweeps down the ages and trickles away
Into every conceivable mould on the way.
Courage and cancer, madness and sin,
Mathematics, tragedy, capital, gin,
Are its manifestations; so are heaven and hell—
God and the Devil pre-exist in the cell.
Chameleon of compounds! Protean goo!
I sing thee who sing in, from, and with you.

. . . .

19. WHETHER INTELLIGENCE IS A DISADVANTAGE
[UNDATED MANUSCRIPT]

Intellect is a dubious advantage if we suppose that it increases
the range of potential suffering along with the range of enjoyment.
That it is better to be a pig satisfied than a Socrates dissatisfied is at
least an arguable thesis, not to be rejected, as Plato and Mill reject it, out of hand. (And I might point out that it is a perfectly
real issue, for we are actually called upon to decide whether we
shall endow our children with the blessing of general awareness or

leave them in provincial darkness.) For in such a comparison we assume that happiness is a fraction, of which the denominator represents the total range of feeling and the numerator the range of satisfactions or positive feelings; and the pig (or the ignorant human being), with a smaller denominator, might embody the larger ratio.

But such a comparison would be largely unreal. For intelligence, as a rule, does not apply itself like a varnish to an already finished situation. It is not a gratuitous increment, as the parable of the cave might lead us to think. It is an urgent resort, a desperate remedy for the ills already encountered on the level of the pig. Those men were *forced* out of the cave by the nightmare on the walls, by the contradiction, conflict, turbulence, and confusion in the realm of shadows where they lived.

That you do not understand the stresses, strains, and dislocations in the larger world around you does not at all imply that you do not feel them in you. Ignorance and stupidity protect you not at all. The great cracks and tensions in society reach all the way down and create fissures and oppositions within your narrow little soul. Now I cannot think of anything more miserable than to suffer ignorantly. You are like a group of bitter litigants shut up forever in a courtroom without a judge. There is no bench before which the issue can represent itself: it writhes and plays itself out to exhaustion. . . . For, after all, we have not heard of a *Socrates* dissatisfied, though we have heard of dissatisfied intellectuals. Socrates is the symbol of a method, and so forth.

Index

Abell, Walter, 37
Accuracy of valuation, 230
Achievements vs. advantages, 220–22
Adler, Mortimer, 268
Aesthetic assimilation of didactic content, 273–74
Aesthetic attitude, xxv, xxvi, 39–40, 79, 86; toward moral ideas, 274
Aesthetic criticism, 265–66, 380–81
Aesthetic judgment, xii, 119. *See also* Critical judgment; Criticism
Aesthetic object, 70–72
Aesthetic pretension, 182–83. *See also* Pretentiousness
Aesthetic purpose, 55, 58, 60–62
Aesthetic quality, 178; vs. ranking, 189–90; of a sentence, 81
Aesthetic relevance of belief, 87–104, esp. 87–90
Aesthetics: the audience of, xxiii–xxiv, xxvii; the case against, xxi–xxii; primitive questions of, xxxiv–xxxv

Agreement, as a factor in criticism, 90, 276
Aiken, Henry, 87
Alexander, Samuel, 38, 47
Analytical philosophy, xix–xx, 285–301, esp. 285–86
Anscombe, G. E. M., xxvi
Appearance and reality, 129
Appreciation, 37, 86. *See also* Aesthetic attitude
Approval as a source of pride, 217–18
Argument, the nature of critical, 157–61
Aristotle, 25, 55, 59, 107–8, 133, 223, 239
Art
—criticism: moralism in, 86, 89–90, 155, 266–67
—ethical criticism of, 153–55, 181–82, 266–73
—generalizations about: inductive, 29–30, 33–35, 160–61; principles of value, 34, 119
—moral functions of, 267–68, 270–71

—uniqueness of works of, xxii, 35, 57

Assertion vs. framing or imagining, 148–50

Associations, as a factor in art, 38, 39

Auden, W. H., 307

Bacon, Francis, 303

Balzac, Honoré de, 186, 193, 209

Barnes, Albert Coombs, 43

Baudelaire, Charles Pierre, 155, 281

Beardsley, Monroe C., xxvi

Beethoven, Ludwig van, xxxvii, 6, 17

Belief: as a factor in critical evaluation, 87–104, 150–51, 276; as a factor in lying, 251–52, 260; vs. imagining, 74

Bell, Clive, xxviii–xxxii passim, 23, 37

Bentham, Jeremy, 137, 247, 258

Berenson, Bernard, 30

Bergson, Henri, 165, 167

Birkhoff, George D., 50, 112

Blake, William, 26, 270, 272–73

Boas, Franz, 36–37

Boas, George, 47

Bodkin, Maud, 291–92

Bohnert, Herbert, 156

Boorishness, 311–12

Bowers, D. F., 38, 49

Bradley, A. C., xxxiii, 287

Breach of promise, 248, 256

Broad, C. D., 247

Brooks, Cleanth, 83

Burke, Kenneth, xxiv, 292

Bush, Douglas, 299

Carew, Thomas, 110–11

Carpenter, Rhys, 24

Cave, the parable of the, 117, 316

Cézanne, Paul, xxix, 23, 25, 35

Chapman, George, 279, 303

Chaucer, Geoffrey, 108

Chinese thought, 199, 201, 211–12

Chirico, Giorgio di, 9

Christian concept of humility, 239–43

Coherence in poetry, 142, 147, 151, 281

Coleridge, Samuel Taylor, 95–96, 113, 302

Collingwood, R. G., 47, 55, 93

Communication: critical vs. ordinary, 163–64; vs. judgment, 215

Contemplation, 75–78. *See also* Aesthetic attitude

Content vs. form. *See* Form-Content problem

Control, by the artist, 58

Corneille, Pierre (*Le Cid*), 7–8

Crane, Hart, 109

Critic, as teacher, 167

Critical argument (reasoning), 157–61

Critical competence of philosophers, xx–xxi, 295–97

Critical judgment(s), xxii, 119, 156, 306–8; comparative, 29–30, 186–94, 297–98, 309

Critical reasons, 157–60, 164–65, 190–91

Critical response, 158–60

Criticism, 156–62, 265–81; art, moralism in, 86, 89–90, 155, 266–67; as communication, 163; as a craft, xxvii, xxxiv, 29–30, 286; vs. evaluation, 210–11; general theory of, 299; as normative, 277–78; as surgery, 311

Croce, Benedetto, xxvi, 35, 53–69 passim, 127, 161, 165, 243

Death, 313

Deliberation, by the artist, 61, 138–53

Deontology, 245–64, esp. 245–48

Design, 19–20, 36–44. *See also* Form

Dewey, John, xxi, xxv, xxxviii, 43, 50, 61, 93, 161
Dickens, Charles, 184–86
Dickinson, Emily, 10
Didactic content in literature, 270, 273, 275
Didacticism in art, 86, 269–73
Didactic poetry, evaluation of, 275–76
Disadvantages, natural, 232–35
Ducasse, C. J., xxxviii, 157, 169

Ego, 220, 222, 225–28, 244. *See also* Self
Egocentricity, 304–5
El Greco, 162, 165–66
Eliot, T. S., xxix, xxxiii, xxxiv, 175–76, 243, 265–66, 278–79
Elton, William, xxxviii
Emerson, Ralph Waldo, 22, 23, 26, 28, 44–45
Empson, William, 292, 293, 295
Emotion, explanation of, 4–7
Empiricism, ethical, 245
Error, 94, 243, 312
Ethical attitude, 153
Ethical criticism of art. *See* Art
Ethical empiricism, 245
Ewing, Ralph, 247
Expression: problem of, xxxiv, 3, 8; as spiritual, 53–54, 66–67
Expression theory of music, xxxiv

False modesty, 219
False pride, 219, 229
Falsity. *See* Truth or falsity
Fechner, Gustav T., 37
Fénelon, François de Salignac de La Mothe-, 313
Fischer, Kuno, 287
Form, 19–20, 22–25, 35; Cézanne as a paradigm for, xxix, 23, 25
Form-Content problem, xxviii, xxxii–xxxiv, 13–16, 22–35, 82–86

Formalism, xxviii–xxxiv, 20–21, 22–35
Formal vs. naturalist vocabulary, 20
Framing of a proposition vs. assertion, 148–50
Francis of Assisi, Saint, 226
Frege, Gottlob, 91–92
Freud, Sigmund, 130, 238–39
Frost, Robert, 138–55
Fry, Christopher, 179
Fry, Roger, xxviii–xxxi, 22–35 passim, 46–47

Garvin, Lucius, 79–80
Generalizations about art. *See* Art
Gide, André, 22–23, 28–29
Goethe, Johann Wolfgang von, 32–33, 176
Goldscheider, Ludwig, 162, 165
Goldwater, Robert, 45
Gray, Thomas, 108–9
Greek concept of hybris, 239–43
Grierson, H. J. C., 7–8

Hamlet, 100, 206, 287–89, 300–301
Hampshire, Stuart, xxii
Hanslick, Eduard, xxxiv, 14
Happiness, 314
Hardy, Thomas, 73, 278
Heine, Heinrich, 85
Herbert, George, 272
History and criticism, 286, 298–99
Homer, 188–89
Homer, Winslow, 72, 77–80, 84
Hopkins, Gerard Manley, 184
Hume, David, 74, 217, 219, 224, 231, 236
Humility, 223–24, 239–43
Hutchinson, A. S. M., 177
Hybris, Greek concept of, 239–43

Ibsen, Henrik, 100–101
Ignorance and stupidity, 235, 311–12, 316

Imagining vs. believing, 74
Imitation: in music, 17–19; in art, 43–44
Importance as a critical concept, 25–29
Inference in poetry, 151
Injustice, as the theme of *King Lear*, 132
Intelligence, 220–21, 225, 233–35; 315; pride of intellect, 243–44
Intention: of the artist, xxv, xxvi; of the liar, 250–53
Intercultural criticism, 199–215
Interpretation, 199–215; prior to evaluation, 200; and evaluation, 210–15; and explanation, 203–10
Intuition: in ethics, 279; in the judgment of art, 279
Intuitionism in ethics, 245–47

James, Henry, 24, 304–5
James, William, 161, 176, 295–96
Jefferson, Thomas, 223
Johnson, Samuel, 10
Jones, Ernest, 289
Jones, Howard Mumford, 293–94
Judgment vs. action, 275. *See also* Critical judgment

Kant, Immanuel, xxi–xxii, 119, 247, 295–96
Keats, John, 88, 91–92, 121
King Lear, 98, 111, 125–37
Kittredge, George Lyman, 288–89, 300
Klee, Paul, 19

Language: as aesthetic object, 70–86, esp. 70–72; for describing music, 12–13; of formalism, 40, 45, 47; ostensive function of, 168; of subject matter, 44–46
Lawrence, D. H., 315
Leibniz, G. W. V., 167
Lenin, V. I., 221, 223

Lewis, C. I., 265–67, 274, 278–79
Literary analogy, in music criticism, 13
Loneliness, 227–28
Longfellow, Henry Wadsworth, 281
Lying: analysis of, 248–56; disvalue of, 258–59, 262–64; ethics of, 245–64; prevalence of, 94; psychology of, 259–62; by Paul Valéry, 311

Macbeth, 84, 127, 136
Maeterlinck, Maurice, 133
Maritain, Jacques, 62
Meaning, 36–52, esp. 50–52; nonreferential, 71–73, 77–79, 84, 86; vs. truth, 156–71, esp. 156, 163
Mencken, H. L., 115
Metaphor, 9, 11–13, 105–21, 141–43
Method: critical, 286–87; formalist, 25, 29–32; the significance of, 290–95
Michelangelo, 32, 192
Milton, John, 7, 109, 159, 280–81
Modesty, 219, 223–24
Moore, G. E., 259
Moral attitude, 231
Moral functions of art, 267–68, 270–71
Moralism, in art criticism, 86, 89–90, 155, 266–67
Moralizing, about taste, 89–90
Music and ideas, xxxiv–xxxvi, 3–21
Music: criticism of, 8–9, 13–21; power of, xxxv–xxxvi, 3–8; program, xxxvi–xxxvii, 13–21; pure, xxxiv, 13–15, 29–30
Musical simile, 10–11
Mysticism, 302

Newman, Ernest, 14
Nietzsche, Friedrich Wilhelm, 80–82

Obscurity, 302–4
Originality of the artist, 56, 58
Othello, 85, 136–37, 253

Pathological vice, 238
Pattern, 19–20, 36–44. *See also*
 Form
Perception of depth, 48–50
Philosophers, critical competence
 of, xx–xxi, 295–97
Philosophical analysis, xix–xx, 285–
 86
Philosophy, inflated, in poetry,
 145–47
Plato, xxix, 34, 55, 84–85, 88, 97,
 117, 258, 316
Poetry, coherence in, 142, 147, 151,
 281; criticism of, 138–55 passim;
 didactic, 275–76; inference in,
 151. *See also* Metaphor
Poussin, Nicolas, 27, 31
Prall, David Wright, xxxviii, 41,
 70–71, 161, 165
Presentational aesthetic, 38
Presumption, 181, 243–44
Pretentiousness, 145–47, 153, 172–
 83, 186, 279
Pride, 134, 216–44, esp. 216–27,
 243–44
Primitive questions of aesthetics,
 xxxiv–xxxv
Prior, Moody E., 291–92
Process of art, 61, 64–65, 68–69
Program music, xxxvi–xxxvii, 13–
 21
Protoplasm, 315
Psychology: of aesthetic response,
 169–71, 278; Freudian, 130, 220–
 28, 238, 244, 289; Roger Fry's,
 26; Gestalt, 169, 257, 291;
 Hume's, 74, 217; of lying, 250–
 53, 259–61; of pride, 220–21;
 textbooks, 277

Quality: of a sentence, 81; vs.

ranking, 189–90

Racine, Jean Baptiste, 136
Realism, 44, 302
Reasons. *See* Argument; Critical
 reasons
Recognition, 41
Religion, 241, 302, 313
Representation, 36, 39, 40, 50–51
Representationalists, 14–15, 23, 30.
 See also Form-Content problem
Resemblance in difference, 107–12,
 118–19, 161
Resignation, 314–15
Richards, I. A., 88, 119, 161, 212–13
Rimsky-Korsakov, Nikolai A.,
 xxix, xxxvii, 17–20
Romanticism, 60, 62, 302
Ross, W. D., 247–48
Ryle, Gilbert, 109

Santayana, George, xxxviii, 38, 70,
 93, 265, 277–78
Scholes, Peter A. (*Oxford Com-
 panion*), 13–14
Schopenhauer, Arthur, 14
Schücking, Levin Ludwig, 287–89
Self, as intruding into poetry, 141
Self-approbation, 223
Self-centeredness, 304–5
Self-consciousness, 140–41, 226
Self-satisfaction, 223, 226
Shame, 216–44, esp. 227–39
Shakespeare, William, xxiii, 3, 5,
 97–98, 111, 185, 188–89, 195; on
 music, 8–11 passim; *Hamlet*, 98,
 100, 127, 165, 206, 287–89, 300–
 301; *King Lear*, 98, 111, 125–37;
 Macbeth, 84, 127, 136; *Measure
 for Measure*, 178; *Othello*, 85,
 98, 136–37, 253; *The Tempest*,
 83, 96, 100–101
Shaw, George Bernard, 315
Shelley, Percy Bysshe, 83, 314
Sidgwick, Henry, 245–47

Silence, the power of, 129–31, 135–37

Simile, 10–11, 106. *See also* Metaphor

Skepticism about aesthetics, xix–xxii

Smith, Chard Powers, 291–92

Sophocles, 270

Spencer, Herbert, 161

Spinoza, Baruch, 176, 216, 223, 228, 236, 237, 239, 312

Standards in art criticism: arguments against, 119, 161; from ethics, 147, 153–55; from logic, 144, 147–51

Stevenson, C. L., 76

Stoll, Elmer Edgar, 301

Stravinsky, Igor, 20–21

Subject matter: of aesthetics, xxi; of art, xxviii, xxxiii, 36–52. *See also* Form-Content problem

Subjectivist theory of beauty, 33

Subtraction, method of, 31

Superlatives, 184–95, esp. 184–90, 194–95

Supposition, 80–81

Swinburne, Algernon Charles, 97–98, 300

Taine, Hippolyte Adolphe, 206

Taste: antinomy of, xxi–xxii; judgment of, xxii, 119. *See also* Critical judgment; Criticism

Tchaikovsky, Peter Ilich, 11–13

Teaching, 313–14; the critic as teacher, 167

Technique in art, 53–69, esp. 58–60

Teleological ethics, 245

Textbooks: in aesthetics, xx, 70; in psychology, 277

Thomas, Dylan, 190

Thoreau, Henry David, 10, 203–8

Tillyard, E. M. W., 291–92, 294–95

Tolstoy, Leo, 73, 133

Translation, 201–3, 213–15

Truth or falsity: of interpretation, 299–300; of metaphor, 11–13; of poetry, 82, 90–94, 147, 249

Tuve, Rosamund, 291–92, 294, 299

Uniqueness, of works of art, xxii, 35, 57

Unity in variety, 113–15

Urban, Wilbur Marshall, 83

Utilitarianism, 245–48, 263

Valéry, Paul, 310–11

Vice, ugliness of, 176

Vivas, Eliseo, 90

Weitz, Morris, xxx–xxxi

Whistler, James McNeil, xxviii, xxxiii, 47

Wimsatt, William K., xxvi

Winters, Yvor, xxiv

Wishengrad, Morton, 226

Wittgenstein, Ludwig, xxxv

Wolfe, Thomas, 172, 177

Woolf, Virginia, 306–10